THE WORD OF THE CROSS

THE WORD OF THE CROSS

- READING PAUL -

JONATHAN A. LINEBAUGH

WILLIAM B. EERDMANS PUBLISHING COMPANY
GRAND RAPIDS, MICHIGAN

Wm. B. Eerdmans Publishing Co.
4035 Park East Court SE, Grand Rapids, Michigan 49546
www.eerdmans.com

28 27 26 25 24 23 22   2 3 4 5 6 7

ISBN 978-0-8028-8167-0

Library of Congress Cataloging-in-Publication Data

Names: Linebaugh, Jonathan A., author.
Title: The word of the cross : reading Paul / Jonathan A. Linebaugh.
Description: Grand Rapids, Michigan : William B. Eerdmans Publishing
    Company, 2022. | Includes bibliographical references and index. | Summary:
    "A collection of exegetical, historical, and theological essays on Paul's letters,
    including reception history and comparative readings in conversation with
    other texts"—Provided by publisher.
Identifiers: LCCN 2021041069 | ISBN 9780802881670
Subjects: LCSH: Paul, the Apostle, Saint. | Bible. Epistles of Paul—Theology. |
    BISAC: RELIGION / Biblical Commentary / New Testament / Paul's Letters |
    RELIGION / Christian Theology / General
Classification: LCC BS2651 .L56 2022 | DDC 227/.06—dc23
LC record available at https://lccn.loc.gov/2021041069

The author and publisher gratefully acknowledge permission to reprint materials
listed on pp. 231–32.

For my teachers

To quote one of them:
"For the many & for the two"
who have studied and also shared
τὸν λόγον τὸν τοῦ σταυροῦ

Contents

FOREWORD

Those who have read or heard the scholarly work of Jonathan Linebaugh will know his trademark qualities: incisive analysis of texts, arresting turns of phrase, and a deep resonance with the theology of Paul. It is, therefore, especially exciting to see twelve of his essays (two previously unpublished) here made accessible to a wider public. There are few people today who can trace the contours of Paul's theology with such sensitivity or utilize the history of theological interpretation with such creativity, and I am confident that everyone will come away from reading this book both enriched and provoked to think harder about the theology of Paul.

Contemporary scholarship on Paul is in an unusual place. There are innumerable historical investigations of Paul's work and context that are resolutely nontheological (sometimes antitheological), fascinated with every aspect of Paul's life except the one thing that made him significant—that he was an apostle charged with communicating "the good news" issuing from the event of Jesus Christ. Among those who do show interest in the theological content of his message, few have the depth of understanding necessary to discern and deploy the rich history of theological engagement with Paul. We are fortunate that Jonathan Linebaugh has both the interest and the capacity to fill this gap, and he offers in these essays at least three significant gifts.

First and foremost, he is concerned to trace what he calls the "grammar" of Pauline theology, its characteristic pattern or shape. What is important, he shows, is not just the relative prominence of this or that motif, or the individual items of vocabulary, but the ways in which Paul's theology is shaped by an antithetical "not, but." That is more than a rhetorical form: it is an echo of the crucifixion and resurrection of Jesus, a "death to the world" that is paradoxically the site of the new creation (Gal 6:14–15). This pattern shapes Paul's language of justification ("not by works of the Law, but by faith in Jesus

Christ"). But more broadly it is the shape of "merciful surprise" whereby God works in grace and power from the "nothingness" of human capacity or worth. Lest we think this is obvious and ordinary, Linebaugh here places Paul into well-chosen comparison—with the Wisdom of Solomon and the Epistle of Enoch—to bring out how outrageous Paul's theology both was and is. But he also shows how this grammar creates a "rhyme scheme" across so much of Paul's thought. If there is one thing that students of Paul need to grasp about his theology it is his captivation by the God who gives life to the dead, who is powerful in weakness, who justifies the ungodly, who enriches the poor, and who calls the unworthy. This is Paul's "word of the cross," centered, as Linebaugh puts it, on "Jesus Christ, the gift who contradicts the old and creates the new." Nowhere is this word better understood and communicated than in the essays contained in this volume.

The second gift of these essays is its deep engagement with the early Reformation and the Lutheran tradition across the span of its development up to today. Luther has not been in fashion among Pauline scholars in the last few decades, but Linebaugh here shows that there is no stream of interpretation that better grasps some of the essential features of Paul's theology. What does Paul mean when he says "I have been crucified with Christ. It is no longer I who live, but Christ who lives in me. And the life I now live . . ." (Gal 2:19–20)? The more one reflects on those sentences the more puzzling they become, but by channeling Luther, Linebaugh makes more sense of them than anyone else I know. How does Paul find hope for Israel in Romans 9–11, where he grapples with the fact that many of his fellow Jews have not believed in Christ? Against those who find Paul here simply inconsistent, Linebaugh's brilliant reading of these chapters finds resources in the Lutheran emphasis on God's undeserved mercy that explains the logic of these chapters (and at the same time counters the Lutheran tendency toward anti-Judaism). In these and many other examples, Linebaugh demonstrates how a deep knowledge of the reception of Paul brings resources that we badly need, even if we (think we) know a lot more about the ancient context of Paul's life and thought.

Third, Linebaugh brings sustained reflection on the work of interpretation, both through his attention and also through close engagement with Johann Georg Hamann. I would wager that few New Testament scholars are familiar with this important philosopher, but Linebaugh's deployment of his thought brings clarity to the role of interpreters in their conversation with the text and thus makes explicit our agency and responsibility as interpreters of Paul. Readers of these essays will notice throughout a deep pastoral sensitivity to our human cries for comfort and hope. The COVID-19 pandemic has made those cries both louder and more urgent: it has required us to face death with greater realism, it has exposed our insecurities, and it has made us ask more plaintively: Where can we find a reliable love? Like Luther, we have become familiar with "trembling," "troubled," and "fearful" hearts, and, as Linebaugh here shows, there is no message more liberating and assuring than the truth of God's unconditioned grace in Christ. In an era when Christianity is considered "useful" only for its social or political contribution, it is good to be shown that Paul has a message that also addresses the depths of our psychological anxieties and existential distress.

Ever since our first meeting in Durham, Jonathan Linebaugh and I have learned much from each other. His stimulus and advice greatly benefited my *Paul and the Gift*, and readers may notice in these essays our convergence at several significant points. I am indebted to Jonathan for his expertise on multiple fronts and for his highly perceptive readings of Paul, and nothing delights me more than the fact that these outstanding contributions, expressed in his scintillating prose, will now be shared widely to the benefit of us all.

JOHN M. G. BARCLAY

PREFACE

A MERCIFUL SURPRISE

> *Nothing can save us that is possible,*
> *we who must die demand a miracle.*
>
> —W. H. Auden, *For the Time Being*

"The word of the cross." This Pauline phrase is both a summary and a surprise. "We preach Christ crucified," Paul announces (1 Cor 1:23; cf. 2:2; 15:3). But this sermon is a scandal: "a stumbling block to Jews and foolishness to Greeks" (1 Cor 1:23).[1] The cross is the site of weakness and shame, of degradation and death. According to "the word of the cross," however, God acts in and at the nothingness of "Christ crucified" to contradict and overcome the conditions of the possible: "the cross is folly . . . but (δέ) it is the power of God" (1 Cor 1:18); "Jews demand signs and Greeks seek wisdom, but (δέ) we preach Christ crucified" (1:23); this news is scandalous and foolish, "but (δέ) to those who are called it is Christ: the power of God and the wisdom of God" (1:23–24); not many among the Corinthians were "wise" or "powerful" or "of noble birth, but (ἀλλά) God chose what is foolish and weak in the world to shame the wise and

---

1. Paul emphasizes that Jesus not only died but that he was crucified (1 Cor 1:17, 18, 23; 2:2, 8). The shame associated with crucifixion under the Roman Imperium intensifies the shock of epitomizing the message of salvation with a phrase like "the word of the cross." See especially M. Hengel, *Crucifixion* (London: SCM, 1977). Philippians 2:6–8, as Susan Eastman notes, emphasizes that the one who was "in the form of God" not only came "in human likeness" but "took the form of a slave" (δοῦλος), not only suffered death but "death on a cross" (σταυρός), indicating that Christ participated in the human condition at its most liminal and derelict and so finally dignified and redeemed human creatures at their most degraded, oppressed, and shamed; see *Paul and the Person: Reframing Paul's Anthropology* (Grand Rapids: Eerdmans, 2017), 126–75, 177.

the strong; God chose what is insignificant and despised in the world, even things that are not (τὰ μὴ ὄντα), to bring to nothing things that are" (τὰ ὄντα, 1:26–28). For Paul, this pattern is a promise, a sermon that proclaims the gospel as a merciful surprise: out of the grave of Good Friday—at the place of foolishness, sin, bondage, and death—God, "in Christ Jesus," creates "wisdom" and "righteousness," "liberation" and "life" (1 Cor 1:30).[2]

W. H. Auden captures something of this merciful surprise, as impossible as it is strange: "nothing can save us that is possible, / we who must die demand a miracle."[3] There is a diagnosis here as deep as death. In this tomb, anything less than a "miracle"—anything that is "possible"—can only be what George Eliot calls "feeble words."[4] The word of the cross, however, proclaims a hope beyond the horizon of what can be. The gospel, Paul insists, is not the possible but "the power of God" (1 Cor 1:18, 24; cf. Rom 1:16), not "feeble words" but what Thomas Cranmer called "comfortable words" (cf. 2 Cor 1:3–7). "We preach Christ crucified": this announcement, weak and foolish though it seems, is a wisdom beyond the world, a power beyond the possible, and a miracle whose name is Jesus Christ.

This pattern of grace, or what might be called the Pauline grammar of the gospel, emerges at the point where the honest diagnosis collides with and is overcome by the hope of mercy. Paul is an apostle of a double apocalypse. "The wrath of God is revealed" (ἀποκαλύπτω, Rom 1:18). The diagnosis, according to Paul's announcement, is sin and death, a captivity and need that runs beneath any human divide: deeper than "us" as opposed to "them," Paul's preaching unveils the reality that "there is no distinction, for all sinned and lack the glory of God" (Rom 3:23; cf. 3:9). "We," to return to Auden, are those "who must die," and "we . . . demand a miracle." But "the righteousness of God is revealed" (ἀποκαλύπτω, Rom 1:17). This, for Paul, is the miracle, the good news that opens the grave: "but now the righteousness of God is manifested" and the "all sinned" gives way to the "are justified as a gift by God's grace through the redemption that is in Christ Jesus" (Rom 3:21–24). God's righteousness is revealed where "none are righteous" (Rom 3:10), but instead of this collision leading to condemnation (cf. Rom 3:19–20), the gift of Christ comes into the

2. I remember lying to my doctoral supervisor only once. John Barclay had asked me why I wanted to study Paul and, nervous applicant that I was, I replied with some half-truths about history, culture, and theology. The honest answer was—and is—that the word of cross, however unexpected and countercultural, is a word of comfort.

3. W. H. Auden, *For the Time Being: A Christmas Oratorio*, in *W. H. Auden: Collected Poems*, ed. E. Mendelson (New York: Vintage International, 1991), 353.

4. G. Eliot, *Janet's Repentance* (London: Hesperus, 2007 [1858]), 130.

condition of bondage and sin and redeems and creates righteousness.[5] As Cervantes has the ever-realistic Sancho Panza say, "What is called need is found everywhere, and extends to all places, and reaches everyone." Such honesty resonates with Paul's "there is no distinction," and it provides grounds for solidarity and compassion ("Lift every roof, and you will find seven puzzled hearts," wrote Thornton Wilder). But diagnosis is not Paul's final word. To quote Cervantes's character who can always see past what can be, in the gospel that gives Christ to the bound and the dead and so sets free and makes alive, "one finds," as Don Quixote puts it, "the reality of all the impossible."[6]

THE WORD OF THE CROSS. It is sometimes said that titles are a first interpretation, a way of signaling a core or unifying theme. While none of the studies in this book focus on 1 Corinthians 1, the theme of that passage suggests itself as a leitmotif when the chapters are read together. Each chapter is an instance of "Reading Paul," but only the first part does so without reference to other texts or traditions. The second section reads Paul in conversation with early Jewish literature and the third reads Paul with later readers of Paul. What varies, in other words, is the method. What emerges as consistent is the motif: the Pauline gospel is a merciful surprise.

Again, Auden's lines gesture toward a Pauline grammar. For Auden, "we" are those who "must die" and therefore "nothing can save us that is possible." Paul's diagnosis runs this deep: it announces a "we" beyond and beneath every "us" and "them" (see chap. 6), a fundamental bondage and need that "demands a miracle" of redemption and resurrection out of captivity and death (see chap. 4). But Paul does not preach the possible. In Christ, and then in Israel's canonical history (see chap. 3), he encounters the creator who promises beyond the possible: the God who, "according to grace" (Rom 4:4, 16), "justifies the ungodly" and also "gives life to the dead and calls into being that which is not" (Rom 4:5, 17; see chap. 2). For Paul, the gospel is Good Friday: it is Christ going into and given for those in the grave. But the word of the cross is also an Easter sermon that rolls away the stone. This, according to Paul, is the grammar of the gospel: not the old or the possible but only the "grace of God" that is "the son of God who loved me and gave himself for me" (Gal 2:20–21). This grace is christological, incongruous, and creative: God's gift of Christ,

5. U. Wilckens, *Der Brief an die Römer*, 3 vols., EKKNT (Zurich: Benziger; Neukirchen-Vluyn: Neukirchener, 1978–82), 1:188: "die Sünde aller also der Ort, an dem die Gottesgerechtigkeit wirksam wird."

6. M. de Cervantes, *Don Quixote*, trans. E. Grossman (London: Vintage Books, 2003), 91.

given at the site of sin, fear, slavery, and death, creates righteousness, peace, freedom, and life (see chap. 9).[7]

This pattern emerges in a particular way through both comparative readings of Paul and reception historical interpretations.[8] Read in conversation with other early Jewish texts, Paul both shares a tradition and stands out within it: he reads the same scriptures but interprets them differently (see chaps. 2, 3, 5, and 8); he considers the relationship between Israel and the nations, but announces a fundamental solidarity "under sin" and "in Christ" (cf. the phrase "there is no distinction" in both Rom 3:23 and 10:12–13; see chaps. 6 and 7); he speaks the language of righteousness and grace, but this inherited and canonical vocabulary is defined by the particular gift of Christ that reveals God's righteousness as it is given to sinners and re-creates them as righteous (see chaps. 1, 7, and 8). The reception historical studies consider readers of Paul—Martin Luther and Thomas Cranmer—who sensed and tried to find new ways to speak the merciful surprise. For Cranmer, this meant saying, "hear what comfortable words . . . St. Paul saith." Luther emphasizes the surprise and the mercy, calling the gospel "strange and unheard of" while also insisting that it gives "rest to your bones and mine."[9] For both, this rest and this comfort is anchored in the incongruity of grace: "Christ Jesus came to save sinners," quotes Cranmer, and as Luther writes, "God accepts no one except the abandoned, makes no one healthy except the sick, gives no one sight except the blind, brings no one to life except the dead," and "makes no one holy except sinners."[10] These Reformation interpretations sometimes entail translating Paul into new contexts and idioms, but the deep exegetical question is not so much whether later interpreters used the same words as Paul. The question is whether they proclaim the same word as Paul: the word of the cross.[11]

---

7. Cf. J. M. G. Barclay, *Paul and the Power of Grace* (Grand Rapids: Eerdmans, 2020), 115: "At every point salvation works out of its opposite, righteousness from sin, life from death. It is as if Paul bends all his theological grammar into the shape of the death and resurrection of Jesus, so that every facet of God's saving power is first crucifixion then resurrection, first disaster then salvation, first death then life."

8. Chapter 5 focuses on (and chap. 12 includes a discussion of) the methodological questions associated with, respectively, comparative and reception historical research.

9. LW 26:159, 177–78.

10. *WA* 1:183.39–184.7.

11. Oswald Bayer's description of the touchstone of preaching can also serve as a criterion for reception historical interpretations: "the gospel can ever be proclaimed anew, without ever saying anything new." See O. Bayer, "Preaching the Word," in *Justification is for Preaching: Essays by Oswald Bayer, Gerhard O. Forde, and Others*, ed. V. Thompson (Eugene, OR: Pickwick, 2012), 196–216.

The word of the cross. As it is for Paul in 1 Corinthians, this phrase summarizes this book and indicates its surprise. The Pauline gospel does not promise the possible. According to Paul's diagnosis, "we who must die"—or we who are dead—"demand a miracle." But as Ernst Käsemann preached the gospel he learned from Paul, the "impossible is not the boundary of hope," because "hope" is born "where graves cannot hold the dead."[12] That is the merciful surprise: God gives Christ, incongruously, to the bound, sinful, and dead; and Christ, impossibly, creates freedom, righteousness, and life.

IN HIS PROLOGUE to *Don Quixote*, Cervantes describes an experience that resonates with my own.

> I wanted to offer it to you plain and bare, unadorned by a prologue ... that [is] usually placed at the beginning of books. For I can tell you that although it took me some effort to compose, none seemed greater than creating the preface you are now reading. I picked up my pen many times to write it, and many times I put it down again because I did not know what to write.[13]

My hope has been to "offer" these readings of Paul "plain and bare, unadorned" by an extended introduction that situates and summarizes them in advance. What I have attempted instead, after (literally) picking up and putting down my pen many times, is to sound a theme: these various essays, which both read different passages of Paul and read Paul in conversation with different texts, come together as studies of a merciful surprise.

There are, however, two words that "I did . . . know to write": thank you. All but two of the chapters have appeared previously and I am grateful to the original publishers of these essays for the permission to include them in this collection. I also want to express my gratitude to Eerdmans, and especially to Trevor Thompson and James Ernest, for encouraging me to bring this material together with the new essays and create this book. The years of writing the essays are better marked by relationships than by the calendar. My children don't exactly make writing easier, but they do make it possible by loving me while not caring at all about my *curriculum vitae*. The same and so much more could be said for my wife, Megan, who both cares and doesn't care in the deepest ways. There are also friends and colleagues, many of whom have

---

12. E. Käsemann, *Commentary on Romans*, trans. G. W. Bromiley (Grand Rapids: Eerdmans, 1980), 124, 166.

13. Cervantes, *Don Quixote*, 4.

been readers and also wells of encouragement: Wesley Hill, Beverly Gaventa, Orrey McFarland, Michael Allen, Simon Gathercole, Susan Eastman, Ashley Null, Dan Siedell, Dorothea Bertschmann, Simeon Zahl, Zac Hicks, Nate Lee, and Gil Kracke.

And finally, there are my teachers, to whom I dedicate this book. To borrow a dedication from one of them (who died in 1788), this is for the many, and for the two: John Barclay and Paul Zahl, teachers and also friends who have both studied and shared "the word of the cross."

Abbreviations

AB	Anchor Bible
ATD	Das Alte Testament Deutsch
BBET	Beiträge zur biblischen Exegese und Theologie
BC	The Book of Concord
BEvT	Beiträge zur evangelischen Theologie
BSLK	Die Bekenntnisschriften der evangelisch-lutherischen Kirche
BZNW	Beihefte zur Zeitschrift für die neutestamentliche Wissenschaft
CBQ	*Catholic Biblical Quarterly*
CEJL	Commentaries on Early Jewish Literature
CGC	Cranmer's Great Commonplaces
Ebib	Etudes bibliques
EC	*Early Christianity*
EKKNT	Evangelisch-katholischer Kommentar zum Neuen Testament
EvT	*Evangelische Theologie*
FRLANT	Forschungen zur Religion und Literatur des Alten und Neuen Testaments
HBT	*Horizons in Biblical Theology*
HNT	Handbuch zum Neuen Testament
HTR	*Harvard Theological Review*
ICC	International Critical Commentary
Int	*Interpretation*
JAAR	*Journal for the American Academy of Religion*
JBL	*Journal of Biblical Literature*
JRT	*Journal of Religious Thought*
JSNT	*Journal for the Study of the New Testament*
JSNTSup	Journal for the Study of the New Testament Supplement Series

JSOTSup	Journal for the Study of the Old Testament Supplement Series
KEK	Kritisch-exegetischer Kommentar über das Neue Testament (MeyerKommentar)
KNT	Kommentar zum Neuen Testament
LQ	*Lutheran Quarterly*
LQB	Lutheran Quarterly Books
LW	*Luther's Works*, ed. J. Pelikan, H. C. Oswald, H. T. Lehmann, and C. B. Brown, 55 vols. St. Louis: Concordia, 1958–86
MNTC	Moffatt New Testament Commentary
NIB	*The New Interpreter's Bible*
NICNT	New International Commentary on the New Testament
NovT	*Novum Testamentum*
NovTSup	Novum Testamentum Supplement Series
NSBT	New Studies in Biblical Theology
NTS	*New Testament Studies*
PG	Patrologia Graeca
PL	Patrologia Latina
PVTG	Pseudepigrapha Veteris Testamenti Graece
SJT	*Scottish Journal of Theology*
SNT	Studien zum Neuen Testament
SNTSMS	Society for New Testament Studies Monograph Series
SNTW	Studies of the New Testament and Its World
StPatr	*Studia Patristica*
TDNT	*Theological Dictionary of the New Testament*
Them	*Themelios*
ThZ	*Theologische Zeitschrift*
TJT	*Toronto Journal of Theology*
TJTM	*Trinity Journal for Theology and Ministry*
TLZ	*Theologische Literaturzeitung*
USQR	*Union Seminary Quarterly Review*
WA	*D. Martin Luthers Werke*, Kritische Gesamtausgabe, ed. J. F. K. Knaake et al., 57 vols. Weimar: Böhlau, 1883–
WABr	*D. Martin Luthers Werke*, Kritische Gesamtausgabe. *Briefwechsel*, 18 vols. Weimar: H. Böhlau, 1930–85
WA DB	*D. Martin Luthers Werke*, Kritische Gesamtausgabe. *Die deutsche Bibel*, 15 vols. Weimar: H. Böhlau, 1906–61
WATr	*D. Martin Luthers Werke*, Kritische Gesamtausgabe. *Tischreden*, 6 vols. Weimar: H. Böhlau, 1912–21

WBC	Word Biblical Commentary
WdF	Wege der Forschung
WUNT	Wissenschaftliche Untersuchungen zum Neuen Testament
WW	*Word and World*
ZNW	*Zeitschrift für die neutestamentliche Wissenschaft und die Kunde der älteren Kirche*
ZTK	*Zeitschrift für Theologie und Kirche*

PART ONE

READING PAUL

CHAPTER 1

Righteousness Revealed

THE DEATH OF CHRIST AS THE DEFINITION OF THE RIGHTEOUSNESS OF GOD IN ROMANS 3:21–26

> *He had his own strange way of judging things. I suspect he acquired it from the Gospels.*
>
> —Victor Hugo, *Les Misérables*

"I had been captivated with a remarkable ardour for understanding Paul in the epistle to the Romans . . . but a single saying in chapter one [δικαιοσύνη θεοῦ] . . . stood in my way."[1] This autobiographical reminiscence from Martin Luther describes the experience of countless readers of Romans. When the phrase δικαιοσύνη θεοῦ first appears in Romans (1:17), Paul's syntax—note the γάρ that links 1:16 and 1:17—suggests that his reference to "the righteousness of God" is explanatory. But the spilt ink (and blood) in which the *Wirkungsgeschichte* of this Pauline phrase is written tells a different story: this part of Paul is "hard to understand" (2 Pet 3:16).

But George Herbert can help:

> Oh dreadful Justice, what a fright and terror
> Wast thou of old,
> When sin and error
> Did show and shape thy looks to me,
> And through their glass discolor thee!

This poetic description resonates with Luther's recollection of "hat[ing] the phrase 'the righteousness of God'" because "according to use and custom" he

---

1. M. Luther, *Preface to the Complete Edition of Luther's Latin Writings*, in LW 34:336–37.

understood it as "the active righteousness by which God is just and punishes unrighteous sinners." Herbert's lines echo this experience. The interpretative problem is not just grammatical; it has to do with what (or who) reveals the definition of righteousness. "When sin and error did show and shape" the "look" of God's justice the result was "fright and terror." But something changes between stanzas two and three: "But now," Herbert says with a Pauline phrase (Rom 3:21):

> that Christ's pure veil presents thy sight
> I see no fears:
> Thy hand is white,
> Thy scales like buckets, which attend
> And interchangeably descend,
> Lifting to heaven from this well of tears.

Where "sin and error" revealed a frightful justice, "Christ's pure veil presents" a righteousness that results in "no fear." Like Luther before him, who "mediated day and night" until the "connections of [Paul's] words" overcame "use and custom" with an exegetical entrance "into paradise itself," Herbert's transition from "fright" to "no fear" occurs at that Pauline point—"but now"—where Christ reveals the meaning of "the righteousness of God."

And this, I want to suggest, is an apocalyptic rendering of δικαιοσύνη θεοῦ in the most precise Pauline sense: It is in "the gospel . . . about God's son . . . Jesus Christ" (Rom 1:1-4, 16) that "the righteousness of God" is "unveiled" (ἀποκαλύπτω, Rom 1:17). For Luther, this meant a new definition: "the righteousness of God" is not the divine justice that punishes the unrighteous but the gift of Jesus that justifies the ungodly.[2] For Herbert, a poem:

> God's promises have made thee mine;
> Why should I justice now decline?
> Against me there is none, but for me much.[3]

This is not always what apocalyptic means when used as a description of Paul and his theology. Luther and Herbert are apocalyptic readers of Paul in

---

2. LW 34:336–37. For Luther's christological understanding of "the righteousness of faith," see chap. 11, "The Christocentrism of Faith in Christ."

3. The above lines are all from a poem entitled "Justice II" that occurs in "The Church" section of Herbert's The Temple, Sacred Poem and Private Ejaculations. Notice that not only the "but now" of Herbert's poem echoes Romans 3:21, but his "against me there is none" also conjures Romans 8:31.

the sense that they interpret God's gift of Jesus Christ as an apocalypse (cf. Gal 1:12): "Christ's pure veil presents" the meaning of righteousness, sings Herbert, echoing Paul's insistence that "the righteousness of God is made visible" in "the redemption that is in Christ Jesus" (Rom 3:21, 24). Here, apocalyptic names an interpretative movement, not from traditional "use and custom" to "the connection of [Paul's] words," but the other way around: from a revelatory occurrence to the definition of God's righteousness it discloses. But apocalyptic, when used primarily to identity the history-of-religions background of Paul's theology, sometimes serves to make the opposite point. Where apocalyptic names the "from whence" of Pauline concepts, this identification can invite a reading of Paul in which "use and custom" determine the definition of Paul's vocabulary—not least the phrase δικαιοσύνη θεοῦ.

Ernst Käsemann provides a representative and influential example. His interpretation of "'The Righteousness of God' in Paul," to quote the title of his 1961 address to the Oxford Congress, is an instance of a larger history-of-religions reconstruction.[4] His celebrated thesis that "apocalyptic is the mother of all Christian theology" is, in the first instance, an historical rather than a theological claim.[5] It is a judgment about "Die Anfänge christlicher Theologie" and represents a shift from Käsemann's pre-1950 answer to the history-of-religions question in terms of Hellensitic and gnostic backgrounds.[6] From the start, the definition of "apocalyptic" proved elusive, but for Käsemann its use was necessary because the near equation in Germany of "eschatology" and a doctrine of history made it impossible to say "eschatology" and mean "*Endgeschichte*."[7] Apocalyptic, in Käsemann's use and context, refers to a spe-

---

4. E. Käsemann, "'The Righteousness of God' in Paul," in *New Testament Questions Today*, trans. W. J. Montague (London: SCM, 1969), 168–82. Käsemann's lecture-turned-essay crystalized the earlier work of A. Oepke ("Δικαιοσύνη Θεοῦ bei Paulus," *TLZ* 78 [1953]: cols. 257–63) and was subsequently expanded, defended, and tweaked by C. Müller, *Gottes Gerichtigkeit und Gottes Volk*, FRLANT 86 (Göttingen: Vandenhoeck & Ruprecht, 1964); K. Kertelge, *"Rechtfertigung" bei Paulus* (Münster: Aschendorff, 1967); P. Stuhlmacher, *Gerechtigkeit Gottes bei Paulus*, FRLANT 87 (Göttingen: Vandenhoeck & Ruprecht, 1965).

5. E. Käsemann, "Die Anfänge christlicher Theologie," *ZTK* 57 (1960): 180; ET, "The Beginnings of Christian Theology," in *New Testament Question of Today*, trans. W. J. Montague (London: SCM, 1969), 82–107.

6. On this shift, see D. V. Way, *The Lordship of Christ: Ernst Käsemann's Interpretation of Paul's Theology* (Oxford: Oxford University Press, 1991), 122–24.

7. See, for example G. Ebeling's call for a definition in "Der Grund christlicher Theologie," *ZTK* 58 (1961): 230. Cf. David Congdon's observation that Ebeling's search for the "Grund" of Christian theology, together with Fuchs's identification of its "Aufgabe," is the scholarly context for Käsemann's claim about the "Anfänge" of Christian theology. "Escha-

cific kind of eschatology characterized by a constellation of features related to *Endgeschichte*: the expectation of an imminent parousia, a cosmic rather than individualistic orientation, the antithetical correspondence of *Urzeit* and *Endzeit*—all of which work together to pose an apocalyptic question: Who is the world's true Lord?[8]

Käsemann's interpretation of "the righteousness of God" in Paul is shaped by this *religionsgeschichtliche* thesis, especially in terms of method. Working in the tradition of Hermann Cremer's programmatic suggestion that Paul's expression, "the righteousness of God," is derived from and consonant with the Old Testament understanding of righteousness as a "relational concept" (*Verhältnisbegriff*), Käsemann's hermeneutic works to the Pauline definition of δικαιοσύνη θεοῦ from the pre-Pauline meaning of the phrase.[9] In his words, "I begin my own attempt to interpret the facts by stating categorically that the expression δικαιοσύνη θεοῦ was not invented by Paul."[10] For Käsemann, δικαιοσύνη θεοῦ is a "formulation which Paul has taken over," a formulation stemming from Deuteronomy 33:21 and mediated to Paul via apocalyptic Judaism as evidenced by the use of the phrase in Testament of Dan 6:10; 1QS 10:25; 11:12; 1QM 4:6.[11] This means that, from where Paul stands in the history of his religion, δικαιοσύνη θεοῦ is a "feste Formel," a traditional phrase with a trajectory of use that pre-defines the phrase as used by Paul.[12] Thus, while

---

tologizing Apocalyptic: An Assessment of the Present Conversation on Pauline Apocalyptic," in *Apocalyptic and the Future of Theology: With and beyond J. Louis Martyn*, ed. J. B. Davis and D. Harink (Eugene, OR: Cascade, 2012), 119–20. For the decision not to use the term "eschatology," see E. Käsemann, *Exegetische Versuche und Besinnungen*, vol. 2 (Göttingen: Vandenhoeck & Ruprecht, 1964), 105n1.

8. See, for instance, Käsemann, *Exegetische Versuche und Besinnungen*, 94, 104n1. Because apocalyptic carries this constellation of features, Käsemann's history-of-religions claim is able to do theological work: apocalyptic is, for Käsemann, a "twofold 'correction' to Bultmann's theology, emphasizing "the 'theology' pole of the theology-anthropology dialectic" and interpreting "both theology and anthropology in light of the lordship of Christ" (Way, *Lordship of Christ*, 138).

9. H. Cremer, *Die paulinische Rechtfertigungslehre im Zusammenhange ihrer geschichtlichen Voraussetzungen* (Gütersloh: Bertelsmann, 1899).

10. Käsemann, "'The Righteousness of God,'" 172.

11. Käsemann, "'The Righteousness of God,'" 172, 173. Several passages from the *Hodayoth* are also noted (1QH 4:37; 7:14, 19; 11:17–18, 30–31; 13:16–17; 15:14–15; 16:10), but none of them contain the exact phrase. Stuhlmacher's attempt to supplement this list could only cite 1 (Ethiopic) Enoch 71:14; 99:10; 101:3; 4 Ezra 8:36 as definitive (*Gerechtigkeit Gottes*, 11, 98).

12. E. Käsemann, "Gottesgerechtigkeit bei Paulus," *ZTK* 58 (1961): 367–78. The claim of Oepke, Käsemann, and (the earlier) Stuhlmacher that δικαιοσύνη θεοῦ is a *terminus technicus* is seriously problematized by the limited number of Old Testament and early

Käsemann can say, with reference to Philippians 3:9 and Romans 3:22, that "whatever else God's eschatological righteousness may be, at any rate it is a gift,"[13] he insists on "der Machtcharakter der Gabe" because "the formulation which Paul has taken over"—δικαιοσύνη θεοῦ—"speaks primarily of God's saving activity, which is present in his gift."[14]

The hermeneutic, governed by the *religionsgeschichtliche* thesis, is that defining δικαιοσύνη θεοῦ in Paul requires finding δικαιοσύνη θεοῦ outside of and before Paul. Käsemann knows what Paul means when he writes "the righteousness of God"—"God's lordship over the world which reveals itself eschatologically in Jesus"[15]—because he knows that "in the field of the Old Testament and of Judaism in general" the same phase is used to describe God's saving action undertaken in faithfulness to those with whom he is in covenant relationship.[16] To borrow Luther's words to describe Käsemann's method, pre-Pauline "use and custom," what we might call the theological lexicon of the Old Testament and apocalyptic Judaism, interpret "the connection of [Paul's] words." Hence David Way's suggestive observation: "although [Käsemann] pays a great deal of attention to the historical background of the theme . . . he does not treat the actual occurrences of [δικαιοσύνη θεοῦ] in Paul's letters in any detail."[17]

Jewish texts that actually contain the formula and the linguistic flexibility with which Paul expresses the correlation of δικαιοσύνη and θεός (Rom 1:17; 3:5, 21, 22, 25, 26; 10:3; 2 Cor 5:21; Phil 3:9); see especially E. Güttgemanns, "'Gottesgerechtigkeit' und strukturale Semantik: Linguistische Analyse zu δικαιοσύνη θεοῦ," in *Studia linguistica Neotestamentica*, BEvT 60 (Munich, 1971), 5–98.

13. E. Käsemann, *Commentary on Romans*, trans. G. W. Bromiley (Grand Rapids: Eerdmans, 1980), 94.

14. E. Käsemann, *Exegetische Versuche und Besinnungen*, 2:183, 185; ET from *New Testament Questions for Today* (London: SCM, 1969), 172.

15. This is a modified translation of Käsemann, *Exegetische Versuche und Besinnungen* 2:192, provided by Way, *Lordship of Christ*, 201. For a discussion of this theme, and Käsemann's reading of justification more generally, see especially P. F. M. Zahl, *Die Rechtfertigungslehre Ernst Käsemann* (Stuttgart: Calwer, 1996).

16. The influence of Cremer on Käsemann's interpretation of the meaning of righteousness in the Old Testament and early Judaism is evident in his insistence that in this "field . . . righteousness does not convey primarily the sense of a personal, ethical quality, but of a relationship" ("'The Righteousness of God' in Paul," 172). It is notable that Käsemann does see Paul expanding or editing the received definition of divine righteousness, interpreting it not as God's saving action in reference to the covenant with Israel but as the creator coming on the scene of creation in power to establish his right; see, e.g., *Romans*, 35, 56, 93, 123; *Exegetische Versuche und Besinnungen*, 2:100.

17. Way, *Lordship of Christ*, 201. For recent examples of this methodological tendency

But that is not to say that Käsemann is necessarily wrong. Rather, what this juxtaposition with Luther and Herbert exposes is that the word "apocalyptic" can function in a variety of ways. This, perhaps, is both its peril and potential. But in this case it is necessary "to call a thing what it is" (Luther).[18] For Käsemann, to say that "apocalyptic is the mother of [Paul's] theology" is to say that δικαιοσύνη θεοῦ is a "formulation which Paul has taken over," a "feste Formel" which he employs to interpret God's saving actions in Jesus Christ. By contrast, to call Luther and Herbert apocalyptic readers of Paul is to say that for them Jesus Christ is the apocalypse, the unveiling of God's righteousness, and thus the one who defines the phrase δικαιοσύνη θεοῦ. As an answer to the question concerning the religious and theological context for Paul's "righteousness of God" phrases, I regard Käsemann's identification of Jewish apocalyptic as both broadly correct and necessary. Paul's announcement of God's righteousness has eschatological judgment as its theological register, a prominent if not universal feature of the early Jewish apocalypses. Furthermore, an examination of righteousness language prior to and contemporaneous with Paul is an indispensable task in establishing what these lexemes have and can mean and thus why they are apropos as an articulation of the Pauline gospel. The problem is not in the identification of Jewish apocalyptic as the history-of-religions background of Pauline theology. The problem occurs when this *religionsgeschichtliche* thesis morphs into a hermeneutic that defines Pauline terms by antecedent usage and thereby (ironically) fails to interpret the gift of Christ as itself the apocalypse that reveals the definition of "the righteousness of God."[19]

WRITTEN IN SCRIPTURE, REVEALED IN CHRIST

Paul's use of the phrase δικαιοσύνη θεοῦ resists definition by an inherited, even canonical, lexicon. As Romans 9:30–10:4 demonstrates, Paul's scriptural

---

see M. F. Bird, *The Saving Righteousness of God: Studies on Paul, Justification and the New Perspective* (Milton Keynes: Paternoster, 2006), 15; G. Turner, "The Righteousness of God in Psalms and Romans," *SJT* 63.3 (2010): 285–301; and N. T. Wright, "The Letter to the Romans," in *NIB* 10, ed. Leander E. Keck (Nashville: Abingdon, 2002), 403. For review of research on δικαιοσύνη, especially but not only in Paul, see chap. 1 of C. L. Irons, *The Righteousness of God: A Lexical Examination of the Covenant-Faithfulness Interpretation*, WUNT 2.386 (Tübingen: Mohr Siebeck, 2015).

18. "The Heidelberg Disputation" (1518), LW 31:35–70.

19. For a critique of defining δικαιοσύνη θεοῦ on the basis of the concept's "prehistory," see H. Conzelmann, "Current Problems in Pauline Research," *Int* 22 (1968): 80; cf. S. K. Williams, "The 'Righteousness of God' in Romans," *JBL* 99 (1980): 244.

and theological heritage names δικαιοσύνη and incites Israel to pursue it (Rom 9:31), but, for Paul, the content of God's righteousness cannot be dislocated from its unveiling in Christ (Rom 1:17; 3:21–26; 10:4). In using the expression δικαιοσύνη θεοῦ, Paul is speaking the language of Deuteronomy, David, Deutero-Isaiah, and Daniel. Yet as Paul interprets the crisis of his present, it is precisely the readers of these scriptural texts who are "ignorant of the righteousness of God" (ἀγνοοῦντες τὴν τοῦ θεοῦ δικαιοσύνην, Rom 10:3; cf. Phil 3:4–9). Thus, while "the law and prophets witness to the righteousness of God," it is not in the law and the prophets that the righteousness of God is revealed. Rather, "the righteousness of God is revealed in the gospel" (Rom 1:17).[20] To locate the definition of the specifically Pauline use of the phrase δικαιοσύνη θεοῦ in the lexicon of the Old Testament and early Judaism is thus to find its meaning in a place Paul never put it. For Paul, "the righteousness of God" is not a conceptual *a priori* that enables him to gauge the soteriological significance of Jesus's history. "The righteousness of God" is that which "has been made visible" (φανερόω) in the event Paul calls "the redemption that is in Christ Jesus" (Rom 3:21a, 24) and "continues to be unveiled" (ἀποκαλύπτω) in the proclamation of the same (Rom 1:16–17). In the words of the first edition of Barth's *Römerbrief*, "Die Wirklichkeit der Gerechtigkeit Gottes im Christus ist das Neue im Evangelium."[21]

To suggest that Paul theologizes from an inherited notion of God's righteousness to an interpretation of God's act in Christ is to read Paul backwards—to read him, in the most basic sense, un-apocalyptically. Paul does not employ δικαιοσύνη θεοῦ to make sense of what happens in Jesus; for Paul, δικαιοσύνη θεοῦ is what happens in Jesus. The unveiling of the righteousness of God, for Paul, occurs, "in it"—that is, in "the gospel" (Rom 1:16–17). And because, according to the opening lines of Romans, "God's son" is the subject

20. Cf. the discussion of Paul's "localizing" reference to the "righteousness of God" that is revealed "in the gospel" in M. A. Seifrid, *Christ, Our Righteousness: Paul's Theology of Justification*, NSBT 9 (Leicester: Apollos, 2000), 46. A full discussion of "the righteousness of God" would include a consideration of "the law and the prophets" as witnesses to this righteousness, both in terms of Paul's explicit references to Habakkuk 2:4 and Genesis 15:6 and the way Paul hears scripture "promising beforehand" (Rom 1:2) and "pre-preaching" (Gal 3:8) the gospel in which the righteousness of God is revealed. For Christ and scripture as mutually interpreting, though with Christ as scripture's "now of legibility," see J. A. Linebaugh, *God, Grace, and Righteousness in Wisdom of Solomon and Paul's Letter to the Romans: Texts in Conversation*, NovTSup 152 (Leiden: Brill, 2013), 177–226, and chap. 3 of this volume, "Not the End."

21. K. Barth, *Der Römerbrief (Erste Fassung) 1919*, Gesamtausgabe 2: Akademische Werke, ed. Hermann Schmidt (Zürich: Theologischer Verlag, 1985), 23.

matter of "God's gospel" (εὐαγγέλιον θεοῦ . . . περὶ τοῦ υἱοῦ αὐτοῦ, 1:1, 3), Paul's evangelical definition of δικαιοσύνη θεοῦ is a christological definition.[22] Jesus Christ, in his comprehensive and constitutive history—"the one who was born of the seed of David" and "the one who was designated Son of God by resurrection" (1:3-4), the one "who was handed over for our trespasses and who was raised for our justification" (4:25)—is the content of the gospel, and as such, the one in whom "the righteousness of God is revealed."[23] As Luther might say, "omnia vocabula," or at least the phrase δικαιοσύνη θεοῦ, "in Christo novam significationem accipere."[24] To interpret "the righteousness of God" apocalyptically in this sense is to deduce its definition from the saving history of Jesus in which Paul sees God's righteousness "unveiled" (Rom 1:17). Only if, in Eberhard Jüngel's words, we let Paul "decide on what a righteous God is like, not on the basis of the normal use of concepts, but only on the basis" of the gift that "justifies the ungodly," can we sing George Herbert's song: "But now . . . Christ's veil presents thy sight."[25]

THE DEATH OF CHRIST AS THE APOCALYPSE OF GOD'S RIGHTEOUSNESS

Romans 3:21-26, at least in part, is Paul's attempt to define δικαιοσύνη θεοῦ by announcing the evangelical event that manifests, demonstrates, and constitutes it. As the three purpose clauses of Romans 3:25-26 indicate, God's act of putting Jesus forward as a ἱλαστήριον is teleological: the cross of Jesus Christ intends the demonstration (ἔνδειξις, 3:25, 26a) and establishment (εἰς τὸ εἶναι, 3:26b) of God's righteousness. Earlier in Romans, Paul locates the "revelation of God's righteous judgment" (ἀποκαλύψεως δικαιοκρισίας τοῦ θεοῦ, 2:5) "in

22. R. Hays, *Echoes of Scripture in the Letters of Paul* (New Haven: Yale University Press, 1989), 85, suggests taking περὶ τοῦ υἱοῦ αὐτοῦ with γραφαῖς ἁγίαις rather than εὐαγγέλιον θεοῦ, but the christological focus of 1:3-4 indicates that περὶ τοῦ υἱοῦ αὐτοῦ identifies the subject matter of the gospel (so most commentators, e.g., Calvin, Cranfield, Dunn, Käsemann).

23. See Origen's even stronger claim: "*Haec ergo iustitia Dei, quae est Christus*" (PG 14.944). Cf. Käsemann's observation that "Paul" in Romans 1:16-17 "interpreted the christological statement of 1:3f. soteriologically" and that this also runs "conversely" (*Romans*, 95). This mutually interpreting christology-soteriology dialectic problematizes N. T. Wright's claim that the gospel is "Jesus Christ is Lord" and thus not "you can be saved"; see, e.g., "New Perspectives on Paul," in *Justification in Perspective: Historical Developments and Contemporary Challenges*, ed. B. L. McCormack (Grand Rapids: Baker Academic, 2006), 249.

24. M. Luther, *Disputatio de divinitate et humanitate Christi* (1540); WA 39.2: 94, 17.

25. E. Jüngel, *Justification: The Heart of Christian Faith*, trans. J. F. Cayzer (London: T&T Clark, 2001), 78.

the day of wrath" (ἐν ἡμέρᾳ ὀργῆς), a time when "God will repay each one according to their deeds" (κατὰ τὰ ἔργα). In this context, the initially generic "one who works the good" (2:7) is specified in Romans 2:13 as a "doer of the law." In this eschatological judgment the law is the criterion. But because "all are under sin" (3:9) and "no one is righteous" (3:10), the revelation of God's righteousness in accordance with this criterion can only mean wrath (3:5). Thus, when the eschatological judgment described in Romans 2:5–16 is imagined in Romans 3:20, the confrontation of universal human unrighteousness and the forensic criterion of the law ends in universal condemnation: ἐξ ἔργων νόμου οὐ δικαιωθήσεται πᾶσα σὰρξ ἐνώπιον αὐτοῦ.

This is the rhetorical and theological prelude to Paul's announcement that "the righteousness of God is made visible" (3:21). In the forensic and nomological terms of Romans 2:5–3:20, this statement should mean an eschatological revelation of God's righteousness according to the law that results in the condemnation of the unrighteous. But Paul announces a "righteousness of God" that is "manifest apart from the law" (3:21) and that effects the justification rather than the judgment of sinners (3:23–24).

One way to hear Paul's proclamation about God declaring the unrighteous righteous through the death of Christ as the demonstration rather than the disqualification of God's righteousness is to read Romans 3:24–26 in conversation with Romans 2:4–10. The universal non-justification of the unrighteous announced in Romans 3:20 reads like the only and inevitable conclusion of the coming judgment. In its wake, Paul's location of God's righteousness in an event that calls the unrighteous righteous sounds like, to borrow Kant's characterization of the cross, a "moral outrage."[26] For Paul, however, the righteousness of God is seen and instantiated in God's justifying act of putting Jesus forward as a ἱλαστήριον because, rather than circumventing the eschatological judgment envisioned earlier in the letter, Romans 3:21–26 interprets the cross of Christ as the enactment of that eschatological judgment in the "now" of Jesus's death.

There is an oft-noted lexical connection between Romans 2:4 and 3:26a (ἀνοχή), but it is seldom observed that this divine patience functions within parallel plotlines.[27] In both Romans 2:4–10 and 3:24–26, ἀνοχή is used to characterize an era in contrast to a time defined by the disclosure of God's righteousness (δικαιοκρισίας τοῦ θεοῦ, 2:5; δικαιοσύνη αὐτοῦ, 3:26). As Gün-

---

26. I. Kant, *Religion within the Limits of Reason Alone* (New York: Harper & Row, 1960), 164.
27. C. E. B. Cranfield, *A Critical and Exegetical Commentary on the Epistle to the Romans*, 2 vols., ICC (Edinburgh: T&T Clark, 1975), 1:211, is a partial exception.

ther Bornkamm remarks, in Romans "the periods of salvation history" are "placed in contrast to each other as the time of patience and the time of the showing of righteousness."[28] This observation is offered by Bornkamm as an interpretation of Romans 3:25-26, but as it stands, it is an equally apt description of the implicit plotline of Romans 2:4-5: the present is the time of God's kindness and patience and concludes with the coming apocalypse of God's righteous judgment. Within this narrative sequence, the end of the era of divine patience is the arrival of the eschaton in the form of a future judgment (2:5-10).

Romans 3:24-26 tells a similar story, but with a surprising temporal twist. Romans 2:4-5 contrasts the present era of patience with the future enactment of justice in the form of a judgment κατὰ τὰ ἔργα. Romans 3:25-26, by contrast, presents the past as the time of the ἀνοχή τοῦ θεοῦ, the time in which God delayed the revelation of his righteous-judgment "by passing over former sins" (διὰ τὴν πάρεσιν τῶν προγεγονότων ἁμαρτημάτων).[29] And this era is juxtaposed, not with the future "day of wrath," but with the present demonstration of divine righteousness that is the cross of Jesus Christ. In narrative terms, God's act of putting Jesus forward as a ἱλαστήριον in Romans 3:25-26 is parallel to "the revelation of God's righteous-judgment" of Romans 2:5.[30] In other words, the death of Jesus Christ is the demonstration of God's righteousness in that the "now" (νῦν) of Golgotha is the eschatological enactment of the final judgment.[31] Expressed in terms of the parallel between Romans 2:5 and

28. G. Bornkamm, "The Revelation of God's Wrath," in *Early Christian Experience* (New York: Harper and Row, 1966), 49.

29. The connection between Romans 2:4-5 and 3:25-26 tells against W. G. Kümmel's insistence that πάρεσις should be translated "forgiveness" rather than "passing over," "Πάρεσις und ἔνδειξις. Ein Beitrag zum Verständis der paulinschen Rechtfertigungslehre," in *Heilsgeschehen und Geschichte: Gesammelte Aufsätze: 1933-1964*, ed. W. G. Kümmel (Marburg: Elwert Verlag, 1965), 260-70.

30. Paul's use of ἱλαστήριον in Romans 3:25-26 operates within an interpretation of the cross as eschatological judgment. Together with the liberative (ἀπολύτρωσις) metaphor, the cultic evocations conjured by the use of ἱλαστήριον do not function as independent though complementary "lines of approximation" (K. Barth, *Church Dogmatics* [CD], vol. IV/1: *The Doctrine of Reconciliation*, ed. G. W. Bromiley and T. F. Torrance, trans. G. W. Bromiley [Edinburgh: T&T Clark, 1956], 274) to the ultimately nonmetaphorical truth of God's salvific act. Rather, in Romans 3:25-26, ἱλαστήριον and ἀπολύτρωσις are coordinated by, and thus contribute to, an interpretation of the cross as God's eschatological judgment.

31. See H. U. von Balthasar, *Mysterium Paschale*, trans. A. Nichols (Edinburgh: T&T Clark, 1990), 119: the cross is "the full achievement of the divine judgment." For a discussion

3:25–26a, the present "demonstration of divine righteousness" (ἔνδειξιν τῆς δικαιοσύνης αὐτοῦ, 3:25, 26a) is the occurrence of the promised "revelation of God's righteous judgment" (ἀποκαλύψεως δικαιοκρισίας τοῦ θεοῦ, 2:5).[32] The "now" of the cross is the "day of wrath" (2:5), the day God reveals his "righteous judgment" (2:5) and thereby shows himself to be righteous (εἰς τὸ εἶναι αὐτὸν δίκαιον, 3:26; cf. 3:5).

As the καί that links the predicates "just" and "justifier" in Romans 3:26b indicates, however, the cross is both the demonstration of God's righteousness and the declaration that those of Christ-faith are righteous. The death of Christ is the demonstration of God's righteousness as the proleptic enactment of God's eschatological judgment. But—and here we approach what Jüngel calls "the deepest secret of God's righteousness"[33]—this carrying out of God's contention with sinful humanity effects, not as its counterpart but as its consequence, the "nevertheless" of justification.[34] In judging unrighteousness on the cross, God justifies the unrighteous. For Paul, "the righteousness of God" revealed in the gospel is this christological act of justifying judgment. Or, to anticipate my interpretation of Romans 3:21–24, "the righteousness of God" is God's eschatological demonstration and declaration of righteousness enacted and spoken in the gift of Jesus Christ.

---

of Paul's description of the death of Christ in relation to the final judgment imagined by an early Jewish apocalypse, see chap. 7, "Debating Diagonal Δικαιοσύνη."

32. This does not mean, as Barth claims, that the "day" of Romans 2:5 (cf. 1:18; 2:16) *refers* to the cross, *A Shorter Commentary on Romans*, trans. D. H. van Daalen (London: SCM, 1959), 24–26. What it suggests, paradoxically, is that the future judgment referred to in 2:5–10 occurs on the cross. While Paul continues to affirm the futurity of judgment (Rom 14:10–12; 1 Cor 3:12–15; 4:4–5; 2 Cor 5:10), his consideration of its soteriological shape in Romans 8:31–34 is determined by God's prior and ongoing act in his Son (cf. the greater-to-lesser logic of Rom 5:9). The relationship between present and future justification is thus the reverse of what Wright suggests: present justification is not an accurate "anticipation of the future verdict" ("The New Perspective on Paul," 260); rather the future word of justification is an echo and effect of the justifying judgment enacted in the cross.

33. Jüngel, *Justification*, 87.

34. It is therefore accurate to gloss "the righteousness of God" as *iustitia salutifera* (so, Cremer, *Die paulinische Rechtfertigungslehre*, 33) not because it is opposed to divine judgment but because in the death of Jesus, as Seifrid comments, "the contention between the Creator and the fallen creature is decided in God's favor and yet savingly resolved," see "Paul's Use of Righteousness Language against Its Hellenistic Background," in *Justification and Variegated Nomism*, vol. 2: *The Paradoxes of Paul*, ed. D. A. Carson et al. (Tübingen: Mohr Siebeck, 2004), 59; cf. G. Theißen, *Erleben und Verhalten der ersten Christen: Eine Psychologie des Urchristentums* (Munich: Gütersloher, 2007), 315–16.

Defining Δικαιοσύνη θεοῦ as the Righteousness of God through Faith in Jesus Christ

In Romans 2:1–3:20, eschatological judgment is not just the location of the revelation of God's righteous judgment (2:5), it is also the context in which God recognizes "the doers of the law" as righteous (2:13, 16; cf. 3:20). Both judgment and justification occur in this forensic future. And here, judgment is carried out "according to works" (κατὰ τὰ ἔργα)—that is, as Romans 2:13 specifies, God's pronouncement will correspond to one's nomistic observance: "the doers of the law will be declared righteous." Or conversely, and because "none are righteous" (3:10) inevitably, "by works of law no flesh will be declared righteous" (3:20). Because God's righteousness operates in accordance with the criterion of the law, it confronts sinners only with a word of condemnation.[35]

"But"—which is a very different word than "accordingly"—"the righteousness of God has been made visible apart from law" (χωρὶς νόμου, Rom 3:21). Within the sphere of the law, divine and human justification are mutually exclusive: the justification of God (Rom 3:4–5) entails the non-justification of sinners (3:19–20). But it is just this impossibility that Romans 3:21–26 proclaims: the divine act that is the cross of Jesus Christ establishes God as both "just" and "justifier" (3:26b). As in Romans 2:13 and 3:19–20, divine and human justification are located in the event of eschatological judgment. But in Romans 3:21–26 the arrival of that eschaton in the "now" of Jesus's death rewrites God's future word of justification in the present tense (3:24; cf. 3:28 and the aorist in 5:1).[36] Justification is not a separate verdict from the one God will speak at final judgment, nor is it only "an anticipation of the future verdict."[37] Justification is the final verdict—a forensic word from the future spoken in the enactment of God's eschatological judgment that is the "now" of Jesus's death (and resurrection; cf. Rom 4:25).[38]

35. See Philo's insistence that, as a matter of principle, δικαιοσύνη works κατ' ἀξίαν (*Leg.* 1.87; *Mos.* 2.9; *Sobr.* 40)—that is, in accordance with some criterion of "fit" or correspondence between human worth and divine action. For "correspondence" as the defining characteristic of God's righteousness in at least some early Jewish texts, see chaps. 2 and 7 in Linebaugh, *God, Grace, and Righteousness*.

36. Peter Stuhlmacher is therefore right to argue that "justification involves an act of judgment" and is "decidedly located in the final judgment," but he underemphasizes the Pauline stress on the "now-ness" of this justifying judgment. See *Revisiting Paul's Doctrine of Justification: A Challenge to the New Perspective*, trans. D. P. Bailey (Downers Grove, IL: IVP Academic, 2001), 14.

37. Wright, "New Perspective on Paul," 260.

38. The term "forensic" indicates more than the legal connotations of the δικ- word

Hence the shock of Paul's announcement: those declared righteous in this judgment are not "the doers of the law" but "sinners." Whereas Romans 2:5 describes a future judgment in which human action and juridical fate correspond (κατά τὰ ἔργα), Paul, in Romans 3:21–26, locates the operations of God's righteousness in the contradiction between human unrighteousness and the somehow stronger word of justification: "All sinned . . . and are declared righteous" (Rom 3:23–24). Grammatically, the objects of the divine saving action implied in the passive participle δικαιούμενοι (3:24) are the sinners of 3:23, and thus, as James Dunn construes this Pauline paradox, "it is precisely those who have sinned and fallen short of God's glory who are justified."[39] The "scandal and folly" of this "word of the cross" is not hard to hear: what Paul calls "the righteousness of God" appears to be—and within the sphere of law described in Rom 1:18–3:20 is—an instance of injustice in which God, with what looks like forensic schizophrenia, accurately diagnoses the unrighteous (Rom 3:23; cf. 3:10) only to rename them with the word of justification (3:24).

For Paul, however, the declaration that sinners are righteous is not a groundless divine fiat. It is a pronouncement grounded in a gift. The adversative δέ that opens Romans 3:21 serves what Jochen Flebbe describes as a "logisch-rhetorischen Funktion in der Opposition zu V.20."[40] In antithesis to the (excluded) possibility of justification before God by works of law (3:20), Romans 3:21 announces a manifestation of the righteousness of God "apart from law." This logical contrast, however, is not between two abstract soteriological theses; it is between reality before and after the "now" of God's "gift" (χάρις) that is "the redemption which is in Christ Jesus" (3:24). The "now" of Romans 3:21 rhymes with the ἐν τῷ νῦν καιρῷ of 3:26a, indicating that the manifestation of δικαιοσύνη θεοῦ (3:21) cannot be isolated from the demonstration of God's righteousness in the eschatological judgment that is the death

---

group; it describes the enactment of final judgment in the arrival of the eschaton that is the death of Jesus Christ. The related phrase, "declare righteous," likewise indicates more than the verdict of a judge: it is, as God's word, the effective pronouncement of the creator that calls and so re-creates sinners as righteous.

39. Following Cranfield, *Romans*, 1:205, I take as the subject of 3:24 the "all" of 3:23 while recognizing that 3:24 continues the main theme from 3:21–22. Douglas Campbell is probably correct to see the anthropological statement of 3:23 as an elaboration of the "all the believing ones" of 3:22 such that the subject of the passive form of δικαιόω in 3:24 is doubly qualified by the "all of faith" and the "all sinned." *The Rhetoric of Righteousness in Romans 3:21–26*, JSNTSup (Sheffield: Sheffield Academic Press, 1992), 86–92. For the quotation from James D. G. Dunn, see *Romans 1–8*, WBC 38A (Waco, TX: Word, 1988), 168.

40. J. Flebbe, *Solus Deus: Untersuchungen zur Rede von Gott im Brief des Paulus an die Römer*, BZNW 158 (Berlin: de Gruyter, 2008), 68.

of Christ (3:25–26). The contrast between Romans 3:20 and 3:21 is thus properly eschatological. νυνὶ δέ signals the arrival of the eschaton in the event of grace that is the cross of Jesus Christ.[41]

It is in this new time—what Paul calls the "now-time" (3:26a)—that "the righteousness of God is made visible." Here and now and not according to law (χωρὶς νόμου), the righteousness of God is revealed as the "righteousness of God through faith in Jesus Christ" (Rom 3:21–22). As Simon Gathercole notes, "apart from law" and "through faith" are mutually-interpreting: "χωρίς in verse 21 is clearly the opposite of διά in verse 22."[42] "Apart from law" is therefore a negative definition of the "righteousness of God through faith in Jesus Christ": "'by faith,'" writes Francis Watson, "*means* 'apart from law.'"[43] In Karl Barth's words, "*sola fide*" is the "great negation," it identifies the absence of law-defined righteousness and so names the nothingness from which God re-creates sinners as righteous.[44] This suggests that "the righteousness of God," as "the righteousness of faith," is not determined by the law-defined correspondence between human worth and God's judgment. Rather, as the incongruity between human worth ("sinners," 3:23) and God's word ("declared righteous," 3:24) indicates, "the righteousness of God" is characterized by creative contradiction. Just as Abraham's faith lived where his body and Sarah's womb were dead (νέκρωσις, Rom 4:19) and trusted "the one who gives life to the dead and calls into being that which does not exist" (4:17), so Paul sets faith in the vacuum created by the absence of law (χωρὶς νόμου, 3:21) and works (ὁ μὴ ἐργαζόμενος, 4:5; χωρὶς ἔργων, 4:6) and identifies the God it trusts as "the one who justifies the ungodly" (4:5). Nothingness, death, and sin—for Paul, these are the site at which God utters a creative counterstatement: creation, life, righteousness.[45]

Faith, in the first instance, is this anthropological negation, the site of sin, death, and nothingness at which God operates out of the opposite. Defined by

41. Cf. Käsemann, *Romans*, 93.

42. S. J. Gathercole, *Where Is Boasting? Early Jewish Soteriology and Paul's Response in Romans 1–5* (Grand Rapids: Eerdmans, 2002), 224. He adds, "the 'righteousness of God revealed apart from the Law' in 3:21 is equivalent to 'the righteousness of God through faith' in 3:22."

43. F. Watson, *Paul and the Hermeneutics of Faith* (London: T&T Clark, 2004), 72.

44. Barth, *CD* IV/1, 621.

45. For the linking of the liturgical predictions of Romans 4:5 and 4:17 and the related claim that *creatio e contrario* describes a *modus operandi* that connects the divine acts of creation, resurrection, and justification, see Linebaugh, *God, Grace, and Righteousness*, 152–54; Käsemann, *Romans*, 123; cf. chap. 9, "The Grammar of the Gospel."

what it is not (i.e., law and works), faith "speaks," as Oswald Bayer puts it, "in the *via negationis*."[46] Facing the human, faith says "no." It hears God's impossible promise—"I will give you a son by Sarah" (Gen 17:6)—looks at Abraham's age and Sarah's barrenness, and laughs (Gen 17:7; Rom 4:19). But faith's focus is not the believing human; it is the "God" who is "able to do as he promises" (Rom 4:21). And looking here, faith laughs again: "the Lord did to Sarah as he promised . . . and Sarah said, 'the Lord has made laughter for me'" (Gen 21:6). As Paul reads Genesis, Abraham's "faith was counted to him as righteousness" (Gen 15:6; Rom 4:3, 22) "because" (διό, 4:22) it is this double laughter: even as faith considers Abraham's age and Sarah's barrenness and says, "death" (Rom 4:19), it hears the promise and "believes the God who gives life to the dead" (4:17; 4:20–21).[47]

This brings us back to Romans 3:21–22. The "righteousness of God through faith," because it is defined by the absence of law, is first an anthropological negation. With Romans 3:20, it says "no" to the possibility of righteousness before God by works of law. But as with Abraham, the laughter of faith's "yes" is louder than the laughter of its "no." And if "apart from law" identifies faith's "no," it is the name "Jesus Christ" that defines faith's "yes." In Romans 3:21–22, the contrast between "law" and "faith" is asymmetrical. Whereas "law" is joined to a preposition (χωρίς), "faith" gets both a preposition (διά) and a name, Jesus Christ. The effect of this imbalance is to "christologize" faith. It is not faith in abstract antithesis to law that defines "the righteousness of God." Rather, "the righteousness of God" is the "righteousness of God through faith in Jesus Christ." Hence Barth's question: "what is the *sola fide* but a faint yet necessary echo of the *solus Christus*?"[48] "Through faith in Christ" is the Pauline way of saying "Christ alone." Defined in antithesis to "works of law," it excludes law-defined worth as the grounds of justification. Defined by the name Jesus Christ, it confesses Christ as the *one* by, in, and on the basis of whom God

---

46. O. Bayer, *Martin Luther's Theology: A Contemporary Interpretation*, trans. Thomas H. Trapp (Grand Rapids: Eerdmans, 2008), 172.

47. Cf. Watson, *Hermeneutics*, 169: "Paul sets faith on the border between despair and hope and sees it facing in both directions. Faith is both despair of human capacity and hope in [the] saving act of God." The passive forms of ἐνδυναμόω and πληροφορέω in 4:20 and 4:21 suggest that even Abraham's believing is generated by God through the promise (cf. Rom 10:17). It is suggestive that when Paul gives voice to "the righteousness of faith," he hears it saying an anthropological no—"Do not say in your heart who will ascend to heaven . . . or who will descend to the abyss?"—and a christological yes—"The word is near you" (Rom 10:6–8).

48. Barth, *CD* IV/1, 632.

justifies the ungodly. "All sinned," says Paul, "and are justified . . . in Christ Jesus" (Rom 3:23–24).

To say that "the righteousness of God" is "the righteousness of God through faith in Jesus Christ" is to say that God's eschatological act of judgment and justification is irreducibly singular: it is Jesus Christ. As Luther puts it, "faith justifies because it takes hold of and possesses this treasure, the present Christ," and therefore "the true Christian righteousness" is not the human act of believing; it is "the Christ who is grasped by faith . . . and on account of whom God counts us righteous."[49] Rather than qualifying this christological singularity (*solus Christus*), *sola fide* is the apophatic affirmation of the "gift" that is "the redemption which is in Christ Jesus" (Rom 3:24): διὰ τοῦτο ἐκ πίστεως, ἵνα κατὰ χάριν (Rom 4:16).[50] To borrow Thomas Cranmer's image, "faith" is the

---

49. LW 26:130 = WA 40.1:229, 22–30. Read with the hindsight of Romans 3 and 4, Paul's opening announcement that "the righteousness of God is revealed in the gospel . . . just as it is written, 'the one who is righteous by faith will live'" (Rom 1:16–17, quoting Hab 2:4) can be heard as an expression of the christological yes that positively defines "the righteousness of God through faith." To read Romans 1:17 as saying that God's righteousness is gifted to faith is, as filled out by Romans 3:22, to say that Christ, who is "our righteousness" (1 Cor 1:30) is given to faith in the gospel.

50. Käsemann, *Romans*, 101: "Precision is given to *sola gratia* by *sola fide*." Cf. Jüngel, *Justification*, 149–226, 236–59, who demonstrates that the reformational *solas* are ordered in such a way as to preserve *solus Christus*. The common charge that the objective genitive reading of πίστις Χριστοῦ is anthropological rather than christological is simply false at the level of historical theological description. For this and a further consideration of the πίστις Χριστοῦ debate, see chap. 11, "The Christocentrism of Faith in Christ." Once the theological objections are addressed, the strong semantic case for something like the objective genitive can be heard: (1) Paul's instrumental faith clauses are derived from the ἐκ πίστεως of Habakkuk 2:4, which does not (*pace* R. B. Hays, *The Conversion of the Imagination: Paul as Interpreter of Israel's Scripture* [Grand Rapids: Eerdmans, 2005], 119–42) employ ὁ δίκαιος as a christological title but as a reference to the generic, believing human, a point confirmed by the appeal to Abraham in Romans 4 and Galatians 3 (Francis Watson, *Paul, Judaism and the Gentiles: Beyond the New Perspective* [Grand Rapids: Eerdmans, 2007], 240). (2) In Paul, Jesus is never the subject of the verb πιστεύω and Paul's habit of interpreting an instance of the verb in a citation with reference to the noun (e.g. Rom 4:3, 5; 9:32–33 10:5–11, 16–17) indicates that the meaning of the noun and verb have not drifted apart (R. B. Matlock, "Detheologizing the ΠΙΣΤΙΣ ΧΡΙΣΤΟΥ Debate: Cautionary Remarks from a Lexical Semantic Perspective," *NovT* 42 [2000]: 13–14; cf. Watson, *Paul, Judaism and the Gentiles*, 243). (3) The question of redundancy in Rom 3:22, Gal 2:16; 3:22, and Phil 3:9 points to "a much wider pattern of repetition of πίστις/πιστεύω in Galatians and Romans, rooted in Genesis 15:6 and Habakkuk 2:4" that functions to disambiguate the genitive phrase (R. B. Matlock, "Saving Faith: The Rhetoric and Semantics of πίστις in Paul," in *The Faith of Jesus Christ: Exegetical, Biblical and Theological Studies*, ed. M. F. Bird and P. M. Sprinkle [Peabody, MA: Hendrickson, 2009], 89).

finger of "St John Baptist," pointing away from the self and to "the lamb of God that takes away the sins of the world."[51]

Paul's definition of "the righteousness of God" as "the righteousness of God through faith in Jesus Christ" is thus an instance of what Käsemann calls "applied Christology."[52] "The righteousness of God" is a description of the eschatological demonstration of righteousness and the eschatological declaration of righteousness that is God's gift of Jesus Christ. This means that Paul does not look in the lexicon of early Judaism to define δικαιοσύνη θεοῦ. He deduces his definition from the gift of Christ that makes God's righteousness visible by demonstrating it in the enactment of eschatological judgment that both judges unrighteousness and justifies the unrighteous. "The righteousness of God" is not a "feste Formel" that Paul "takes over" from apocalyptic Judaism. Rather, God's gift of Jesus Christ is the apocalypse—the event that unveils "the righteousness of God." Käsemann, in this specific sense, reads Paul backwards: Paul does not employ a traditional concept to interpret what God has done in Christ; for Paul, "the righteousness of God" is what God has done in Christ. It is not "use and custom" that define the Pauline phrase δικαιοσύνη θεοῦ. Rather, "Christ's pure veil presents th[e] sight" of divine justice. As Origen put it, the "*iustitia Dei . . . est Christus*"—"the righteousness of God" is the gift of Jesus Christ in whom "we become the righteousness of God" (2 Cor 5:21) and who himself is "our righteousness" (1 Cor 1:30). For Paul, δικαιοσύνη θεοῦ is not just a concept from apocalyptic Judaism; δικαιοσύνη θεοῦ is what is apocalypsed in the gospel of Jesus Christ. Paul's apocalyptic definition of "the righteousness of God" is a christological definition: Jesus Christ, as both the eschatological demonstration and the gift of God's righteousness, is the revelation of "the righteousness of God." In Romans 3:21–26, the divine act that is his death defines δικαιοσύνη θεοῦ.

The Pauline definition of δικαιοσύνη θεοῦ is a christological redefinition: it is deduced from and descriptive of God's gift of Jesus Christ. Barth captures this:

> The Christian message does not at its heart express a concept or an idea . . . it recounts a history . . . in such a way that it declares a name. . . . This means that all the concepts and ideas used in this report [δικαιοσύνη θεοῦ, for example] can derive their significance only from the bearer of this name

51. J. E. Cox, *Miscellaneous Writings and Letters of Thomas Cranmer* (Cambridge: Parker Society, 1846; repr., Vancouver: Regent College Publishing, 2002), 132–33.

52. Käsemann, *Romans*, 96.

and from his history, and not the reverse. . . . They cannot say what has to be said with some meaning of their own or in some context of their own abstracted from this name. They can serve only to describe this name—the name of Jesus Christ.[53]

Victor Hugo's description of the merciful Monseigneur Bienvenu, however, seems the more fitting conclusion. "He had his own strange way of judging things," Hugo writes in *Les Misérables*, "I suspect he acquired it from the Gospels." For Paul, God has his own strange way of judging; he reveals it in the gospel.

---

53. Barth, *CD* IV/1, 16–17. This does not mean that "the law and the prophets" do not "bear witness to" God's righteousness revealed in the gospel, but it does suggest they do so precisely as voices that "pre-preach" (Gal 3:8) and "promise beforehand" the "gospel . . . about God's Son, Jesus Christ" (Rom 1:1–4). The crucified and risen Christ is the definition of δικαιοσύνη θεοῦ both before and after the "now" of the gospel, but it is only in this "now" that the "mystery kept secret" in "the prophetic writings" is "disclosed"; so Romans 16:25–26, echoing the revelatory vocabulary (φανερόω) of Romans 3:21.

CHAPTER 2

PROMISES BEYOND THE POSSIBLE

GRACE AND THE GOD WHO . . . IN ROMANS 4

The Real is what will strike you as really absurd.

—W. H. Auden, *For the Time Being*

"The grave," says the god Apollo, is "an end." Earlier, in Act I of Thornton Wilder's play *The Alcestiad*, the figure of Death expresses the same finality: "I am here forever. I do not change." Apollo, however, is on the scene "to set a song in motion," to tell "a story" after and out of the end. But after-the-end is impossible: "There is no lesson you can teach me," shouts Death.

Within the drama, Death is not so much wrong as limited, incapable of imagining the impossible. The grave is an end, and there is, within the realm of what can be, no after, no out of, no opening. As W. H. Auden put it, "Nothing can save us that is possible, / we who must die demand a miracle." Apollo's song, however, has miracle as its theme: "You broke the ancient law," complains Death as the god opens the grave, "the living are the living and the dead are the dead."

What Death has to learn, it seems, is the same "lesson" Paul announces in Romans 4: the "impossible," in Ernst Käsemann's words, "is not the boundary of hope"—when and where "that hope" is "in the promise of the God who raises the dead."[1] Christ was crucified, Paul confesses. But that grave, by grace, is not the end: he "was raised" (Rom 4:25). Apollo's conclusion captures the apostle's proclamation: "Death, the sun is risen. You are shaking. . . . Start accustoming yourself to change."

In Romans 4, Paul is accustoming himself to change. The one who died on a cross has been resurrected and this—strangely, somehow, at the site of sin—is

1. E. Käsemann, *Commentary on Romans*, trans. G. W. Bromiley (Grand Rapids: Eerdmans, 1980), 124.

a redemption that reveals and a grace that gives righteousness (Rom 3:21–26). Death and life, however, like sin and righteousness, are opposites; and nothing, as Friedrich Nietzsche observes, can "originate in its antithesis. . . . Such origination," he says, "is impossible."[2] And yet—or as Paul might put it, "but now"—the God who speaks and gives in the gospel is the one who promises beyond the possible, "the one who," in Paul's phrases, "gives life to the dead," "calls into being that which is not," and "justifies the ungodly" (Rom 4:5, 17).

For Paul, however, accustoming himself to change is not only about reconceiving the possible. It is also entails returning to and reading the past. "What then shall we say," Paul asks, "that Abraham, our forefather according to the flesh, has discovered?" That the christological gospel prompts this canonical question suggests that, for Paul, Israel's scripture is not, as Gotthold Ephraim Lessing once described it, an "antiquated" and "exhausted primer," a once helpful "hint" that can be "dispensed with" and torn "from the child's hand" in the course of "the education of the human race."[3] The scriptural words, rather, as Paul reads them, are not just in the past. They are a promise: they "were written," he says in Roman 4:24, "for us." To an apostle accustomed to change, pages from the past are proclamations of the gospel (Rom 1:1–4; Gal 3:8): Abraham's history, as Paul hears it, is κατὰ χάριν (Rom 4:4, 16), a story written according to the grammar of a grace given, incongruously, to the ungodly and the dead and that, impossibly, creates righteousness and life.[4] That this hearing happens—that canonical history becomes apostolic homily—suggests that Paul's present, to borrow a phrase, is scripture's "now of legibility"—the time when the gospel accustoms the apostle to the evangelical impossibilities of the past (cf. Rom 3:21; 16:25–27).[5]

2. F. Nietzsche, *Beyond Good and Evil: Prelude to a Philosophy of the Future*, trans. R. J. Hollingdale (London: Penguin Books, 1973), 33.

3. *Lessing's Theological Writings*, trans. H. Chadwick (Stanford: Stanford University Press, 1957), 82–98.

4. For the notion of grammar in relation to the shape or pattern of Paul's theology, see chap. 9, "The Grammar of the Gospel."

5. G. Agamben, *The Time That Remains: A Commentary on the Letter to the Romans*, trans. P. Dailey (Stanford: Stanford University Press, 2005), 145, uses the phrase "Das Jetzt der Lesbarkeit" to summarize the hermeneutic of Walter Benjamin. See Benjamin, "Theses on the Philosophy of History," in *Illuminations: Essays and Reflections*, ed. H. Arendt, trans. H. Eiland and K. McLaughlin (Cambridge: Harvard University Press, 1999), 253–64. J. D. Dawson, *Christian Figural Reading and the Fashioning of Identity* (Berkeley: University of California Press, 2002), 134, refers to the way the gospel reveals the "gospelness" of prior events. For a similar account of Paul's hermeneutic, one which sees "Das Alte Testament als integraler Bestandteil des Evangelium" while insisting that the Old Testament is "ein

"What then shall we say Abraham has discovered?" Romans 4 is, at once, an exegetical and an evangelical answer: the God who raised Jesus is and ever has been the one who, by grace, opens the grave. Old and barren, ungodly and dead: these are, in Romans 4, the tombs of what is and what can be. Isaac and heirs, righteousness and resurrection: these name the impossible that God both promises and performs. In Apollo's almost apostolic announcement, "the sun is risen." And that dawn, as Oswald Bayer writes, "discloses the meaning of all" that "comes after" and "all" that "comes before."[6] The possible and the past are both children of the promise. To read and preach in the light of the risen son, as Paul does in Romans 4, is to become accustomed to change, to see beyond the shadow of death and hear a hymn in which hope and history rhyme: as in the gospel God is, so in Genesis God was, and over graves God will be—the one who promises beyond the possible.

The Pattern of Promise

Readings of Romans 4 often emphasize either 4:1–8 or 4:9–17 and, correspondingly, interpret the chapter as, in Käsemann's words, a "Schriftbeweis" for "die Glaubensgerechtigkeit" or, as Richard Hays counters, insist that "the crucial issue . . . is not how Abraham got himself justified but rather whose father he is."[7] For Paul, however, God's justifying pronouncement and God's promise share a shape—they are both κατὰ χάριν (Rom 4:4, 16). This phrase, "according

---

integrales Element" of the gospel "in seiner *Interpretatio Christiana*," see F. Hahn, *Theologie des Neuen Testament*, 2 vols. (Tübingen: Mohr Siebeck, 2005), 1:195–201; cf. 2:38–142. For a fuller discussion of the reciprocal yet asymmetrical relationship between Christ and scripture, see J. A. Linebaugh, *God, Grace, and Righteousness in Wisdom of Solomon and Paul's Letter to the Romans: Texts in Conversation*, NovTSup 152 (Leiden: Brill, 2013), 177–226; cf. chap. 3 of this volume, "Not the End."

6. O. Bayer, *Theology the Lutheran Way*, ed. and trans. J. G. Silcock and M. C. Mattes, LQB (Grand Rapids: Eerdmans, 2007), 2000. Cf. Bayer, *A Contemporary in Dissent: Johann Georg Hamann as a Radical Enlightener*, trans. R. A. Harrisville and M. C. Mattes (Grand Rapids: Eerdmans, 2012), 219: the gospel is the one history by which one "learns to spell history."

7. E. Käsemann, *An die Römer*, HNT 8a (Tübingen: Mohr Siebeck, 1973), 99, 110; R. Hays, *The Conversion of the Imagination* (Grand Rapids: Eerdmans, 2005), 83. Hays's proposed punctuation and translation of Romans 4:1 reflects this either/or interpretation; it is also grammatically unlikely given the definite article with προπάτωρ; see Hays, "Have We Found Abraham to Be Our Forefather According to the Flesh? A Reconsideration of Rom 4:1," *NovT* 27.1 (1985): 76–98. For an earlier iteration of this debate in German scholarship, compare G. Klein, "Römer 4 und die Idee der Heilsgeschichte," *EvT* 23 (1963): 424–47; and U. Luz, *Das Geschichtsverständnis des Paulus* (Neukirchen: Neukirchener Verlag, 1968), 168–86.

to grace," describes a pattern that holds together the origin and horizon of Abrahamic history: Abraham is righteous "according to grace"; Abraham is a father "according to grace."

To adapt a question from Orrey McFarland, however, "Whose Abraham? Which grace?"[8] Paul is part of a chorus of interpreters who sense that the pattern of Israel's history is present at its Abrahamic start. And yet, the shape of Paul's reading is a surprise: life from death, righteousness from sin, creation from nothing, hope against hope. κατὰ χάριν captures this pattern of the impossible. It also catches Paul accustoming himself to change.

What Abraham discovered is what Paul reads: "Abraham believed God and it was reckoned to him as righteousness" (Rom 4:3, quoting Gen 15:6). Where Genesis is silent, however, early Jewish commentators often speak: Abraham is called righteous because, in some sense, he is: virtuous or philosophic, obedient or opposed to idolatry, Abraham is, as Wisdom of Solomon explicitly says, δίκαιος (Wis 10:5–6).[9] For Paul, however, the silence itself says something. Genesis does not identify anything about Abraham before or beyond Genesis 15:6 that makes the patriarch a fitting recipient of righteousness. And this lack, on Paul's reading, speaks loudly: Abraham is not righteous because he is; rather, as the silence says, he is declared righteous even though he isn't. It is almost possible to hear Paul reciting lines from Samuel Taylor Coleridge's "The Rime of the Ancient Mariner": "No voice they did impart— / No voice; but O! the silence sank / Like music on my heart" (part 4, lines 524–26). The silence, for Paul, names a nothingness, an absence in relation to Abraham of any symbol of value that would make him a worthy or fitting recipient of God's grace. And so, as Simon Gathercole writes, "God's declaration of Abraham as righteous" is "the word of the God who calls 'nonentities' into being as 'entities,'" who "speaks in opposition to reality and thereby transforms it."[10] Justification, in other words, is not a description of what is but the creation of what was not: out of ungodliness God calls and thereby creates righteousness. Paul emphasizes this mismatch between the previous conditions of the possi-

---

8. O. McFarland, "Whose Abraham, Which Promise? Genesis 15:6 in Philo's *De Virtutibus* and Romans 4," *JSNT* 35.2 (2012): 107–29.

9. See, for example, Philo, Jubilees, Sirach, Liber Antiquitatum Biblicarum, 1 Maccabees, the Damascus Document, Wisdom of Solomon, and Josephus. For a fuller consideration and comparison of Paul with these and other early Jewish texts, see F. Watson, *Paul and the Hermeneutics of Faith* (London: T&T Clark, 2004), 167–272, and S. J. Gathercole, *Where Is Boasting? Early Jewish Soteriology and Paul's Response in Romans 1–5* (Grand Rapids: Eerdmans, 2002), 216–51; cf. Linebaugh, *God, Grace, and Righteousness*.

10. Gathercole, *Where Is Boasting*, 243.

ble and God's promise by insisting that Abraham's μισθός—his "reward"—is not a payment that corresponds to work (Rom 4:4; cf. Gen 15:1). It is, rather, a gift characterized by incongruity: the blessing of righteousness, read according to the grammar of this grace, is God not counting sin but covering it, God reckoning righteousness in the absence of works; it is, against the possible, God justifying the ungodly (Rom 4:5–8).[11]

The same pattern shapes Paul's reading of God's promise to Abraham: "I have made you the father of many nations." Like the blessing of righteousness, the promise of Abraham's paternity is κατὰ χάριν (Rom 4:16–17). In both instances, "according to grace" indicates an antithesis: not by works or through law, but through faith and as a gift (4:4–5, 13–16). Read according to this grammar, Abraham's justification is an unconditioned and creative act: apart from works and to the ungodly, God speaks and thereby gives righteousness. As the pattern of God's promise, "according to grace" says "no" to a possible reading of Genesis—the promise is "not through law"—even as it insists on another interpretation: the promise is "through the righteousness of faith" (4:13–16). In Romans 4, then, from beginning to end, κατὰ χάριν is the grammar according to which Paul reads Genesis.

Resonating behind Paul's language—not law or works but faith and grace—is also an echo of Romans 3:21–31, one which, in context, expands the confession of Romans 3:30: the *one* God will justify *all*.[12] The difference between Jew and gentile may have marked the previous border of the possible. Now, however, accustomed to change and reading again the story of Abraham, Paul discovers that the conditions and the timing of the blessing remove any restraints on the scope of Abraham's family: as the ungodly and before being circumcised, Abraham is justified (Rom 4:9–12). "Not through law" thus explodes a limit: the promise is not only for "those who are of the law." It is a promise that "Abraham" would be "heir of the world," a promise that he would be "the father of us all" (4:13, 16). Heard "according to grace," this promise, in Käsemann's words,

11. For Paul's distinctive use of the wage/gift distinction in this context, see Barclay, *Paul and the Gift* (Grand Rapids: Eerdmans, 2015), 479–89. N. T. Wright, "Paul and the Patriarch: The Role of Abraham in Romans 4," *JSNT* 35.3 (2013): 207–41, suggests that it is not Abraham but his gentile heirs who are identified as "ungodly" in Romans 4:5. For counter arguments, see especially J. Lambrecht, "Romans 4: A Critique of N. T. Wright," *JSNT* 36.2 (2013): 189–94, and D. Shaw, "Romans 4 and the Justification of Abraham in Light of Perspectives New and Newer," *Them* 40.1 (2015): 50–62.

12. For the lexical connections between Romans 3:27–31 and Romans 4, see D. Campbell, *The Deliverance of God: An Apocalyptic Rereading of Justification in Paul* (Grand Rapids: Eerdmans, 2009), 725–27.

"burst apart the circle of receivers": walls at the edge of what can be, when built by human difference, collapse where God gives before and in the absence of worth.[13] As John Barclay notes, the justification of the ungodly "marks" both the breadth and the basis of Abraham's fatherhood: a family as wide as the world is possible only where a promise—a gift—disregards the systems of value that divide. Incongruous grace, in other words, signals "both the goal" of Paul's "Gentile mission" (the creation of a Jew and gentile family) and also the good news that is Paul's gospel (Christ, given to the dead, makes alive).[14]

The promise, then, is "not through law" insofar as law functions as a line that draws the circle of inheritance only around those who are ἐκ νόμου (4:14). More fundamental than this divide, however, is the announcement that "there is no distinction" (Rom 3:23). The law, because it occasions transgressions and works wrath, offers a diagnosis that does not differentiate between human persons; it reduces all, without distinction, to a common denominator: *homo peccator* (4:15; cf. 3:9, 19–20, 23).[15] According to the possible, the law, in Paul's words, is the "emptying" and the "end" of the promise (4:14). But: "by faith" and "according to grace," the apparently barren promise is pregnant: "I have made you the father of many nations" (Rom 4:17 quoting Gen 17:5).

As the addressee of this promise—as the one to whom God said, "so shall your offspring be" (Rom 4:18 quoting Gen 15:5)—Abraham hears and hopes in a God whose grace is beyond the possible: "he believed," says Paul, "the one who gives life to the dead and calls into being that which is not" (Rom 4:17). To call God the creator is both to read Genesis from the beginning and to emphasize the omnipotence of the God of Abraham and of Isaac. Nothingness is no barrier for the one who calls into being because, as Roman 4:21 has it, for this God, what is promised is possible: ὃ ἐπήγγελται δυνατός ἐστιν καὶ ποιῆσαι. More startlingly, however, Paul's confession interprets the birth of Isaac from the conditions of advanced age and infertility as a miracle of life out of death. Old and barren, Paul reads; dead and dead, Paul writes (νεκρόω; νέκρωσις, 4:19). What God promised—"so shall your offspring be"—is, according

13. E. Käsemann, "The Faith of Abraham in Romans 4," in *Perspectives on Paul*, trans. M. Kohl (Philadelphia: Fortress, 1971), 88–89.

14. Barclay, *Paul and the Gift*, 482: "the scope and means of justification are interlinked . . . justification by faith marks both the goal (the inclusion of Gentiles with Jews) and the means (the disregard of the normal tokens of value)" of Paul's "mission to Gentiles."

15. Cf. Watson, *Hermeneutics of Faith*, 168–69: "Paul's reading of scripture is a reading in black and white." Replacing an interpretation of scripture in which "the boundary between light and darkness" is "set at the border between the holy people and the idolatrous realm of the Gentiles," Paul redraws "the border" at the site of the distinction "between God and humankind." See chap. 6, "Announcing the Human."

to Paul, beyond the possible. But the impossible is, again and again on Paul's reading, what God says and gives: out of Abraham's ungodliness God calls and creates righteousness; out of Abraham and Sarah's deadness God promises and creates a child. As Paul says later in Romans, Isaac is a "child not of the flesh" but, at and out of the impossible, a "child born by the promise" (9:8).

What then does Paul say that Abraham has discovered? A pattern of promise: God speaks and gives, incongruously, to the ungodly and the dead; and this word, this gift, impossibly, creates righteousness and makes alive. To read Genesis this way—to perceive history "according to grace"—is to be accustomed to change. As Wesley Hill observes, Paul's interpretation of Genesis is marked by "a kind of chronological confusion": the apostle's reading of patriarchal history is forged in the events of Good Friday and Easter.[16] That Paul hears silence and says "ungodly" in the narrative of Abraham's justification suggests that he reads from the announcement that, as Romans 5 has it, "Christ died for the ungodly" (Rom 5:6–8)—a death that is at once a demonstration of God's love and a redemption that, as grace, creates righteousness and gives righteousness (Rom 3:21–26). Similarly, to interpret old and barren as a deadness from which birth is the miracle of being made alive is to read Genesis according to the confession of the gospel: "we believe in the one who raised our Lord Jesus from the dead" (Rom 4:24).

In making these moves Paul becomes, in Walter Benjamin's sense, "a historian," one who "grasps the constellation which his own era has formed with a definite earlier one."[17] Reading from the end, Paul returns to a canonical history that is "in narrative terms the beginning, but" which, in the pattern and language of Paul's interpretation, is, as John Barclay writes, a "reflection of the startling incongruity that believers have experienced in the gift of" the crucified and risen "Christ."[18] Abraham's ungodliness is not the end, but only because Christ died for and gives righteousness to the ungodly. Sarah's empty womb is not the end, but only because of the empty grave.

The Laughters of Faith: Hope against Hope

In Romans 4, κατὰ χάριν expresses a pattern of promise that holds Abrahamic history together: at the site of sin, righteousness; where human difference

16. W. Hill, *Paul and the Trinity: Persons, Relations, and the Pauline Letters* (Grand Rapids: Eerdmans, 2015), 56. Cf. U. Wilckens, *Die Brief an die Römer*, EKKNT 6 (Zurich: Benziger; Neukirchen-Vluyn: Neukirchener, 1978–82), 1:279–85.
17. Benjamin, "Theses on the Philosophy of History," 263, Thesis A.
18. Barclay, *Paul and the Gift*, 486.

divides, one family; from nothing, calling into being; out of death, life. All this, "according to grace." As Paul reads Genesis, however, Abraham's faith is not in grace. Rather, "Abraham believed God." But God—the God of Abraham and of Isaac—is also the God of Easter. "Abraham believed God," says Genesis; "we believe in the God who raised Jesus from the dead," confesses Paul. This confession defines an identity: the God of Genesis is the God of the gospel. Just so, however, the events of the gospel—"Jesus was handed over for our trespasses and raised for our justification," as Paul proclaims them in Romans 4:25—disclose both the pattern of the promise and also the identity of the one who promises. To use Paul's own language, the gospel unveils not only grace, but also "the God who . . ."[19]

This formulation—God as "the one who . . ."—appears at the end of Romans 4 as an announcement of Easter: God is "the one who raised our Lord Jesus from the dead." This proclamation of the gospel, however, also patterns earlier identifications of the God of Genesis. God is, in Romans 4:5 and 4:17, "the one who": justifies the ungodly, gives life to the dead, and calls into being that which is not." In each instance, as in the confession of resurrection in Romans 4:24, God is named with a substantive participle: the one who—raised, justifies, gives life, calls. And in each instance, God's action is directed to and creates out of the opposite: God raised, the crucified; justifies, the ungodly; calls, that which is not; gives life, to the dead. Martin Luther captures the pattern. "It is of the nature of God," he says," that he makes something out of nothing." As creator, God does the impossible. As giver, Luther adds, God's grace is incongruous: "Thus God accepts no one except the abandoned, makes no one healthy except the sick, brings no one to life except the dead, [and] makes no one holy except sinners."[20] Like Luther—who is taking his cues from Paul—Romans 4 links the language of creation and salvation and gestures toward a God whose giving rhymes in three radical forms: *creatio ex nihilo*, *resurrectio mortuorum*, and *iustificatio impii*.[21] This suggests, on the one hand, that the creator is the unconditioned giver: "out of nothing" means "by grace

19. For the way Paul's language about God in Romans 4 is shaped by the gospel, see Hill, *Paul and the Trinity*, 56, and J. Flebbe, *Solus Deus: Untersuchungen zur Rede von Gott im Brief des Paulus an die Römer*, BZNW 158 (Berlin: de Gruyter, 2008), 257.

20. WA 1:183.39–184.7. Käsemann continues this line of thought: "daß Gott immer nur dort schafft, wo irdisch nichts vorhanden ist" (*Römer*, 117).

21. See O. Bayer, "The Ethics of Gift," *LQ* 24 (2010): 452. For the linking of the liturgical predictions of Romans 4:5 and 4:17 and the way they together describe a *modus operandi* that connects the divine acts of creation, resurrection, and justification, see Linebaugh, *God, Grace, and Righteousness*, 152–54; cf. Käsemann, *Römer*, 116–17.

alone"—it means in Oswald Bayer's words, creation as "an absolute, categorical giving, that finds nothing in its recipients" but contradicts their nothingness by calling them into being.[22] The traffic runs both ways, however. As the God of the gospel, God is also the God of Genesis: the giver is and acts as the creator. Concerning "the divine work of justification," writes Luther, Romans drives its reader to "say with Paul that we are nothing at all, just as we have been created out of nothing." As the recipient of God's gift, the *homo peccator* is, from this "nothing," "called righteous" and so is, *ex nihilo*, "a new creature."[23]

What Luther is tuned into is a pattern in Romans 4 according to which the disjunction between what God says and those to whom God speaks suggests that verbs like καλέω and δικαιόω are *verba Dei* that do the *opera Dei*—words of God that are and enact the works of God. It is that which is not (τὰ μὴ ὄντα) that God calls (καλέω) into being (4:17). It is to the ungodly (ἀσεβής) that God says, and so gives and creates, righteousness (4:5).[24] It is the dead (νεκρός) who are the direct objects of the verbs of resurrection (ζῳοποιέω, 4:17; ἐγείρω, 4:24) and so, as in the Gospels, it is those who are not living who listen to the words "get up," "come out," and, as Ephesians has it, "wake up, sleeper, rise from the dead." God's word does not merely describe reality. It determines reality: what is and what can be are what God's promise establishes and opens.

It is this God—the one who as Psalm 33:9 proclaims, "spoke and it was done"—whom Abraham hears and in whom Abraham hopes. What God promises is beyond the possible: creation from nothing, the justification of the ungodly, life from the dead. But precisely where the earthly calculus of what can be is in the grave, God creates and God gives. Abraham considered the human conditions: his body was dead and Sarah's womb was dead (Rom 4:19). Hope has no home in what Barclay calls "the previous conditions of the possible."[25] But: the impossible, when it is what God promises, is possible: ὃ ἐπήγγελται δυνατός ἐστιν καὶ ποιῆσαι (Rom 4:21). This, in Käsemann's words, is

---

22. Bayer, "The Ethics of Gift," 452; cf. W. W. Schumacher, *Who Do I Say That You Are? Anthropology and the Theology of Theosis in the Finnish School of Tuomo Mannermaa* (Eugene, OR: Wipf & Stock, 2010), 151: "*ex nihilo* is the *sola gratia* of the doctrine of creation."

23. LW 34:113, 156.

24. According to Bayer's reconstruction, Luther's reformation breakthrough is tied up with a development in his understanding of language: rather than a word functioning only as a sign (*signum*) that refers to a reality (*res*), Luther came to see that God's words (*verba Dei*) are God's work (*opera Dei*), that divine speech establishes rather than merely refers to reality. The *signum* is the doing of the *res*. Luther describes the divine address as a *verbum efficax*, LW 5:140; cf. O. Bayer, *Promissio: Geschichte der reformatischen Wende in Luthers Theologie*, 2nd ed. (Darmstadt: Wissenschaftliche Buchgesellschaft, 1989).

25. Barclay, *Paul and the Gift*, 412.

where grace and faith meet: in an "exodus" from the horizons of what can be into the promise land of mercy and miracle where "God in his sole efficacy and grace is the first and last word."[26]

Abraham's faith flies the banner under which faith always lives: "in hope, against hope, he believed." It is not that faith is a generic openness to the absurd. Rather, faith is created by and clings to a promise that is, at once, beyond the possible and yet—as the word of God—the definition of what can and will be, of what, by being spoken by the creator, is. As in the Abrahamic narrative, faith, for Paul, is a double laughter. Hearing the impossible promise—"I will give you a son by Sarah"—Abraham looks at his age and Sarah's barrenness and, as Genesis says, "fell on his face and laughed" (Gen 17:15–17). But that is not the last laughter. "The Lord visited Sarah as he had said, and the Lord did to Sarah as he had promised." So faith laughs again: "Sarah said, 'God has made laughter for me; everyone who hears will laugh over me'" (Gen 21:1–7). As Francis Watson writes, "Paul sets faith on the border between despair and hope and sees it facing in both directions."[27] Its motto, to borrow a phrase, is "with people this is impossible, but with God all things are possible" (Matt 19:26). Such faith, Paul says, does what the world of Romans 1 refused: it "gives glory to God" (Rom 4:20), trusting that God's will and God's word is the only frontier of what can be. In Martin Luther's words, Paul's reading of the Abraham narrative "preaches nothing but the glory of God," that is, it "confesses our impossibility and God's possibility."[28]

Abraham's "faith," according to Paul, "was counted to him as righteousness" (Gen 15:6; Rom 4:3, 22) "because" (διό, 4:22) it is this double laughter: even as it considers Abraham's age and Sarah's barrenness and says, "death" (Rom 4:19), faith hears the promise and "believes the God who gives life to the dead" (4:17; 4:20–21).[29] Located in this land of sin and death, faith faces earthly reality and "speaks in the *via negationis*": impossible.[30] Following the finger of John the Baptist, however, faith looks away from the human conditions and listens

26. Käsemann, "The Faith of Abraham in Romans 4," 93; cf. Käsemann, *Romans*, 124.

27. Watson, *Paul and the Hermeneutics of Faith*, 169. Cf. A. Nygren, *Romans*, 179–81.

28. LW 32:156. See E. Adam, "Abraham's Faith and Gentile Disobedience: Textual Links Between Romans 1 and Romans 4," *JSNT* 65 (1997): 47–66; cf. Käsemann, *Romans*, 124–25. For Luther's reflections on the way faith fulfills the first commandment and can even be called "the creator of the deity," though "not in God but in us," see LW 26:227; WA 40.1:360, 8.

29. The passive forms of ἐνδυναμόω and πληροφορέω in 4:20 and 4:21 suggest that Abraham's faith is created by God through the promise (cf. Rom 10:17).

30. Bayer, *Martin Luther's Theology: A Contemporary Interpretation*, trans. T. H. Trapp (Grand Rapids: Eerdmans, 2008), 172.

instead to the divine word: what to the eye cannot be, becomes, as God's word to the ear, what is.

God's promises are beyond what is humanly possible. And so faith's first laughter, against hope, considers what can be and laughs with Abraham: "Impossible." Faith's final laughter, however, in the hope carried by the word that calls forth light from darkness and life from death, sounds more like Sarah: "Impossible? Perhaps. But God has done what God has promised." To quote Käsemann once more, even at the null point—barren, ungodly, nothing, dead—there is "hope . . . for those who have no hope," because "faith" lives where "natural possibilities" die and "hope" is born "where graves cannot hold the dead."[31]

W. H. Auden was right: "Nothing can save us that is possible, / we who must die demand a miracle." But God, answering a prayer Augustine once uttered, gives what death demands: the impossible we cannot do, God has promised. As another poet put it, "Death, thou wast once / . . . Nothing but bones, / The sad effect of sadder groans. "But"—the poet continues with a characteristically Pauline contrast that announces something new—"since our Saviour's death has put some blood / Into thy face, / Thou art grown fair and full of grace" (George Herbert, "Death"). As in *The Alcestiad*, death and resurrection proclaim the dawn: "Death, the sun is risen. You are shaking. . . . Start accustoming yourself to change." Apollo's song is Paul's confession: "We believe in the one who raised from the dead our Lord Jesus, who was handed over for our trespasses and raised for our justification" (Rom 4:24–25). This gospel—this righteousness and this resurrection—shapes the way Paul reads. The God of Abraham and of Isaac is "the one who": justifies the ungodly, gives life to the dead, and calls into being that which is not. "In the beginning, God said . . ." And from the beginning, Paul might say, the pattern of that promise has been grace: God gives, incongruously, to the ungodly and the dead and God creates, impossibly, righteousness and life. Such promises are beyond the possible. But the son is risen and the apostle invites us to accustom ourselves to change: where we could only look and weep at the conditions of sin, nothingness, and death, we can now listen and laugh as God promises righteousness, creation, and life.

31. Käsemann, *Romans*, 124, 166.

CHAPTER 3

Not the End

THE HISTORY AND HOPE OF GOD'S UNFAILING WORD IN ROMANS 9–11

> *The whole of history [is] a concealed witness, a riddle that cannot*
> *be solved, without plowing with another heifer than our reason.*
>
> —Johann Georg Hamann, *Socratic Memorabilia*

Paul knows the future. That, at least, is what the contrast between the present Paul describes in Romans 9 and 10 and the mystery he unveils in Romans 11:25–32 suggests. With grief, pain, and prayer (9:2; 10:1), Paul confronts the apparent collateral damage of the "word" by which God has "called a not my people, my people" (9:25): the advent and proclamation of Israel's Christ (9:5; 10:14–18) has occasioned Israel's stumble (9:32; cf. 11:11). In the words of Romans 3:3, "some did not believe" (ἀπιστέω); and in Romans 9–11 that "some" sounds more like "most" (9:27; 11:2–5, 7). The Israelites, Paul's "kindred according to the flesh" (9:3; cf. 11:1), to whom "belong the adoption, the glory, the covenants, the giving of the law, the promises, and the patriarchs" (9:4–5) are, in Paul's present, "hardened" (11:25) and "disobedient" (10:21; 11:30–32); they are, through unbelief (ἀπιστία, 11:20, 23), like branches broken off from the root that the sustains their life (11:17). "Great sorrow" and "unceasing anguish" indeed.

But what did Bob Dylan say? "When you're standing at the crossroads / That you cannot comprehend / Just remember that death is not the end."[1] Paul, in Romans 9–11, is standing at a crossroads, and Paul remembers: "now" is "not the end." While the present requires two terms to describe Israel—the "remnant" (11:5) and "the rest" (11:7)—this is, for Paul, the middle rather than

---

1. "Death Is Not the End," written and performed by Bob Dylan, on *Down in the Groove* (Special Rider Music, 1988).

32

the end of history, it is a "now" that persists only "until." And it is that "until," described in Romans 11:25 as "until the fullness of the Gentiles comes in," that names the horizon of hope: "all Israel will be saved" (11:26).

It is here, however, that the sphinx of Romans 11 poses its riddle: How does Paul know the future? By what theological and emotional path does Paul travel from the anguished prayer that opens chapters 9 and 10 to the euphoric poem that closes chapter 11? How, to put it plainly, does Paul know "all Israel will be saved"? As Ernst Käsemann asked the question, how can "the long detour" of Romans 9–10 be understood as a "meaningful and necessary" road to Romans 11:25–32?[2]

At its root, this question about the relationship between Romans 9–10 and Romans 11 is a specific way of asking the perennial question about the relationship between, in Käsemann's words, justification and salvation history: is Paul's soteriology a subplot that finds its meaning within the story of God, Israel, and the nations or is the gift of Jesus that calls sinners righteous the hermeneutical unveiling, the event in time that gives meaning and voice to all times?[3] To get at this issue, however, I want to ask a more specific question: is Paul's revelation about the salvation of "all Israel" commensurable with the pattern of thought developed in Romans 9–10 or does it stand in irresolvable tension with the arguments that precede it? Proponents of the latter reading are not without evidence. If Paul's insistence that the "word of God has not failed" (9:6a) is not disqualified by the reduction of Israel to a remnant, is it not confused to assume, as Romans 11:11–32 seems to, that God's faithfulness will mean the erasing of the line between the remnant and the rest?[4] Does not the assertion that Israel is "loved on account of their fathers" (11:28) revert to precisely the genealogical calculation of election that Romans 9:6–13 dismantled ("it is not the children of the flesh who are the children of God," says 9:8)?[5] Is it not the case that the juxtaposition of theses such as "there is no difference between

2. E. Käsemann, *Romans*, trans. G. W. Bromiley (Grand Rapids: Eerdmans, 1980), 314.

3. E. Käsemann, "Justification and Salvation History in the Epistle to the Romans," in *Perspectives on Paul* (Philadelphia: Fortress, 1971), 60–78. For a discussion of this theme, and Käsemann's reading of justification more generally, see especially P. F. M. Zahl, *Die Rechtfertigungslehre Ernst Käsemann* (Stuttgart: Calwer, 1996).

4. See T. Donaldson, "'Riches for the Gentiles' (Rom 11:12): Israel's Rejection and Paul's Gentile Mission," *JBL* 12 (1993): 81–98: "While in Romans 9:1–11:10 the thrust of the argument is that the present situation is in no way inconsistent with God's promises to Israel, the argument from 11:11 proceeds on the assumption that the present situation has to be overcome if God is to be proved faithful" (89).

5. Cf. B. W. Longenecker, "Different Answers to Different Issues: Israel, the Gentiles and Salvation History in Romans 9–11," *JSNT* 36 (1989): 95–123.

Jew and Greek" (10:12) and "all Israel will be saved" (11:26) reflects a wrestling with the dual themes of God's impartiality and Israel's election that ends not in a satisfying answer but in an antimony?[6]

This chapter is a "no" to these questions. Unexpected though Paul's confidence about Israel's future feels in the wake of his grief and prayer, it is a confidence about the future forged in the history of God's word in the present and the past. At its core, the contention of Romans 9:6–11:10 is that the divine economy reflected in Israel's scriptures is consonant with the habits of divine action that characterize Paul's present: as "the one who calls" (9:11), God is and has been "the one who has mercy" (9:16). Considered in conversation with the voices of Israel's historians and prophets, the surprising dealings of God in the present look less like an aberration than a *modus operandi*—a pattern that unites past and present and thereby reveals the rhyme scheme of history in all its tenses. And here, in the harmony of history present and past, is the ground of Paul's hope: God is the one who has mercy; God was the one who has mercy; God will be the one who has mercy. Because the present, together with the past it makes legible, are connected by the operations of God's unconditioned and incongruous mercy, the witness of history in present and past tenses engender, to borrow a phrase from Johann Georg Hamann, "a like hope," a confidence that the future will rhyme with the present and the past as God's promise once again performs the miracle of mercy: "and this will be my covenant with them: I will take away their sins" (11:27).

My thesis then: Paul knows the future because he knows the present and the past. It is the pattern of divine action that is revealed in the present and read in the past that Paul promises as the future. Tracing this movement means standing with Paul in his present and, from that now of pain and grief, following his gaze, first backwards as he rereads Israel's scriptures, and then forward as he imagines Israel's salvation. Paul's promise, "all Israel will be saved" (11:26), is made at and as the end of this dynamic interplay between present, past, and future. Hope, you might say, is the child of history, and for Paul, in Romans 9–11, it is the union of history present and past that makes a promise: now is "not the end."

---

6. For this theme, see especially C. Cosgrove, *Elusive Israel: The Puzzle of Election in Romans* (Louisville: Westminster John Knox, 1997), 27–38, 65–90. For variations of the thesis that Romans 11:11–32, or at least Romans 11:25–27, is ultimately incompatible with Romans 9:6–10:21 (or 9:6–11:10), see H. Räisänen, "Paul, God, and Israel: Romans 9–11 in Recent Research," in *The Social World of Formative Christianity and Judaism*, ed. J. Neusner et al. (Philadelphia: Fortress, 1998), 178–208; J. Lambrecht, "Israel's Future according to Romans 9–11: An Exegetical and Hermeneutical Approach," in *Pauline Studies* (Leuven: Peeters, 1994), 34–54; M. Wolter, "Das Israelproblem nach Gal 4, 21–31 und Röm 9–11," *ZTK* 107 (2010): 25–29.

THE PRESENT

Strange reversals shape Paul's present: Israel has stumbled in their race to "the law of righteousness" (9:31; cf. 11:9, 11), while gentiles, without running, find themselves at the finish-line of the "righteousness of faith" (9:30; cf. 10:4, 20); whereas Israel is hardened (11:25), reduced to a remnant (9:27–29; 11:5; cf. 11:7–10), disobedient (10:21; 11:30–32), and disconnected from their life-giving root (11:17), the gentiles, though not God's people and unloved, are called "my people," "loved," and "children of the living God" (9:25–26). Vis-à-vis the nations, this signals the success of Paul's gentile mission (cf. 11:13); but it is, at the same time, a source of sorrow: "I am not lying," says Paul, "I have great pain and constant anguish" and "my heart's desire and prayer to God for them is that they may be saved" (9:2; 10:1).[7]

Romans 9–11 is written from this open wound. But in this now of pain and prayer Paul also makes a promise: "The word of God has not failed."[8] As we will consider below, this means that the past history of God's word shares a shape with the surprises of Paul's present (9:6b–29; 11:1–10), but it also indi-

---

7. The pathos here confirms Wolter's observation that "das Israelproblem" is about Israel *qua* Israel rather than Israel as representative of some more general theological question ("Das Israelproblem," 20–21). This resists the tendency to make Israel into a Pauline parable of either sin (e.g., Paul's critique of justification by works "strikes the hidden Jew in all of us") or salvation (e.g., Israel's redemption in Romans 11 is an illustration of the justification of the ungodly); see, respectively, E. Käsemann, "Paul and Israel," in *New Testament Questions of Today* (London: SCM, 1969), 186, and *Romans*, 260, 266, 317. This recalls the method of Moses Mendelssohn, who attempts to express Judaism as a natural, rational, and universal religion by filtering out the contextual and historical elements (the "temporal truths of history," in Lessing's phrase), leaving a religion that is supposedly identical to the "eternal truths" deducible through reason (*Jerusalem oder über religiöse Macht und Judentum*, 1783). This tendency to make Israel a representation or cipher rather than allow the concreteness of history to stand, together with all instances of reducing people (or better: persons) to a parable, are liable to Hamann's critique of Mendelssohn: he "severs . . . the temporal from the eternal" and leaves, where there was a living whole, "two dead halves." See "Golgotha and Scheblimini," in *Hamann: Writings on Philosophy and Language*, ed. K. Haynes (Cambridge: Cambridge University Press, 2007), 179.

8. For the programmatic significance of Romans 9:6a for Romans 9–11 as a whole, see C. E. B. Cranfield, *A Critical and Exegetical Commentary on the Epistle to the Romans*, 2 vols., ICC (Edinburgh: T&T Clark, 1975), 2:473; E. Lohse, *Der Brief an die Römer*, KEK 4 (Göttingen: Vandenhoek & Ruprecht, 2003), 270; cf. Jochen Flebbe's observation that Romans 9:6a indicates that, for Paul, the "Israelproblem" is also and more deeply a "Gottesfrage," *Solus Deus: Untersuchungen zur Rede von Gott im Brief des Paulus an die Römer*, BZNW 158 (Berlin: de Gruyter, 2008), 268–69.

cates that, for Paul, the paradoxes of what he calls "the now time" (11:5), far from disqualifying God's faithfulness, lay bare the grammar of God's word: God's word performs what it promises, both "carrying out" the divine "sentence" (9:27) and calling without condition (9:25–26). That Paul locates this double-effect both in the present and as an effect of God's word is evident as he reapplies the voice of Hosea to describe the calling of the gentiles—"her who was not loved I will call 'loved'" (9:25–26)—and as the reduction of Israel to a remnant is heard as the content of Isaiah's cry: "Though the number of the sons of Israel be as the sand of the sea, only a remnant of them will be saved" (9:27–29).[9] This suggests that, for Paul, as he reads his current and canonical history together, there is a twofold relation between past and present. First, the present is consistent with the scriptural past: as "scripture says of Elijah . . . in the same way there is, at the present time, a remnant" (11:3, 5). Second, the present is the proper tense for the voice of Israel's prophets: Israel's stumble is occasioned by the placement of Isaiah's promised "rock of offense" (9:33, fusing Isa 8:14 to Isa 28:16),[10] and the gentiles' reception of righteousness (9:30) is God's "yes and amen" to Hosea's prophecy: "in the very place where it was said of them, 'You are not my people,' there they will be called 'children of the living God'" (9:26; Hos 2:1).

As Paul listens to Israel's prophets, however, he hears more than a promised future that is his present; he hears an announcement that the future will be the aftermath of an event. The prophets, as Paul lets them speak in the present-tense, say that salvation and stumbling are the double-effect of a single cause. This is, perhaps, most evident as Paul invites Isaiah to provide the color commentary for the race to righteousness he announces in Romans 9:30–33. In a competition that Calvin describes as a "singular paradox," the "Gentiles, who did not pursue righteousness, attained righteousness," while "Israel, run-

---

9. For Paul's appropriation of Hosea 2:25 and 2:21 in Romans 9:25 and 9:26 respectively, see J. R. Wagner, "'Not from the Jews Only, but Also from the Gentiles': Mercy to the Nations in Romans 9–11," in *Between Gospel and Election*, ed. F. Wilk and J. R. Wagner, WUNT 257 (Tübingen: Mohr Siebeck, 2010), 422. For the remnant motif indicating judgment in Romans 9:24–33, see F. Wilk, *Die Bedeutung des Jesajabuches für Paulus*, FRLANT 179 (Göttingen: Vandenhoeck & Ruprecht, 1998), 186; cf. U. Wilckens, *Der Brief an die Römer*, 3 vols., EKKNT (Zurich: Benziger; Neukirchen-Vluyn: Neukirchener, 1978–82), 2:198; Lohse, *Der Brief an die Römer*, 276, 283.

10. The lexemes that Paul lifts from Isaiah 8:14 are πρόσκομμα and πέτραν. For a full discussion of Paul's textual emendations to Isaiah 28:16 and an accompanying suggestion that Paul was writing from "a Septuagint text that had been reworked . . . to bring it closer to a Hebrew exemplar," see J. R. Wagner, *Heralds of the Good News: Isaiah and Paul "In Concert" in the Letter to the Romans*, NovTSup 101 (Leiden: Brill, 2002), 130.

ning after the law of righteousness, did not catch up with the law" (9:30–31).[11] A bizarre result, to be sure; but as Paul reads Isaiah from the finish-line, he discovers that this surprise is in scripture. By adding the words "stumbling" and "rock" from Isaiah 8:14 to Isaiah 28:16, Paul, as Francis Watson notes, "creates a text that announces a forthcoming divine act with two contrasting outcomes": "Behold, I am laying in Zion a stone of stumbling, and a rock of offense; and whoever believes in him will not be put to shame" (Rom 9:33).[12] God, Paul hears Isaiah say, will place a stone that will simultaneously occasion stumbling and salvation.[13] Well . . . for Paul, what's promised is present: the rock has reduced Israel to a remnant as it has, at the same time, created a "my people" out of the gentiles.

Paul's diagnosis of his present does not stop here, however. It is more concrete—it is, in a word, more christological. While Romans 9–11 invites us to say, as Käsemann does, that "Salvation history is . . . the history of the word which . . . accomplishes election and rejection,"[14] Paul, in Romans 10, is more particular: the word that both calls and cuts short is, in Paul's phrases, "the word of faith that we proclaim" (10:8); it is "the word of Christ" (10:17). For Paul, the word of God that has not failed, the word spoken by the prophets and fulfilled in Paul's present, is active now as the apostolic announcement of Jesus Christ. Where Isaiah speaks of "those who proclaim good news" (Isa 52:7; 10:15) and "the message" (Isa 53:1; Rom 10:16), Paul hears a reference to the preaching of "the gospel" (Rom 10:16). And it is this gospel, this "word of Christ," that is the agent of judgment and grace as rejection and election are concretely realized in and as unbelief and faith: "not all have obeyed the gospel" (10:16) and, conversely, "faith comes by hearing" (10:17).

This means, on the one hand, that Israel's stumble is the failure to "submit to the righteousness of God revealed in Christ" (Rom 10:3–4); the symptoms of

---

11. J. Calvin, "Acts 14–28 and Romans 1–6," in *Calvin's Commentaries*, vol. 19, trans. J. Owen (Grand Rapids: Baker, 2003), 377.

12. F. Watson, *Paul, Judaism and the Gentiles: Beyond the New Perspective* (Grand Rapids: Eerdmans, 2007), 323.

13. For the future form of καταισχύνω as a reference to final judgment and thus as a reference to eschatological salvation when qualified by the negative particle (οὐ), see R. Bultmann, "αἰσχύνω κτλ," in *TDNT* 1, ed. G. Kittel, trans. G. W. Bromiley (Grand Rapids: Eerdmans, 1964), 189. For Israel's stumble as the result of intentional divine action, see M. Theobald, *Studien zum Römerbrief*, WUNT 136 (Tübingen: Mohr Siebeck, 2001), 374–78; F. Avemarie, "Israels rätselhafter Ungehorsam: Römer 10 als Anatomie eines von Gott provozierten Unglaubens," in *Between Gospel and Election*, ed. F. Wilk and J. R. Wagner, WUNT 257 (Tübingen: Mohr Siebeck, 2010), 299–320.

14. Käsemann, *Romans*, 273.

Israel's "spirit of stupor" (11:8) are the pursuit of the law "as if by works" (9:32) and ignorance (10:2) of the "Christ" who "is the end of the law" (10:4); the "ears that would not hear" (11:8) can listen to Moses's words about "the righteousness of the law" as a summons to life via the law (10:5), but they are deaf to the presence of Christ in the promise spoken by the "righteousness of faith": "The word is near you" (10:6–8). However one reads the disputed references to "works," "law," and "their own righteousness," it is evident that Israel, according to Paul's diagnosis, assumes that God's calculation of righteousness will factor in their nomistic privileges and/or practices whereas Paul insists that in the divine economy the only currency is Christ.[15] This is, to the Jew, an offense because in rendering their possession and observance of the law irrelevant for salvation, Paul effectively voids the soteriological value of what John Barclay calls "their pre-existing capital."[16] But this offense is, at the same time, an open door: "there is no distinction between Jew and Greek; for the same Lord is Lord of all, bestowing his riches on all who call on him" (10:12).

Here is the other side of the christological coin: though offensive in its unconditional distribution, the wealth of God given in Christ is, precisely because of its unconditional operations, given to all. This can be seen as much in the call that chooses the remnant as in the call that creates beloved children from the gentiles. For Paul, Isaiah's promise that "a remnant will be saved" (Isa 10:22; Rom 9:27) is fulfilled in the present existence of "a remnant chosen according to grace" (Rom 11:5). This grace, defined negatively by the clause "not by works" (11:6), connects the call of the remnant both to the "calling-into-being of Israel" and to the current calling of the gentiles.[17] Like those who did "not bow the knee to Baal" in the time of Elijah because God acted, saying "I have kept for myself" (11:2–4),[18] like Jacob who was chosen "not because of works but because of him who calls" (9:11), and like the gentiles who in contrast to

---

15. Käsemann, *Romans*, 277, 281–82, and Cranfield, *Romans*, 2:515, articulate the view that Paul's critique is of a nomistic practice, problematic both because of transgression and, more deeply, because of the *ambitio divinitatis* that motivates it. For the view that Paul's polemic targets a presumption rooted in Israel's privileges, especially election and the possession of the law, see, for example, J. D. G. Dunn, *Romans 9–16*, WBC 38B (Waco, TX: Word, 1988), 595.

16. J. M. G. Barclay, *Paul and the Gift* (Grand Rapids: Eerdmans, 2015), 539. How this voiding relates to what appears to be its refunding in the references to election, the root, and the fathers in Romans 11 will be explored below.

17. B. R. Gaventa, "On the Calling-into-Being of Israel: Romans 9:6–29," in *Between Gospel and Election*, ed. F. Wilk and J. R. Wagner, WUNT 257 (Tübingen: Mohr Siebeck, 2010), 255–69.

18. Paul adds the reflexive pronoun to the divine speech of 3 Kingdoms 19:18, thereby signaling an emphasis on divine initiative that is sharpened to exclusivity by the antithesis that follows: "by grace, not by works" (11:4, 6).

Israel "did not pursue righteousness . . . as if by works" (9:30, 32), the remnant is constituted, not "by works," but according to a grace that is active when works are absent and/or irrelevant (11:6).[19] This grace, as just noted, is the rock that causes those who race for righteousness "as if by works" to stumble (9:31–32), but it is also, in a world in which "none is righteous" (Rom 3:10) and God "has imprisoned all in disobedience" (11:32), the only rock on which to stand. Because Christ is present in the word without assistance or condition, because he is "near" without being brought either down from heaven or up from the abyss (10:6–8), God's grace can be defined in antithesis to works and as the gift of Christ to all (10:12; 11:6; cf. 9:11). The remnant exists, in other words, not because they, in distinction from the "rest," have met mercy's conditions but only because God, as the one who has mercy, is the one who calls without condition.[20]

As with Israel, so with the gentiles, though whereas the grace that calls the remnant can be described as a *creatio continua*—an ever-present act of creation that keeps that which mercy has already created—the calling of the gentiles, as Paul depicts it, is a *creatio ex nihilo*. Paul's own image is that of the non-runners winning the race to righteousness, but it is his re-voicing of the prophets that most pointedly captures the paradox of God's creative call. Isaiah: "I have been found by those who did not seek me; I have shown myself to those who did not ask for me" (Isa 65:1; Rom 10:20). Hosea: "I will call the not my people, my people, and the not loved I will call loved. And in the place where it was said to them, 'You are not my people,' there they will be called 'children of the living God'" (Hos 2:23 and 2:1; Rom 9:25). These dramatic mismatches—not seeking but finding, not loved but loved, not asking but seeing, not a people but a people—reveal both the power and the pattern of God's word: God's word is creative and unconditioned—that is, it performs the paradoxical promise it speaks, creating from the nothingness of the gentiles beloved sons and daughters of God.

So far Paul's present. The prophets announced an event and its impact, a divine act that would mean both stumbling and salvation. These promises are, according to Paul, the present: the cutting short of Israel and the incongruous calling of the gentiles are the double effect of the one "word of Christ." It is, in

19. The contrast here between ἔργα and χάρις also echoes Paul's description of the justification of Abraham in Romans 4:4–5.

20. Cf. John Barclay's discussion of the remnant as a sign of God's mercy on the ungodly rather than God's preservation of the godly in "Paul's Story: Theology as Testimony," in *Narrative Dynamics in Paul: A Critical Assessment*, ed. B. W. Longenecker (Louisville: Westminster John Knox, 2002), 151–52.

other words, the preached Christ that both occasions and makes sense of the paradoxes of Paul's present. But what of his past? If the word of God that has not failed is both the scriptural word and the word of faith, if it is, in other words, spoken in the past and the present, then the creative and unconditioned word operative in the present must cohere with the habits of God's word in Israel's canonical history. Paul thus becomes, in Walter Benjamin's sense, "a historian," one who "grasps the constellation which his own era has formed with a definite earlier one."[21] In returning to Israel's scriptural past, Paul does not so much construct as uncover a history written with the grammar revealed in the gospel. He is, in other words, more reader than writer. And thus, while it is the word of Christ that makes legible the words of scripture, this, for Paul, is not a reason to forget the canonical past; rather the christological legibility of scripture is an invitation to read—to remember.[22]

The Past

"To articulate the past historically," writes Walter Benjamin, "means to seize hold of a memory as it flashes up at a moment of danger."[23] This captures the pathos of Romans 9–11, the grief and pain that prompts Paul to remember. But it also describes Paul's response to his "moment of danger": he seizes hold of a memory by rereading Israel's scriptures. The present moment of danger is occasioned and shaped by God's creative and unconditioned word, a word Paul defines as "the word of Christ" which both reduces Israel to a remnant

21. W. Benjamin, "Theses on the Philosophy of History," in *Illuminations: Essays and Reflections*, ed. H. Arendt, trans. H. Eiland and K. McLaughlin (Cambridge: Harvard University Press, 1999), 263, Thesis A.

22. For Paul, then, unlike G. E. Lessing, Israel's scripture is not an "antiquated" "primer" or once helpful "hint" that can be "dispensed with" in the evolution of "the education of the human race" (*Lessing's Theological Writings*, trans. H. Chadwick [Stanford, CA: Stanford University Press, 1957], 97, 91, 94). Hamann, riffing on Lessing, is closer to the Pauline suggestion that the time of the gospel, rather than rendering Israel's scriptures outdated, opens the present as a new time of reading: "the entire history of the Jewish people [is] a living, mind- and heart-rousing primer of all historical literature in heaven, on and under the earth,—an adamantine hint forward to the Jubilee year" ("Golgotha and Scheblimini," 191–92). For Lessing, Christ comes to "tear the exhausted primer from the child's hand" (91); for Hamann, the scriptural scrolls are sealed until Christ comes and breaks them, but this breaking of seals is the opening of the scrolls and thus an invitation to read them—a point reflected in the allusive texture of the Pauline texts (not least Romans 9–11). Cf. J. A. Linebaugh, *God, Grace, and Righteousness in Wisdom of Solomon and Paul's Letter to the Romans: Texts in Conversation*, NovTSup 152 (Leiden: Brill, 2013), 177–226.

23. Benjamin, "Theses on the Philosophy of History," 255 (Thesis VI).

and creates a people by calling those who are no-people. For Paul, however, the word of God that has not failed has a past as well as a present: it is the word spoken to Abraham, "In Isaac your seed will be called" (Rom 9:7; Gen 21:12) and "I will come and Sarah will have a son" (Rom 9:9; Gen 18:14); it is the word spoken to Rebekah, "The older will serve the younger" (Rom 9:12; Gen 25:23); it is the word spoken to Moses, "I will have mercy on whom I have mercy" (Rom 9:15; Exod 33:19); it is the word spoken to Pharaoh, "For this reason I raised you up, that I might demonstrate my power in you" (Rom 9:17; Exod 9:16).

These scriptural words, for Paul, are not just a record of the past. They are a promise. According to Romans 1:1–4, Paul reads the "holy scriptures" as a pre-saying of the gospel (cf. Gal 3:8), but, as Romans 3:21 indicates, the hermeneutical transition from promise to witness occurs in the "now" of the revelation of God's righteousness that is "the redemption that is in Christ Jesus" (3:21–24). In the words of Romans 16:25–26, scripture "now" (νῦν) speaks the mystery it long kept secret because the preaching of Jesus Christ unveils "the law and the prophets" (3:21) as witnesses to the gospel.[24] It is as the time of the preaching of Jesus Christ that Paul's present constitutes what Agamben calls scripture's "now of legibility,"[25] the time at which the proclamation and impact of the gospel reveal, as if by retroactive echo, the "gospelness" of prior events.[26]

It is in this "now of legibility" that Paul rereads his canonical past. What he hears is a history originated, ever newly created, and shaped by the same unconditioned and creative word at work in his present. Three antitheses

24. For a similar account of Paul's hermeneutic, one which sees "Das Alte Testament als integraler Bestandteil des Evangelium" while insisting that the Old Testament is "ein integrales Element" of the gospel "in seiner *Interpretatio Christiana*," see F. Hahn, *Theologie des Neuen Testament*, 2 vols. (Tübingen: Mohr Siebeck, 2005), 1:195–201; cf. 2:38–142.

25. G. Agamben, *The Time That Remains: A Commentary on the Letter to the Romans*, trans. P. Dailey (Stanford: Stanford University Press, 2005), 145, uses the phrase "Das Jetzt der Lesbarkeit" to summarize and define the hermeneutic of Walter Benjamin. See Benjamin, "Theses on the Philosophy of History," 253–64, and *The Arcades*.

26. J. D. Dawson, *Christian Figural Reading and the Fashioning of Identity* (Berkeley: University of California Press, 2002), 134. This relationship between scriptural past and christological present is aptly described with the term *typology* as long as the "Innergeschichtlichkeit" of the *figura* and its fulfillment is maintained; so E. Auerbach, "Figura," *Istanbuler Schriften*, vol. 5, *Neue Dantestudien* (Istanbul, 1944): 54. Rather than dislocating a past event from its location in history and dissolving it into the antitype it anticipates, typology, as a description of Paul, is descriptive of the way the gospel unveils anticipations of itself in Israel's scripture. For a different description of typology, see Agamben, who argues that the type/antitype conceptuality indicates "a caesura that divides the division between times . . . in which the past is dislocated into the present" and thus points to the "inseparable constellation" of typos and antitypos (*The Time That Remains*, 74).

structure Paul's interpretation of the material from Genesis and Exodus he considers. First, the ascription of sonship to Isaac by the words "through Isaac your seed will be called" means that "it is not the children of the flesh who are children of God, but the children of the promise are reckoned as his seed" (Rom 9:8). This curious notion of a promise giving birth recalls Paul's reading of the same narrative in Romans 4. There, the birth of Isaac is described as an act of resurrection in which the "God who gives life to the dead and calls into being that which does not exist" (4:17) creates life out of the deadness of Sarah's womb and Abraham's body (Rom 4:19). In Romans 9, Paul reads God's promise to Abraham as undercutting the assumption that being a child is determined by genealogy. In the case of Isaac, the status "son" is not constituted by parentage; it is called into being (καλέω, 9:7) by the "word of promise" (9:9). Isaac is a child of God because he is born as such by God's future-tense word: "I will come and there will be . . ." (9:9). Read this way, the Isaac narrative underwrites Paul's thesis that "it is not the case that all who are descended from Israel are Israel" (9:6b) by demonstrating that, from their origins, Israelites are God's children, not on the basis of their genealogical relation to Abraham, but because they are, as the reformers liked to say, *creatura verbi Dei*.[27] Beverly Gaventa captures this: "the entity known as 'Israel' is not and never has been defined by birth but only by God's creation; it is not a biological but a theological category."[28] Just as Abraham was reckoned (λογίζομαι, 4:3, 5) righteous before and apart from works (4:1–13), so Isaac, irrespective of his parentage, is, by a promise, reckoned (λογίζομαι, 9:8) a child. The second generation of Israel, in other words, like the first, is called into being by the creative and unconditioned word of the one who both justifies the ungodly (4:5) and creates life out of death (4:17–19).

The third generation intensifies this. By recalling that Jacob and Esau are sons of the same sexual act (9:10), Paul emphasizes their similarity, thus accentuating his observation that the twins "are made dissimilar only by the divine words recorded in scripture": "The older will serve the younger" (Gen 25:23; Rom 9:12).[29] Working from the scriptural word to Rebecca, "before the twins

---

27. Stephen Westerholm notes that Paul does not deny a relation between Abrahamic descent and divine election; he only insists that Abrahamic descent is not the basis for nor identical with being a child of God. "Paul and the Law in Romans 9–11," in *Paul and the Mosaic Law*, ed. J. D. G. Dunn (Tübingen: Mohr Siebeck, 1996), 221–22.

28. Gaventa, "On the Calling-into-Being of Israel," 259. Gaventa's broader argument in this section is that Paul is not apologizing for the current division within Israel but insisting that "the only Israel that exists is the one God brought into being through promise and call" (260).

29. Watson, *Paul, Judaism and the Gentiles*, 309–10.

were born" and therefore before they "had done anything good or bad," Paul constructs his second antithesis: "not by works but by the one who calls" (9:11–12). For Paul, the timing of this promise, as well as its content, preclude any correlation between the divine decision and the worthiness of Jacob.[30] The emphasis here, as in the case of Isaac, is less on the "who" of election than the "how." That is, Paul is tracing the pattern of election and interprets both the Isaac and the Jacob narratives as exemplifications of the unconditionality and provenience of God's word: God's choice does not respond to or recognize an antecedent human reality; it is, to quote Gaventa again, "an act of creation."[31] The purpose clause embedded in Romans 9:11 (ἵνα ἡ κατ᾽ ἐκλογὴν πρόθεσις τοῦ θεοῦ μένῃ) accents this, concentrating the explanation for election exclusively in the pre-choice of God, the προ-prefix indicating that election precedes and therefore precludes any and all human criteria. Thus, as Paul reads the story of Jacob and Esau, he hears a word of election and rejection that neither corresponds to nor is contingent upon prior human difference. Jacob and Esau are the same; it is only God's choice that creates a difference. Rather than attempting to explain the rationale behind God's selection, Paul concludes with a ruthless restatement of God's pre-choice from Malachi: "Jacob I loved; Esau I hated" (Rom 9:13; Mal 1:2–3).

That this scriptural quotation is supposed to sting is confirmed by the question that follows: "What then shall we say, is there injustice with God?"[32]

30. Philo, alert to the destabilizing potential inherit in God's prenatal and unexplained choice of Jacob over Esau, appeals to divine foreknowledge and thus argues that while God's election of Jacob precedes his deeds, it is nevertheless proleptically based on them (*Leg. All.* 3.88–89). For this, see my "Rational or Radical: Origen on Romans 9.10–14," *StPatr* 52 (2011). Cf. *Jubilees* 19 in which the antenatal choice is erased and the Jacob and Esau narrative is rewritten to highlight the correspondence between divine choice and human character.

31. Gaventa, "On the Calling-into-Being of Israel," 260. As in the citation of Genesis 21:21 in Romans 9:7, the use of καλέω here, especially as a divine predicate (ὁ καλῶν, 9:12), recalls the predication of God as ὁ καλῶν τὰ μὴ ὄντα ὡς ὄντα (Rom 4:17) and thereby evokes the creational connotations of the Pauline "calling" motif. For the creative connotations of καλέω in Paul, see S. J. Chester, *Conversion at Corinth: Perspectives on Conversion in Paul's Theology and the Corinthian Church*, SNTW (London: T&T Clark, 2003), 59–112.

32. The history of interpretation of Romans 9:6–14 is, in part, a history of answering this question for Paul. Chrysostom, in his *Homiliae in epistulam ad Romanos*, Homily 16 on Romans 9, followed Philo and explained election in relation to divine foreknowledge. Origen, who, like Augustine after him (see, e.g., *De Spiritu et Littera*), read "not by works" as categorical rather than time-specific, still argued that the election of Jacob and rejection of Esau "did not happen without a reason" (*quomodo haec non extra rationem fiant*) by insisting that Jacob was considered "worthy of God's love" before birth "according to the merits of his previous life" (*praecedentis videlicet vitae meritis*) (*De Principiis* 2.9.7).

Paul's μὴ γένοιτο, however, is not grounded in an uncovering of the previously hidden criteria that distinguished Isaac from Ishmael and Jacob from Esau, but rather in God's words to Moses in the aftermath of the golden calf idolatry: "I will have mercy on whom I have mercy and I will have compassion on whom I have compassion" (Rom 9:15). As in the narrative of Exodus 32–34, for Paul, mercy is not the restoration of the righteous; it is the rebirth of the unrighteous, "the generative divine force that brings something into existence."[33] "Therefore," as Paul's third antithesis deduces from the Exodus quotation, "it is not of the one who wills, or of the one who runs, but of the God who has mercy" (9:16). The references to willing and running add human disposition and achievement to the list of excluded explanations for election, but the striking thing about this antithesis is not so much what is precluded as what is proposed. In tune with Paul's explanation of God's call solely in terms of God's identity as "the one who calls" (9:12), his accounting of the operations of mercy is reducible to a predication: God is "the one who has mercy."[34]

Mercy, however, is not the whole story. Scripture also speaks a word to Pharaoh: "For this reason I raised you up, so that I might demonstrate my power in you and so that my name might be proclaimed throughout the entire earth" (Rom 9:17; Exod 9:16).[35] Paul's silence about Pharaoh's role in the hardening of his own heart (see Exod 8:28; 9:34; 13:15; cf. 1 Sam 6:6) allows him to read God's word to Pharaoh as a counterpart to his word to Moses: "God has mercy on whom he wills and hardens whom he wills" (9:18). Here, as in the contrast between love and hate in the Jacob and Esau narrative, the difference between mercy and hardening is reducible to the sheer fact that "God wills" (θέλει, 9:18). This duality is picked up in Paul's question about "vessels of wrath" and "vessels of mercy" in Romans 9:22–23. In this context, however, the two purpose clauses from God's word to Pharaoh (see the double ὅπως in Rom 9:17) seem to push the relationship between hardening and mercy "from symmetry to teleology."[36] God, as Paul insists by way of the image of the potter, is free to make different objects from the same lump of clay, but his

---

33. J. M. G. Barclay, "'I Will Have Mercy on Whom I Have Mercy': The Golden Calf and Divine Mercy in Romans 9–11 and Second Temple Judaism," *EC* 1 (2010): 100. For Exodus 32–24 as an account of Israel's re-creation parallel to Genesis 6–10, see W. Moberly, *At the Mountain of God: Story and Theology in Exodus 32–34*, JSOTSup 22 (Sheffield: JSOT Press, 1983), 91–93.

34. Cf. Wagner, *Heralds of the Good News*, 50–52.

35. This is most likely an adapted quotation of Exodus 9:16 LXX, substituting ἐξεγείρω for διατηρέω and δύναμις for ἰσχύς; cf. Wagner, *Heralds of the Good News*, 55n36.

36. Watson, *Paul, Judaism and the Gentiles*, 191.

freedom is focused not on the destruction of "vessels of wrath"—an end that never actually occurs in the text—but on the revelation of "the riches of his glory upon the vessels of mercy."[37] For Paul, the twofold effect of God's word is both asymmetrical, enduring vessels of wrath while making known his glory to vessels of mercy, and teleological: God "patiently endures the vessels of wrath . . . in order to (ἵνα) make known the wealth of his glory."

Mercy, then, while free and willed rather than natural and necessary as the potter motif recalls, is nevertheless, as Paul reads the canonical past, "the very fundament of history"[38]—that toward which the divine acts of hatred and hardening are directed. There is hope here. If Isaac and Jacob are called irrespective of their pedigree and performance (9:7–13), if Israel is re-born by mercy in the wake of idolatry (9:15–16), if God hardens in order to have mercy (9:17–23), then maybe the disobedient and hardened "rest" of Israel are not outside the range of God's unconditioned and re-creative grace. That the past and present grammar of God's word is one is evident as Paul connects the vessels of mercy with "us whom he calls, not only from the Jews but also from the Gentiles" (9:24). Like the present word of Christ that both reduces Israel to a remnant (9:27–29) and creates a people out of a no-people (9:25–26), the scriptural word both hardens and has mercy, both hates and loves. But if, as the call of the gentiles reveals, "the word of Christ" says "loved" to those who are not loved, then maybe there is hope on the far side of hatred and hardening. Maybe there is a future. Maybe now is not the end.

THE FUTURE: "A LIKE HOPE"

Romans 10 ends in crisis and in hope. Israel is still a "disobedient and contrary people," but Isaiah's image of God's outstretched arms leaves Paul's prayer for Israel unanswered yet open (10:21). Romans 11 makes a promise as an answer to this prayer: "all Israel will be saved" (11:26). This can feel jarring. The opening of Romans 11 says "no" to the question "has God rejected his people" (11:1) by linking the current division within Israel between the remnant (11:1–6) and the rest (11:7–10) with, on the one hand, those God kept for himself in the time of Elijah and, on the other hand, imprecatory passages from Deuteronomy

---

37. For the potter motif as establishing divine freedom rather than denoting divine caprice, see R. Feldmeier, "Vater und Töpfer? Zur Identität Gottes im Römerbrief," in *Between Gospel and Election*, ed. F. Wilk and J. R. Wagner, WUNT 257 (Tübingen: Mohr Siebeck, 2010), 377–90.

38. Barclay, "The Golden Calf and Divine Mercy," 101.

(29:4 LXX) and the Psalms (68:23–24 LXX). In Romans 11:11, however, Paul expresses a new hope—a horizon beyond the present division in which those who have stumbled are found to be within the sphere of God's mercy.

As noted in the introduction, it is here that some are inclined to call Paul's bluff, suggesting that the future he imagines for Israel is grounded either on nothing or the very premises he rejected to make sense of his present and past. Romans 9 is written to erase every "because" that could conceivably provide a human criterion that identifies or explains why God's mercy was attracted to an Isaac or Jacob rather than an Ishmael or Esau: not family, not social status, not works. In the void left by the denial of a rationale for election in terms of differentials in human worth, Paul names God: "the one who calls"; "the one who has mercy." Or again, in Romans 10, human action and initiative— whether ascending and descending, seeking and asking, or even observing the commandments—are excluded as explanations for the distribution of God's wealth. And again, where there is only nothingness in terms of the human canons of worth, Paul places one name: Jesus Christ (see 10:6, 7, 9; also vv. 11, 12, 13, 17).[39] But then there is Romans 11:28: Israel, as it concerns election, is loved on account of their ancestors. As Ross Wagner remarks, this "appeal" to the patriarchs "has struck some interpreters as a *deus ex machina*," a wish anchored in ancestry that forgets Paul's earlier insistence that "it is not the children of the flesh who are the children of God" (9:8).[40]

But the next verse tells a different story. Paul's argument does not run "all Israel will be saved because Israel is loved on account of their ancestors," but rather "Israel is loved on account of their ancestors because (γάρ) the gifts and calling of God are irrevocable" (11:29). Here, as in Romans 9, it is God's gifts and God's call, not Israel's ancestors, that ground election. As Barclay writes in relation to the identity of the "root" in the olive tree metaphor (11:17–24), "What matters about the patriarchs is that they were rendered significant by

39. For the christological references in Romans 10:11–13, see especially C. K. Rowe, "Romans 10:13: What Is the Name of the Lord?," *HBT* 22 (2000): 135–73; cf. Linebaugh, *God, Grace, and Righteousness*, 197–204.

40. Wagner, "Mercy to the Nations," 429. One way to circumvent this apparent tension is to read "all Israel" in Romans 11:26 as a reference to the one people of God, gentile as well as Jewish believers; so N. T. Wright, "The Letter to the Romans," in *NIB* 10, ed. L. E. Keck (Nashville: Abingdon, 2002), 620–99, and *Paul and the Faithfulness of God* (Minneapolis: Fortress, 2013), 1239–45. This interpretation is unlikely, however, as it leaves the division between the remnant and rest untouched, requires "Israel" to have two meanings in 11:25–26, is unable to account for the contrast between the "part" of Israel that is currently hardened and the "all" Israel that will be saved, and fails to make meaningful Paul's references to the "acceptance" and "fullness" of Israel (11:12, 15).

a grace and calling which bore no relation to their intrinsic worth." It is not the "patriarchs themselves" that sustain Israel or engender Paul's hope; it is "the calling or election of God," his "unconditioned favor."[41] By anchoring his hope for Israel in God's grace and call, Paul connects the future with the present, linking Israel with both the remnant chosen by grace and the gentiles who are God's people and loved because of God's call. At the same time, this future-by-grace also evokes Israel's creation-by-grace, thereby uniting Israel's origin and destiny: as Israel was called into being by a word of unconditioned mercy, so Israel, though hardened and disobedient now, will be reborn by the unconditioned grace and creative call of God.

Hence my thesis: Paul's hope is anchored in history. But "history," as Hamann puts it, "is a sealed book, a concealed witness, a riddle that cannot be solved."[42] Paul's promise that "all Israel will be saved" is not the obvious end to a story he's read from beginning to middle. Rather, for Paul, the past as much as the future is revealed. To borrow from Oswald Bayer, Paul's historiography works "from a key event that discloses the meaning of all events that come before and after it."[43] It is as God reveals himself in the gift of Jesus Christ as the one who gives irrespective of human prerequisites that Israel's scriptural past becomes legible as a history of this God and this grace. Israel's history, in other words, echoes Paul's christological present: as unveiled in the giving of Jesus, God is and has been the one whose grace is operative at the point of sin, nothingness, and death and as the gift that brings, salvation, creation, and life (cf. Rom 4:5, 17). Jesus, to use the language of Romans 10, is the "word" (10:8, 17) that unearths the grammar of all God's words.[44] The present and the past, as revealed in Jesus and read in scripture, is a history of the God who is speaking and has spoken in but one style: the grammar of grace. And it is here,

41. Barclay, *Paul and the Gift*, 550: "everywhere Paul discusses the patriarchs he is concerned to elucidate not *that* they were the origin of Israel, but *how* this was the case (Gal 3:6–19; 4:21–31; Rom 4:1–23; 9:6–13)."

42. Hamann, "Socratic Memorabilia," in *Sämtliche Werke*, 2:65.

43. O. Bayer, *Theology the Lutheran Way*, LQB, ed. and trans. J. G. Silcock and M. C. Mattes (Grand Rapids: Eerdmans, 2007), 200.

44. Cf. Hamann's reference to "the *stylus curiae* of the kingdom of heaven" in "Cloverleaf of Hellenistic Letters, First Letter," in *Hamann: Writings on Philosophy and Language*, ed. K. Haynes (Cambridge: Cambridge University Press, 2007), 40. Cf. Hamann, "Gedanken über meinen Lebenslauf": "I found the unity of the divine will in the redemption of Jesus Christ, so that all history . . . and works of God flowed towards this center." See also U. Luz, *Das Geschichtsverständnis des Paulus* (Munich: Kaiser Verlag, 1968): "Im Lichte der eschatologischen Gnade Gottes wird für Paulus die Einheit des Heilshandelns Gottes durch die Geschichte hindurch sichtbar."

in this history, that there is "a like hope": the word of mercy that now calls the gentiles and has always created Israel will be the word that re-grafts (11:23–24) and resurrects (11:15) "the rest" (11:7).[45]

The history Paul promises as Israel's future, then, like the present and the past, is the history of God's word. As is the case with the gentiles and the remnant, and as was the case in Israel's formation and history, the future is determined by God's call (11:29; 9:7, 12, 25–26), God's election (11:28; 9:11; 11:5, 7), God's mercy (11:30–32; 9:15–18), and God's grace (11:29; 11:5). The earlier use of these words reveals particular definitions which Paul deduces from God's gift of Jesus: God calls without condition; his election precedes and precludes all human criteria; his mercy is not the restoration of the righteous but the re-creation of the sinful; and his grace is what he gives in giving Jesus (i.e., peace to enemies, salvation to sinners, justification to the ungodly, and life to the dead; cf. Rom 5:6–10, 17–18). The recurrence of this vocabulary as Paul imagines Israel's future is an indication that the salvation of Israel will share this shape. Israel is now an enemy (11:28), disobedient (11:31–32), guilty of transgression (11:12), sinful (11:27), ungodly (11:26), lost (11:15), and in need of nothing less than life (11:15). And it is this Israel—disobedient, hardened, stumbling, excluded, and broken off—that Paul promises God will accept (11:15), include (11:12), forgive (11:27), save (11:26; cf. 11:14), have mercy upon (11:31–32), and resurrect (11:15).

That the future Paul promises is patterned by the same unconditioned grace revealed in the christological present and thereby made legible in Israel's scripture indicates that the salvation of Israel is not, for Paul, a soteriological sleight-of-hand, some dream that won't die even if Paul's own arguments have killed it. Rather, the gospel of Jesus Christ uncovers the grammar of God's word and thus illuminates the "gospelness" not just of the past but of the future. The God who is and has been the one who, in mercy, raises the dead and justifies the ungodly (cf. Rom 4:5, 17) will be the one who resurrects and redeems Israel (Rom 11:15, 26). And in fact, for Paul, this is easier to imagine than the current miracle of grace at work in the calling of the gentiles. Through the repeated use of "greater to lesser" rhetoric, Paul asks if the gentiles, though wild branches, are grafted onto the cultivated olive tree, "how much more" (πόσῳ μᾶλλον) will the God who is able to re-graft natural branches (11:23) do exactly that (11:24). Or again: if Israel's trespass and loss mean wealth and reconciliation for the world, "how much more" (πόσῳ μᾶλλον) will their "fullness" and "acceptance" mean (11:12, 15)?[46]

---

45. For more on the "grammar" of Paul's theology, see chap. 9, "The Grammar of the Gospel."
46. Cf. Wagner, "Mercy to the Nations," 429.

More important for our purposes than that Paul knows Israel's future, however, is how he knows it. The "greater to lesser" logic suggests not just that Paul has always assumed the story ends with Israel's salvation but that the nature of grace seen in the unconditioned call of the gentiles reveals the grammar of God's word and thus engenders the assurance that the ever unexpected yet ever spoken word of mercy will again be addressed to Israel. In this sense, the histories of Israel and the gentiles are deeply interwoven. Israel's trespass occasions the gentiles' salvation, which in turn has the potential to provoke Israel to jealousy (11:11).[47] There is one root and one olive tree, but God, with an arboricultural approach as unnerving and hopeful as his grace, breaks off the natural branches (Israel) to make room for the wild branches (the gentiles), and yet is both able and intending to regraft those branches that have been broken off (11:17–24). Israel's disobedience has led to the reception of mercy by the disobedient gentiles, and somehow this mercy generates a momentum that will also mean mercy for Israel (11:30–31). It is notable that in these interwoven histories, neither Israel nor the gentiles become the subject of salvific verbs: "salvation belongs to the Lord," suggests Paul's grammar.[48] In the case of the gentiles it is, as Wagner writes, "not as active agents, but . . . as recipients of blessings promised to Israel that these gentiles provoke God's people."[49] Similarly, while gentiles are shown mercy because of Israel's disobedience, it is God who has mercy (11:30; cf. 9:16).

Here, however, it is necessary to remember what Paul has already said: the event that renders Israel disobedient, even as it is mercy for the gentiles, is specific and concrete: it is the advent and announcement of Israel's Christ (9:30–10:17). That Paul has not forgotten this is evident both as he describes Israel's instrumentality in relation to the salvation of the gentiles and as he imagines the future salvation of Israel. To say that Israel's rejection or loss (ἀποβολή) occasions the reconciliation (καταλλαγή) of the world (11:15) is to interpret the scriptural ordering of rejection and election (cf. the use of Exod 9:16 in Rom 9:16–24) through the crucified and risen Christ. That sin or

---

47. For the jealousy motif, see R. H. Bell, *Provoked to Jealousy: The Origin and Purpose of the Jealousy Motif in Romans 9–11*, WUNT 2.63 (Tübingen: Mohr Siebeck, 1994).

48. The verbs of salvation that have God as the (implied) subject include ἐγκεντρίζω (11:17, 19, 23, 24), σῴζω (11:26), ἀφαιρέω (11:27), ἐλεέω (11:30, 31, 32). The one exception is that Paul is the subject of σῴζω in 11:14, but, as Wagner suggests, this is an exception that proves the rule: "[Paul] portrays himself as the sole active intermediary" ("Mercy to the Nations," 426). The nouns that name Israel's salvation also point to God as the acting subject: πλήρωμα, 11:12; πρόσλημψις, 11:15.

49. Wagner, "Mercy to the Nations," 426.

transgression can lead to salvation (11:11–12) is an unheard of idea that Paul brings to his present from the saving history of Jesus: "where sin abounded, grace super-abounded" (Rom 5:20). Just as the death of God's son means the reconciliation of God's enemies (Rom 5:10), so the loss of God's people means the reconciliation of the world. Similarly, Israel's salvation is described in terms that suggest a christological imagination. According to Paul's diagnosis, Israel is lost (11:15) and imprisoned in disobedience (11:32), and therefore salvation must mean "life from the dead" (11:15) and mercy (11:31–32). Because it is God who both breaks off and regrafts, who both loses and resurrects—because grace operates on the other side and out of divine judgment—this saving history is always hidden under the sign of its opposite. But for Paul, the life, death, and life again of Jesus, God's unconditioned gift to the ungodly, while itself foolish, scandalous, and *sub contrario* (cf. 1 Cor 1:18–25), is the one history according to which, as Bayer puts it, "one learns to spell history."[50] Rejection and resurrection, in others words, are descriptive of Israel's current situation and coming salvation only as Israel's present and future are reimagined around the rejected and resurrected Jesus. Just as Paul brings God's christological acts of justification and resurrection to the Abraham narrative in Romans 4, interpreting Abraham's reckoning of righteousness as the justification of the ungodly (4:3–5) and Abraham's age and Sarah's barrenness as conditions of deadness that require resurrection (4:17–21), so in Romans 11 Paul tells Israel's ongoing story in the shape of the crucified and risen Christ.

This suggests that while Jesus, in Romans more than in, say, Galatians, is integrated into the history of Israel as "the seed of David" (Rom 1:3), "the root of Jesse" (15:12), and the "Messiah from [Israel] according to the flesh" (9:5), the hermeneutical direction is not, in the first instance, from Israel's story to Israel's Christ. It is, rather, from Israel's Christ to Israel's story.[51] Jesus, to return to Agamben's suggestive phrase, is history's "now of legibility," the time in which the mysteries contained but kept secret in Israel's scriptures are unveiled and given voice (cf. Rom 16:25–26). Hence the mystery Paul discloses in Romans 11:25–27:

---

50. O. Bayer, *A Contemporary in Dissent: Johann Georg Hamann as a Radical Enlightener*, trans. R. A. Harrisville and M. C. Mattes (Grand Rapids: Eerdmans, 2012), 219.

51. For a fuller discussion of the reciprocal yet asymmetrical relationship between Christ and scripture, see Linebaugh, *God, Grace, and Righteousness*, 177–226. As I say on p. 178n3: "Paul's 'hermeneutic,' as J. L. Martyn remarks, 'works from the previously unknown and foolish gospel of the cross to the previously known and previously misunderstood scripture' and, as Martyn does not say, back again," quoting J. L. Martyn, "John and Paul on the Subject of Gospel and Scripture," in *Theological Issues in the Letters of Paul* (Edinburgh: T&T Clark, 1997), 221.

the salvation of "all Israel" will occur "as it is written" (11:26a).[52] But as Paul's conflation of two texts from Isaiah indicates (59:20–21 and 29:7a LXX), the ability to read requires revelation. While Paul lifts the words "he will remove ungodliness from Jacob" (ἀποστρέψει ἀσεβείας ἀπὸ Ἰακώβ) verbatim from Isaiah as he describes the work of the "the redeemer" (ὁ ῥυόμενος, cf. 1 Thess 1:10), the context of the Isaiah text (especially 59:16–21 LXX) suggests that the coming of the redeemer "on account of Zion" (ἕνεκεν Σιων) will mean the salvation of Israel from their ungodly enemies. Paul's context by contrast, has the redeemer coming "from Zion" (ἐκ Σιων) to a hardened, lost, stumbling, cut off, and disobedient Israel not in order to save them from the ungodly but to save Israel as the ungodly.[53] The addition of Isaiah 27 confirms this. Paul, by adding Isaiah 27 to Isaiah 59, lets the prophet interpret his own promise: "this will be the covenant from me to them" (59:21a), "when I take away their sins" (27:9a).

This future echoes Israel's origin. Just as Abraham, according to Paul's reading of Genesis, was called without condition (Rom 4:10), justified though ungodly (4:5), and blessed by the forgiveness of sins (4:7–8), so Israel has a future because God's covenant is unconditioned—it is "a covenant from me" and "for them"—and because God will banish Israel's ungodliness and forgive Israel's sin. Or again: the God who called Isaac and Jacob before and irrespective of their lives and who remade Israel by mercy after the golden calf idolatry (9:7–16) will again come and re-create Israel through an unconditioned word: "I forgive you."

For Paul, however, while his reading of the past and his promise about the future rhyme, it is the present that reveals the rhyme scheme. The end will be like the beginning, but both beginning and end are legible from the middle. It is Paul's "now" that finally grounds his hope: "just as (ὥσπερ) you [gentiles] were once disobedient to God but now (νῦν) receive mercy, in the same way also (οὕτως καί) [Israel] is now (νῦν) disobedient . . . so that they might receive mercy" (11:30–31). It is God's present-tense word of mercy to gentiles, what

---

52. For the modal interpretation of καὶ οὕτως (11.26a), together with the proposal that μυστήριον refers "to one particular . . . aspect of God's plan of salvation" (i.e., Israel's salvific instrumentality), see M. Bockmuehl, *Revelation and Mystery in Ancient Judaism and Pauline Christianity*, WUNT 2.36 (Tübingen: Mohr Siebeck, 1990), 170–75, 226. When read with the phrase ἄχρι οὗ (11:25), καὶ οὕτως unveils the divinely appointed means and the redemptive historical order of Israel's salvation.

53. For the significance of the change from ἕνεκεν Σιων to ἐκ Σιων, see Linebaugh, *God, Grace, and Righteousness*, 221; cf. Wilk, *Die Bedeutung des Jesajabuches für Paulus*, 39–40; H. Hübner, *Gottes Ich und Israel*, FRLANT 126 (Göttingen: Vandenhoeck & Ruprecht, 1984), 115–16.

Paul calls "the word of Christ," that reveals the pattern according to which God is, has been, and therefore will be "the God who has mercy" on Israel. What the call of the once disobedient gentiles tells Paul is that Israel's current disobedience, rather than disqualifying them from God's grace, puts them in the one and only meeting place of mercy. It is at the site of sin and death that God creates righteousness and life. "Grace," in Marilynne Robinson's phrase, "is an ecstatic fire," at once reducing to ashes all hopes anchored in human worth as it kindles a hope that even disobedience and death cannot burn.[54] As Käsemann writes, "there is hope always only for those who have no more hope."[55] And so: there is hope for Israel.

It is, then, to answer the question that opened this paper, the history of God's creative and unconditioned mercy, revealed to Paul in the gift of Jesus and thus legible in Israel's scriptures, that engenders "a like hope" for the future: "all Israel," disobedient though they now are, "will be saved." Naming this ground of hope, however, also hints at the answers to the implicit question about the relationship between the history of Jesus and the history of Israel and the nations that precede and follow it. As Paul's conclusion indicates, the grace revealed in the giving of Jesus underwrites Paul's hope for Israel's future because it unveils the grammar of God's history-writing word: now, then, and always—"God shut up all in disobedience in order that he might have mercy on all" (11:32).[56] History may be, to return to Hamann, "a riddle that cannot be solved"—hidden under the opposite and ever beyond calculation because mercy is always unconditioned.[57] But, to add Paul's voice to Hamann's words, "the entire riddle of [history], the impenetrable night of its terminus a quo and terminus ad quem, are dissolved by the charter of the Word [of Christ]."[58]

54. M. Robinson, *Gilead* (London: Virago, 2004), 224.

55. Käsemann, *Romans*, 303.

56. See Peter Stuhlmacher's description of Romans 11:32 as "the quintessential structural law of God's gracious work" and "history's fundamental principle," in *Revisiting Paul's Doctrine of Justification: A Challenge to the New Perspective*, trans. D. P. Bailey (Downers Grove, IL: IVP Academic, 2001), 30, 71; cf. Käsemann, "Justification and Salvation History," 70, 75–76.

57. Hamann, "Socratic Memorabilia," in *Sämtliche Werke*, 2:65.

58. J. G. Hamann, "Zweifel und Einfälle" (1776), in *J. G. Hamann 1730–1788: A Study in Christian Existence*, ed. and trans. Ronald Gregor Smith (New York: Harper & Brothers, 1960), 59.

CHAPTER 4

"The Speech of the Dead"

IDENTIFYING THE NO LONGER AND NOW LIVING "I"
OF GALATIANS 2:20

Methinks we have hugely mistaken this matter of Life and Death.

—Herman Melville, *Moby-Dick*

"Where I am not I," writes Saint Augustine, "I am more happily I." This is, as Augustine admits, a strange way of speaking. In context, however, it is provoked by another surprising confession: "I have been crucified with Christ and I no longer live, but Christ lives in me" (Χριστῷ συνεσταύρωμαι· ζῶ δὲ οὐκέτι ἐγώ, ζῇ δὲ ἐν ἐμοὶ Χριστός, Gal 2:19–20). For Augustine, this Pauline pattern of speech generates a genre: "the speech of the dead." It is, Augustine insists, "they who are already dead" who are "living."[1]

The history of reading Galatians 2:20 is characterized by similar shock: "Strange and unheard of," says Luther; "inconceivable" and an "enigma," adds Schweitzer.[2] For E. P. Sanders, "the real bite of Paul's theology" is expressed in the "participatory categories" of texts like Galatians 2:20.[3] And yet, when it comes to what John Riches calls "the task for interpreters" to account for and understand "the language of participation and mystical union which [Paul] uses," Sanders waves the white flag of hermeneutical surrender:

---

1. Augustine, *On Continence* 29, translated by C. L. Cornish, in *Nicene and Post-Nicene Fathers*, series 1, ed. P. Schaff, vol. 3 (Christian Literature Publishing Company, 1887), 392 (translation altered).

2. LW 26:159; A. Schweitzer, *The Mysticism of Paul the Apostle*, trans. W. Montgomery (New York: Seabury Press, 1931), 3; cf. S. Eastman, *Paul and the Person: Reframing Paul's Anthropology* (Grand Rapids: Eerdmans, 2017), 1, who refers to the "puzzle of Pauline anthropology."

3. E. P. Sanders, *Paul and Palestinian Judaism: A Comparison of Patterns of Religion* (Minneapolis: Fortress, 1977), 502, 549.

We seem to lack a category of "reality"—real participation in Christ—which lies between naïve cosmological speculation and belief in magical transference on the one hand, and a revised self-understanding on the other. I must confess that I do not have a new category of perception to propose here.[4]

Riches is content to respond to Sanders with pregnant understatement: "This is a strange view to take of a text which has exercised such influence throughout 2000 years of human history."[5] Kevin Vanhoozer, however, is more diagnostic: to say "participation is central to Paul's theology but largely inaccessible today" is symptomatic of a fragmented theological context in which "various ditches, some uglier than others, have created divides and led to misunderstandings between biblical studies" and "historical . . . and systematic theology."[6] Vanhoozer's interpretative prescription is to "name and navigate" these ditches: "we have a better chance of responding to [the] questions" raised by Paul's language of "union with and participation in Christ" if we take "into account exegetical, historical, and systematic theological perspectives."[7] The act of exegesis, in others words, raises interpretative questions that invite and even require theological retrieval and "*ressourcement*" as integral aspects of "exegetical reasoning."[8]

This invitation to engage in theological retrieval and attend to reception history has been accepted by some. Richard Hays answered Sanders's interpretative agnosticism with a set of possible concepts with which to understand Paul's language of participation. Some of Hays's suggestions are contextual or critical possibilities (e.g., familial and political solidarity or narrative participation). But one has a rich historical and theological pedigree: "My own guess is that" a consideration of Paul's language "would be . . . clarified by careful study of participation motifs in patristic theology, particularly the thought of the Eastern fathers."[9] This guess has generated further research. Michael Gorman,

4. Sanders, *Paul and Palestinian Judaism*, 522–23. The quotation is from John Riches, *Galatians through the Centuries* (Oxford: Blackwell, 2013), 137.

5. Riches, *Galatians*, 137.

6. K. J. Vanhoozer, "From 'Blessed in Christ' to 'Being in Christ': The State of the Union and the Place of Participation in New Testament Exegesis and Systematic Theology Today," in *In Christ in Paul: Explorations in Paul's Theology of Union and Participation*, ed. M. J. Thate, K. J. Vanhoozer, and C. R. Campbell (Grand Rapids: Eerdmans, 2018), 6–7.

7. Vanhoozer, "From 'Blessed in Christ' to 'Being in Christ,'" 11.

8. M. Allen, "'It Is No Longer I Who Live': Christ's Faith and Christian Faith," *JRT* (2013): 5. See also G. Macaskill, *Union with Christ in the New Testament* (Oxford: Oxford University Press, 2013), 3–4.

9. R. Hays, "What Is 'Real Participation in Christ'? A Dialogue with E. P. Sanders on

for instance, makes regular recourse to the language of *theosis* to interpret Paul: "To be in Christ is to be in God . . . this means that for Paul . . . conformity to the crucified Christ . . . is really theoformity, or theosis."[10] For Grant Macaskill, "Gorman's work represents a welcome attempt to offer a coherent account of Paul's theology . . . and to do so with a willingness to draw upon theological conceptualities."[11] That said, Gorman's deployment of *theosis* in the service of Pauline exegesis exhibits, as Macaskill points out, "some serious problems." Despite Hays's call for a "careful study" of the Eastern fathers, "Gorman does not actually engage with the patristic writings, nor does he offer much by way of an actual definition of *theosis*." This latter point is particularly problematic as the term is "theologically plastic." The language of *theosis* is used within and as part of a theological synthesis in which its potential to confuse or merge creator and creation is constrained by both incarnational and Trinitarian dogma—a constraint that appears absent in Gorman both as he claims too little (e.g., cruciformity as a moral trope indicating a manner of living patterned after the crucified and risen Christ) and as he claims too much (e.g., *theosis* suggests that "obedience and faith" amount to "a participation in the being . . . of God").[12]

Gorman's recourse to doctrinal history is necessary and welcome; and at the same time it is a reminder that theological retrieval for the sake of exegesis is a demanding and difficult task: it requires patient attention to the sources, an awareness of the history and debates surrounding doctrines, an understanding of the ways terms and concepts are borrowed, baptized, and embedded within larger frames by Christian theology, as well as an openness to tracing the relationship between texts and the theological resources that have been utilized in the service of reading them. In this sense, Macaskill's book, *Union with Christ in the New Testament*, which offers covenant and divine presence as ways to conceptualize union in terms of representation and interpersonal

---

Pauline Soteriology," in *Redefining First Century Jewish and Christian Identities: Essays in Honor of Ed Parish Sanders*, ed. F. E. Udoh (Notre Dame, IN: University of Notre Dame Press, 2008), 336–51; R. Hays, *The Faith of Jesus Christ: The Narrative Substructure of Galatians 3:1–4:11*, 2nd ed. (Grand Rapids: Eerdmans, 2002), xxxii.

10. M. Gorman, *Inhabiting the Cruciform God: Kenosis, Justification, and Theosis in Paul's Narrative Soteriology* (Grand Rapids: Eerdmans, 2009), 4.

11. Macaskill, *Union with Christ in the New Testament*, 27.

12. Macaskill, *Union with Christ in the New Testament*, 27, 74–75. This latter formulation says "too much" because it uses the language of *theosis* to express an idea that the Palamite tradition, most notably, labored to guard against: that the sanctified creature participates in the being or essence of the divine. For an account of Pauline soteriology that engages with patristic theologies of theosis in both depth and detail, see B. C. Blackwell, *Christosis: Engaging Paul's Soteriology with His Patristic Interpreters* (Grand Rapids: Eerdmans, 2016).

communion, is a model: it engages the scriptural and early Jewish backgrounds as well as the reception historical and theological foregrounds of union with Christ before exploring that theme across the New Testament. The cost of this breadth, of course, is depth. Macaskill calls Galatians 2:19–20 "the most obviously participatory language in Galatians," and yet he only devotes seven lines to its analysis.[13]

My aim in this chapter is to join those who have accepted the invitation to read Paul with recourse to reception history and theological reflection, but to do so in a more focused manner. For this reason, I will limit myself to one principal dialogue partner, Martin Luther, and one primary text, Galatians 2:20.

Which brings us back to "the speech of the dead." Paul's confession gestures toward a strange and surprising simultaneity: "I no longer live," says Paul; "the life I now live," he adds. Listening to Augustine while reading Galatians indicates that the bishop is endeavoring to speak according to Paul's *modus loquendi*: "I am not I, I am"; or again, "they who are already dead [are] living." To attend to—to be addressed by and to learn to speak—according to this Pauline pattern is to encounter a question: Who—or even which I—am I? Expressed in terms of the text: Is (or are) the I that no longer lives and the I that now lives the same I? Pursuing this question is the purpose of this essay, and I will do so with reference to Luther's reading of Galatians, which, in contrast to some other theologies stemming from Augustine, captures the Pauline pattern according to which the "I" both is not, but also is, the same someone.

Identifying the No Longer Living "I"

"One speaks theologically about the human being," Oswald Bayer comments on Luther's *Disputatio de homine*, "from three vantage points": as creature, as sinner, and as redeemed.[14] The question concerns the relationship between

---

13. Macaskill, *Union with Christ in the New Testament*, 220–21. For a dogmatic account that resonates with Macaskill's, see M. Allen, who refers to "personal union" as "the stuff of covenant and communion." *Sanctification* (Grand Rapids: Zondervan, 2017), 225. Another recent study that explores conceptual resources with which to understand and translate Paul's participatory account of human personhood is found in S. Eastman, *Paul and the Person*. Eastman, however, does not engage the theological tradition so much as bring Paul into conversation with contemporary research in developmental psychology and philosophy of mind. For interaction with Eastman, see J. A. Linebaugh, "Participation and the Person in Pauline Theology," *JSNT* 40.4 (2018): 516–23.

14. O. Bayer, *Martin Luther's Theology: A Contemporary Interpretation*, trans. T. H. Trapp (Grand Rapids: Eerdmans, 2008), 154.

these three designations. David Kelsey, for instance, insists that while the categories of creation, salvation from sin, and eschatological completion share
the same anthropological structure (i.e., each emphasizes that human being
is dependent being), they are not a single but three stories of the self. In his
words, "the canon is made whole by three kinds of inseparable narratives,
each of which has a distinct plot or narrative logic that cannot be conflated
with either of the other two." Consequently, "the array of claims made in theological anthropology" in "Holy Scripture . . . cannot be ordered into a single
systematic structure."[15] For Luther, by contrast, while the ruptures between
creation and sin and between sin and salvation are real and radical, the three
aspects are more closely related: "the human is God's creation"; this creature
"was subjected after Adam's fall to the power of the devil, which means, under
sin and death"; "only through the Son of God, Christ Jesus, can [the person]
be freed and be given eternal life as a gift."[16]

Galatians 2:20 confesses an I that no longer lives and an I that now lives.
The relationship between these two lives is described as death: "I have been
crucified with Christ." The exegetical challenge is both to identify each I and
also to ask if and in what sense each I can be identified with the other: who
no longer lives, who now lives, and are the two related despite being divided
by death?

Martinus de Boer stands out somewhat among commentators on Galatians
in that he explicitly asks who or which I Paul describes as having died. Taking
his cue from Galatians 2:19a and its announcement of a death "to the law,"
de Boer suggests that the expression "to die to" is "metaphorical and means
to become separated from." It is thus Paul's life with respect to the law that
ends, his "nomistic I," to use de Boer's phrase.[17] Beverly Gaventa protests at
this point, insisting there is "no sign that this death and life are the death and
life of the nomistic self only." On the contrary, for Gaventa, as Paul's more
obviously comprehensive statements about dying with Christ in Romans 6
and 2 Corinthians 5 indicate, Galatians 2:20 puts "the whole of the *ego*" in the
grave.[18] Part of what pressures de Boer in this direction, however, is, to quote
Luther again, the "strange and unheard-of" confession of Paul. It is, de Boer

15. D. Kelsey, *Eccentric Existence: A Theological Anthropology* (Louisville: Westminster
John Knox, 2009), 10, 897.

16. LW 34:148; WA 39.1:176.7–13.

17. M. de Boer, *Galatians* (Louisville: Westminster John Knox, 2011), 159–61.

18. B. Gaventa, "The Singularity of the Gospel Revisited," in *Galatians and Christian
Theology: Justification, the Gospel, and Ethics in Paul's Letter*, ed. M. W. Elliott et al. (Grand
Rapids: Baker Academic, 2014), 193.

sees, in being "crucified with Christ" that the "nomistically determined I died," but such language, while said to be "realistic and serious," is finally labeled "metaphorical and hyperbolic" and thus "cannot be taken literally."[19]

It is, however, just this assumption that Paul's confession resists. Galatians 2:20 is not an analogy between Christ's death and a deathlike experience of the I. Galatians 2:20, rather, is an announcement that Christ's death is the death of the I. To retreat to the language of nonliteral and hyperbolic is to miss the radical reframing required by Paul's language. In Gerhard Ebeling's words, "it is not life and death as they are that set the terms within which" Galatians 2:20 "must be made to fit." On the contrary, "it is the all-inclusive relationship to Jesus Christ that sets the terms by which the decision is made as to the meaning of life and death. Christ is not given his place in the order of life and death." Instead, "life and death are given their decisive place in Christ."[20] As Death says to the god Apollo after a resurrection-like rescue in Thornton Wilder's play, *The Alcestiad*, "You broke the ancient law and order of the world: that the living are the living and the dead are the dead." Apollo's response: "Death, the sun is risen. You are shaking. . . . Start accustoming yourself to change."[21]

Reoriented in this way, it is possible to avoid de Boer's conclusion that "the extreme language of crucifixion with Christ gives expression to . . . the loss of a previous manner of life."[22] According to Galatians 2:20, it is not only a manner of life that is lost; it is life that is lost: "I no longer live." But this only sharpens the question: Who no longer lives? What is this life that ends in death with Christ?

Luther both asked and answered this question: "Who is this me? It is I, an accursed and damned sinner."[23] For Luther, the human *qua peccator* is precisely the human not living according to their nature *qua creatura*: created to live outside the self through faith in God and love for others, the sinner is curved in on and in love with the self; created in and for freedom, the sinner is bound yet still answerable; created to worship and receive from God, the sinner idolizes and attempts to save her or himself.

Paul, like Luther, knows of a creation in which sin is unnatural, into which "sin came" (Rom 5:12). But he also knows that into this creation, sin did in fact

19. De Boer, *Galatians*, 159–61.

20. G. Ebeling, *The Truth of the Gospel: An Exposition of Galatians*, trans. D. Green (Minneapolis: Fortress, 1985), 143.

21. T. Wilder, *The Alcestiad*, in *The Collected Short Plays of Thornton Wilder*, ed. A. T. Wilder (New York: Theatre Communications Group, 1998), 2:224.

22. De Boer, *Galatians*, 161.

23. LW 26:177.

come, and since then, "from Adam," Paul says, "death reigned" (Rom 5:14). The initial I of Galatians 2:20, the I who no longer lives, is thus the I that exists east of Eden and in Adam. There are several Pauline phrases that describe this "life" (e.g., "under sin" and "according to the flesh"), but they converge in a common diagnosis: this life is death.[24] However much the Pauline authorship of Ephesians continues to be disputed, the opening lines of Ephesians 2 are indisputably Pauline: "dead in your trespasses and sins." As Luther argued within but also against his inherited Augustinian tradition, the person *qua peccator* is not merely incomplete and wounded (and thus only in need of a grace that perfects and heals); the sinner is captive, complicit, and a corpse (and thus in need of a grace that sets free, forgives, and resurrects). In Galatians, the linguistic web of curse, imprisonment, slavery, sin, and death all gesture in the direction of this diagnosis. In our passage, however, it is expressed in the unexpected dative phrases about dying to the law in order to live to God: if death in one relationship is required for there to be life in the most fundamental relationship (i.e., life in relation to God), then the most basic thing to say about the present life is that it is not life. To borrow another provocative yet profoundly Pauline sentence from Augustine, "In comparison with [life with God], what we have now should be called death."[25]

Two theological consequences follow from the depth of Paul's diagnosis. First, the movement from—or perhaps better, the rupture between—creation and sin is a movement from life to death. Sin came, says Paul, and death reigned. And that suggests, second, that Paul's diagnosis requires a redefinition of death. Death is not, at least according to Paul's deepest sense, what waits at the end of life in the flesh; death is life in and according to the flesh. In Bonhoeffer's words, "this life is dead," not because "one no longer exists," but rather because the relation with God that defines and grounds the human creature is contradicted: instead of living with and from God, the sinner "lives out of" the self and in relation to sin "and thus is dead."[26] To bring this definition of death closer to the Pauline pattern of Galatians 2:20, to be dead is to live with death before rather than behind you: death is life before and apart from death with Christ.

So again: Who is the I who no longer lives? One way to answer this question with Paul is to say: the I who dies is the one who is dead.

24. Cf. Ebeling, *The Truth of the Gospel*, 142: Paul "describes Adamic life as death."

25. Augustine on Psalm 119. Cf. Kelsey's designation of "sin as living death" (*Eccentric Existence*, 864).

26. D. Bonhoeffer, *Creation and Fall* (Minneapolis: Fortress, 2004 [1937]), 90–91.

DEATH WITH AND LIFE IN CHRIST

If the proclamation of Christ crucified is foolishness to Greeks, the Pauline announcement of crucifixion with Christ has been a stumbling block to interpreters. The scholarly habit of classifying Paul's confession as "nonliteral," "figurative," and "hyperbolic" is, if unsatisfying, at least unsurprising: "the speech of the dead" is a difficult language.[27] There is, however, another and older tradition that, as Luther concludes, also domesticates Paul's confession of death. Thomas Aquinas, for example, can capture the image of some of Paul's most startling claims: "I have been crucified with Christ," reads Thomas, and then he writes, "the love of Christ . . . on the cross for me brings it about that I am always nailed with him."[28] The death that occurs in this case, however, is not that of a who but of a what: it is not the person that is crucified with Christ on Thomas's reading but rather, in his words, "concupiscence or the inclination to sin, and all such have been put to death in me."[29] Similarly when commenting on Paul's confession of "new creation," Thomas's exegetical echo feels somewhat muted: there is not new life but rather what he calls a "new manner of life."[30] As insisted in relation to de Boer's use of the same phrase, however, in Galatians 2:20 it is not only a manner of life that is lost and newly created; it is life that is lost and newly given: "I no longer live," but, by grace, "Christ lives in me."

For Thomas, "the justification of the unrighteous is a movement . . . from the state of sin to the state of justice," a movement that is nontemporal but nevertheless ordered: first, an infusion of grace; second, a movement of the will toward God in faith; third, a movement of the will away from sin; and fourth, the remission of guilt.[31] Within this movement, the person is radically altered. Human nature, both as created and fallen, is, by grace, perfected and healed. But the maxim holds: *gratia non tollit naturam sed perficit* ("grace does not destroy but perfects nature"). When reading Galatians, this means, for Thomas, that when Paul announces a "new creation" (Gal 6:15), he is actually naming a new creature, a person who in turn is not so much new as renewed:

---

27. For representative uses of these terms to describe Galatians 2:19–20, see J. L. Martyn, *Galatians: A New Translation with Introduction and Commentary* (New York: Doubleday, 1997), 278; de Boer, *Galatians*, 160; Ebeling, *The Truth of the Gospel*, 144 (though Ebeling is arguing against rather than for a "figurative" interpretation).

28. Thomas Aquinas, *Commentary on Saint Paul's Epistle to the Galatians by St. Thomas Aquinas*, trans. F. R. Larcher (Albany: Magi, 1966), 63.

29. Thomas Aquinas, *Galatians*, 62.

30. Thomas Aquinas, *Galatians*, 53–55, 205–6.

31. *Summa Theologica* IaIIae, q. 113.

this is not a new life but instead what Thomas calls a new "manner of life," a habit of living characterized by "faith formed by love."[32] The I, in other words, survives their salvation. The movement is drastic—from the state of sin to the state of justice—but it does not include or go through death. As Heiko Oberman summarizes what he calls the "unanimous medieval tradition"—exhibited not just in Thomas but also in "Duns Scotus, Gabriel Biel" and "the Council of Trent"—"the *iustitia Dei* remains the finis, the goal . . . of the *viator* who is propelled on his way . . . by the *iustitia Christi* (i.e., by the infusion of grace)."[33] "Life," in Daphne Hampson's words, "is a *via* for our transformation," a road to righteousness along which one's new manner of life, caused by grace and characterized by faith working through love, is the form of righteousness.[34]

But here is Luther's alternative: "where they speak of love" as the form righteousness, "we speak of faith" which "takes hold of Christ" because "he is the form"—he is "true Christian righteousness."[35] As Luther reads Paul's negation of ἔργα νόμου and his announcement of righteousness διὰ πίστεως Ἰησοῦ Χριστοῦ, he hears the apostle locating justification outside of the person and, as per Galatians 2:17, "in Christ." In his words, "when it is necessary to discuss Christian righteousness, the person must be completely rejected" because, negatively, the "I, as a person distinct from Christ, belongs to death and hell" and, positively, because Christ "is our righteousness and life."[36] Oberman captures the contrast: For the medieval tradition the "*iustitia Dei*" is "the *Gegenüber*," the "standard according to which" a human life "will be measured in the Last judgment." For Luther, "the heart of the Gospel is that the *iustitia Christi* and the *iustitia Dei* coincided" such that "the sinner is"—now and definitively—justified, a reality that "forms the stable basis and not the uncertain goal of life."[37] Interpreting Galatians this way, Luther not only can but is also compelled to embrace the language of death. Speaking *in persona Pauli*, Luther demonstrates his fluency in the speech of the dead: "I am not living as Paul now, for Paul is dead . . . my own life I am not living."[38]

32. Thomas Aquinas, *Galatians*, 53–55, 205–6.

33. H. Oberman, *"Iustitia Christi* and *Iustitia Dei*: Luther and Scholastic Doctrines of Justification," in *The Dawn of the Reformation: Essays in Late Medieval and Early Reformation Thought* (Edinburgh: T&T Clark, 1986): 104–25.

34. D. Hampson, *Christian Contradictions: The Structures of Lutheran and Catholic Thought* (Cambridge: Cambridge University Press, 2001), 83, see also 2–3, 56–96.

35. LW 26:129–30, cf. 126–28.

36. LW 26:166–67.

37. Oberman, *"Iustitia Christi* and *Iustitia Dei*," 19, 20, 25.

38. LW 26:170.

Returning to Galatians from this history of reading it, Paul's confession of crucifixion with and new life in Christ sounds like a dramatic depiction of an I who suffers a rupture as deep as death and as radical as resurrection. If the Pauline diagnosis of the movement from created to "under sin" is that it is a movement from life to death, the Pauline declaration of the movement from "under sin" to "in Christ" names a movement from (and through) death to life.

One way to get textual traction on this counter-intuitive claim is to attend to Paul's use of the dative case and prepositional phrases and prefixes in Galatians 2:19–20. As Susan Eastman notes, "Paul's astounding self-description is all about death and life."[39] The order, however, is alarming: death dominates v. 19 whereas life follows in v. 20. The effect, as Ebeling points out, is that "what is said about life begins and ends with references to death: the death of the self ('I no longer live') and the death of and with Christ ('the son of God gave himself for me' and 'I have been crucified with Christ')."[40] Life, for Paul, is not the existence of the I before death; life is what emerges out of and after death. This Pauline pattern—both the unexpected order and the implied redefinitions—unsettles the assumption that life and death are only the subsistence or cessation of a created substance. According to Paul's grammar, death and life are not absolute concepts, they are relative—or better: relational. In Galatians 2:19, life and death are first defined with the dative: death is death to the law and life is life to God. As the confession continues, prepositions color in these relations christologically: Christ died for me (ὑπὲρ ἐμοῦ), which is itself the concrete gift (Gal 2:21) that grounds and includes my having been crucified with (σύν) Christ and on the far side of which "Christ lives in me" (ἐν ἐμοί).

Luther caught the implications: when defining death and life theologically (and, as will be argued below, when identifying the I), "we cannot think in terms of the category of substance, but only in the category of relation."[41] Attempting to answer a perennial exegetical question—what is the nature of the believer's crucifixion with Christ and how does it occur?—Luther offers what he takes to be a Pauline and relational answer: "I have been crucified and have

39. Eastman, *Paul and the Person*, 153.

40. Ebeling, *The Truth of the Gospel*, 137.

41. WA 40.2:354. For "relational ontology" in Luther, see W. Joest, *Ontologie der Person bei Luther* (Göttingen: Vandenhoeck & Ruprecht, 1967), and G. Ebeling, *Dogmatik des christlichen Glaubens* (Tübingen: Mohr Siebeck, 1979). For the application of this category to Paul, see E. Rehfeld, *Relationale Ontologie bei Paulus: Die ontische Wirksamkeit der Christusbezogenheit im Denken des Heidenapostels*, WUNT 2.326 (Tübingen: Mohr Siebeck). Though in dialogue with different fields and voices, Eastman's *Paul and the Person* also argues for a thoroughly relational account of Pauline anthropology.

died with Christ. How? Through grace and faith." This reply is shaped by the terms given in Galatians: righteousness is through faith and the death of Christ is the "grace of God" that gives righteousness (2:16, 21). For Luther, however, grace and faith also specify the fundamental form of the divine-human relationship: "God," who as creator and redeemer is giver, "does not deal with us ... except through" grace—that is, "through the word of promise. We, in turn, cannot deal with God except through faith."[42] Named from the giving side, this relation is called grace; named from the being-given-to side, the relation is called faith. To say, then, that one is crucified with Christ "through grace and faith" is to say, in Ebeling's words, that "dying" is "caught up in our relationship with" Christ just as Paul's dative and prepositional phrases—"live to God" and "Christ lives in me"—indicate that "living" is "defined with reference to" and in relationship with God and Christ.[43]

This connection between a relational understanding of the self and a realistic reading of Paul's language of death and life is evident in Susan Eastman's recent study, *Paul and the Person*. "Insofar as the self is always a self-in-relationship," she writes, the relational rupture occasioned by crucifixion with and life in Christ—that is, the rupture between being a self-in-relation to sin and being a self-in-relation to Christ—is the death of the old I even as it is the birth of the new.[44] There is, in Ian McFarland's words, a "shift in relation" that "comes entirely from God's side" and, as "grace," "has no ground in human being" even as it grounds human being: "our lives are ... defined and sustained not by our natural capacities or incapacities but solely by God's word."[45] The Pauline pattern of defining death and life in relation to Christ is thus a form of preaching the Pauline gospel: a person is not determined by what they have inherited or achieved—not by biology or biography, by pedigree or performance—but by God's gift of Jesus Christ.

What this requires, however, is attending to the soteriological register of death and resurrection in which Paul writes. Learning this language with and from Paul entails following a pattern of speech in which the divine acts of creation and salvation are spoken together. In Romans 4:5 and 4:17,

42. LW 36:42. For God as giver in both creation and redemption, see Luther's exposition of the three articles of the creed in his *Confession Concerning Christ's Supper* (LW 37:66; WA 26:505, 38–506).

43. Ebeling, *The Truth of the Gospel*, 138–40.

44. Eastman, *Paul and the Person*, 160.

45. I. A. McFarland, "The Upward Call: The Category of Vocation and the Oddness of Human Nature," in *The Christian Doctrine of Humanity: Explorations in Constructive Dogmatics*, ed. O. D. Crisp and F. Sanders (Grand Rapids: Zondervan, 2018), 231, 235.

for instance, God's unconditioned grace rhymes in three radical forms: *creatio ex nihilo, resurrectio mortuorum,* and *iustificatio impii.*[46] Picking up this pattern, Luther offers mutually interpreting accounts of creation and justification. In his explanation of the first article in the Small Catechism, creation is confessed with recourse to soteriological categories: "God has created me together with all creatures . . . purely because of his fatherly and divine goodness and mercy, without any merit or worthiness on my part."[47] The antithetical grammar and technical vocabulary of justification are used here in relationship to creation: not by or in consequence of human merit or worth, but purely through divine mercy and goodness—that is, through grace. The effect is a confession of *creatio ex nihilo* in the language of salvation *sola gratia*: "out of nothing" means "by grace alone"—it means, in Oswald Bayer's words, creation "as an absolute, categorical giving," a gift "that finds nothing in its recipient" but contradicts that nothingness by calling them into being.[48] If Paul describes a divine *modus operandi* in Romans 4 by linking the predications of the God who justifies, creates, and resurrects, Luther channels Paul as he characterizes God as the one whose way is to "make something out of nothing," who, as creator, always operates with incongruous grace: God "accepts no one except the abandoned, makes no one healthy except the sick, brings no one to life except the dead, [and] makes no one holy except sinners."[49]

As this begins to indicate, the interpretative traffic runs both ways for Luther. In the Heidelberg Disputation, for example, Luther brings language from the doctrine of creation to a soteriological thesis: "the love of God does not find but creates that which is pleasing to it."[50] A similar move is evident in a series of later disputations prompted by Romans 3:28: "in the divine work of justification," argues Luther, "the negation of works and the incongruity between human unrighteousness and God's pronouncement of righteousness forces us to "say with Paul that we are nothing at all, just as we have been created out of nothing." In being justified, the *homo peccator* is, from this "nothing," "called

---

46. See O. Bayer, "The Ethics of Gift," *LQ* 24 (2010): 452; cf. J. A. Linebaugh, *God, Grace, and Righteousness in Wisdom of Solomon and Paul's Letter to the Romans: Texts in Conversation,* NovTSup 152 (Leiden: Brill, 2013), 152–54, and E. Käsemann, *An die Römer,* HNT 8a (Tübingen: Mohr Siebeck, 1973), 116–17.

47. BSLK 510.33–511.8.

48. Bayer, "The Ethics of Gift," 452.

49. WA 1:183.39–184.7; cf. Käsemann, *Römer,* 117: "daß Gott immer nur dort schafft, wo irdisch nichts vorhanden ist."

50. LW 31:41; WA 1:354–35: "Amor dei non invenit, sed creat suum diligibile."

righteous" and so, *ex nihilo*, constituted as "a new creature."[51] What Luther
is tuned into is the way the disjunction in Paul between what God says and
those to whom he speaks suggests that words like καλέω and δικαιόω function
as verbal verbs—works of God enacted as words of God.[52] God's calling, for
instance, calls into being: where there was a "not my people" God calls and
thereby creates "my people"; to those who were "not loved" God calls and so
creates the "loved" (Rom 9:24). Or again, to those who are sinners and unrighteous, God does the verbal verb δικαιόω and thereby creates the opposite: "all
sinned . . . and are justified" (Rom 3:23–24; cf. 4:5; 5:6–10; Gal 2:15–21).[53]

Luther is thus reading with the grain of Paul's theology. In Galatians, the
grammar of the gospel is christological and just so incongruous, creative, and
charismatic: it is Christ, the χάρις or gift of God, given at the site of sin and
death, that creates righteousness and life.[54] As 2 Corinthians 4:6 has it, it is
the creator who said, "Let light shine out of darkness" who shines into us by
speaking the re-creative and redemptive word of "Jesus Christ." Citing both
this verse and Romans 4, Luther insists that neither creation nor new creation are the kindling of a "spark" "out of a gleaming coal," but rather "out of
darkness light; out of death life, out of sin righteousness."[55] To bring Paul and
Luther together by borrowing from Kathryn Tanner, for both the apostle and
his Reformation reader, "the grace" that saves "us has its analogue in the divine
act that created us—from nothing."[56]

Paul's good news is thus as deep as his diagnosis. "Sin came," "death reigned,"
and life in Adam and "under sin" is death. Correspondingly, redemption takes
the form of resurrection as the I who is dead dies with Christ and new life is

51. LW 34:113, 156.

52. According to Bayer's reconstruction, Luther's reformation breakthrough is tied up
with a development in his understanding of language: rather than a word functioning only
as a sign (*signum*) that refers to a reality (*res*), Luther came to see that God's words (*verba
Dei*) are God's work (*opera Dei*), that divine speech establishes rather than merely refers to
reality. The *signum* is the doing of the *res* and therefore, in the tradition of Psalm 33:9—"God
spoke and it was done"—Luther describes the divine address as a *verbum efficax*; see LW
5:140; cf. O. Bayer, *Promissio: Geschichte der reformatischen Wende in Luthers Theologie*, 2nd
ed. (Darmstadt: Wissenschaftliche Buchgesellschaft, 1989).

53. Consider this line from a Lutheran hymn: "Thy strong word bespeaks us righteous."
Cf. U. Wilckens, *Der Brief an die Römer*, 3 vols., EKKNT (Zurich: Benziger; Neukirchen-
Vluyn: Neukirchener, 1978–82), 1:188n39: "die Sünde aller [ist] also der Ort, an dem die
Gottesgerechtigkeit wirksam wird."

54. See chap. 9, "The Grammar of the Gospel."

55. LW 8:39.

56. K. Tanner, *Christ the Key* (Cambridge: Cambridge University Press, 2010), 64–65.

READING PAUL

created as grace opens the grave. In Luther's most succinct formulation: "death and resurrection . . . is full and complete justification."[57]

What this reading requires is a christological and relational definition of life to pair with the previous definition of death: if being dead is living with death before you, being alive is living with death behind you. Or again, to make the christological relation more explicit: death is life before and apart from death with Christ; life is life after and out of death with Christ.[58]

Identifying the Now Living "I"

The opening question still stands: Is (or are) the I that no longer lives and the I that now lives the same I?

No: I Am Not Me

The divide between the creature and the sinner is life and death; that between the sinner and the new creature is death and life. "I died to the law," "I have been crucified with Christ," "I no longer live"—these moments of Paul's confession gesture toward a discontinuity as deep as death. "Christ lives in me," "the life I now live"—these indicate a rupture as fundamental as resurrection.[59] There are, to borrow an image from Lou Martyn, "no through trains" from the old I to the new: "not development or maturation," comments Eastman on Galatians 2:20, but "death and resurrection . . . are the watchwords of Christian existence."[60] To hear Paul's confession is to encounter, as Tanner puts it, a "dis-

57. LW 36:67.
58. Consider Poem 816 by Emily Dickinson:

> A Death blow is a Life blow to Some
> Who till they died, did not alive become—
> Who had they lived, had died but when
> They died, Vitality begun.

59. Cf. J. M. G. Barclay, *Paul and the Gift* (Grand Rapids: Eerdmans, 2015), 386: Paul's "language of 'death' and 'life' . . . marks a radical disjunction."
60. J. L. Martyn, *Theological Issues in the Letters of Paul* (Nashville: Abingdon, 1997), 221; Eastman, *Paul and the Person*, 174. Cf. S. Chester, "Apocalyptic Union: Martin Luther's Account of Faith in Christ," in *In Christ in Paul: Explorations in Paul's Theology of Union and Participation*, ed. M. J. Thate, K. J. Vanhoozer, and C. R. Campbell (Grand Rapids: Eerdmans, 2018), 378: for Luther, Galatians 2:19–20 describes "not . . . the gradual healing of the self but . . . its death." See also Hampson, *Christian Contradictions*, 101: "there is no linear progress from being a sinner to being justified."

continuous radical leap between qualitatively different conditions," a passage from "next to nothing" to "everything."[61]

As Luther works to communicate the nonidentity of the no longer and now living I, he starts, again, to speak "the speech of the dead": "I am dead; by my own life I am not living."[62] For Luther, the Pauline insistence that "I no longer live" generates a corresponding confession, captured succinctly and with full shock in the phrase, "Thank God, I am not me" (Bob Dylan). With the phrase ζῶ οὐκέτι ἐγώ, Luther comments, "Paul clearly shows how he is alive," locating life outside of rather than "in my own person or substance."[63] As *The Freedom of a Christian* concludes, "a Christian lives not in him or herself," but rather, to return to Luther's Galatians commentary, the gospel "snatches us away from ourselves and places us outside ourselves" (*nos extra nos*).[64] For Luther, as Wilfried Joest suggests, the essence (or *Wesen*) of a person lies not in but out—a person *is* not *in sich und für sich* but *extra se*.[65] Existence, to borrow Kelsey's title, is eccentric.

That the person lives outside the self, however, does not imply that they live nowhere. According to Galatians 2:20, life is specifically located: "Christ lives in me"; "I live in faith."[66] These dative clauses are debated. Christ living ἐν ἐμοί, as the majority of commentators argue, can be locative, but it is also possible, with Calvin, to read it as a dative of respect: Christ, who is not me,

61. Tanner, *Christ the Key*, 65.
62. LW 26:170.
63. LW 26:166.
64. LW 26:387; WA 7:69, 12–13.
65. Joest, *Ontologie der Person bei Luther*, 234, 249. Cf. McFarland, "The Upward Call," 224: "the determining factor," when identifying who a person is, "is not anything intrinsic to and thus located within the individual, but extrinsic: constituted entirely by God's address."
66. Paul also locates life "in the flesh," a phrase that Luther interprets as follows: "I do live in the flesh, yet not on the basis of the flesh or according to the flesh" (LW 26:172). As Eastman argues, this localizing of life "in the flesh" also indicates that the person is always embodied and socially embedded (*Paul and the Person*, 156–60). The other crucial question raised here, but not considered in this paper, is the relationship between the I in grace and the I in glory (i.e., between the person redeemed and in Christ and the person resurrected and with Christ). Both Romans 8 and 1 Corinthians 15 point to a material continuity, but the latter's language of "spiritual body" catches something of the dialectic explored here: it is the body that is raised, but precisely that body is new. The Easter narratives capture this as well: the body of the risen Christ is different, but that it is the body of Jesus is evident as the tomb is empty and the wounds remains. Allen suggests that one way to express this double "nature of the new" is to say that we are dealing not with "transubstantiation" but with "transfiguration" (*Sanctification*, 225).

lives for me.[67] Similarly, life ἐν πίστει may, as most take it, be instrumental (i.e., "by faith"), though as de Boer contends, it could be a dative of sphere, indicating the "territory where Christ is Lord."[68] Whatever one decides, for Luther, the datives define life in relationship, specifically in relationship to Christ in whom I trust and who lives in and for me. The corollary to living *extra se*, according to Joest, is that one is "carried" by another.[69] Luther's way of emphasizing this in the Galatians commentary is to say that the life of the I that is ex-centric is also alien. There is, he writes, "an alien life, that of Christ in me."[70] As Luther's early lectures on Romans have it, we live both outside ourselves and in another: *extra nos et in Christo*.[71] The life that is confessed as "not I, but Christ in me" is grounded outside of the self and in relationship to Christ. Barclay is thus reading Paul with Luther when he describes this "wholly reconstituted existence" as "suspended by" and "founded on . . . the life of another, the life of 'Christ in me.'"[72]

Galatians 2:19–20 can therefore be said to "disclose and require," as Eastman argues, "an intersubjective account of the person," an account in which to be is, in Ebeling's phrase, to be "in relationship" (*in relatione*).[73] This is, according to Luther, precisely the sort of definition Paul provides in Romans 3:28. As thesis 32 of the *Disputatio de homine* asserts: "the human being *is* justified by faith."[74] On Luther's reading, to "live by faith in the Son of God" defines human being because it locates life in relationship to the one who "loves me and gave himself for me." Faith, in other words, is not a predicate of a self-defined person; it is, rather, a name for the relation with Christ that creates and carries the person—it is being grounded in gift. This definition encompasses

67. See M. Allen, *Justification and the Gospel: Understanding the Contexts and Controversies* (Grand Rapids: Baker Academic, 2013), 104.

68. De Boer, *Galatians*, 157.

69. Joest, *Ontologie*, 261–62.

70. LW 26:170. Joest introduces the term "exzentrisch" (*Ontologie*, 233–353). For variations, see, e.g., ecstatic (Oberman), a-centric (Allen), and eccentric (Kelsey).

71. WA 56:159; LW 25:136.

72. Barclay, *Paul and the Gift*, 379, 386.

73. Eastman, *Paul and the Person*, 152; Ebeling, *Lutherstudien*, 156–57. Cf. N. Slenckza, "Luther's Anthropology," in *Oxford Handbook of Martin Luther's Theology*, ed. R. Kolb, I. Dingel, and L. Batka (Oxford: Oxford University Press, 2015), and R. Saarinen, "Martin Luther and Relational Thinking," in *Oxford Research Encyclopedia of Religion* (Oxford: Oxford University Press, 2017).

74. LW 34:139. As Bayer points out, because this is a definition, Luther's Latin—"Hominem iustificari fide"—is better rendered, "the human being is human in being justified by faith" (*Martin Luther's Theology*, 155n3); cf. Slenckza, "Luther's Anthropology."

both creation and new creation: out of nothing, by grace, God creates; out of sin and death, by grace, God redeems and resurrects.[75]

On Luther's reading of Paul, faith is righteousness because of the one to whom it relates: "faith . . . takes hold of Christ . . . the One who is present in faith."[76] In Galatians 2:19–20, Paul's language and grammar gesture in this direction. Death and life are situated to and with and in—that is, with and in relationship—to God and Christ: "live to God;" "crucified with Christ;" "Christ lives in me;" "I live by faith in the Son of God."[77] Luther's image of the "happy exchange" is a way of depicting these dynamic relationships: it is not just an exchange of properties (i.e., our sin for Christ's righteousness); it is a communion of persons. Because Christ "took upon himself our sinful person and granted us his innocent and victorious person," because he became "Peter the denier, Paul the persecutor . . . David the adulterer" and "the person of all people," Luther invites us to sing, "mine are Christ's living and dying" and, joining with the Song of Songs, "my beloved is mine and I am his."[78]

Such a song is only sung east of Easter, on the far side of the divide Paul calls death. This life, in other words, is not a given; it is given—it is a gift. According to Galatians 2:20–21, "the grace of God" with which I die and in which I live is the self-giving of the "Son of God who loved me and gave himself for me."[79] The content of grace, as Barclay suggests, is Christ crucified and risen. Correspondingly, the character of grace is incongruity: a gift that comes as God's "counter statement to the previous conditions of the possible," giving righteousness at the site of sin and creating life out of death.[80] As another Pauline confession puts it, "by grace, I am" (1 Cor 15:10).

The life of the now living I can thus be called christological—I am in Christ—but also ex-centric, alien, and charismatic. I am: outside myself, in

75. Cf. Bayer, *Martin Luther's Theology*, 156: "As created being, human existence is justified-through-faith existence. As justified-through-faith existence, it is created existence."

76. LW 26:129–30. See chap. 11, "The Christocentrism of Faith in Christ."

77. For Luther, the phrases *extra se*, *coram deo*, and *in Christo* are ways of referring to these relationships.

78. LW 26:280–84; *Freedom of the Christian*, 287. Cf. Eastman who argues that Paul's language of "union discloses a relational notion of the person" (*Paul and the Person*, 153) and Vanhoozer who plays with the resonance between union, communion, and communication ("From 'Blessed in Christ' to 'Being in Christ,'" 27–28).

79. See Bayer who, with reference to Galatians 2:19–20, speaks of "a gift from someone else, by whose life I live" (*Martin Luther's Theology*, 235). Bonhoeffer offers another definition of death in these terms: being dead is "having to live." Being alive, then, is having life—death is life as demand; life is life as gift (*Creation and Fall*).

80. Barclay, *Paul and the Gift*, 412.

another, as gift. Or again, to combine Dylan and Luther, I am both "not me" and, by grace, "as Christ."[81]

Yes: I Am Loved

Daphne Hampson asks a question at this point that forces us to ask our opening question one more time.[82] Recognizing that Luther's reading of Paul is in the tradition of what William James calls "twice born" religion, Hampson provides an apology for the "once born" variety. "I should not," she says, "wish to base myself on that which lies outside myself. . . . I am interested in what I should call being 'centered' in oneself (as opposed . . . to living *extra se*). . . . I am concerned for the transformation of the self, rather than the breaking of the self." Her rationale here is deep: marginalized and oppressed persons are not helped but harmed by being "told that [the] self needs to be" shattered.[83] This protest contains a crucial question: are soteriologies of death and resurrection—that is, accounts of salvation like we encounter in Galatians and Luther's reading of it—finally opposed to the human person? Does the announcement of the death of the I eliminate the possibility of God's love for the I? If I only am outside myself and in Christ, does God ever look at and love me?

These questions are an acute way of asking whether and in what sense there is continuity between the no longer living and the now living I. One possible answer is to ground personal continuity in creation. For Thomas Aquinas, as we have seen, created life is not lost—sin is not defined as death—and therefore God always and ever loves God's creatures and, in grace, it is precisely their natures as created and fallen that are perfected and healed so that it is finally

---

81. LW 26:168: "by [faith] you are so cemented to Christ that he and you are one person, which . . . declares: 'I am as Christ,' and Christ, in turn, says, 'I am as that sinner.'"

82. Hampson also asks about the place of love in Luther's theology. If Christ and the Christian are, in Luther's words, "so cemented" that he and they "are as one person," does not the otherness of the I and Christ collapse? But love, Hampson contends, is "bi-polar"; it demands two rather than one and so, by definition, disappears if the "distance" and distinction between persons is lost (*Christian Contradictions*, 29–39, 246). For Luther, however, oneness with Christ does not, as Bayer puts it, "denote an identity without distinction" (*Martin Luther's Theology*, 229n31). To be "as one person" with Christ, Luther writes, is to be in a relation "more intimate than a husband and wife." Personal union, in other words, is a relational notion; it names a communion of persons even as it anchors one (the creature) in the other (Christ). Cf. W. Elert, *The Structure of Lutheranism*, trans. W. A. Hansen (St. Louis: Concordia, 1962), 176, and Ebeling, *The Truth of the Gospel*, 149.

83. Hampson, *Christian Contradictions*, 237–41; see also Hampson, "Luther on the Self: A Feminist Critique," *WW* 8.4 (1988): 334–42.

they who are beheld and beloved.[84] In Galatians 2:20, however, the drama and "disjunction between old and new . . . entails," as John Webster notes, "the exclusion of certain ways of understanding the continuity of the self." It is not, for instance, that "the old and new are points on a continuum" that only indicate "different dispositions of a subject that is [finally] self-identical."[85] The discontinuity is more fundamental—it is death, and after and out of death, it is life. To capture this, readers of Paul refer to "a radical break" and a "reversal" or "counter-movement . . . that is wholly incongruous with the prior conditions" and possibilities of "human history."[86]

But that is not the whole story. Both Barclay and Eastman, whom I just quoted, also point to a paradoxical congruity and continuity. For Barclay, God's incongruous gifts are "entirely congruous" with God's promises and, as Eastman adds, the "continuity of the person" is anchored in being addressed by God's promise and call. In Luther's phrase, as both creature and new creature, the person is *creatura verbi*—a creature of the word: called, by grace and from nothing, into being and called, by grace and out of sin and death, righteous and alive.[87]

But again: is (or are) the I as created and fallen and re-created the same? If the distance between the old and new is death, and if the "life I now live" is *extra se, in Christo*, and *sola gratia*, does the person persist? Galatians 2:20 gestures toward an answer to this question in a way that responds directly to Daphne Hampson's concern about the elimination of love. According to Paul's

---

84. For two recent engagements with Catholic reflection on nature and grace and what Protestant theology might learn from and contribute to that conversation, see Allen, *Sanctification*, 212–25, and McFarland, "The Upward Call."

85. J. Webster, "Eschatology, Ontology, and Human Action," *TJT* 7.1 (1991): 5. In one sense, this chapter is an attempt to engage Webster's question about the anthropological and ontological entailments of Paul's language in places like Galatians 2:20 and 2 Corinthians 5:17 (4–5). What Webster calls for is a "metaphysics of the *solus Christus*" (10).

86. Eastman, *Paul and the Person*, 174; Barclay, *Paul and the Gift*, 412–14. McFarland also asks about the "discontinuity between human existence as created and redeemed" and argues that while "there is nothing in our natures . . . that serves as the pivot point . . . that guarantees that the beings we are now . . . subsist across that divide," we can nevertheless say that "our natures are not destroyed or left behind" because it is "we, body and soul, who live with God in glory" even though "we do not do so because of the qualities of our souls or bodies" ("The Upward Call," 236).

87. That the person is anchor by a word of address entails that humans are, as McFarland points out, "the sort of creatures that can respond when called"—that they are spoken to precisely as the kind of creatures who are both receptive and response-able ("The Upward Call," 224; O. Bayer, *Freedom in Response*).

confession, there is a "me" that Christ loved and gave himself for. *Pro me*—for me: for Luther, "this brief pronoun"—"me"—is "true power." "Anyone who can speak" and "apply it to her or himself," he says, "defines Christ properly" as "grace" and "savior," as "mercy" and as he who "gives and is given." The power is the meeting of the christological past and a personal pronoun, a pairing that gives peace to "a trembling and troubled heart" and "rest to your bones and mine."[88]

What this picks up is the Pauline identification of those whom Christ loves and those to whom he gives himself: Christ gave himself to deliver "us," says Galatians 1:4; the son of God loved and gave himself for me," adds Galatians 2:20. Luther wants to know, "Who is this me?" His answer, "It is I, an accursed and damned sinner," resonates especially with Romans 5:6–10. The me—the us—that Jesus loved and gave himself for is me as a sinner and an enemy, me when I was weak and ungodly: "God demonstrated his love like this: while we were still sinners Christ died for us" (Rom 5:8). The I may no longer live, but the I was and is loved. According to Paul, the self does not survive salvation: "one died for all therefore all died" (2 Cor 5:14). But the gospel is an Easter sermon that rolls away the stone: it says, in the words of the novelist Walker Percy, "I love you dead" (cf. Eph 2:1–4); and it also sings, to quote Ephesians, "Wake up sleeper, rise from the dead."[89]

The persistence of the person, in other words, is not grounded in the person. I am: not me but, by grace, in Christ. But it is exactly this grace and this Christ—the one who loved me and gave himself for me—that establishes a kind of continuity, what might be called the passive persistence of the person. The cross is, at once, a death that breaks the story of the self into two even as it is a gift and love that has a way of holding it together. I may no longer live, but, in the dative and accusative cases if you will—in the cases of the creature and receiver—there is and was and will be a me who is persistently loved and graced by God.[90]

So finally: Is (or are) the no longer and now living I the same? The stubbornness of this question confirms Käsemann's caution: "the mysteriousness of existence remains." But moving toward a Pauline answer is also to hear his final hint: "Only the gospel has the clue to the hieroglyph" we translate

---

88. LW 26:177–78.

89. W. Percy, *Love in the Ruins* (New York: Picador, 1971), 68.

90. See Bayer, who refers to the "dative of gifted-existence" in "The Being of Christ in Faith," *LQ* 10 (1996): 142.

human.[91] Paul's "strange and un-heard of" confession requires a dialectical conclusion, one that both unburdens those carrying the weight of their own worth even as it says "I love you" to those whose lives feel like an endless and failing audition for affection. No: death and life divide the no longer and now living I and the life of the latter is gifted, ex-centric, and in Christ. But also yes: though I no longer live, there is a me that is ever and always loved. To speak "the speech of the dead," it seems, is to talk twice: life and death and death and life separate the self. And yet, in and across the passages of creation, sin, grace, and glory there is a me that is loved and loved and loved and loved. To combine the confession: I am—outside myself, by grace, and in Christ a me whom God did, does, and will ever love.

91. E. Käsemann, "On Paul's Anthropology," in *Perspectives on Paul*, trans. M. Kohl (Philadelphia: Fortress, 1971), 30.

PART TWO

READING PAUL IN CONTEXT
AND CONVERSATION

CHAPTER 5

RELATIONAL HERMENEUTICS AND COMPARISON AS CONVERSATION

The text lives . . . by coming into contact with another text.

—Mikhail Bakhtin

"Where does the riddle of a book lie? In its language and content? In the plan of its author or in the mind of the interpreter?—" Johann Georg Hamann asked this question in a Christmas letter in 1784. It still haunts hermeneutics.[1]

Hamann's question identifies three possible locations for the "riddle of a book": the text, the author, the interpreter. Does a text mean, in other words, as words on a page ("language and content"), as a mediation of the *mens auctoris* ("the plan of the author"), or as a reader's interpretation ("the mind of the interpreter")? The form of Hamann's question, however, resists the alternatives. Instead of an answer, he offers an em dash: "—." But consider the context of the question:

> God, nature, and reason have as intimate a relation to one another as light, the eye, and all that the former reveals to the latter, or like the center, radius, and periphery of any given circle, or like author, book and reader. Where does the riddle of a book lie? In its language and content? In the plan of its author or in the mind of the interpreter?—

The riddle of the book, for Hamann, is not located in author or text or interpreter; it is the "relation" between author and text and interpreter.

There is a story here. Hamann's relational hermeneutic, while present from

---

1. J. G. Hamann, *Briefwechsel*, ed. W. Ziesemer and A. Henkel, 8 vols. (Wiesbaden: Insel Verlag, 1955–75), 5, Nr. 784, 272:14–18; ET, G. Griffith-Dickson, *Johann Georg Hamann's Relational Metacriticism* (Berlin: de Gruyter, 1995), 338.

at least 1759, takes its most suggestive form in a 1762 essay entitled *Aesthetica in nuce*. Hamann was prompted to write, in large part, in response to Johann David Michaelis's pioneering research on philology and biblical interpretation following the Danish expedition to Arabia.[2] Hamann countered Michaelis's scholarly pilgrimage, which aimed at resurrecting scripture through understanding the "extinct" Hebraic languages, with his own "philological crusade." His quest was also a question: not so much about how scholarship can resurrect the language of scripture, but rather how can the language of the "poet of heaven and earth" resurrect us?[3]

This debate is programmatic, positioned as it is at the dawn of modern biblical scholarship. For Michaelis, comparative research is indispensable: it deepens linguistic understanding, colors in historical contexts, and can disclose genealogical connections. But this study, as undertaken by Michaelis, is governed by what Hamann labels "monastic rules," method as a medicine proscribed to protect against "passion."[4] For Hamann, by contrast, philology, interpretation, and comparison are more dynamic—more self-involving and passionate, more relational.

With hindsight, Michaelis's approach looks like the forerunner of much comparative research, whether genealogical or analytic—that is, whether the aim is to determine derivation and influence or to arrange texts synoptically and explore their similarity and difference. But Hamann is a reminder that there might be another way. This chapter does not pretend to offer a comprehensive history, theory, method, or rationale for the practice of comparing texts. It will, rather, remember Hamann's relational riposte. Hamann's relational hermeneutic invites a form of comparison in which texts are not so much placed side by side and observed as they as brought by an engaged interpreter into relationship, face to face—and because the interpreter is a relational participant we have to add, to face. After considering the salient features of Hamann's relational account of interpretation (in occasional dialogue with Ricoeur, Gadamer, and Bakhtin), I will suggest a relational approach to

2. See J. D. Michaelis, *Beurtheilung der Mittel, welche man anwendet, die ausgestorbene Hebräische Spache zu verstehen* (Göttingen, 1757). The expedition was funded by the king of Denmark and led by Karsten Niehbur, but it was undertaken at the behest of Michaelis, whose research was part of an emerging historical approach to interpretation associated with figures such as Siegmund Jakob Baumgarten, Johann August Ernesti, and Johann Salomo Semler.

3. *Aesthetica in nuce* was published as part of a collection entitled *Crusades of a Philologian*.

4. J. G. Hamann, *Sämtliche Werken*, ed. J. Nadler, 6 vols. (Vienna: Verlag Herder, 1949–57), 2:208.20.

comparative research in which comparison is understood as a conversation between the comparanda as well as with the comparator. Finally, a comparative sample drawn from my previous study of *Wisdom of Solomon* and Romans will attempt to put some flesh on the theoretical bones by hosting and participating in a conversation between and with the texts.

RELATIONAL HERMENEUTICS WITH J. G. HAMANN

Hamann's relational approach to reading and writing is on display from the opening dedication of his initial authorial experiment, the *Socratic Memorabilia* (1759). This "flying leaf," as Hamann called his writings, has a "double dedication": to "nobody" and "to Two."[5] The two here are Hamann's "friends," Christoph Berens and Immanuel Kant. Hamann hopes that their relationship will enrich their reading, whether that results in "biased praise" or "biased criticism."[6]

This may seem like an incidental detail, but it gestures toward a fundamental aspect of Hamann's hermeneutic. The language of friendship recurs in the *Socratic Memorabilia* in relation to the interpretation of its titular subject: "Socrates often visited the workshop of a tanner who was his friend" and who "was the first to have the idea of writing down the conversations with Socrates." Hamann's hope is to "understand my hero as well as Simon the tanner," to understand Socrates as a friend.[7]

In the *Socratic Memorabilia*, this hermeneutic of friendship entails passionate commitment to the friend, what Hamann calls "a thirsting ambition for truth," and also the capacity to feel with the friend: "as one must oneself know the affliction [of hypochondria] to understand a hypochondriac . . . perhaps one must have sympathy for ignorance in order to understand the Socratic variety."[8] In addition to these relational postures, Hamann also suggests a relational procedure: an "interpreter must" place "texts" in "connection with others," must "couple" them because "words" and so texts mean in "relations."[9] Texts are

---

5. Hamann, *Sämtliche Werken*, 2:57. For English translations, in addition to Griffith-Dickson, *Relational Metacriticism* see J. G. Hamann, *Writings on Philosophy and Language*, ed. K. Haynes (Cambridge: Cambridge University Press, 2007), 3.

6. Hamann, *Sämtliche Werken*, 2:61.32–33.

7. Hamann, *Sämtliche Werken*, 2:65.24–31.

8. Hamann, *Sämtliche Werken*, 2:63.34; 70.28–32. See too Griffith-Dickson, *Relational Metacriticism*, 381, 388.

9. Hamann, *Sämtliche Werken*, 2:71.25–34. The most significant "comparison" in *Socratic Memorabilia* is Hamann's coupling of the inscription at Delphi ("know thyself") and the Socratic confession of ignorance.

compared—or "coupled"—because, as Griffith-Dickson writes, they "achieve their meaning and power when viewed in their relations," and this "relational fertility is such" that "new light is shed on both by their new relation."[10]

All of these themes reappear and are developed in *Aesthetica in nuce*. If Hamann's relationship with Kant and Berens occasioned the *Socratic Memorabilia*, this 1762 essay from his *Crusades of a Philologian* is part of an ongoing engagement with Michaelis. Hamann's earlier *Cloverleaf of Hellenistic Letters* had already interacted with Michaelis, whose scholarship he seems genuinely to have admired and whose philology he worried was too truncated. His appraisal of Michaelis in these "letters" does at times, as Hamann admits, "extend frankness into impertinence."[11] But Michaelis also seems to have inspired Hamann. Between 1759 and 1763, Hamann did indeed undertake a philological crusade: in addition to studying a range of authors from Horace to Luther, this "great study scheme" included Greek, Hebrew, and Arabic.[12]

This intensive study is evidence that Hamann's relational hermeneutic is not a replacement for linguistic and contextual research. Rather a relational understanding of reality means that research has to be less about "monastic rules" and more a "rhapsody," less constrained and more "kabbalistic." These unexpected descriptions, taken from the subtitle of the essay ("a rhapsody is kabbalistic prose"), are not an exercise in obscurantism: they name the genre and genealogy of the hermeneut. Interpretation is kabbalistic because an interpreter is not a reader after the order of Melchizedek—"without father or mother, without genealogy, without beginning of days or end of life" (Heb 7:3). Kabbala gestures toward tradition and transmission, and for Hamann is a reminder that each interpreter has a location and a life, an inheritance and a history. As a rhapsody, Hamann's philological and comparative research is like the poems of the rhapsodists, both in the sense that they selected and "stitched together" pieces of previous poetry and in that they were, as Hamann's reference to Plato's *Ion* indicates, "interpreters of interpreters."[13]

---

10. Griffith-Dickson, *Relational Metacriticism*, 65.

11. *Writings on Philosophy and Language*, 59. Perhaps the most obvious example is Hamann's remark that a "reader who hates the truth may find much in *Opinion on the Means Used to Understand the Defunct Hebrew Language* to comfort him" (*Writings on Philosophy and Language*, 53). These "letters" also afforded Hamann the opportunity to express his original take on the then *en vogue* question about the quality of New Testament Greek: the Greek of the New Testament is humble because the "*stylus curiae*" of the self-giving God is "the *genus humile dicendi*" (*Writings on Philosophy and Language*, 40).

12. For fuller details, see Griffith-Dickson, *Relational Metacriticism*, 76.

13. Hamann, *Sämtliche Werken*, 2:217. 20. See Griffith-Dickson, *Relational Metacriticism*, 82–83, for an excellent discussion of the significance of the subtitle.

If the kinds of relationships that go under the name research involve selection, coupling, and interpretation—if research is a kabbalistic rhapsody—then, for Hamann, the moments and movements of these relationships can also be specified. Francis Bacon, who is among the muses of *Aesthetica in nuce*, divided learning into three: history with memory, philosophy with reason, and poetry with phantasy. Hamann followed suit, but added some job descriptions or jurisdictions: with regard to the data (Hamann would say *dicta*) of nature and history, which are forms of "address" and yet heard as "jumbled verse," it is "for the scholar to gather these; for the philosopher to interpret them; to imitate them—or even bolder—to bring them into order is the poet's part."[14] Within this division of labor, Michaelis's research has an essential role, but it also oversteps its limits when it imagines archeological research and exegetical rules can resurrect the language of "the poet at the beginning of days."

For Hamann, research is reception, interpretation, and response. These moments are not so much a method as modes of relating: of listening, of engaging, and of speaking. This suggests a fundamental anthropological asymmetry: the human creature is addressed and only so able to answer, is receptive and only so responsive, is a reader and only then a writer. Hamann's relational hermeneutic, in other words, is part of a more comprehensive relational anthropology. In an age in which the unions between contingent and necessary truth, subject and object, and rationality and sensuousness were being dissolved by what Hamann criticized as "the art of divorce" (*Scheidekunst*), he insisted on the "art of marriage" (*Ehekunst*).[15] This is ultimately a christological contention, rooted in the "*communicatio* of the divine and human *idiomata*" and reflected in the title of a 1784 essay that references both the self-emptying and exaltation of Jesus, *Golgatha und Scheblimini*.[16] But this is not a narrowly christological confession. For Hamann, the christological *communicatio* discloses a relational understanding of reality: it is a "fundamental law and master-key of all our knowledge and of the whole visible economy."[17]

---

14. Hamann, *Sämtliche Werken*, 2:199.1–3. John Milton, in *Areopagitica*, writes of "Truth" being "hewed . . . into a thousand pieces and scattered to the four winds" such that the "sad friends of truth," like "the careful search that Isis made for the mangled body of Osiris," must go "up and down gathering up limb by limb" the scattered "members" of "virgin Truth."

15. On this theme, see O. Bayer, *A Contemporary in Dissent: Johann Georg Hamann as a Radical Enlightener*, trans. R. A. Harrisville and M. C. Mattes (Grand Rapids: Eerdmans, 2012), xii–xiii, 14; Griffith-Dickson, *Relational Metacriticism*, 1–15.

16. *Scheblimini* is taken from Psalm 110:1 and means "sit at my right hand." The quotation is from "The Last Will and Testament of the Knight of the Rose-Cross" (1772), Hamann, *Sämtliche Werken*, 3:27.11–14.

17. Hamann, *Sämtliche Werken*, 3:27.11–14 (see *Writings on Philosophy and Language*, 99). Goethe, for whom Hamann was "the brightest mind of his time," was among the first

In *Aesthetica in nuce* this "whole visible economy" is interpreted as an "address (*Rede*) to the creature through the creature."[18] For Hamann, then, to be a creature is to be addressed, to be one "whose existence is relative" or "constituted by a relation" of reception and response.[19] The human person lives from an address and as an answer.[20] For this reason, as Oswald Bayer argues, "hermeneutical" characterizes Hamann's understanding of human existence: it points to "the linguistic character of . . . communication," the way this communication requires "time" and "translation," and theologically the "cascade from the speaking God to the receptive human being." Here Hamann anticipates Gadamer. Hermeneutic describes life as interpretative existence—the relational reality Hamann would call "being created."[21] Furthermore, Hamann's relational hermeneutic resonates with Gadamer's insistence that reading is a relationship: a text, for Gadamer, is "ein echter Kommunikationspartner" and thus to describe reading he speaks "vom einem hermeneutischen Gespräch."[22]

Hamann makes the same point: while author and reader are among the communication partners who participate in the hermeneutical conversation, interpretation is also and always a relationship with "the given letters"—with the text.[23] This attention to the given resists what Bayer calls "a twofold impatience," the interpretative urge to get behind or away from the text to either "the self-understanding of the author" or "the self-understanding of the reader."[24] As Ricoeur puts it, interpretation occurs "before the text"—along

---

to interpret Hamann along the lines of the necessity of unification and the problem of isolation. Goethe's estimation of Hamann was shared by many and surpassed, perhaps, only by Kierkegaard who named Hamann, along with Socrates, as the "most brilliant minds of all time." For these and other descriptions of Hamann, see J. R. Betz, *After Enlightenment: The Post-Secular Vision of J. G. Hamann* (Oxford: Wiley-Blackwell, 2012), 2–3.

18. Hamann, *Sämtliche Werken*, 2:198.29.

19. O. Bayer, "God as Author: On the Theological Foundations of Hamann's Authorial Poetics," in *Hamann and the Tradition*, ed. L. M. Anderson (Evanston, IL: Northwestern University Press, 2012), 165.

20. Hamann would call the address the human lives from the Word or grace and the answer life is lived as either unbelief or faith and love: faith and love are engendered by the antecedent address and are modes of relating to another, whether that other is God (related to in faith) or the neighbor (related to in love). Here, as Hamann said he was always doing, he "Lutherizes" (*Briefwechsel*, 307, quoted in Betz, *After Enlightenment*, 33).

21. Griffith-Dickson, *Relational Metacriticism*, 354.

22. H.-G. Gadamer, *Wahrheit und Methode: Grundüzge einer philosophischen Hermeneutik*, Gesammelte Werke 1 (Tübingen: Mohr Siebeck, 1990), 364, 391.

23. From a letter to Jacobi, cited in Griffith-Dickson, *Relational Metacriticism*, 129.

24. O. Bayer, "Hermeneutical Theology," *SJT* 56.2 (2003): 144.

the "detour" of attention to "signs" and "symbols."[25] In this sense, it is possible, indeed necessary, to talk about the "relative autonomy of the text over against the author as well as over against the reader."[26] To quote John Milton, "books are not absolutely dead things, but do contain a potency of life . . . they are as lively, and as vigorously productive, as those fabulous dragon's teeth." This does not mean, as Griffith-Dickson points out, that the text is a "self-sufficient" subject: a text derives from an author and depends on a reader. But it is not dominated by either.[27] Precisely as a text—as signs, symbols, and detour—it detains; it resists and relates. Relative autonomy, in other words, is "relational autonomy."[28] Hamann is just as opposed to an "exegetical materialism" that forgets the author as an "other" as he is to an "exegetical idealism" that leaps over the "given letters."[29] Author, text, and reader—these are the communication partners who engage in a hermeneutical conversation.

As in the *Socratic Memorabilia*, the relational hermeneutic of *Aesthetica in nuce* entails passion, but also participation. "Do not," Hamann warns, "venture into the metaphysics of the fine arts without being initiated into the orgies and Eleusinian mysteries."[30] Passion, in other words, is not a problem but a prerequisite: Michaelis "sets monastic rules—Passion alone gives abstractions as well as hypotheses hands, feet, wings."[31] The contrast with Michaelis is telling. According to Hamann's diagnosis, strict exegetical methods—"monastic rules"—are motivated by "fear": fear of subjectivity and of misinterpretation, but also "fear of the spirit and life of the prophets."[32] While Hamann's relational hermeneutic calls for rather than prohibits passion, he is resolutely opposed to a one-sided subjectivity, to those who "flood" the text by "dreaming up their own inspiration and interpretation."[33] His solution, however, is not rules; it

25. P. Ricouer, "Erzählung, Metapher und Interpretationstheorie," *ZTK* 84 (1987): 232–53, quoted in Bayer, "Hermeneutical Theology," 143.

26. Bayer, "Hermeneutical Theology," 143. Related to this is Gadamer's contention that "understanding is never a subjective relationship towards a given 'object' but belongs rather to the effective history" of the text or artifact, *Wahrheit und Methode*; ET, *Truth and Method* (New York: Continuum, 1997), xix.

27. See Griffith-Dickson, *Relational Metacriticism*, 129–30. As Hamann reads Socrates, he imagines him talking back to his interpreter: "What does this young fellow," Plato in this case, "mean to make of me?" (*Sämtliche Werken*, 2:65.29–30).

28. Bayer, "God as Author," 173.

29. The terms are Griffith-Dickson, *Relational Metacriticism*, 129, 337.

30. Hamann, *Sämtliche Werken*, 2:201.12–14.

31. Hamann, *Sämtliche Werken*, 2:208.20–21.

32. Hamann, *Sämtliche Werken*, 2:204.26–27.

33. Hamann, *Sämtliche Werken*, 2:207.22 and 208.6.

is the relationship. Hamann talks about an interpreter being "true" to their communication partners, of sympathy, and of reading as a form of relating as a "friend." What this amounts to, as Griffith-Dickson puts it, is that the "safeguards" against exegetical "abuse . . . arise from the respectful relationship with the author and the text." And she adds, "There are no further safeguards for this than there are against misunderstanding in any other relationship."[34]

The flipside of this is that the possibilities of understanding are the same as in other relationships. Hamann's hermeneutic emphasizes certain capacities and practices that enable us to come to know another. Perhaps the most essential, for Hamann, is being addressed or, more simply, listening—the patient mode of receiving the other as they give themselves to us. But coming to know another also requires empathy and engagement. Hamann talks about "sympathy" and "initiation," forms of relating that require imagination and experience. George Eliot's explanation of the role of realism in literature resonates with Hamann: "We want to be taught to feel . . . for the peasant in all his coarse apathy and the artisan in all his suspicious selfishness." Art, according to Eliot, can engender this "feeling for" because "it is a mode of amplifying experience and extending our contact with our fellowmen beyond the bounds of our personal lot."[35] At the limits of the imagination, Hamann also invites initiation "into the orgies and Eleusinian mysteries"—into relationships and experiences. As Melville puts it in *Moby-Dick*, if you want to understand "the experience of whaling," then "go a-whaling."[36] There are, to use a term employed by many religious and philosophic traditions, "ways" of life that to know are to live. That this is so, and that a person only lives one life, is the central insight of Kavin Rowe's *One True Life*. This does not mean, as Rowe is sometimes misread as suggesting, that "rival traditions of life" cannot converse. Rather it specifies, in such cases, the relationship that comparison is: a relation between "rivals" who can nevertheless be friends in sympathetic but still honest conversation.[37]

34. Griffith-Dickson, *Relational Metacriticism*, 128.

35. *Essays of George Eliot*, ed. T. Pinney (Milton Park: Routledge & Kegan Paul, 1968), 170–71.

36. Consider also the note found next to Martin Luther's deathbed: "No one can understand Virgil in his Bucolics and Georgics unless he has spent five years as a shepherd or farmer. No one understands Cicero in his letters unless he has served under an outstanding government for twenty years. No one should believe that he has tasted the Holy Scriptures sufficiently unless he has spent one hundred years leading churches with the prophets." WATr, no. 5677; 317.

37. It is essential to stress that strong traditions that invite living as the deepest mode of understanding can nevertheless converse and relate, can share experiences and empathize. It is precisely a lack of the kind of empathy suggested by Eliot, an "incapacity to think . . .

This kind of conversation brings us back to comparison. Mikhail Bakhtin says, "The text lives only by coming into contact with another text."[38] Hamann could almost have written that. He would agree that a text only lives by coming into contact with another, though that other could be a reader rather than another text. Drop the "only," however, and you've got Hamann: the text lives by coming into contact with another text. Stitching together or "coupling" texts and traditions is a hermeneutical act that is both rhapsodic and relational. "By creating new relationships," writes Griffith-Dickson, the interpreter "creates a new world of possible meanings and insights," a world in which "new light is shed on both [texts or traditions] by their new relation."[39] This relational and rhapsodic approach resists forms of comparison in which material is simply juxtaposed and analyzed by a personally uninvolved interpreter. For Hamann, texts and traditions should not, in this side-by-side sense, just be compared; they should be coupled: brought into relationship, face to face.

But again, because the interpreter is also engaged in the relationship, this comparative relation is best described as face-to-face-to-face. And this suggests that the illumination that occurs in the comparative relationship does not apply only to the texts. The interpreter also "lives by coming into contact with another." Hamann explores this theme under the question of self-knowledge. Through reading and comparative research—that is, by relating to others—we come to know not just the other but also ourselves. "Self-knowledge begins with the neighbor, the mirror."[40] As Hamann's stitching together of Socratic and Pauline ignorance suggests, however, this knowledge is less about "knowing something" than it is about "being known" by someone (1 Cor 8:2–3). "Self knowledge comes from being known."[41] To read and compare and relate to others is, in T. S. Eliot's words, to "explore" the "unknown," the "unremem-

---

from another person's point of view," that Hannah Arendt diagnoses as the "banality of evil" in *Eichmann in Jerusalem: A Report on the Banality of Evil* (London: Penguin Books, 2006 [1963]), 252, xiii.

38. M. Bakhtin, "Toward a Methodology for the Human Sciences," in *Speech Genres and Other Late Essays*, ed. C. Emerson and M. Holquist; trans. V. W. McGee (Austin: University of Texas Press, 1986), 162.

39. Griffith-Dickson, *Relational Metacriticism*, 65, 133. Within the larger theological horizon of *Aesthetica in nuce*, this coupling is underwritten by and ultimately hears "the testimony of Christ," the "divine word" that both interprets scripture and is the "master-key" that unlocks the books of nature and history. Hamann's hermeneutic is thus characterized by the relationship between the one and the any: the one word of Christ makes legible and can be read in any book, whether it be the book of scripture, nature, or history.

40. Hamann, *Briefwechsel*, 6:281.

41. G. Griffith-Dickson, "God, I, and Thou: Hamann and the Personalist Tradition," in

bered," and the "half-heard." But the "end of all our exploring" is not only a better understanding of others. The "end" is the self-knowledge that comes from being known—the end "will be to arrive where we started, and know the place for the first time."[42]

ENGAGED EXEGETICAL EAVESDROPPING: COMPARISON AS CONVERSATION

After suggesting that "the text lives . . . by coming into contact with another text," Bakhtin adds a significant gloss: "joining a given text to a dialogue" creates "the point of . . . contact between texts" at which "a light flashes."[43] This description of comparative research resonates with Hamann's relational hermeneutic. For Bakhtin, texts are not just studied in juxtaposition; they are joined. And this joining or, in Hamann's word, this coupling creates a point of contact, a conversation.

The aim of this section is to suggest that this understanding of comparison as conversation provides a way to conceive and conduct comparative research that is informed by Hamann's relational hermeneutic. Comparison is a dynamic relationship between the comparanda and with the comparator. This relational dynamism, however, resists the attempt to translate Hamann's hermeneutic into a fixed comparative method. Living relationships cannot be controlled by "monastic rules." What Hamann invites, rather, is a consideration of the relationship that comparison is and the conditions by which an interpreter might facilitate and participate in that relationship. One way to capture this relationship is to call it engaged exegetical eavesdropping.

First, exegetical eavesdropping: texts sound different when they talk, not just to a reader, but to another text. This is the insight behind Bakhtin's insistence that "joining a given text to a dialogue" creates "the point of . . . contact between texts" at which "a light flashes." Texts come alive when they connect, when they converse about what they share and where and why they differ. Hamann's description of the act of interpretation as a rhapsody points in the same direction: stitching texts and traditions together introduces a "couple" that engages in a conversation and "creates a new world of possible meanings and insights." The relational results of this flash of light or new world of possible meanings cannot be controlled or predicated: familiar sentences may become

---

Hamann and the Tradition, ed. L. M. Anderson (Evanston, IL: Northwestern University Press, 2012), 56.

42. From "Little Gidding," which is the last of Eliot's *Four Quartets*.

43. Bakhtin, "Toward a Methodology for the Human Sciences," 162.

strange, once insignificant passages may speak with surprise and urgency, apparently novel ideas may prove commonplace, and claims that seem routine may emerge as radical. But whatever the results, the relationship between the texts can impact the relationship the reader has with the texts. As the texts talk to each other, their otherness—their demand of a detour and their difference as given letters—resist and relate to the reader by requiring an act of reception, of listening. Exegetical eavesdropping describes this movement of comparative interpretation: comparison involves listening in on a conversation between the comparanda.

But texts don't just talk to each other. As Jonathan Z. Smith puts it, "It is the scholar who makes their cohabitation . . . possible."[44] The interpreter, in other words, creates the conversation through the "postulation of similarity which is the ground of methodological comparison" and by "bringing differences together."[45] Comparison is a relationship not just between texts but also with the interpreter. Exegetical eavesdropping is thus necessarily engaged: the comparator listens to but also facilitates and participates in the conversation. Hosting the conversation entails "bringing together" the comparanda and "the focused selection of significant aspects of the phenomena" being compared; participating in the conversation includes, in Hamann's terms, the kind of interpretation and response that involves friendship, passion, empathy, and experience.[46]

Both of these relational roles raise possible problems. E. P. Sanders argues in his comparison of Paul and Palestinian Judaism that "the two principal difficulties" of placing texts in conversation can be "summarized by the words imbalance and imposition."[47] The former, "imbalance," refers to the problems associated with comparing a single text or author with a more expansive tradition and the tendency such disproportion has toward over generalization. Reducing a diverse tradition to a common denominator that is useful for comparison may conceal rather than capture the tradition or texts in question. The second difficultly, "imposition," identifies a temptation in comparative research to allow one participant in the relationship, whether one of the comparanda or

---

44. J. Z. Smith, *Drudgery Divine: On Comparison of Early Christianities and the Religions of Late Antiquity* (Chicago: University of Chicago Press, 1990), 51.

45. Smith, *Drudgery Divine*, 51.

46. Smith, *Drudgery Divine*, 51, 53; cf. his endorsement of F. J. P. Poole's remark that "comparisons do not deal with phenomena *in toto* or in the round, but only with the aspectual characteristic of them."

47. E. P. Sanders, *Paul and Palestinian Judaism: A Comparison of Patterns of Religion* (Minneapolis: Fortress, 1977), 19.

the comparator, to function as the control or canon—the standard according to which the other communication partners are measured.[48] There are some procedural strategies that can alleviate these problems: limiting the comparanda to two or three texts that can converse reduces the risks of imbalance and reading the texts that bear less family resemblance to the reader first and without initial reference to the other text(s) mitigates against imposition. But methodological rules, for Hamann, are "a negative quality" that can reduce risk but can "never replace" the relationship."[49] As Volker Hoffman describes Hamann's hermeneutic, "an element comes into interpretation that cannot be reduced to a rational method; indeed only through this it seems can the aliveness of interpretation be guaranteed."[50] Any attempt to gain "analytic control over the framework of comparison" amounts, in Hamann's view, to a return to Michaelis's "monastic rules."[51] Both the risks and the possibility of reducing them stem from what reading is: a relationship.

One way to express the freedom and constraints that shape the hermeneutical relationship is to say that the reader is responsible, or better: response-able. That a reader is *able* to respond indicates a critical and creative freedom; that this freedom is a *response* indicates that it depends on and is constrained by an antecedent word.[52] This dialectic of "freedom in response" can be seen in

48. Sanders's own study is a telling example of this error: the normative status of Pauline patterns of soteriology result in the conclusion that, to quote Westerholm's summary, "Jews are said, in effect, to have been good Protestants after all." *Perspectives Old and New: The "Lutheran" Paul and His Critics* (Grand Rapids: Eerdmans, 2004), 341.

49. Griffith-Dickson, *Relational Metacriticism*, 128. Thus, while I agree with T. Engberg-Pedersen that comparative work requires deep familiarity with "each figure to be compared," I am reluctant to call this requirement a rule or, as he does, a *lex*. "Self-Sufficiency and Power: Divine and Human Agency in Epictetus and Paul," in *Divine and Human Agency in Paul and His Cultural Environment*, ed. J. M. G. Barclay and S. J. Gathercole (London: T&T Clark, 2008), 118.

50. V. Hoffman, *Johann Georg Hamanns Philologie: Hamanns Philologie zwischen enzyklopädischer Mikrologie und Hermeneutik* (Stuttgart: Verlag W. Kohlkammer, 1972), 190 (quoted in Griffith-Dickson, *Relational Metacriticism*, 128).

51. See Smith, *Drudgery Divine*, 53. For Hamann, it is "fear" that motivates method, and Smith does at least seem to have a concern: if comparison lacks "analytic control" and "a clear articulation of purpose, one may derive arresting anecdotal juxtapositions . . . but the disciplined constructive work of the academy will not have been advanced, nor will the study of religion have come of age" (53). I suspect Hamann would respond to this academic eschatology with an ageless aesthetic: "Let us now hear the conclusion of this newest aesthetic, which is the oldest: Fear God and give Him glory" (*Sämtliche Werken*, 2:217.15–17).

52. This notion of responsibility within an interpretative relationship bears some resemblance to Habermas's concept of "Mündigkeit" as the criterion of truth within an "un-

the way similarity and difference play out in comparative research.[53] Smith insists, "there is nothing 'natural' about the enterprise of comparison. Similarity and difference" are not properties of a single text; they exist in the act of comparison that creates the "cohabitation" of texts that makes "sameness" and "difference" possible. But even Smith concedes the "postulation of similarity" involves "the selection of significant aspects of the phenomena."[54] Therefore, as Hamann says of knowledge, similarity is "neither mere invention nor mere recollection."[55] Similarity is specified and named as such by an interpreter, but what is selected as similar is supplied by the texts or traditions. This "sameness," in other words, is at once activated by the interpreter and anchored in the texts. And as Smith suggests, "similarity . . . is the ground of methodological comparison"; it makes it possible.[56] In relational terms, similarity enables dialogue by providing the points of continuity between texts that serve as conversational commonplaces—topics for the texts to talk about. But as Poole puts it, if "similarity makes [comparison] possible," then "difference makes [it] interesting."[57] Difference, however, like similarity, is neither simply created nor uncovered, "neither mere invention nor mere recollection." Rather, the interpreter invites texts into a dialogue so difference can be discovered. This difference is found by the interpreter, but it is found in the "given letters" as they detain and address, resist and relate. To adapt Poole, similarity makes dialogue possible; difference invites an interesting form of dialogue: debate.

It is these relational dynamics that I am attempting to capture with the phrase engaged exegetical eavesdropping. Comparison, in this relational

---

constrained dialogic relation." For Habermas, however, all communication is both ordered to and, because "reason can become transparent to itself," capable of understanding (see both *Knowledge and Human Interests* [Cambridge: Polity, 1987], 287 and the introduction to the fourth edition of *Theory and Practice* [London: Heinemann, 1974], 17). But reason, as Hamann pointed out in his *Metakritik* of Kant, is not a hypostatic something that can vaccinate us against our histories and traditions. Rather, reasoning is a human activity that is performed by persons who think and converse in language and as those who have a life and location.

53. The phrase is the title of a collection essays by Oswald Bayer, *Freedom in Response* (Oxford: Oxford University Press, 2007).

54. Smith, *Drudgery Divine*, 51, 53.

55. Hamann, *Sämtliche Werken*, 3:41.11–12.

56. Smith, *Drudgery Divine*, 53.

57. F. J. P. Poole, "Metaphor and Maps: Towards Comparison in the Anthropology of Religion," *JAAR* 54 (1986): 417. One thinks of Mr. Darcy, in Jane Austen's *Pride and Prejudice*, whose love for Elizabeth Bennet is less interested in the ways she is like other women than it is in the ways she is different and so distinctively her.

frame, involves the interpreter facilitating a conversation between texts but also participating in a conversation with texts. The comparative form is thus face to face—as the texts talk to each other—and to face—as the interpreter brings together, listens to, and talks with the texts.

WISDOM AND ROMANS (AND ME) IN CONVERSATION

A comparison of *Wisdom of Solomon* and Paul's letter to the church in Rome is a particular relationship. These are texts that share a language, social and religious locations, a scriptural inheritance, and a set of theological concepts and concerns. The particularities of this relationship are also affected, in this instance, by the fact that I am conducting this comparison between *Wisdom* and Romans. I have a long and studied relationship with *Wisdom* and, in Hamann's words, feel like a "friend" to this text and its tradition. But I am a Christian. I read Paul within a confession that is both shared with and shaped by Paul's letters. Specifying all this neither rules out comparison nor means that "monastic rules" are necessary to control the conversation. What this naming does, to quote Luther, is "call a thing what it is." This comparison is a real relationship—between *Wisdom* and Romans and with me.

Wisdom and Romans have a lot to talk about. Both texts consider the relationship between Jew and non-Jew, both explore the meaning and operations of God's righteousness and grace, and both think theologically in conversation with Israel's scriptures. But as an icebreaker, consider Jacob. For *Wisdom*, Jacob is "righteous" (δίκαιος) and so when Sophia "guides" and "gives to" him (Wis 10:10) this beneficence exemplifies a theological maxim: "Wisdom rescues from trouble those who serve her" (10:9) and "she seeks those who are worthy (ἄξιος) of her" (6:16). In Romans, Jacob is again a recipient of divine blessing, but here the rationale is not his righteousness. Rather, as Paul's exploitation of the prenatal promise emphasizes, Jacob's election is "not based on works" but only on "the one who calls" (Rom 9:9–13). This continuity together with contrast invites a conversation.[58]

Wisdom is a sermon addressed to sufferers. It is difficult to reconstruct the socio-historical details alluded to by *Wisdom*, but the tone and content of the pastoral address indicate that the situation was serious enough to generate a series of questions about the moral order of the world, the patterns of history,

---

58. For my attempt to facilitate this conversation between *Wisdom* and Romans, see *God, Grace, and Righteousness in Wisdom of Solomon and Paul's Letter to the Romans: Texts in Conversation*, NovTSup 152 (Leiden: Brill, 2013).

and the past, present, and future justice of God. Into this crisis—a crisis that appears to be characterized by the present flourishing of the ungodly and the suffering of the righteous (Wis 2–5)—the author of *Wisdom* announces a word of hope: the God of illimitable love is ineluctably just.[59]

This is bedrock: "You are just and you rule all things justly" (12:15). It is this God who "arranged all things by measure and number and weight" (11:20). Within this precisely calibrated cosmos, justice has a reliable shape: the non-condemnation of the righteous (12:15) and "God's fitting judgment" (ἀξίαν θεοῦ κρίσιν) of the unrighteous (12:26). The paradigmatic instantiation of this pattern is the Exodus. At the Red Sea, the "righteous" and the "ungodly" (10:20) encounter, respectively, deliverance and destruction: "Sophia led the righteous through deep waters, but she drowned their enemies" (10:18–19). In *Wisdom*, this correspondence is a criterion. Whether *Wisdom* is diagnosing the present, remembering the past, or promising a future, the shape is the same: as in the Exodus, God's justice is evident in the congruence between the form (judgment or mercy) and object (ungodly or righteous) of God's action. Adam, Noah, and the patriarchs are rescued and rewarded by Sophia because they are, in some sense, "worthy of her" (10:1–14; cf. 6:16).[60] Solomon receives Sophia as a "gift" (χάρις, 8:21), but this giving is conditioned by correspondence: Solomon was "good" (ἀγαθός, 8:20). In *Wisdom*'s telling of the events of the Exodus, there is symmetry between the judgment experienced by the "ungodly" Egyptians and the mercy shown to Israel, a "holy people and blameless race" (Wis 10:15–19:22). And the final hope is anchored in a promise that the eschaton will be like the Exodus: the present chaos will be overcome by correspondence as the God of justice acts to judge the unrighteous oppressors and vindicate the righteous sufferers (Wis 2–5).

As the Exodus shapes *Wisdom*'s theology and hermeneutic, it also necessarily shapes its anthropology. The symmetry of divine justice requires both

---

59. The consensus, which is probable though not definite, places *Wisdom* in Alexandria between 220 BCE and 20 CE; see C. Larcher, *Le Livre de la Sagesse, ou La Sagesse de Salomon* (Paris: Gabalda, 1983), 1:141–61; D. Winston, *The Wisdom of Solomon*, AB 43 (Garden City, NY: Doubleday, 1979), 20–25; H. Hübner, *Die Weisheit Salomons*, ATD Apokryphen 4 (Göttingen: Vandenhoeck and Ruprecht, 1999), 15–19. While it is difficult to have an explicit relationship with anonymous or unknown authors, sensitivity to social setting and occasion helps to avoid treating the text in what Griffith-Dickson calls an "anti-human fashion" and remembers that language and its truth is not just correspondence and representation, but communication and relationship.

60. In most cases, this worthiness is identified as being "righteous," though in the case of Adam it is his status as the "first formed father of the world" (10:1).

the righteous and the unrighteousness. This is assumed throughout *Wisdom*, but it is argued in chapters 13–15. The extended polemic against gentile idolatry and immorality serves to pick out Israel as the innocent and so reinforce the irreducible difference between Israel *qua* the righteous and non-Israel *qua* the ungodly. "All people" might be "ignorant of God" (13:1), idolatrous (13:10–14:11, 15–21; 15:7–13) and so immoral (14:12–14, 22–29), but not Israel: "We will not sin, knowing that we are counted as yours. . . . For the evil intent of human art has not deceived us" (15:1–4). The Exodus enacts justice because it is judgment for the ungodly and "deliverance" for Israel *qua* a "holy people and blameless race" (Wis 10:15). Again, the Red Sea crossing gives the criterion. The Egyptians are named the "enemy" (ἐχθρός, 10:19) and the "ungodly" (ἀσεβής, 10:20) and so they suffer "God's fitting judgment" (ἀξίαν θεοῦ κρίσιν). Israel is "holy" (ὅσιος, 10:17) and "righteous" (δίκαιος, 10:20) and her rescue is thus, precisely as grace, "a reward (μισθός) for her labors" (10:17). The Exodus embodies justice: judgment for the unrighteous and mercy for the righteous. For *Wisdom*, this is the protological order, the canonical past, and the promise: as it was in the beginning, even if it is not now, it ever will be. This is hope—for the righteous.

But here Romans interjects: "all, both Jew and Gentile, are under sin" (Rom 3:9). *Wisdom* 13–15 and Romans 1:18–32 are connected by vocabulary and an argumentative sequence. Both texts argue from a squandered creation-related knowledge of God (Wis 13:1–9; Rom 1:19–20) to a corresponding turn to idolatry (Wis 13:10–14:11, 15–21 and 15:7–13; Rom 1:21–23), which in turn occasions a litany of immorality (Wis 14:12–14, 22–29; Rom 1:24–31) and invites a fitting exercise of divine judgment (Wis 14:30–31; Rom 1:32). At the end of this argument, however, *Wisdom* insists on Israel's innocence; Paul announces Israel's inclusion. "We will not sin" and "human art has not misled us," writes *Wisdom*. At this very moment in the argument, in what Richard Hays has called a "rhetorical sting operation," Romans asks, "Do you think, you human being, when you judge others who do such things and yet do the same things yourself, that you will escape the judgment of God?" (Rom 2:3).[61] For *Wisdom*, the polemic against gentile idolatry and immorality serves to reinforce a distinction: the non-Jewish world is ungodly, Israel is righteous. According to Romans, however, "there is no distinction" (Rom 3:22). The story of sin that Paul proclaims in Romans 1:18–32 is *human* history. God's wrath is revealed against the unrighteousness and ungodliness of human beings (ἄνθρωπος, 1:18), and the creational context (1:19–21) and echoes of both Eden

---

61. R. B. Hays, *The Moral Vision of the New Testament* (San Francisco: Harper, 1996), 389.

and Israel (1:23) universalize Paul's diagnosis: "none are righteous" (3:9) and "all sinned" (3:23).[62] Thus, in contrast to *Wisdom*'s polemical insistence on the irreducible difference between righteous Israel and the ungodly gentiles, Paul's proclamation reduces that anthropological fraction to a single denominator: he announces the human and names a common condition—*homo peccator*.

For *Wisdom*, this can only have one conclusion. Because God's justice meets ungodliness with judgment, universal unrighteousness can only end in universal condemnation. And at Romans 3:20 Paul appears to agree: "No human being will be justified before God by works of the law." But, Paul declares, "the righteousness of God is made manifest," with the result that those who "sinned and lack the glory of God" are "justified as a gift by God's grace" (Rom 3:21–24). This announcement is uttered in language *Wisdom* also speaks: θεός, δικαιοσύνη, and χάρις. But the configuration and usage of the words are off. The enactment of God's righteousness, in *Wisdom*, entails judgment for the sinner and grace for the righteous. But Paul's "good news" proclaims a revelation of divine righteousness that is grace for the sinner. In Romans, then, grace is not, as it is in *Wisdom* (and most of Greco-Roman society and Jewish theology), an unearned yet fitting gift given to a worthy recipient. Grace, in Romans, is the incongruous gift God gives at the site of sin and death that creates out of the opposite: righteousness and life (cf. Rom 4:4–5, 17).

For Paul, however, this definition of grace is not a given; it is given. It is deduced from a specific gift of God. As Romans 3:24 puts it, sinners are recreated as righteous by receiving the incongruous gift that is "the redemption that is in Christ Jesus." This, for Paul, is the event that enacts and establishes the righteousness of God (Rom 3:21–22, 25–26) and the event that is the grace of God (see, e.g., Rom 8:32; Gal 2:21). This suggests that while the language Paul

---

62. A telling contrast is that whereas *Wisdom* avoids the golden calf episode, Romans 1:23 alludes to it:

And they exchanged the glory (καὶ ἠλλάξαντο τὴν δόξαν) that was theirs for the likeness (ὁμοίωμα) of a grass-eating ox. (Ps 105:2 LXX)

And they exchanged the glory (καὶ ἤλλαξαν τὴν δόξαν) of the immortal God for the likeness (ὁμοίωμα) of the image of a mortal man and of birds and four-footed animals and creeping creatures. (Rom 1:23)

This echo includes Israel in the history of Adamic sin, a link which is further developed in Romans 5:12–14 (and arguably Rom 7). Furthermore, as Simon Gathercole notes, Romans 2:21–24 and 3:9–18 provide what he calls "phenomenological evidence" and "scriptural evidence" for Israel's inclusion in the story of sin, *Where Is Boasting? Early Jewish Soteriology and Paul's Response in Romans 1–5* (Grand Rapids: Eerdmans, 2002), 201.

uses is contextual and canonical, his lexicon is christological. In Karl Barth's words, "The Christian message . . . recounts a history . . . in such a way that it declares a name." And "this means that all the concepts and ideas used in this report can derive their significance only from the bearer of this name and from his history. . . . They can serve only to describe this name—the name of Jesus Christ."[63] Righteousness and grace, as descriptions of the history of Jesus Christ, announce the event in which God both judges ungodliness and thereby justifies the ungodly in Christ—the "one who loved me and gave himself for me" (Gal 2:20), the one who "died for us while we were sinners" (Rom 5:8), the one who is "our righteousness" (1 Cor 1:30). Paul's christological definitions of divine righteousness and grace would no doubt cause *Wisdom* to say, as Victor Hugo does in *Les Misérables*, "he had his own strange way of judging things." But Paul could respond just as well with Hugo's next words: "I . . . acquired them from the Gospel."

This suggests that, from the perspective of Paul, the divide between *Wisdom* and Romans runs along a christological fault-line. But if their points of contrast are christological, the source of their common ground is, in large part, canonical. As Francis Watson writes, "Paul and his fellow-Jews read the same texts, yet them read them differently."[64] The shared language and *loci communes* that characterize the conversation between *Wisdom* and Romans are not coincidences but are the family grammar given by a shared scriptural tradition. But if this similarity makes the conversation possible, it is the different readings that make the conversation interesting. To use Watson's words, what connects *Wisdom* and Romans is a canon—they read the same texts— what differentiates them is a hermeneutic—they read these texts differently.

Wisdom reads the Red Sea crossing as the paradigm of divine justice and rewrites the rest of pentateuchal history according to this criterion: as the righteous were delivered and the ungodly were destroyed, so Adam, Noah, and the patriarchs were the worthy whom *Wisdom* rescued, and so righteous Israel was only tested but finally blessed in the wilderness while the ungodly Egyptians were judged by the plagues that fittingly befell them (Wis 10–19). In Romans 4 and 9–11, by contrast, the hermeneutical criterion does not seem to be correspondence but rather incongruous and creative grace. God's gift to Abraham is not a reward but a re-creation of him as righteous (Rom 4:4-5, 17), nor is the birth of Isaac a rewarding of the righteous but rather a resurrection from the dead (4:19-25). Whereas *Wisdom* identifies the worthiness of Jacob

---

63. K. Barth, *Church Dogmatics*, vol. IV/1: *The Doctrine of Reconciliation*, ed. G. W. Bromiley and T. F. Torrance, trans. G. W. Bromiley (Edinburgh: T&T Clark, 1956), 16–17.

64. F. Watson, *Paul and the Hermeneutics of Faith* (London: T&T Clark, 2004), ix.

that ensures that his blessing is just (Wis 10:10), Paul insists that in the cases of Isaac and Jacob no genealogical, social, or moral worth can account for their calling, which is anchored only in the God who promises and calls without condition: "not the children of the flesh, but the children of the promise"; "not by works, but by the one who calls" (Rom 9:7–13). *Wisdom*, at this point, would want to ask Paul's own question: "Is there injustice with God?" (Rom 9:14). Paul, as *Wisdom* would hope, says "by no means," but he does so on the basis of God's words to Moses in the aftermath of the golden calf: "I will have mercy on whom I have mercy and compassion on whom I have compassion" (Rom 9:14–15). This is unexpected mercy at the site of sin, not the predictable pattern of fitting judgment and grace that *Wisdom* calls justice. Paul, I suspect, would grant that this is unpredictable but precisely so full of promise.

It is the unlooked for and incongruous mercy of God that "calls those who are not my people my people" and "her who was not loved, loved" (Rom 9:25). And it is this unconditioned and creative grace—this pattern of promise that shapes the christological present and the canonical past—that funds Paul's hope for the future: "all Israel will be saved" (11:26), not because Israel is righteous and will be rewarded, but because Israel, though stumbling and trespassing (11:11–12), is at the site of God's salvation: though disobedient and dead, God has mercy and makes alive (11:15, 32). In Romans, then, as in *Wisdom*, there is a rhyme scheme and a righteousness that shapes history. For *Wisdom* the pattern is the predictable and just correspondence that orders the cosmos, is exemplified in the Exodus, and so will shape the eschaton. For Paul, the history of Jesus Christ that embodies God's righteousness and is God's gift that justifies the ungodly unveils a calculus of incongruity that means the grace of God is never predictable, but is always a promise: "He shut up all in disobedience, so that he can have mercy on all" (Rom 11:32).[65]

The comparison might end here, but not, as Hamann reminds us, the relationship. In his terms, by gathering and interpreting I have done the work of the "scholar" and the "philosopher," but the work of the "poet"—that is, the work of the person—remains. I have played an active role in the dialogue between *Wisdom* and Romans, curating the conversation through selection and interpretation, but Hamann insists that the relationship that research is includes reception, reflection, *and response.*[66]

---

65. For more on these readings of Romans 3:21–26 and Romans 9–11, see chaps. 1 and 3, respectively, "Righteousness Revealed" and "Not the End."

66. If such engagement seems out of place as part of what Kierkegaard calls "a scientific aloofness from life," I would quote some further words from this most famous fan and follower of Hamann: "the sort of learning that is 'indifferent'" is "an inhuman sort of curiosity" and can be contrasted with "concern" which implies a "relationship to life." *Sickness unto*

To use Hamann's language, I can "sympathize" with *Wisdom*. In a context of social oppression and suffering, the memory and promise of God's judgment against the enemy and mercy for the marginalized is hope. The Pauline gospel of God's justification of the ungodly through the incongruous gift of Christ, under these conditions, sounds "scandalous and foolish"—it sounds like less good news than today's horrifying headline. And yet, for me, a sermon to righteous sufferers doesn't quite get to the bone. When I read *Wisdom* and Romans together, Paul's diagnosis reveals too much and resonates too deeply for me to hope that mercy for the righteous means mercy for me. Listening to Romans, I feel more like *Wisdom*'s Egyptians than its Israelites, more like the Pauline ἄνθρωπος, more like Janet in George Eliot's *Janet's Repentance*, who knew how "weak and how wicked" she was and who was left with only one question—my question: "Is there any comfort—any hope?" Paul's "word of the cross," though "scandalous and foolish," is a sermon not just for sufferers, but a sermon for sufferers and sinners—for Israelites and Egyptians, for me. And so, while I can sympathize with *Wisdom*'s likely conclusion that the Pauline gospel "turned the world upside down" (Acts 17:6), I can also confess with Paul that the "good news" of God's incongruous and creative grace in Christ is "the power of God unto salvation" (Rom 1:17).

Death (New York: Doubleday, 1954), 142. For Kierkegaard's admiration of and (imperfect) attempt to follow Hamann, see J. R. Betz, "Hamann before Kierkegaard: A Systematic Theological Oversight," *Pro Ecclesia* 16.3 (2007): 299–333.

CHAPTER 6

Announcing the Human

RETHINKING THE RELATIONSHIP BETWEEN
WISDOM OF SOLOMON 13–15 AND ROMANS 1:18–2:11

> What is called need is found everywhere, and extends to all places,
> and reaches everyone.
>
> —Miguel de Cervantes, *Don Quixote*

The story of sin starts in Eden (Wis 2:23–24; Rom 5:12). If the beginning of a story was the whole story, then Romans and the *Wisdom of Solomon* would have a similar tale to tell. And many have assumed they do. Since Grafe alerted the world of Pauline scholarship to the unusually close connection between Romans 1:18–32 and *Wisdom* 13–14, readers of Romans have typically read Romans 1:18–32 as a condensed but consistent restatement of *Wisdom*'s aniconic polemic.[1] Nygren's Romans commentary problematized this textual relationship by extending the comparison into Romans 2 and *Wisdom* 15, but even here the theological affinity between Romans 1:18–32 and *Wisdom* 13–14 was affirmed (and exploited).[2] According to his programmatic reading—a reading that dominates modern commentaries[3]—Romans 1:18–32 reactivates *Wisdom*'s

---

1. E. Grafe, "Das Verhältniss der paulinischen Schriften zur Sapientia Salmonis," in *Theologische Abhandlungen: Carl von Weizsäcker zu seinem siebzigsten Geburtstage 11. December 1892 gewidmet* (Freiburg: Mohr Siebeck, 1892), 251–86. W. Sanday and A. C. Headlam, *The Epistle to the Romans*, ICC (New York: Scribner's, 1896), 51–52, 267–69, introduced these parallels to English-speaking scholarship. For a detailed survey of scholarship, see J. R. Dodson, *The "Powers" of Personificaiton: Rhetorical Purpose in the Book of Wisdom and the Letter to the Romans*, BZNW 161 (Berlin: de Gruyter, 2008), 4–13.

2. A. Nygren, *Commentary on Romans*, trans. C. C. Rasmussen (London: SCM, 1952), cf. 112 with 114–17.

3. J. D. G. Dunn, *Romans 1–8*, WBC 38A (Waco, TX: Word, 1988), 82–83; J. A. Fitzmyer,

polemical attack on *gentile* idolatry and immorality and *then* (Rom 2:1–11), in what Richard Hays calls a rhetorical "sting operation,"[4] establishes the hamartiological equality of Jew and gentile. Interpreted this way, Romans 1:18–32 is still about gentile sin; 2:1–11 simply undermines *Wisdom's* immunization of Israel (Wis 15:1–4) by pointing to the impartiality of divine judgment (2:6–11) and the presence of sin within the elect nation (2:1–5, 21–24). Douglas Campbell, following the unpopular proposals of Schmeller and Porter,[5] has recently radicalized this interpretative trend, arguing that the affinities between Romans 1:18–32 and *Wisdom* 13–14 are so close that Romans 1:18–32 is properly read as an un-Pauline summary of *Wisdom's* polemic.[6] The crucial point for our purposes is that these construals, despite their diversity, assume that while Paul critiques *Wisdom* 15:1–4 in Romans 2:1–11, Romans 1:18–32 stands as a compressed but theologically faithful re-presentation of *Wisdom* 13–14.

In this respect, Kathy Gaca is something of an outlier. As she reads Romans 1:18–32, Paul, while speaking within the "tradition of Hellenistic Jewish polemic," has introduced a "problematic innovation": whereas the polemical tradition charges the gentiles with theological ignorance, Paul ascribes received theological knowledge to gentiles, thereby accusing them not just of ignorance but of apostasy.[7] For Gaca, however, while Paul alters the accusation (apostasy not ignorance), the identity of the accused (gentiles) remains unchanged.

Romans, AB 33 (London: Geoffrey Chapman, 1992), 298; D. J. Moo, *The Epistle to the Romans*, NICNT (Grand Rapids: Eerdmans, 1996), 133; E. Lohse, *Der Brief an die Römer*, KEK 4 (Gottingen: Vandenhoeck & Ruprecht, 2003), 86, 99.

4. R. B. Hays, *The Moral Vision of the New Testament* (San Francisco: Harper Collins, 1996), 389.

5. T. Schmeller, *Paulus und die "Diatribe": Eine vergleichende Stilinterpretation* (Münster: Aschendorf, 1987), 225–86; C. L. Porter, "Romans 1:18–32: Its Role in the Developing Argument," *NTS* 40 (1994): 210–28.

6. D. A. Campbell, *The Deliverance of God: An Apocalyptic Rereading of Justification in Paul* (Grand Rapids: Eerdmans, 2009), 542–93. In Campbell's reconstruction, it is not *Wisdom* that speaks, but an adversarial teacher for whom *Wisdom* was a theologically formative text.

7. K. L. Gaca, "Paul's Uncommon Declaration in Romans 1:18–32 and its Problematic Legacy for Pagan and Christian Relations," *HTR* 92.2 (1999): 165–98. Others have noticed that Romans 1:18–32 differs from *Wisdom* in a number of ways, but this has generally been used as evidence against Pauline interaction with *Wisdom*; e.g., R. Bell, *No One Seeks for God: An Exegetical and Theological Study of Romans 1.18–3.20*, WUNT 106 (Tübingen: Mohr Siebeck, 1998), 76. However, as Francis Watson notes, this assumption "implies that 'influence' and 'differences' are mutually limiting . . . In fact . . . the depth of Paul's engagement with this text is evident precisely at the points he also differs from it." *Paul and the Hermeneutics of Faith* (London: T&T Clark, 2004), 405n77.

The terms in which Paul's rhetorical trap is sprung, however, invite a reconsideration of Paul's polemical target in Romans 1:18–32. The one who judges the other (κρίνεις τὸν ἕτερον, 2:1)—the other being the presumed target of the invectives of 1:18–32—is liable to condemnation because this judge is guilty of the other's sins (τὰ αὐτὰ πράσσεις, 2:1; ποιῶν αὐτά, 2:3). The effect of this rhetorical move is to eliminate the self-imposed distance between the judge and the other, thereby subjecting the judge to their own condemnation (σεαυτὸν κατακρίνεις, 2:1). Functionally, then, the indictment of Romans 1:18–32 becomes, at least retroactively, an indictment of the Jew as much as the gentile.[8] It is this implication that necessitates a reexamination of Romans 1:18–32, one which attends more closely to the *dramatis personae* Paul actually presents and exhibits a corresponding sensitivity to the inclusion of Israel within the scope of Israel's own polemical tradition.[9]

Because this reading is retrospective—occasioned as it is by the terms of the rhetorical turn at 2:1–11—it is necessary to allow our argument to develop in parallel with Paul's own rhetorical strategy. For this reason, our (brief) first pass through Romans 1:18–32 will emphasize the similarities between this unit and *Wisdom* 13–14 in an effort to highlight the crucial break which occurs at 2:1. What makes this investigation unique, however, is that it intends to take up the invitation to reread Romans 1:18–32 in light of the polemical twist of Romans 2. This rereading will attempt to situate Paul's accusatory announcement of 1:19–32 within the kergymatic progression of Romans 1:16–18 and consider the rhetorical function and theological significance of Paul's alterations to the Hellenistic Jewish polemical tradition. It will be argued that the contextualization of the Pauline polemic within the apostle's apocalyptic keryma (Rom 1:16–18), together with his "supra-natural theology" (1:19–20), allusive inclusion of Israel within the history of sin (1:23), insertion of divine agency into the causal link between idolatry and immorality (1:24, 26, 28), and collapsing of *Wisdom*'s differentiation between types of idolatry (1:24–25) require an interpretation of Romans 1:19–32 according to which its polemical target includes, as 1:18 indicates, "all . . . humankind."

Thus my thesis: Paul's polemic in Romans 1:18–32, rather than standing as a compressed but consistent restatement of *Wisdom* 13–14, serves the opposite

---

8. That the interlocutor of Romans 2:1–16 is the same figure explicitly identified as a self-proclaimed Jew in 2:17 will be argued below.

9. R. Jewett, *Romans*, Hermeneia (Minneapolis: Fortress, 2007), 152–54, like R. Dabelstein, *Die Beurteilung der "Heiden" bei Paulus*, BBET 14 (Bern: Lang, 1981), 73–79, before him, argues for the inclusion of Israel within the polemical scope of Romans 1:18–32, but this argument is made at the expense of Paul's engagement with *Wisdom* rather than, as this essay intends, on the basis of a close comparison between Romans 1:18–32 and *Wisdom* 13–15.

rhetorical and theological function of *Wisdom* 13–15. This is not to say that these texts exhibit no continuity. On the contrary, the often noted lexical, thematic, and argumentative parallels between Romans 1:18–2:5 and *Wisdom* 13–15 indicate an engagement which is situated within an antithetic argument. *Textual dependence* serves the rhetorical function of establishing *theological difference*. Whereas *Wisdom*'s polemic serves to reinforce the anthropological distinction between Jew and gentile (*qua* non-idolaters and idolaters), Paul reworks the aniconic tradition to reveal that "there is no distinction" (Rom 3:23): "all, both Jew and Greek, are under sin" (Rom 3:9).[10]

ROMANS 1:19–2:5 AND *WISDOM OF SOLOMON* 13–15: AN INITIAL READING

Wisdom 13–15 and Romans 1:18–2:5 are connected by a series of lexical and thematic links and, perhaps more significantly, by a unique argumentative structure.[11] As Watson observes, "The argument of Romans 1:18–32 develops in parallel to *Wisdom* 13:1–14:31" and, as Campbell remarks, "the two argumentative progressions are unique to the Wisdom of Solomon and Romans 1."[12] Both texts argue from a squandered creation-related knowledge of God to a corresponding turn to idolatry that in turn occasions a litany of social and moral perversities, thereby inviting an appropriate exercise of divine judgment. This broad structural continuity conceals numerous significant theological differences that will be explored after the rhetorical turn of Romans 2:1 has been

---

10. C. E. B. Cranfield, *A Critical and Exegetical Commentary on the Epistle to the Romans*, 2 vols., ICC (Edinburgh: T&T Clark, 1975), 1:104n1, seems to have intuited a similar reading, but he never developed it outside a footnote. Paul's theology engages with, responds to, and dignifies—and so does not elide or erase—human particularity and difference (see the section on the divine "yes" in chap. 4, "'The Speech of the Dead'"). He does, however, both reframe inherited and achieved symbols of identity (see, e.g., Gal 3:28; 1 Cor 1:18–31; Phil 3:3–14) and, at the bedrock of need and hope (Rom 3:23; 10:12), declare a fundamental lack of distinction deeper than real but relative human difference.

11. For a detailed list of the lexical parallels, see T. Laato, *Paul and Judaism: An Anthropological Approach*, trans. T. McElwain (Atlanta: University of South Florida, 1995), 94–95.

12. Watson, *Hermeneutics*, 405; Campbell, *Deliverance of God*, 360. While this argumentative sequence is particular to Romans and *Wisdom*, Philo's *De decalogo* offers something of a parallel to *Wisdom* in that its denunciation of false-worship moves from the less deplorable act of worshiping heavenly elements or bodies (52–56; Wis 13:1–9) to the absurd practice of worshiping created images (66–77; Wis 13:10–14:10; 14:15–21; 15:7–13) which finds its most risible expression in Egyptian animal-worship (77–81; Wis 15:18–19); cf. J. M. G. Barclay, *Jews in the Mediterranean Disapora: From Alexander to Trajan (323 BCE–117 CE)* (Berkeley: University of California Press, 1996), 186.

considered. Situating this discontinuity, however, requires that the following analysis emphasize the points of contact between Romans and *Wisdom*, in order to underline the dramatic twist of Romans 2, which will then point us back to Paul's unique reworking of the polemical tradition in Romans 1.

(1) A (possible) creation-related knowledge of God has been squandered:
Wisdom *13:1–9; Romans 1:19–20*

Wisdom's claim that the animal plagues function as the appropriate divine recompense for Egyptian animal worship (11:15–16; 12:23–27; 15:18–16:1) invites an extended reflection on the origin of idolatry and the corresponding divine judgment that confronts it (13:1–15:13).[13] Theological knowledge is universally available because, as *Wisdom* 13:5 states, "the greatness and beauty of the created" (κτίσμα) provides an "analogous perception (ἀναλόγως θεωρεῖται) of the creator" (ὁ γενεσιουργός). Similarly, Paul insists that the "knowledge of God" (τὸ γνωστὸν τοῦ θεοῦ) has been evident "since the creation of the world (ἀπὸ κτίσεως κόσμου) because his eternal power and divinity (θειότης, cf. Wis 18:9) are perceivable in the things that have been created/done" (τοῖς ποιήμασιν, Rom 1:19–20). In both texts, however, this (possible) knowledge of the creator is forfeited by worthless (μάταιος, Wis 13:1; ματαιόω, Rom 1:21) fools who either fail to reason from creation to creator (Wis 13:1–9) or neglect to honor the God they know (Rom 1:21–22). Stupidity, however, is "no excuse": both the ignorant idolaters of *Wisdom* and the rebels against revelation of Romans are ἀναπολόγητος (Rom 1:20; Wis 13:8).

(2) This wasted opportunity to know the true God manifests itself
in false religion: Wisdom 13:10–14:11, 15–21 (and 15:7–13); Romans 1:21–23

Paul and *Wisdom* appear to agree that humans are fundamentally worshipers, and thus turning from true worship can only be a turning to its opposite—idolatry. *Wisdom* offers a detailed review of the origin of idolatry: leftover lumber becomes a household god (13:10–19), a sailor's fear of the sea provokes prayer to the powerless (14:1), an image designed to console a bereaved father

13. For a detailed analysis of this section see M. Gilbert, *La critique des dieux dans le Livre del la Sagesse (Sg 13–15)* (Rome: Biblical Institute Press, 1973); cf. M. McGlynn, *Divine Judgement and Divine Benevolence in the Book of Wisdom*, WUNT 2.139 (Tübingen: Mohr Siebeck, 2001), 132–69; D. Wintson, *The Wisdom of Solomon*, AB 43 (Garden City, NY: Doubleday, 1979), 247–91.

gains religious momentum until it achieves legal apotheosis (14:15–16a), the absence of a monarch occasions the fashioning of his image which slips from respect to worship in the popular imagination (14:16b–21), profiteers trade in idols, actively capitalizing on the senseless piety of their customers (15:7–13) and, most deplorably, Egyptians worship animals even God failed to bless (15:18–19).[14] Paul, choosing succinctness over subtlety, condenses this complex genesis of idolatry into a single sentence: καὶ ἤλλαξαν τὴν δόξαν τοῦ ἀφθάρτου θεοῦ ἐν ὁμοιώματι εἰκόνος φθαρτοῦ ἀνθρώπου καὶ πετεινῶν καὶ τετραπόδων καὶ ἑρπετῶν (Rom 1:23). Paul's compactness has the advantage of emphasizing the oppositeness of idolatry and true worship implicit in much of *Wisdom*'s rhetorical devaluation of the natural origin and impotence of idols. Artifacts which are created by human artisans are obviously, if only implicitly, not them- selves creators (cf. Isa 44:9–20) and thus, as creatures of creatures, are powerless in response to prayer (Wis 13:16–14:1 cf. Ps 115:5–7). Paul captures this contrast between the creator and the creature in the antithetical presentation of the incorruptible God (ἄφθαρτος θεός) and the corruptible human (φθαρτὸς ἄν- θρωπος). Furthermore, Paul's focus on creaturely idolatry (i.e., animals rather than artifacts) appears to follow the distinctive emphasis of *Wisdom*'s aniconic polemic which ultimately has Egyptian animal worship as its target.[15]

(3) The turn to idols occasions a corresponding decline into immorality:
Wisdom *14:12–14, 22–29; Romans 1:24–31*

The point is explicit in *Wisdom*: "For the idea of idols was the beginning of sex- ual perversion (ἀρχὴ πορνείας) and the discovery of them was the destruction of life" (14:12). And again, "for the worship of nameless idols is the beginning and cause and end (ἀρχὴ καὶ αἰτία καὶ πέρας) of every evil" (14:27). Without compromising this basic aetiology (idolatry leads to immorality), Paul empha- sizes the divine agent within the causal process. God delivers idolaters over to sin because (διό, 1:24; cf. 1:26, 28) they exchanged his glory and truth and failed to acknowledge his divinity (1:23, 25, 28). The effect, in Romans, is an ethical de- cline, rooted in the meta-sin of idolatry, which spirals downward into sexual sin (1:24, 26–27) and then overflows into a smorgasbord of nonsexual immorality (1:29–31).[16] While *Wisdom* mixes sexual and non-sexual sins (14:23–26), the

---

14. For a detailed tracing of *Wisdom*'s polemic see Gilbert, *La critique*, 245–57; cf. C. Larcher, *Le Livre de la Sagesse, ou, La Sagesse de Salomon* (Paris: Gabalda, 1983), 1:122.

15. Watson, *Hermeneutics*, 407.

16. E. Klostermann, "Die adäquate Vergeltung in Röm 1,22–31," *ZNW* 32 (1993): 1–6; cf.

Pauline emphasis on sexual denaturalization is reflected in *Wisdom*'s vice list as it repeatedly refers to the defilement of marriage (1:24), sex inversion (γενέσεως ἐναλλαγή), marital disorder (γάμων ἀταξία), and adultery (μοιχεία, 1:26).

(4) A fitting divine judgment awaits those guilty of idolatry and the corresponding immorality: Wisdom 14:30–31; Romans 1:32

Divine judgment upon sin is evident within the historical depreciation of human religion and ethics, but in neither Romans nor *Wisdom* is God's confrontation with the sinner reducible to anthropological history. In *Wisdom*, those whose history is characterized by the movement from idolatry to immorality will be overtaken by "just penalties" (τὰ δίκαια),[17] not because their idols are powerful, but because "the just penalty" (ἡ δίκη) for their sins will "always overtake the transgression of the unrighteous" (14:30–31). It is difficult to fix the juridical context for this coming judgment, but 14:11 appears to indicate that *Wisdom*, consistent with its earlier eschatology (Wis 2–5), expects a future divine visitation upon idols and idolaters. According to Paul, idolaters, though theologically ignorant (1:22), are nevertheless aware of the divine decree "that the ones who practise such things (i.e., the idolatry and immorality catalogued in 1:23–31) are worthy of death (ἄξιοι θανάτου, Rom 1:32; cf. Wis 1:16). That the execution of this decree awaits an eschatological act of divine judgment is explicitly stated in Romans 2:5–10.

THE RHETORICAL TURN

In Romans 2:1 Paul addresses a generic individual (ἄνθρωπος) who is characterized by an ironic combination of judging the people depicted in 1:19–32 and practising the vices of 1:19–32. The effect of this combination—a combination which is paradoxically expressed in the contrast between ἕτερος and αὐτός—is to remove the self-imposed distance between the judge and the other. The judge's condemnation of the other, because the judge does the same things (τὰ αὐτὰ πράσσεις), is necessarily self-condemnation (σεαυτὸν κατακρίνεις). To expose this identification of the judge and the other, however,

---

S. Gathercole, "Sin in God's Economy: Agencies in Romans 1 and 7," in *Divine and Human Agency in Paul and His Cultural Environment*, ed. J. M. G. Barclay and S. J. Gathercole (London: T&T Clark, 2006), 162–63.

17. Codex Alexandrinus (A) has ἄδικα instead of δίκαια; see McGlynn, *Divine Judgement*, 158n73.

Paul does not introduce a new set of criteria by which the judge's religion and morality is assessed. On the contrary, the judge's judgment is shown to be self-referential on the basis of the theological principles which shaped the polemic of 1:19–32.[18] The repeated use of πράσσω (2:1, 2) and ποιέω (2:3) in conjunction with αὐτός (2:1) and τοιοῦτος (2:2, 3) includes the judge within the pattern of idolatry and immorality outlined in 1:18–32 and, in particular, with the phrasing of 1:32: οἱ τὰ τοιαῦτα πράσσοντες. Effectively, then, by their own standards, the judge is an object of the revelation of divine wrath (1:18) and thus under the divine death sentence of Romans 1:32.

The judge, however, appears to disagree. This raises the dual question of the judge's identity and the rationale behind their assumed immunity from both the logic of their own judgment and, more fundamentally, the judgment of God (τὸ κρίμα τοῦ θεοῦ, 2:3). As to identity, despite some continued scholarly protest,[19] the generic judge of 2:1–5 should be associated with the Jew of 2:17. While the evidence for this assertion includes matters of genre, scriptural quotation and thematic links between 2:1–6 and 2:17–24,[20] the most compelling (and relevant) evidence is that Paul's argument assumes that the judge of 2:1–5 endorses his critique of false-religion in 1:18–32 and thus the entirety of 2:1–24 operates within the parameters of what Wischmeyer calls "der innerjüdische Israel-Diskurs."[21] More specifically, Romans 2:1–5 engages with *Wisdom* by arguing from theological principles articulated in *Wisdom*. Thus, to say that the judge is a Jew is only a partial answer. Paul's continued engagement with *Wisdom* in Romans 2:1–5 establishes both the Jewishness of his interlocutor's theology and, more specifically, forces us to say with Ernst Käsemann that 2:1–11 "ist einzig Polemik gegen jene jüdische Tradition begreiflich, welche sich am deutlichsten und teilweise mit gleicher Begrifflichkeit in Sap. Sal 15,1ff. äußert."[22] In other words, Paul's interlocutor is neither a generic human nor a generic Jew. The judge is a Jew in the theological tradition of the *Wisdom of Solomon*.

18. Campbell refers to this rhetorical tactic as "universalization," an "argumentative concession that can be forced onto the proponents of any position by insisting that the principles within that position . . . be applied consistently to its proponents" (*Deliverance of God*, 548).

19. See, e.g., S. K. Stowers, *A Rereading of Romans: Justice, Jews, and Gentiles* (New Haven: Yale University Press, 1994), 101–4.

20. So Watson, *Paul, Judaism and the Gentiles*, 198; S. J. Gathercole, *Where Is Boasting? Early Jewish Soteriology and Paul's Response in Romans 1–5* (Grand Rapids: Eerdmans, 2002), 198–99.

21. O. Wischmeyer, "Römer 2.1–24 als Teil der Gerichtsrede des Paulus gegen die Menschheit," *NTS* 52 (2006): 359.

22. E. Käsemann, *An die Römer*, HNT 8a (Tübingen: Mohr Siebeck, 1973), 49.

This association of the judge and the theology of *Wisdom* is evident in the implicit affirmation of the polemical content of 1:18–32, the judge's presumed immunity from divine judgment, and the language in which Paul launches his critique. Paul's indication that his interlocutor assumes they will "escape the judgment of God" (Rom 2:3) alludes to and attacks one of *Wisdom*'s central theological convictions: Israel is different because Israel is not idolatrous. Paul's polemical turn toward Israel in Romans 2:1 occurs at the same argumentative moment, and in much the same language, as *Wisdom*'s polemical pause in relation to Israel at 15:1–4:

> But you our God are kind (χρηστός) and true, patient (μακρόθυ-
> μος) and managing all things in mercy.
> For if we sin we are yours, knowing your power; but we will not
> sin, knowing that we are reckoned as yours.
> For to understand you is complete righteousness, and to know
> your power is the root of immortality.
> For neither has the evil intent of human art deceived us, nor the
> useless labor of painters.

Here, as in Exodus 34:6–9, divine patience and mercy anchor an assurance that sin does not disqualify Israel from being God's people (cf. σοί ἐσμεν, σοὶ λελογίσμεθα, Wis 15:2 with ἐσόμεθα σοί, Exod 34:9 LXX).[23] As John Barclay notes, "the reference to sin ('even if we sin') picks up Moses' confidence that 'you will forgive our sins and our iniquities' (Exod 34:9, LXX)."[24] However, whereas Moses utters these words in the wake of the golden calf episode, *Wisdom* contextualizes this confidence within an assurance that Israel does not and will not worship idols because they know God: "we will not sin (15:2b); "the evil intent of human art has not deceived us" (15:4). Thus, while *Wisdom* echoes Exodus 34:6–9, it decontextualizes divine mercy: "*Wisdom* does not make, and could not make, reference to the Golden Calf."[25] Unlike the ungodly who are ignorant of God (13:1) and thus caught in the inevitable movement from idolatry to immorality (14:12–14, 22–31), Israel knows God and therefore "will not sin" (15:2b). The function of 15:1–4 within *Wisdom*'s critique of false-religion is therefore to establish the irreducible difference between Jew and

23. For the echo of Exodus 34, see Larcher, *Livre*, 3:847–49; cf. H. Hübner, *Die Weisheit Salomons*, ATD Apokryphen 4 (Göttingen: Vandenhoeck & Ruprecht, 1999), 183–84.
24. J. M. G. Barclay, "'I Will Have Mercy on Whom I Have Mercy': The Golden Calf and Divine Mercy in Romans 9–11 and Second Temple Judaism," *EC* 1 (2010): 91.
25. Barclay, "'I Will Have Mercy,'" 91.

gentile on the basis of the non-idolatry of the former and the false-worship of the latter. More concisely, *Wisdom*'s anthropological dualism is built on Israel's immunity from idolatry. It is this foundational presumption that Paul challenges in Romans 1:18–2:5.[26]

Paul's reference to the kindness (χρηστότης) and patience (μακροθυμία) of God (Rom 2:4) echoes *Wisdom*'s echo of Exodus 34. Paul, however, is quick to remind his interlocutor of an essential element of *Wisdom*'s theology: God mercifully "overlooks human sin for the sake of repentance" (εἰς μετάνοιαν, Wis 11:23; cf. Rom 2:4).[27] Whereas *Wisdom* 15:1–4 suggests that an awareness of the divine attributes renders potential sin an actual impossibility, Paul, like Exodus 34, locates the operations of divine kindness and patience within the matrix of human idolatry and immorality. Paul thus disputes the assumed immunity of the judge who, in Romans 2:1–4, appears to base their self-differentiation vis-à-vis the other on the same religious and ethical criteria *Wisdom* employs to construct the distinction between Jew and gentile.[28] Assuming that the history of Romans 1:18–32 is the history of the other, the judge affirms Paul's *theologoumenon*: οἱ τὰ τοιαῦτα πράσσοντες ἄξιοι θανάτου (Rom 1:32). But as Paul's repeated claim that the judge "does the same things" (2:1, 3) implies, Paul's reading of history includes his interlocutor within the story of sin that Romans 1:18–32 rehearses. For Paul, in opposition to *Wisdom*, "the difference between Jew and Gentile"—a difference that Paul maintains as real and significant (e.g., Rom 1:16; 3:1; 9:1–5; 11:11–32; 15:8–13)—"is not," as Watson observes, "the difference between the righteous and the unrighteous."[29] In *Wisdom* 15:1–4 Israel is different because the nation is not guilty of the idolatry and immorality catalogued in *Wisdom* 13:1–14:31. In Romans the gap between

---

26. Gathercole notes that Romans 2:21–24 and 3:9–18 also provide what he terms "phenomenological evidence" and "scriptural evidence" for Israel's sinfulness (*Where Is Boasting*, 211).

27. On Paul's use of *Wisdom*'s theology and language against his interlocutor, see Watson, *Hermeneutics*, 410.

28. *Pace* K. Yinger, *Paul, Judaism and Judgement According to Deeds*, SNTSMS 105 (Cambridge: Cambridge University Press, 1999), who argues that Paul is not disputing a Jew "claiming 'we have not sinned' . . . but Jews or Jewish Christians claiming that they will not be treated the same way as the 'sinners' in the judgement" (152–53). This reflects a tendency among Pauline scholars to abstract *Wisdom* 15:2a ("even if we sin") from the insistence in 15:2b and 15:4 that "we will not sin" and "human art has not misled us." See, e.g., B. W. Longenecker, *Eschatology and the Covenant: A Comparison of 4 Ezra and Romans 1–11*, JSNTSup 57 (Sheffield: JSOT Press, 1999), 182; U. Wilckens, *Der Brief an die Römer*, 3 vols; EKKNT (Zurich: Benziger; Neukirchen-Vluyn: Neukirchener, 1978–82), 1:121–24.

29. Watson, *Hermeneutics*, 410.

the Jewish judge and the other is erased because Paul's interlocutor is guilty of the idolatry and immorality catalogued in Romans 1:19–32. This inclusion of Paul's Jewish dialogue partner within the scope of what initially sounds like a Jewish polemic against non-Jews invites a reconsideration of the subtle but substantive differences between *Wisdom* 13–15 and Romans 1:18–32. To state my thesis in advance, the rhetorical contextualization of Romans 1:19–31 within the kerygmatic proclamation of 1:16–18, together with the Pauline alterations to *Wisdom's* critique of non-Jewish religion, broadens the target of Paul's polemic to include Israel and thus, as Paul announces in 1:18, πᾶς ἀσέβεια καὶ ἀδικία ἀνθρώπων.

Rereading Romans 1:18–32

This rereading will attempt to situate Paul's accusatory announcement of 1:19–32 within the kerygmatic progression of Romans 1:16–18 and consider the rhetorical function and theological significance of Paul's alterations to the Hellenistic Jewish polemical tradition. It will be argued that this rhetorical location, together with Paul's divergence from *Wisdom's* aniconic critique, contribute to a universalizing of Paul's polemical target. The anthropological effect is the essential identification of Jew and gentile as they confront the divine verdict, not as non-idolatrous Jew or idolatrous gentile, but as ἄνθρωποι.[30]

The Kerygmatic Context of Romans 1:19–32

Wisdom's aniconic polemic is situated within an extended reflection on Egyptian animal worship and functions primarily as an argument for Israel's avoidance of idolatry over against non-Jewish religion (12:23–15:18). Paul's polemic finds its rhetorical context within the proclamation of a gospel that addresses both Jew and gentile with the news of God's saving righteousness (Rom 1:16–17). This contextual contrast generates a difference in genre which Bornkamm identifies as a distinction between "Hellenistic apologetic" (*Wisdom*) and "prophetic accusation" (Romans).[31] Understood within the

---

30. While it would be over-determined to argue from Paul's use of ἄνθρωπος to the broadening of his polemical target, it is nevertheless suggestive that ἄνθρωπος is explicitly and intentionally inclusive in Romans 3:28 (cf. Gal 2:16) and 5:12–19. Even in Romans 2:1 where ἄνθρωπος is limited to the Jewish judge, Paul argues from within "der innerjüdische Israel-Diskurs" to "eine universale Verurteilung," and therefore his use of ἄνθρωπος has "universal-anthropologische Dimensionen" (Wischmeyer, "Römer 2.1–24," 376).

31. Bornkamm, "The Revelation of God's Wrath," 54.

double-apocalypse of divine righteousness and wrath (1:17–18), the Pauline proclamation announces an event. Such a claim states a conclusion ahead of its evidence, however. To situate the polemic of Romans 1:19–32 within its apocalyptic and kerygmatic context it is necessary to take a step back and consider the grammatical and theological progression of Romans 1:16–18.

The apocalypse of wrath in Romans 1:18 is connected to the gospel of 1:16 through an argumentative chain linked by successive uses of the explanatory γάρ. Paul is not ashamed of the gospel *because* (γάρ) it is the divine power for salvation *because* (γάρ) the righteousness of God is revealed in it; *for* (γάρ) the wrath of God is revealed. Grammatically, the γάρ of 1:18 relates ἀποκαλύπτεται ὀργὴ θεοῦ directly to the syntactically similar and ultimately salvific (1:16) revelation of divine righteousness in 1:17. The crucial question is what this grammatical connection indicates about the theological link between the revelations of wrath and righteousness in relation to the gospel.

Answers to this question, while diverse, generally take one of two approaches: juxtaposition or progression. According to the former, wrath and righteousness relate as opposites.[32] This reading has always been puzzled by the presence of γάρ in 1:18,[33] but Campbell's radicalized version of this interpretation explains the γάρ as contributing to the structural parallel between the revelations of wrath and righteousness which, according to his reading, represent two antithetical gospels.[34] As Cranfield observes, however, "there would seem to be no justification (apart from a theological presupposition that it is appropriate to contrast δικαιοσύνη θεοῦ and ὀργὴ θεοῦ)" to read Romans 1:17 and 1:18 antithetically.[35] In Campbell's case at least, his exegesis is explicitly motivated by a disinclination to permit a theological association between the syntactically linked revelations of righteousness and wrath. In his words, Romans 1:17 and 1:18 express "fundamentally different conceptions of

---

32. P. Stuhlmacher, *Gerechtigkeit Gottes bei Paulus*, FRLANT 87 (Göttingen: Vandenhoeck & Ruprecht, 1966), 80–81.

33. M.-J. Lagrange, *Saint Paul: Épitre aux Romains*, Ebib 13 (Paris: J. Gabalda, 1922), translates the γάρ with "car," but argues that in this context is has "une légère opposition" (21); cf. C. H. Dodd, *The Epistle to the Romans*, MNTC (London: Hodder and Stoughton, 1932), who refers to the "adversative conjunction *but* in 1.18" (45).

34. The Pauline gospel (1:17), defined by a saving righteousness, is set in juxtaposition to the "Teacher's" gospel (1:18), which is centred on an eschatological exercise of retributive wrath, Campbell, *Deliverance of God*, 542–43. This construal requires reading Romans 1:18–32 as a summary of the rhetorical opening of Paul's opponent whose theology is decisively shaped by *Wisdom*. Such a thesis is seriously called into question by the numerous and significant differences between Romans 1:18–32 and *Wisdom* 13–14.

35. Cranfield, *Romans*, 1:106–7.

God."[36] But this theological interpretation appears to put asunder that which the apostle has joined together. In 1 Thessalonians 1:10 and Romans 5:9, to cite just two examples, salvation is defined as deliverance from divine wrath. Similarly, the natural force of the repeated γάρ of Romans 1:16–18 coordinates the saving righteousness of God with that from which it saves. Thus, in the interpretative tradition of Sanday and Headlam, we can say that the γάρ of 1:18 explains the revelation of righteousness by citing the reason it is required.[37] But we can also say more.

This initial answer may appear to imply a movement from wrath to saving righteousness which in turn would support a progressive reading in which the era of wrath precedes the era of righteousness.[38] There are, however, two related reasons why this cannot be sustained. First, as Bornkamm observes, world history prior to the gospel event is not characterized as an era of wrath. Rather, for Paul, the time before the revelation of divine righteousness is the period of patience (Rom 3:25–26; cf. 2:4).[39] It is this time of divine forbearance that is brought to an end in the present (ἐν τῷ νῦν καιρῷ, 3:26) demonstration of divine righteousness that is the cross of Christ Jesus (3:24–26). The correlation between εἰς ἔνδειξιν τῆς δικαιοσύνης αὐτοῦ (3:25, 26) and δικαιοσύνη θεοῦ ἀποκαλύπτεται (1:17), together with the identical time references indicated by ἐν τῷ νῦν καιρῷ (3:26) and the present tense of ἀποκαλύπτω (1:17), indicate that it is, as the connection between 1:16 and 1:17 suggests, in the gospel that the divine righteousness is revealed. What then of the revelation of wrath in 1:18? The structural parallelism between the revelations of wrath and righteousness, especially the identical present passive form of ἀποκαλύπτω, suggests that the dual revelations are tied to a single reality.[40] Read this way, the apocalypse of divine wrath is not only the reason for the revelation of

36. Campbell, *Deliverance of God*, 543.

37. Sandy and Headlam, *Romans*, 40.

38. H. Lietzmann, *An die Römer*, 3rd ed., HNT 8 (Tübingen: Mohr Siebeck, 1928), 31. A variant of this reading does not relate the two eras chronologically but views wrath and righteousness as two spheres of existence corresponding to being outside (wrath) or inside (righteousness) the gospel, see, e.g., T. Zahn, *Der Brief des Paulus an die Römer*, KNT 6 (Leipzig: Deitchert, 1910), 86–87.

39. Bornkamm, "The Revelation of God's Wrath," 49.

40. Campbell, *Deliverance of God*, 542–43, attempts to soften the syntactical connection between 1:17 and 1:18 by interpreting the present tense verb of 1:18 as "a rare future present"; cf. Bell, *No One Seeks for God*, 14; H.-J. Eckstein, "'Denn Gottes Zorn wird vom Himmel her offenbar warden.' Exegetische Erwägungen zu Röm 1,18," *ZNW* 78 (1987): 74–89. However, the present time reference of the identical occurrence of ἀποκαλύπτεται in 1:17 makes this unlikely.

saving righteousness. It is the underside of the one event that reveals both.[41] The antithesis between wrath and righteousness, therefore, does not indicate the presence of two gospels. Rather it represents the two words of the singular apostolic announcement: wrath and righteousness, condemnation and salvation, death and life, no and yes. In Pauline terms, the cross is the divine enactment of judgment on ungodliness and therefore the justification of the ungodly. Accordingly, the revelation of wrath is, in relation to the gospel, a *novum*—something heretofore concealed but now unveiled.[42]

This brings us back to the difference between *Wisdom* 13–14 and Romans 1:18–32. In *Wisdom* the anthropological situation is fundamentally knowable. Non-Jewish humanity has foolishly failed to exercise their rational potential, but this failure renders them ignorant, not epistemologically incapable. In *Wisdom*'s words, the non-Jewish world should have known that "a corresponding perception of the creator" is derivable "from the greatness and beauty of created things" (Wis 13:5), but, being "foolish by nature," they failed to think from "the good things" to "the one who exists" (13:1). Reading Romans 1:18–32 as if it were *Wisdom* 13–14, Campbell detects what he considers an un-Pauline parallel in the anthropology of Romans 1:18–32. According to Campbell, the polemic of Romans 1 presupposes an epistemological openness to the existence and demands of God which is itself the presupposition for the rational transition from wrath to grace.[43] Thus interpreted, the content of Romans 1:19–32 is es-

---

41. Cf. K. Barth, *A Shorter Commentary on Romans*, trans. D. H. van Daalen (London: SCM, 1959), 24–26; see also *Church Dogmatics*, vol. I/2: *The Doctrine of the Word of God*, ed. G. W. Bromiley and T. F. Torrance, trans. G. W. Bromiley (Edinburgh: T&T Clark), 304–5. While Barth's explicit association of the revealed wrath of Romans 1:18 and the cross is theologically appropriate, it is exegetically premature. Though divine wrath finds its eschatological manifestation on Golgotha, Romans 1:18–3:20 is that part of the apostolic kerygma which announces God's wrath that stands over humankind and which, as Paul only later reveals, is enacted and exhausted on the cross.

42. R. Jewett, *Romans*, Hermeneia (Minneapolis: Fortress, 2007), 150–52. This is not to suggest that God's wrath is not operative prior to the gospel events (cf. Rom 1:24, 26, 28). For the cross as the revelation of God's righteousness that both judges and justifies, see chap. 1, "Righteousness Revealed."

43. Campbell, *Deliverance of God*, 16–17. Campbell's theological concern is to combat a "prospective soteriology" (i.e., plight to solution), which he insists rests on a faulty epistemology that requires an essentially rational rather than revelatory apprehension of the human condition. This is contrasted with a "retrospective soteriology" (i.e., solution to plight), which allows the liberating gospel to inform its object about its prior captivity. This epistemological criticism, however, is neutralized if the anthropological content of Romans 1:19–3:20 is situated within the revelatory disclosure of 1:16–18.

sentially and antecedently known, or at least knowable. But this is precisely the reading that the apocalyptic and kerygmatic context of 1:18 will not allow.

In contrast to *Wisdom*'s invitation to reason "from below," Paul's apocalyptic accusation pronounces the gospel's verdict on the world. The revelation of wrath is thus a constituent part of the Pauline proclamation (cf. Rom 2:16; 1 Thess 1:9–10). Read this way, solution and plight do not exist in a linear relationship that can be plotted in terms of an epistemological process. There can be no sense of a natural, rational awareness of the anthropological situation which somehow functions as a soteriological preface to the proclamation of the gospel. Paul is not arguing from plight to solution or from solution to plight. He is, as Mark Seifrid observes, announcing both the solution (1:16–17) and the corresponding plight which it presupposes (1:18).[44] There is, then, between solution and plight what we might call an antithetical affinity—the problem and the answer fit. However, an apprehension of this fit—this correspondence between the severity of the crisis and the drama of the divine saving act—is the epistemological product of the *theologia crucis*. It is the event and proclamation of the cross that reveals both sin and salvation, both wrath and saving righteousness. Within this kerygmatic context, the revelation of divine wrath is not, in contrast to *Wisdom*, reducible to a process of rational deduction. The revelation of divine wrath, to risk the tautology, is a revelation.

PARADISE LOST: CREATED-THEOLOGY IN ROMANS 1:19–21

Romans 1:19–32 narrates the history of ἀσέβεια and ἀδικία against which God's wrath of 1:18 is revealed. Within the movement of this basic plotline Romans 1:19–21 establishes humanity as recipients of divine truth, thereby legitimating the accusation that people "suppress the truth" (1:18). Paul's reference to "the knowledge of God" (τὸ γνωστὸν τοῦ θεοῦ, 1:19) that has been evident "since the creation of the cosmos" (ἀπὸ κτίσεως κόσμου, 1:20), suggests that, for Paul, the act of creation is the establishment of the divine-human relationship.[45] Within this context, "natural theology" is more properly "created-relationality"; it is the theological knowledge presupposed in the

---

44. M. A. Seifrid, "Unrighteous by Faith: Apostolic Proclamation in Romans 1:18–3:20," in *Justification and Variegated Nomism*, vol. 1: *The Paradoxes of Paul*, ed. D. A. Carson et al. (Grand Rapids: Baker Academic, 2004), 105.

45. Cf. F. Watson, *Text and Truth: Redefining Biblical Theology* (Edinburgh: T&T Clark, 1997), 242–67.

original relationship between human creature and divine creator. For Paul, however, what is primal is past (and prologue).

According to *Wisdom* 13:1–9, knowledge of God is an unactualized potential. Creation offers a corresponding knowledge of the creator (13:5), but the non-Jewish world failed to reason from "the good" to "the one who exists" (13:1). In Romans 1 by contrast: τὸ γνωστὸν τοῦ θεοῦ φανερόν ἐστιν ἐν αὐτοῖς, and this because ὁ θεὸς αὐτοῖς ἐφανέρωσεν. Here knowledge of God is a reality on account of divine revelation (cf. 1:21). As Markus Barth replies to his own question—"What is suppressed?"—it is "the factual knowledge of God."[46] In both *Wisdom* and Romans this possible (*Wisdom*) or actual (Romans) theological knowledge is tied to creation, but it is notable that whereas *Wisdom* argues for a possible theological knowledge derived "from" (ἐκ, 13:1, 5) creation, Paul indicates only that God's revelatory activity has been occurring "since" (ἀπό, Rom 1:20) the creation of the cosmos and that this self-disclosure is somehow related to "the things that have been made." There is a sharp contrast between *Wisdom*'s insistence that though people could and should have known God they are nevertheless ignorant of God (13:1) and Paul's declaration that people, γνόντες τὸν θεόν, have failed to honor him. In the one case the knowable God is unknown (*Wisdom*); in the other the unknowable God (τὰ ἀόρατα, 1:20) is known (Romans).[47]

"For although they knew God . . ." (1:21). This, for Paul, is the problem: not that humanity is ignorant of God, but that humanity knew God. *Wisdom* asserts that Israel's knowledge of God will prevent sin (15:2) and the ungodly are defined as such on the basis of their theological ignorance (e.g., 2:1). From a Pauline perspective, knowledge of God does not prevent sin; it is the precondition for creaturely rebellion.[48] As Watson observes, "we learn in Rom. 1:19–20 that to be human is to be the recipient of God's self-disclosure."[49] But in Romans 1:18–23 we also learn that to be human in history is to be a rebel against this creational revelation. "Suppressing the truth" (Rom 1:18) presupposes "knowledge of God" (1:19). The διότι which connects the two clauses indicates that Paul's emphasis on the actuality of theological knowledge serves to establish the reality of human rebellion and the legitimacy of divine judgment. By relating divine revelation to creation, Paul effectively includes all humanity

---

46. M. Barth, "Speaking of Sin," *SJT* 8 (1955): 288–96.

47. Cf. H. Bietenhard, "Natürliche Gotteserkenntnis der Heiden? Eine Erwägung zu Röm 1," *ThZ* 12 (1956): 275–88.

48. Bornkamm, "The Revelation of God's Wrath," 59.

49. Watson, *Text and Truth*, 258.

within its scope and therefore makes each person a potential rebel. In contrast to *Wisdom*'s charge that people are "without excuse" because they failed to exercise their epistemic potential and therefore know God, Paul insists that humanity is "without excuse" because the self-revealing God is known. To adapt Gaca's provocative proposal, *Wisdom*'s polemic targets idiots; Paul aims at apostates.[50]

This construal captures the implicit plot of Paul's polemical proclamation. There is a definite movement from knowledge of God to ignorance, idolatry, and immorality. Thus, in contrast to *Wisdom*'s summons to reason "from below" (from creation to creator), Paul announces a revelation "from above." Moreover, whereas *Wisdom* envisages a process of epistemological ascent, Paul tells a story of anthropological decline. As Richard Bell remarks, Romans 1:19–31 narrates a "fall."[51] In Watson's words, "the effect of the primal revelation was, simply and solely, its own distortion into idolatry."[52] For Paul, idolatry is not a step in the right religious direction. It is the rejection of revelation. The movement of false religion is not from theological ignorance to the almost excusable worship of creation (as in *Wisdom*). It is the distortion of divine self-disclosure—a suppression of theological truth (1:18) and the exchange of that truth for a lie (1:25).[53] Consequently, within the Pauline polemic an original, creation-related knowledge of God does not represent an alternative route to theological knowledge. This original revelation is fundamentally rejected revelation: it is past. Its function is therefore not to contribute to theology proper but to establish the reality of human "excuselessness" and therefore to ground the necessity of the re-creative revelation of Romans 3:21–22: it is prologue.[54]

ADAM, ISRAEL, AND EVERYONE: ALLUSIVE INCLUSION IN ROMANS 1

Allusions are elusive: they are difficult to identify, and their meaning and rhetorical function is not always clear. The following analysis of the allusive presence of Adam and Israel in Romans 1 concedes the initial ambiguity of the

---

50. Gaca, "Paul's Uncommon Declaration in Romans," 165–98. Barth, *CD* I/2, 304, anticipates Gaca in his suggestion that the gospel's universality implies a corresponding crisis in which "the complaint of apostasy is now expressly and seriously leveled against them all."

51. Bell, *No One Seeks for God*, 94.

52. Watson, *Text and Truth*, 261.

53. Cf. Watson, *Text and Truth*, 274n41, who notes that the Pauline affirmation of primal revelation occurs within a theological interpretation of the phenomena of idolatry.

54. Cranfield, *Romans*, 1:116.

allusions. It is possible that Paul's account of human sin draws freely and some-what indiscriminately from biblical resources. In this broad sense, Stephen Westerholm is correct to describe Romans 1:18–32 as "a dramatized depiction of the human condition, recalling many a biblical account . . . but not retell-ing any one story."[55] However, it is precisely as Paul is drawing together these various stories that he effectively constructs a single story—the human story. As argued above, the terms of the rhetorical turn at 2:1–5 force a rereading of Romans 1:18–32 which is alert to the inclusion of unexpected characters within the narrative. The following argument should thus be read as an exegetical attempt to reread Romans 1:18–32 in light of the implications of 2:1–11.

In *Wisdom* 13–15, the ignorant idolaters do not include Israel (15:2b–4). Paul's polemic permits no such limitations. Subsuming his polemical address-ees under the single term ἄνθρωπος, Romans 1:18–32 tells the tragic tale of human history "since the creation of the cosmos" (ἀπὸ κτίσεως κόσμου, 1:20). This creational context is the first indication that the humanity in question is, both broadly and specifically, Adamic humanity. God's self-revelation began in the beginning (1:20). This brings Adam into the story, but the ingressive ἀπό keeps the narrative moving.[56] Put another way, the story of a primordial knowledge of God which is exchanged for a lie is Adam's story. But for Paul, Adam's story is never Adam's story alone.

In Romans 5:12 Paul traces human sin and the death that accompanies it back to Adam: "Therefore, just as sin came into the world through the one man

---

55. S. Westerholm, *Perspectives Old and New: The "Lutheran" Paul and His Critics* (Grand Rapids: Eerdmans, 2004), 386.

56. Those who find Adam in Romans 1 include J. Jervell, *Imago Dei: Gen 1,26f. im Spätju-dentum, in der Gnosis und in den paulinischen Briefen* (Göttingen: Vandenhoeck & Ruprecht, 1960), 317–18; M. D. Hooker, "Adam in Romans I," *NTS* 6 (1959–60): 297–306; Bell, *No One Seeks for God*, 26; Dunn, *Theology of Paul the Apostle*, 91–93; J. R. Levison, "Adam and Eve in Romans 1.18–25 and the Greek *Life of Adam and Eve*," *NTS* 50 (2004): 519–34. However, see the cautionary article by A. J. M. Wedderburn, "Adam in Paul's Letter to the Romans," in *Studia Biblica 1978*, JSNTSup 3, ed. E. A. Livingstone (Sheffield: JSOT Press, 1980), 3:413–30. The strongest evidence for the presence of Adam in Romans 1 is: (1) 1:23 probably echoes Genesis 1:26a (LXX) in which ἄνθρωπος, εἰκών, and ὁμοίωσις (a possible synonym with Paul's ὁμοίωμα) are all coordinated; (2) the references to "exchange" (Rom 1:23, 25), "desire" (1:24) and service to the creature (1:25) may be allusions to Genesis 1–3 which have been, as Levison ("Adam and Eve," 523) argues, "refracted through the lens of a tradition such as we find in the Greek *Life of Adam and Eve*"; (3) the possible reflection of Jewish traditions about the tree of the knowledge of good and evil in the contrast between presumed wisdom and actual folly in 1:22; (4) the points of contact between Paul's references to sexual immorality and traditions (e.g., 4 Macc. 18:7–8; 2 En. 31:6) about Eve's temptation relating to unchastity.

(δι' ἑνὸς ἀνθρώπου), and death through sin, so death spread to all because all sinned." In Pauline theology, the Adamic trespass means death (5:15), condemnation (5:16, 18) and the status of "sinner" (5:19) for the many who, through Adam's sin, are subjected to the reign of death (5:17, 21).[57] But this universalism also has a particularity. While "all sinned" (5:12), not all sinned "in the likeness of Adam's trespass" (ἐπὶ τῷ ὁμοιώματι τῆς παραβάσεως Ἀδάμ, 5:14). That had to await the coming of the Mosaic Law (5:13–14) and therefore is a distinction unique to Israel. As Gathercole remarks, "Here we see that the primeval 'fall' of Adam and Eve has . . . been brought into association with sin under the Law in the life of the people of Israel."[58]

Romans 7:7–12 makes precisely this point. As in Romans 1, multiple stories appear to be intermixed. The prohibition against desire (ἐπιθυμία, 7:7), the emphasis on deception (ἐξαπατάω, 7:11; cf. Gen 3:13) and, most notably, the reference to a prior period of aliveness apart from the law (ἐγὼ ἔζων χωρὶς νόμου ποτέ, 7:9) indicate the allusive presence of Adam.[59] As Moo and Watson argue, however, the primary focus of Romans 7:7–12 is Israel's encounter with the Mosaic Law.[60] In Watson's words, "The topic here is not the fall but the coming of the law, and the commandment, 'You shall not desire' (v. 7) is drawn not from Genesis but from the Decalogue (Exod 20:17)."[61] The absence of an object in relation to the prohibition indicates, as in Philo (*Decal.* 142–

---

57. While *Wisdom* explains the entrance of death in relation to the devil's agency in Eden (2:23–24), Adam's particular theological significance is not as the archetypal sinner, but rather as the first figure in a long history of Wisdom saving those who are "worthy of her" (10:1–2; cf. 6:16).

58. Gathercole, "Sin in God's Economy," 161n3; cf. N. T. Wright, *The Climax of the Covenant: Paul and the Law in Pauline Theology* (London: T&T Clark, 1991), 39. 4 Ezra 3:7, 20–27 offers a similar account of the replication of Adamic sin in Israel's history.

59. G. Bornkamm, "Sin, Law and Death: An Exegetical Study of Romans 7," in *Early Christian Experience* (New York: Harper & Row, 1969), 87–104; H. Hübner, *Das Gesetz bei Paulus. Ein Beitrag zum Werden der paulischen Theologie*, FRLANT 119 (Göttingen: Vandenhoeck & Ruprecht, 1978), 66–69; Käsemann, *An die Römer*, 186. Early Jewish sources (e.g., Apoc. Mos. 19:3; Apoc. Abr. 24:9) commonly cite "desire" as the root of all sins and therefore link the prohibition against desire to the Eden narrative, see Dunn, *Theology of Paul the Apostle*, 87–88, 98–99.

60. D. J. Moo, "Israel and Paul in Romans 7:7–12," *NTS* 32 (1986): 122–35; Watson, *Hermeneutics*, 335–80. This is established primarily on the basis of Paul's use of νόμος, the similarity between the narrative sequence of this text and, in Moo's words, "a Pauline theological pattern having to do with the redemptive-historical experience of Israel, the citation of the tenth commandment, the link between the law and life (cf. Lev 18:5; Sir 45:5) and the connection between 'desire' and Israel's experience in the desert (cf. 1 Cor 10:1–10)" (123).

61. Watson, *Hermeneutics*, 359.

153) and 4 Maccabees 2:6, that the tenth commandment is cited here as, in Moo's phrase, "a representative summation" of the law.[62] The coming of this command (7:9) is the event of the law's coming, the conclusion of the period referred to in Romans 5:14 (ἀπὸ Ἀδὰμ μέχρι Μωϋσέως). This association of Adam and Israel enables Paul to recast Israel's confrontation with the law in Edenic terms. In this respect, the selection of the prohibition against desire, rather than forcing a choice between a focus on Israel or Adam, has the effect of bringing Sinai and Eden together.[63] As Stephen Chester remarks, Paul "creates a fusion between the giving of the command not to eat in the Garden of Eden" and "the giving of the law at Sinai."[64]

By linking desire and death, however, Paul does more than connect Eden and Israel's sin. He connects quite specifically the Adamic trespass and Israel's experience under the law in the wilderness. As Watson has demonstrated, the "correlation of desire and death derives . . . from Numbers."[65] First Corinthians 10:1–10, reading Numbers 11 in a similar fashion to Psalm 105:14–15, associates Israel's desire in the desert (1 Cor 10:6) with the destruction of nearly the entire wilderness generation (10:5). Here, the first manifestation of this sin-causing illicit desire is the idolatrous incident of the golden calf: "Do not be idolaters as some of them were; as it is written, 'The people sat to eat and drink and rose to play'" (1 Cor 10:7, quoting Exod 32:6). This indicates that the story of desire leading to death that is elusively narrated in Romans 7:7–12 is in part the story of Israel's sin and death at Sinai and in the wilderness. This, crucially, is the story *Wisdom* cannot tell.

This brings us back to Romans 1. By including Israel within the history of Adamic sin, Paul confronts the realities of Israel's past that *Wisdom* is forced to erase or displace. As argued above, *Wisdom* alludes to Moses's confident words in the aftermath of the golden calf, but in the same sentence *Wisdom* exonerates Israel from idolatry (Wis 15:2–4). That Paul faces precisely this history is strikingly evident in the double allusion of Romans 1:23. We have already noted the probable echo of Genesis 1:26a here. But in keeping with the Pauline association of Adamic and Israelite sin, the primary reference of this verse is to the allusion to the golden calf in Psalm 105:20 (LXX):

62. Moo, "Israel and Paul in Romans 7:7–12," 123n8.

63. G. Theissen, *Psychological Aspects of Pauline Theology*, trans. J. Galvin (Edinburgh: T&T Clark, 1987), 204–6; S. J. Chester, *Conversion at Corinth: Perspectives on Conversion in Paul's Theology and the Corinthian Church*, SNTW (London: T&T Clark, 2003), 186n29.

64. Chester, *Conversion at Corinth*, 187n129.

65. Watson, *Hermeneutics*, 363.

And they exchanged the glory (καὶ ἠλλάξαντο τὴν δόξαν) that was theirs for the likeness (ὁμοίωμα) of a grass-eating ox. (Ps 105:20 LXX)

And they exchanged the glory (καὶ ἤλλαξαν τὴν δόξαν) of the immortal God for the likeness (ὁμοίωμα) of the image of a mortal man and of birds and four-footed animals and creeping creatures. (Rom 1:23)

Here, to adapt a phrase, we have an echo of Israel in the polemic of Paul.[66] This allusive inclusion of Israel stands in the sharpest possible contrast to *Wisdom*'s claim that Israel is innocent of idolatry (15:4). There is no room for the golden calf in *Wisdom*'s anthropological dualism. The wilderness is the site of blessing and testing for the holy, idolatry-free nation in symmetrical contrast to the plagues which fittingly befell the unrighteous Egyptians (Wis 11–19). As Barclay notes, "the God-aware people of Israel are in principle averse to idolatry, and hardly liable to worship a Golden Calf."[67] But Paul, as Watson comments, "faces the fact that the author of *Wisdom* strives to suppress: that the holy nation is itself deeply complicit in the idolatry and ungodliness that it prefers to ascribe to the Gentiles."[68] As we have seen, for *Wisdom*, Jew and gentile are irreducibly different *qua* non-idolaters and idolaters. Consequently, Paul's inclusion of Israel within the human history of idolatry effectively eliminates the basis on which *Wisdom*'s anthropological dualism is constructed.

Romans 1:18–32 is a polyvalent narrative. The story of the sin of Adamic humanity is told in the gentile-directed style of the *Wisdom* 13–15. In contrast to that tradition, however, the polemical target is broadened to include Israel. Dunn captures this dynamic by referring to a "blending of traditions" that produces a "twofold indictment," a reference first to "the characteristic Jewish condemnation of Gentile religion and sexual practice" and, secondly, to a "reminder that Israel itself falls under the same indictment."[69] The effect of Romans 1:18–32 is therefore the opposite of *Wisdom* 13–15. Whereas *Wisdom* explicitly disassociates Israel and idolaters, Romans 1:18–32 highlights Israel's idolatry and thereby collapses the difference between Jew and gentile at bed-

66. "All that Paul says about the foolishness of those that think themselves to be wise, and of the fabrication of quadripedal idols, he says by allusions to OT sayings" (Barth, "Speaking of Sin," 291).

67. Barclay, "'I Will Have Mercy,'" 93.

68. Watson, *Hermeneutics*, 411.

69. Dunn, *The Theology of Paul the Apostle*, 93. Dunn appears to overlook the oddity of having these two indictments side by side and that the presence of such a phenomenon represents a significant Pauline alteration to the polemical tradition from which he draws.

rock stratum of human sin. The contrast is between two theological anthro-
pologies: *Wisdom*'s anthropological dualism, which has Israel (righteous) and
non-Israel (sinners) as its lowest, irreducible denominators, is confronted by
Paul's apostolic announcement that further reduces the Jew/gentile distinction
to a single denominator: ἄνθρωπος.

INTRODUCING DIVINE AGENCY

Stanley Stowers observes that "interpreters have not placed enough emphasis
on God's action in [Romans] 1:18–32."[70] We have already considered the contextualization of Romans 1:19–32 within the apostolic announcement of an
ultimately salvific divine act and the explicit references to divine self-revelation
that ground the claims about a primal theological knowledge. In Romans 1,
however, God's agency is not only evident in acts of salvation and revelation.
It is also active in judgment. *Wisdom*'s explanation of the origin and effects
of sin, at least in chapters 13–15, is strictly anthropological.[71] According to
Romans 1:24, 26, and 28, by contrast, "the human situation depicted in Rom 1
derives," as Beverly Gaventa argues, "both from human rebellion against God
and from God's own active role in a cosmic conflict."[72] And "and" makes all
the difference.

Paul's introduction of divine agency into the causal link between idolatry
and immorality is unique in the Hellenistic Jewish polemical tradition. The
significance of this innovation is underlined by the triple use of the phrase
ὁ θεὸς παρέδωκεν (1:24, 26, 28).[73] Gaventa's consideration of both biblical
and nonbiblical uses of παραδίδωμι demonstrates that "handing over virtually
always involves a handing over to another agent."[74] This raises two related
questions: whom did God hand over and to whom did God deliver them?

Taking the latter question first, Romans 1:24, 26, and 28 all identify that to
which people were delivered with an εἰς + accusative clause: εἰς ἀκαθαρσίαν
(v. 24), εἰς πάθη ἀτιμίας (v. 26), and εἰς ἀδόκιμον νοῦν (v. 28). According to
this reading, the phrase ἐν ταῖς ἐπιθυμίαις τῶν καρδιῶν αὐτῶν that separates
the παραδίδωμι and εἰς clauses in 1:24 is interpreted causally. This is consistent
with both the Pauline (1 Cor 10:6) and early Jewish opinion that "desire is the

70. Stowers, *A Rereading of Romans*, 93.
71. *Wisdom* 2:24 does introduce a supra-human cause within the account of death's
origin, but here the nonhuman is demonic (διάβολος) not divine.
72. B. R. Gaventa, *Our Mother Saint Paul* (Louisville: Westminster John Knox, 2007), 113.
73. Cf. Gathercole, "Sin in God's Economy," 162–66.
74. Gaventa, *Our Mother Saint Paul*, 114.

origin of every sin" (Apoc. Mos. 19:3) and means that God hands people over to "uncleanness," "dishonourable passions," and a "worthless mind" because of the desires of their hearts. While these sound more like descriptions of human misbehavior or depravity than agents, the reappearance of these motifs in Romans—Gaventa cites 6:19–20, 7:5, and 8:6–7—seems to subsume these unnatural disorders under the power of sin. This is not quite the same as saying, as Gaventa does, that "uncleanness, dishonorable passions, and a deformed mind are instances of synecdoche; they refer to the anti-God powers, especially the power of Sin."[75] But it does imply that these human conditions are, in part, the effects of sin and therefore point to its oppressive power.

There is, then, a linking of desire and the implicit agency of sin in Romans 1:24. Following a now recurring pattern, this subtly connects the *Verdammnisgeschichten* of Romans 1:18–32 and Romans 7:7–12.[76] Sin as the subject of verbs is a major character of Romans 7:8–11. With the coming of the prohibition against desire (ἐπιθυμέω, 7:7), sin sprang to life and produced "all desire" (πᾶσα ἐπιθυμία, 7:8) in the "I," thus deceiving and killing the human (7:11). The parallel movement from desiring (ἐπιθυμία) to the effects of sin's agency and ultimately death (1:32) in Romans 1:24–28 suggests that Israel, a focus of Romans 7, is not excluded from the account of God handing humanity over to the destructive power of sin in Romans 1:24–28. Tying the effects of sin to the causal effects of desire, with all its associations with Adam and Israel, contributes to the bringing together of Jew and gentile under the single term ἄνθρωπος. Thus, in answer to the second question, God handed over humans—Jew and gentile—to the effects of sin's agency. In Romans 1:18 ἄνθρωπος means ἄνθρωπος: it is an inclusive reference and as such the tragic history of human sin is precisely the *human* story.

Unsubtle Subversion

"God's wrath strikes man's religion."[77] This is true in both *Wisdom* 13–15 and Romans 1. But again, there are crucial differences. There is a subtle differentiation between two types of false worship in *Wisdom* 13:1–9 and 13:10–19. The initial focus (vv. 1–9) is on those things created by the divine artisan. Fire, water, air, wind, stars: these "created things" (κτίσμα, 13:5) were taken to be gods (13:2) with the result that gentile religion became fixed on the pen-

75. Gaventa, *Our Mother Saint Paul*, 119.
76. Cf. Gathercole, "Sin in God's Economy," 159–69.
77. Barth, "Speaking of Sin," 290.

ultimacy of the created rather than its divine cause (13:1, 3–5, 9). In 13:10–19 the focus is no longer on the works of the divine creator, but rather on the artifacts created by humans (cf. 14:15–21; 15:7–13). Under this general topic, *Wisdom* demonstrates an awareness of various forms of idolatry: personal piety (13:11–19), legal cult (14:15–16), and emperor worship (14:17–21). This differentiated reflection on non-Jewish cult displays a level of acculturated sophistication and subtlety.[78]

Whatever Paul is in Romans 1, he is certainly not subtle. In contrast to *Wisdom*'s careful distinguishing of types of idolatry, Paul's account reduces idolatry to images of living creatures (Rom 1:24). A similar lack of subtlety is evident as Paul, unlike *Wisdom*'s sensitive evocation of Israel's aniconic tradition, offers an apparently novel interpretation of idolatry as service to the creature (1:25). *Wisdom*'s emphasis on the human origin of certain idolatrous artifacts (13:10–19; 15:7–13) evokes what Watson calls the "craftsman motif" from Isaiah 44:9–20, and the satirical polemic against the lifeless impotency of idols derives from Psalm 115:5–7.[79] Paul's interpretation, by contrast, seems to come from nowhere. It may be, however, that Paul's language of "exchange" and its connection to, as Levison writes, "the inversion of the human dominion that is established in Gen. 1:26" reflects an interpretative tradition that includes "the exchange of human dominion for subservience to animals" as an effect of the Edenic fall.[80] In the Greek Life of Adam and Eve the wild animals address the woman after her rebellion: ἡμῶν αἱ φύσεις μετηλλάγησαν (11:2). That this exchange includes the forfeiting of Adamic dominion is confirmed both by an extrabiblical linking of the Edenic sin with animal rebellion (24:3) and an eschatological promise that Adam's rule will be reestablished (39), thus indicating that the loss of that rule is presupposed. This connection between Romans 1:23, 25 and an interpretative tradition associated with the Eden narratives further confirms the significance of Adam within Paul's polemic. Importantly, however, Adam himself is not the polemical target. Paul accuses ἄνθρωποι not Ἀδάμ. Accordingly, the effect of this (possible) allusion to Eden is not to focus on humanity's progenitor, but rather to establish human solidarity and thereby to address Jew and gentile as ἄνθρωπος, as Adamic humans.

Read within this rhetorical and theological context, Paul's apparently crude collapsing of types of idolatry takes on new significance. Hidden

78. Barclay, *Jews in the Mediterranean Diaspora*, 392.
79. Watson, *Hermeneutics*, 407.
80. Levison, "Adam and Eve," 530, 533.

within Paul's undifferentiated description of false worship is what we might call an unsubtle sophistication: a subversively unnuanced account of cultic practice which has the effect of collapsing both the difference between types of religion and the associated differences between their practitioners.[81] In *Wisdom*, false religion exists on something of a sliding scale that moves from mildly condemnable (μέμψις ὀλίγη, 13:6) to "most foolish" (πάντες ἀφρονέστατοι, 15:14)—that is, from nature worship (13:1–9) to Egyptian animal worship (15:18–19). It is the object of cultic devotion that distinguishes Egyptian from Greek, and ultimately Egyptian and Greek from Jew. In this variegated religious scheme, Israelite religion is set in contrast to a highly differentiated assortment of false religion. Although all non-Jewish religion is false insofar as it is not directed to the one God of Israel, the object of one's worship remains theologically relevant. Worshiping the works of the creator is closer to the truth than idolizing animals that even the creator did not bless (15:18–19). In this sense, there is true religion (Israel) and progressively less true religion.

Paul's perspective is different. Those who worship human images, birds, four-footed animals, and reptiles are all guilty of the single sin of serving the creature rather than the creator (Rom 1:23). For Paul, cultic practice is not a definitive distinguishing mark of Greeks, Jews, and Egyptians. The differences between types of false religion only serve to conceal a fundamental identity. The particular image of cultic devotion is ultimately inconsequential. Either one worships the one God, or one does not. By relativizing the significance of religious differences Paul effectively broadens his polemical scope. In contrast to *Wisdom*'s portrayal of Israel in juxtaposition to a range of false religion (15:1–4; 18:9), for Paul there is only true worship and its opposite. Despite its diversity non-Jewish religion is essentially a singular entity. And insofar as Israel is complicit in Adamic humanity's history of idolatry—a reality that Paul's allusion to the golden calf episode in Romans 1:23 forces the reader to concede—Israel has been on the wrong side of the true/false worship divide. Here again, Paul's alterations to the Hellenistic Jewish polemical tradition have the effect of producing an antithetical anthropology in relation to *Wisdom*'s essential distinction between Jew and gentile. Whereas *Wisdom* contrasts Israel with various types of idolaters, Paul reduces idolatry to terms reflected in Israel's original Sinai sin and thereby includes Israel within humanity's common hamartiological history.

81. Watson, *Hermeneutics*, 407n82, considers this possibility: "The Pauline conflation might be regarded either as a crude misunderstanding or as a sign of theological sophistication."

Conclusion

In the words of Romans 3:22, "there is no distinction." But for *Wisdom*, there is a distinction. Anthropology is reducible no further than the difference between Jew and gentile because Jews know God and gentiles are idolatrous. *Wisdom* 13–15 serves to reinforce this division by contrasting the idolatry and immorality of non-Jews with Israel's innocence in relation to idols and the consequent immorality. Paul's engagement with *Wisdom* 13–15 makes the opposite point. The contextualization of the Pauline polemic within the apocalyptic and kerygmatic context of Romans 1:16–18, together with the various alterations Paul introduces into the polemical tradition, serve to eliminate the fundamental difference fundamental between Jew and gentile by eliminating the imagined difference between non-idolatry and idolatry. The story of Romans 1:18–32, even as it tells the diverse stories of Adam, Israel, and the gentiles, is, as 1:18 states, the story of the ἄνθρωπος. By narrating these various stories within and as a single story Paul effectively creates a common human history. Thus, in contrast to *Wisdom*'s irreducible anthropological dualism, Paul announces, at the bedrock of human need and *coram deo*, the essential oneness of all. He announces the human.

CHAPTER 7

DEBATING DIAGONAL Δικαιοσύνη

THE EPISTLE OF ENOCH AND PAUL IN THEOLOGICAL CONVERSATION

> *Oh dreadful Justice, what a fright and terror*
> *Wast thou of old. . . .*
> *But now that Christ's pure veil presents thy sight*
> *I see no fears . . .*
> *Lifting to heaven from this well of tears.*

—George Herbert, "Justice III"

If, as is commonly recognized, Jewish apocalyptic provides an essential background for Pauline theology, then a theological dialogue between Paul and his predecessors promises to yield some interpretative fruit.[1] In an attempt to initiate such a conversation, this essay intends to let the Epistle of Enoch and Paul's epistle to the Romans talk to each other. The hope is to offer a reading of, and so get to know, the Epistle of Enoch and then allow this text to direct a reading of Romans 3:21–24. In this way, the questions asked of the familiar Pauline text will, hopefully, be somewhat less familiar. This way of framing things is both an indication of the "freshness" of this approach and something of a disclaimer. The relative inattention given to some of the interpretative issues that fill the pages of modern commentaries (e.g., the πίστις Χριστοῦ debate and the meaning of ἱλαστήριον) is a result of the methodological attempt to let the Enochic author ask the exegetical questions. The questions I imagine our Enochic interlocutor asking Paul are generated by their common self-designation as receivers and conveyers of divine

---

1. R. B. Matlock, *Unveiling the Apocalyptic Paul: Paul's Interpreters and the Rhetoric of Criticism*, JSNTSup 126 (Sheffield: Sheffield Academic, 1996), provides a review of research into Paul's "apocalyptic" theology.

revelation. This commonality, however, only intensifies the incompatibility of the content of the two apocalypses. The Epistle of Enoch articulates an expectation of a future judgment that overcomes the injustice of the present by reconnecting the causal lines between, on the one hand, righteousness and blessings and, on the other hand, wickedness and curses. From this perspective, the Pauline announcement of the present revelation of a divine righteousness that justifies sinners is likely to be heard as dangerously confused, a proclamation that calls the very injustice to which the Epistle of Enoch responds—the link between sinners and soteriological blessings—an expression of divine justice.[2]

Eschatological Justice in the Epistle of Enoch

Imagine there's no heaven . . . The author of the Epistle of Enoch imagined such a reality. And as John Lennon predicted, it was easy. But also horrifying. Easy because locating reality in the empirical requires no imagination. Horrifying because the present, if real, constitutes a complete reversal of the canons of justice. The epistle is shaped by two types of imagining. The one, attributed to the sinners (ἁμαρτωλοί), is an unimaginative assumption that what you see is what you get (e.g., 102:6).[3] The other, ascribed to the righteous, is an imaginative ontology that links actuality with eschatology. The pretension to reality of the unjust present, characterized as it is by the flourishing of the wicked and the oppression of the righteous, is confronted with a no less ontological counter-statement: the present and empirical are less real than the eschatological and heavenly.[4] Nickelsburg catches the rhetorical trick, "These opposites contrast one's perception of an unjust world with the reality of divine justice, which will

---

2. The Epistle of Enoch (hereafter the epistle, i.e., 1 En. 92:1–5; 93:11–105:2) represents a relatively late moment in the Enochic literary history. The composition of both the frame and the body of the epistle probably dates from the period immediately before the Maccabean Revolt, L. T. Stuckenbruck, *1 Enoch 91–108*, CEJL (Berlin: de Gruyter, 2007), 211–15; Nickelsburg, *1 Enoch 1: A Commentary on the Book of 1 Enoch, Chapters 1–36; 81–108*, Hermeneia (Minneapolis: Fortress, 2001), 427–28.

3. When possible, references are to the Greek text in M. Black, *Apocalypsis Henochi Graece*, PVTG 4 (Leiden: Brill, 1970). Otherwise, translation follows Stuckenbruck, *1 Enoch*, though in each case G. W. E. Nickelsburg and J. C. VanderKam, *1 Enoch: A New Translation* (Minneapolis: Augsburg Fortress, 2004), and D. Olson, *Enoch: A New Translation* (N. Richland Hills, TX: BIBAL Press, 2004), have been consulted.

4. For the social setting of the epistle see Nickelsburg, *1 Enoch 1*, 425–28; Stuckenbruck, *1 Enoch*, 211–15.

be enacted in the judgment in the as yet unseen future and which is already in the process of happening in the unseen heavenly realm."[5]

One way into the organizing theological theme of the epistle is to note the contrast between 103:9–15 and 104:1–6. These passages represent alternative readings of reality. In the one case (103:9–15), the historical fact of oppression and poverty constitute "the real." By contrast, 104:1–6 insists that reality cannot be separated from eschatology. The present is a paradox. The lived experience of the righteous is characterized by the covenant curses of Deuteronomy 28–30.[6] "Having hoped to be the head" (γενέσθαι κεφαλή), the righteous "have become the tail" (ἐγενήθημεν κέρκος; 103:11a; cf. Deut 28:13, 44). The question is whether this upside-down existence, implying as it does the inversion of Deuteronomic theology, reflects reality or simply reality's experienced but temporary aberration. The epistle's opinion is clear: at the judgment the righteous "will not be found as sinners" (οὐ μὴ εὑρεθῆτε ὡς οἱ ἁμαρτωλοί, 104:5).[7] Looks can be deceiving. The apparent righteousness of the rich (cf. 96:4) and the assumed disobedience of the downcast (103:9–15) will both be exposed in an eschatological reversal of fortunes (104:5–6).[8] In this way, the symmetrical justice of Deuteronomic theology is preserved by being postponed. At the eschaton the unjust diagonal that presently links sin and blessing will be erased and the straight lines between, on the one hand, righteousness and blessing and, on the other, wickedness and curse will be redrawn.

This pattern reverberates throughout the entire epistle. With the voice of Enoch, the author addresses himself to "my sons . . . and the last generation who will do uprightness and peace" (92:1). Despite the obvious injustices of the present, these "righteous ones" (92:4; cf. 94:3) have no need to "be saddened

5. Nickelsburg, *1 Enoch 1*, 423. Stuckenbruck refers to the "real (eschatological) state of affairs" (*1 Enoch*, 568).

6. Stuckenbruck, *1 Enoch*, 548: "The language in the text . . . consists in large part of words, expressions and whole phrases drawn from the reservoir of curses for breaking the covenant in Deuteronomy 28. . . . The righteous are made to utter a deep disappointment, if not disillusionment, that they themselves are suffering the consequences promised in the covenant to the disobedient (cf. e.g., Lam. 5.1–22; Deut. 31.17b)." See also A. Dillmann, *Das Buch Henoch* (Leipzig: Fr. Chr. Wilh. Vogel, 1853), 322; G. W. E. Nickelsburg, "The Apocalyptic Message of *1 Enoch* 92–105," *CBQ* 39 (1977): 322–33; C. VanLandingham, *Judgment and Justification in Early Judaism and the Apostle Paul* (Peabody, MA: Hendrickson, 2006), 90.

7. Note also the prohibition that introduces the speech of 103:9–15 (μὴ γὰρ εἴπητε) and the oath-formula that opens 104:1–6. These prefaces serve to commend the content of the latter passage while discouraging the attitude expressed in the former.

8. G. W. E. Nickelsburg, "Riches, the Rich, and God's Judgment in 1 Enoch 92–105 and the Gospel According to Luke," *NTS* 25 (1978–79): 324–44.

because of the times, for the Holy and Great One has appointed days for everything" (92:2). This consolation via God's cosmological control epitomizes the epistle. The times of trouble (92:2) and the times of justifying judgment (92:3–5) are fixed on the divine calendar.[9] This gives way to an apophatic celebration of the categorical transcendence of God (93:11–14).[10] Although divine identity and action are inscrutable, however, this in no way implies that they are arbitrary. On the contrary, the respective fates described in 92:3–5 correspond to the two-ways of "righteousness" and "wickedness" (94:1–5). Contained within this moral dialectic is a polarized construal of reality. There is right and wrong, the righteous and the sinners, life and death, justice and injustice. The problem of the present is that theory and perception do not line up. Empirical existence is typified by a relational imbalance. The causal links between wickedness, injustice, and death on the one hand, and righteousness, justice, and life on the other, are destabilized by the observable prospering of the wicked at the expense of the righteous. This tension between perceivable fact and theological imagination necessitates the eschatological relocation of the two-ways *telos*. It is to this task that the main body of the epistle (94:6–104:8) is dedicated.

According to Nickelsburg, "the author's view of reality is paradoxical, literally. Wrongness will be overcome by right and injustice by justice."[11] This paradoxical perspective is evident in the content and structure of the "woe-oracles" that shape the first of three discourses (94:6–100:9).[12] Following the formal pattern of prophetic denunciation, all eight woes exhibit a bipartite structure: (1) a description and indictment of sin and (2) an announcement of the corresponding judgment.[13] In several cases (95:5; 98:12–13; 99:11, 12), the

9. This helps to explain the editorial dislocation of the Apocalypse of Weeks (93:1–10; 91:11–17).

10. That this emphasis on the unknowability of the divine stands in *prima facie* contradiction to the Enochic claim to revealed knowledge about the mysteries of the creator and the creation is regularly observed; see, e.g., F. Martin, *Le Livre d'Hénoch: Documents pour l'étude de la Bible, traduit sur le texte Éthiopien* (Paris: Letouzey et Ané, 1906), 245; J. C. VanderKam, *Enoch: A Man for All Generations* (Columbia: University of South Carolina Press, 1995), 91; Stuckenbruck, *1 Enoch*, 237–38. This tension probably serves to highlight the uniqueness of the Enochic revelation.

11. Nickelsburg, *1 Enoch 1*, 424.

12. For the division of the body of the epistle into three major discourses of varying length (94:6–100:9; 100:10–102:3; 102:4–104:8), see Stuckenbruck, *1 Enoch*, 3. Nickelsburg locates six sub-units: 94:6–96:3; 96:4–98:8; 98:9–99:10; 99:11–100:6; 100:7–102:3; 102:4–104:8 (*1 Enoch 1*, 421).

13. It is in these descriptions of the wicked and their acts of injustice that we learn the most about the religious identity and socioeconomic status of the sinners. The opponents

relationship between the shape of judgment and the act that requires it evinces a principle of *quid pro quo*.[14] To take just one example: "Woe unto you who pay evil to your neighbour, for you shall be repaid in accordance with your deeds" (95:5). This eschatological re-linking of crime and punishment redraws the correlative lines that the injustices of the present appear to disconnect. In Stuckenbruck's words:

> For the writer, the woe-oracles have the crucial function of overcoming the mismatch between the sinners' malevolent activities on the one hand, and their social and economic prosperity, on the other. The denunciatory oracles fulfil this function by drawing a direct line of correlation from the sinners' misdeeds and false teaching to the punishments and judgement that must follow as a consequence.[15]

By both naming sin and describing its inevitable effect, the woes embody the tension of the present and its resolution. As Nickelsburg remarks, "The unrequited deeds of the wicked (part I) stand in tension with the concept of divine justice, which will be enacted in the judgment (part II)."[16] In this way, the woes function as a judicial recalibration, a proleptic enactment of the eschatological restoration of balance and justice.[17] In both their structural and theological symmetry they reflect the moral logic that the epistle insists constitutes (eschatological) reality.[18]

The sin-judgment relationship is only the negative half of the inverted in-

---

appear to be (primarily) Israelites (cf. 96:7; 98:11–15; 99:2; 104:10–13) who have gained material riches (94:8; 96:4; 100:6) in an unrighteous manner (97:8; cf. 94:7; 104:3) and who are abusing their power and leading others astray through some form of false teaching (98:15; cf. 99:7–9). Interestingly, in contrast to their rich oppressors, the in-group is never described as "poor" and only once as "lowly" (96:5). Instead, probably in an effort to highlight the injustice of the present crisis, the author refers to his audience with the label "righteous" (see Nickelsburg, *1 Enoch 1*, 426–25).

14. Nickelsburg, *1 Enoch 1*, 418; Stuckenbruck, *1 Enoch*, 197.

15. Stuckenbruck, *1 Enoch*, 193.

16. Nickelsburg, *1 Enoch 1*, 418.

17. This may imply, as Stuckenbruck, *1 Enoch*, 197, suggests, "that in the narrative world of the text, the 'woe-oracles' play a rhetorical role in bringing the judgement about . . . they function as the testimony against the wicked that will be taken into account at the time of divine judgement; see 96.4, 7; 97.7."

18. For this reason, Nickelsburg can speak of the formal qualities of the woes offering "a capsule summary of the author's worldview and message," containing as they do "a contrast and complementarity between present sin and future judgment" (*1 Enoch 1*, 418).

justice of the present. Not only do the wicked prosper, a problem whose rhetorical remedy is found in the woe-oracles, but the righteous also suffer, often
at the hands of the wicked. For this reason, the woe-oracles are necessarily
paralleled by their formal counterpart: "exhortations."[19] Mirroring the woes,
the exhortations are shaped by a twofold structure: (1) encouragement for the
suffering righteous, often accompanied by an allusion to or description of
some unjust circumstance (e.g., 95:3; 96:3; 102:5; 104:2–3, 6) and (2) a reference
to the future judgment as the grounds for consolation. Again, a single example
makes the point: "You righteous ones, do not fear the sinners, for the Lord will
again deliver them into your hands" (95:3). In contrast to the two-ways exhortation (94:1–5), the body of the epistle addresses its audience under the rhetorical assumption that they are already on the "way of righteousness" (cf. 94:1).[20]
Correspondingly, the exhortations do not contain contrasting moral options,
but rather invite a counter-empirical hope and fearlessness. One's existential
orientation to the coming judgment is determined by one's present status.[21]
"Fear will find" the wicked (100:8) and whatever grounds they imagine they
have for hope will be exposed as self-created illusions (98:10, 12a, 14).[22] By
contrast, the righteous are exhorted to "have hope" (96:1; 102:4 Eth; 104:2,
4 Eth), "take courage" (102:4 Gk; 104:2 Gk), "do not fear/be afraid of" (95:3;
96:3; 102:4 Eth; 103:4; 104:5, Gk 6), and to "have faith" (97:1).[23]

The basis for these competing eschatological perspectives is the soteriological dialectic associated with final judgment. In an act of complete re-balancing,
the judgment will both punish the wicked and reward the righteous.[24] This

---

19. See D. W. Kuck, *Judgment and Community Conflict: Paul's Use of Apocalyptic Judgment Language in 1 Corinthians 3.5–4.5*, SNT 66 (Leiden: Brill, 1992), 72–73, who argues that
the "woes" and "exhortation," together with the final judgment they presuppose, combine
to announce a complete "reversal."

20. Stuckenbruck, *1 Enoch*, 199.

21. This intentionally leaves unanswered the question of how status is determined. This
crucial matter will be picked up below.

22. 94:6b adds that the wicked will have no peace (cf. 1 En. 5:4, 5 Gk), indicating a tendency to describe the fate of sinners with language drawn from the Watchers mythology (cf.
95:4; 97:9; 98:2a, 4b, 11; 100:9b; 103:11c). Stuckenbruck detects in this reactivation "a more
rational cosmology in which discourse about the demonic is downgraded, if not almost
entirely removed" (*1 Enoch*, 211).

23. Stuckenbruck, *1 Enoch*, 199. See also Nickelsburg, *1 Enoch 1*, 419, for a graphical
analysis of the exhortations.

24. As in the Book of Dream Visions (1 En. 83–90), but unlike the Similitudes (1 En. 37–
71), the epistle imagines the righteous avoiding rather than successfully passing through
the judgment.

ᄀ

symmetry, however, is pushed one step further. The epistle envisages not only a reversal of fortunes, but also a reversal of roles. The inverted socio-economic power relationship of the present is turned right-side-up as the oppressors become the oppressed and the oppressed become the oppressors. This is evident in 95:3 and 96:1:

> 95:3—for the Lord will again deliver them into your hand so that you may carry out judgment on them as you wish.

> 96:1—for the sinners will quickly be destroyed before you, and you will have authority on them, as you wish.[25]

That the righteous will have a hand in the punishment of the wicked implies a retributive thoroughness. Both the end (eschatological bliss or destruction) and the instrument (sinners judged by the righteous) of judgment ensure a final state of equitability.

The wicked, however, have a reply (τότε ἐροῦσιν οἱ ἁμαρτωλοί; cf. 102:6): "Open your eyes"! Imaginative speculation about some unseen eschatological reversal is nothing but a fanciful avoidance of the obvious.

> [οἱ] εὐσεβεῖς κατὰ τὴν εἱμαρμένην ἀπεθάνοσαν καὶ τί αὐτοῖς περιεγένετο ἐπὶ τοῖς ἔργοις αὐτῶν; (102:6)

> [The] pious die according to fate and what is gained for them on the basis of their works? (102:6)[26]

The Enochic retort is, of course, that deeds do in fact matter and that death is, at most, penultimate.[27] Within the narrative world of the text, however, these counter-empirical claims are not merely naïve speculation. They are

---

25. Cf. 98:12 and 99:11. This theme is also present in the Apocalypse of Weeks (91:12b) and the Animal Apocalypse (90:19). Both Nickelsburg (*1 Enoch 1*, 418) and Stuckenbruck (*1 Enoch*, 200) suggest that this motif is rooted in the canonical language of Holy War (e.g., Num 21:34; Deut 2:24; 3:2; Josh 6:2; 8:1; 10:8).

26. The introductory ὅταν implies a temporal indeterminacy that is reflected in my "gnomic" translation of the aorist verbs.

27. Stuckenbruck observes that this move requires the epistle to take up, reject, and modify two biblical motifs: "(1) the idea that after death those who inhabit Sheol are not distinguished from one another (cf. 102.6b) and (2) the view that covenant faithfulness is accompanied by reward in this life (cf. 103.9–15)" (*1 Enoch*, 206).

divine revelation. The formal platform for this "disclosure discourse" is the epistle's dual employment of the "oath-formula" (e.g., "I swear to you"; cf. 98:1–3, 4, 6; 99:6–9; 103:1–4; 104:1–6) and revelatory prefaces (e.g., "I know" or "I have seen"; cf. 94:5, 10; 97:2; 98:8, 10, 12; 100:10; 103:2, 7–8; 104:10, 12). The rhetorical function of this formal combination can be seen in 103:1–4. The author is able to address the righteous under oath (καὶ νῦν ἐγὼ ὀμνύω; 103:1) because, having read (ἀναγινώσκω) the urgent writing (τὴν γραφὴν τὴν ἀναγκαίαν),[28] he understands (ἐπίσταμαι) a mystery (μυστήριον), that is, the things written about his righteous readers (τὰ γεγραμμένα . . . περὶ ὑμῶν). These good things (ἀγαθά) include joy and honor (ἡ χαρὰ καὶ ἡ τιμή), which, according to the Ethiopic text, are "the offshoot of your labours."[29] Crucially, the recipients of these eschatological gifts are the pious who have died (τῶν ἀποθανότων εὐσεβῶν). Contrary to the assertion of the sinners in 102:6, death does not disqualify the soteriological pattern announced in 99:10:

> blessed will be those who receive the words of the wise and understand them, to do the commandments (ποιῆσαι τὰς ἐντολάς) of the Most High; and they will walk in the path of his righteousness and not go astray with those who err, and they will be saved (καὶ σωθήσονται).

The epistle's theodicy is not shaped by competing human opinions but rather by the confrontation between human perception and divine revelation. The wicked see reality as it appears, whereas the Enochic author strains the perceptible through the hermeneutical filter of revealed reality and sees things as they are. The oath-formulas present this tension between empirical illusion and revealed (eschatological) reality as a legal debate. Within this rhetorical courtroom, the author's words "under oath" function as a twofold testimony. As Stuckenbruck writes:

> On the one hand, he takes upon himself the function of a witness against the sinners by describing their deeds (98:1–3; 99:6–9) and declaring that their guilt cannot be concealed (98:6–8). On the other hand, in claiming to have received divine revelation, he proclaims the innocence of the righteous and announces that they will be rewarded (103:1–4; 104:1–6). . . . The writer

---

28. It is difficult to determine the original behind the references to "heavenly tablets" in the Chester Beatty text. Stuckenbruck (*1 Enoch*, 516) suggests τὴν γραγὴν τὴν ἁγίαν as a probable source for the Ethiopic ṣeḥfata qedusāta ("holy books").

29. S. Gathercole, *Where Is Boasting? Early Jewish Soteriology and Paul's Response in Romans 1–5* (Grand Rapids: Eerdmans, 2002), 48, notes the stronger reward theology implicit in the Ethiopic addition of "many and good things will be given to you."

believes that his testimony is not only divinely inspired but also provides
a definitive account of the religious state and ultimate fate, respectively, of
the righteous who are innocent and of the sinners.[30]

In this courtroom drama, commonsense is overcome by circularity. The
empirical epistemology of the wicked is trumped by a circular argument from
presupposed justice to eschatological justice. In this logical circle, however,
both presupposition and conclusion are authorized by an appeal to divine
revelation. The epistle's message of an eschatological reordering is a divine
word of reality spoken into the unjust illusion of the present.

The certainty and thorough equitability of the judgment is ensured both
by forces of creation (100:10–102:3) and by the scrupulousness with which
the angels maintain the heavenly books (98:6–8; 103:3; 104:1, 7). The angelic
record-keeping reflects the judicial symmetry which has shaped the epistle's
moral vision. Both the unrighteous deeds of the wicked (98:7–8; 104:7) and
the rewards (103:3) and names (104:1) of the righteous are written down. This
symmetry, however, is slightly skewed. The books appear to contain evidence
against the wicked, whereas it is the identity and destiny of the righteous that
are recorded. For E. P. Sanders this imbalance is paradigmatic:

> While the righteous are also said to be recompensed in the final judgment
> for their labours (103:3), the author characteristically thinks that the reward
> of the righteous in the resurrection will not be earned by works, but be
> given by the mercy of God; even the righteous man's continuing uprightness
> in the new life will be by grace.[31]

The partial correctness of this formulation is confirmed by 92:4a: "He will
be merciful to the righteous one and to him he will give uprightness which is
eternal." But Sanders's one-sided conclusion overlooks the essential structures
of the epistle. The question is not whether the righteous and wicked deserve
their respective fates (although that is, to a degree, assumed in the reward
soteriology of 99:10; 103:3–4 and 104:13–105:1).[32] The question is whether or
not the right people are going to receive the right retribution. In other words,

30. Stuckenbruck, *1 Enoch*, 198–99.

31. E. P. Sanders, *Paul and Palestinian Judaism: A Comparison of Patterns of Religion*
(Philadelphia: Fortress, 1977), 356. Sanders's basic pattern is affirmed with reference to the
Enochic literature by K. K. Yinger, *Judgment according to Deeds*, SNTMS 105 (Cambridge:
Cambridge University Press, 1999), 70.

32. VanLandingham, *Judgment and Justification*, 90–92; Gathercole, *Where Is Boasting*,
46–49. This pattern of thought is also implicit in the two-ways exhortation of 94:1–5.

the basic question is one of justice. The epistle's contention is that the temporal inversion of the Deuteronomic symmetry will give way to an eschatological balance characterized by the merciful reward of the righteous and the just destruction of the ungodly. Mercy is the positive side of a single but bipartite act of eschatological justice. God has mercy on the righteous, but as the epistle's theodicy demands, God has mercy *only* on the righteous.[33]

The implication is that the righteous and the wicked are, in some sense, the appropriate objects of their respective retributions. The grounds for this soteriological fittingness are implicit in the sobriquets that stereotype the competing groups: sinners and righteous. That these are essentially moral categories is evident, on the one hand, in the correlation between the repeatedly described sins of the wicked and their eschatological destruction and, on the other hand, the assumption that the righteous have chosen the path of righteousness and will be rewarded accordingly.[34] Sanders would prefer to ground the status of the righteous in what he sees as the "utter gratuity of election,"[35] but the epistle imagines the righteous choosing for themselves "righteousness and

---

33. Cf. 94:10 which explicitly informs the sinners that there will be no mercy for them. Sanders, it seems, has rightly rejected the proclivity of portraying early Jewish soteriology in the commercial terms of human earning, but his positive proposal overlooks the necessary correspondence between divine action and human suitability evident in the epistle and that is also characteristic of ancient gift-economies in which prizes/rewards/gifts are given to the "fitting." For two discussions of Jewish soteriology in relation to gift-exchange by John Barclay, see "Grace within and beyond Reason: Philo and Paul in Dialogue," in *Paul, Grace and Freedom: Essays in Honour of John K. Riches*, ed. Paul Middleton et al. (London: T&T Clark, 2009), 9–21, and *Paul and the Gift* (Grand Rapids: Eerdmans, 2015).

34. These points are particularly clear in, respectively, the woe-oracles and exhortations.

35. That election was "utterly gratuitous" has become something of a rallying cry in the post-Sanders era. While this refrain is true as far as it goes, it tends, ironically, to import the peculiarly Pauline notion of the un-preconditioned gift into its description of early Jewish theology. Election as a divine χάρις is coordinated with notions of human suitability such that the gift (election) corresponds to the social, intellectual, and/or moral worth its recipient. (For Abraham's election, see, e.g., Jub. 11:14–12:24; L. A. B. 6:1–18; *Ant.* 1.154–185; Apoc. Ab. 1–9; for the election of Abraham's immediate descendants, see, e.g., Jub. 19:13–20; CD 3.1–4; LAB 32:5; for the election of national Israel, see, e.g., 2 Bar. 48:20; 1QM 10.9–11). Interestingly, VanLandingham, *Judgment and Justification*, 20–54, concludes from the affinity between divine choice and prior human value in these texts that, "Considering what 'grace' means . . . election cannot be characterized as such" (27). This, again, reads a distinctively Pauline redefinition of "grace" into the theology of Second Temple Judaism rather than allowing each text's contextual discourse to establish the semantic domain of the terms it employs. For Paul's understanding of grace in relation to his social and theological contexts, see chap. 8, "Scandalous and Foolish."

an elect life" (94:4).[36] What Sanders misses is that for the epistle's theodicy to work, the lines between covenantal obedience and blessings and, conversely, disobedience and covenant curses need to be redrawn. This means both that the righteous and wicked should be, respectively, blessed and cursed and that the righteous and the wicked should be blessed and cursed because they are, respectively, obedient and disobedient. It is this connection that prevents the theodicy from being arbitrary.

Within this theological context mercy cannot operate apart from preconditions. In fact, the injustice of the present is evident precisely in the apparent condition-free favor that characterizes the temporal blessings of the wicked. Put another way, a theology of the rewarded sinner—or, to anticipate a tension with Paul, the justification of the ungodly—is the errant, overly empirical view that the epistle seeks to correct. Divine mercy is not located in the unjust, diagonal link between sinners and blessings, but within a divine act of justice that functions as the eschatological erasure of that line and the reestablishment of a balanced and just correspondence between, on the one hand, wickedness and punishment (judgment) and, on the other hand, righteousness and blessing (mercy).

Enoch Reads Romans 3:21-24

Paul, like the author of the epistle, is a receiver of divine revelation. The gospel that he proclaims is, by his account, emphatically not κατὰ ἄνθρωπον. It is, rather, an apocalypse of Jesus Christ (ἀποκάλυψις Ἰησοῦ Χριστοῦ, Gal 1:11-12). Such a claim is sure to intrigue our Enochic interlocutor. This Paul, it seems, understands that truth is never κατὰ ἄνθρωπον—that is how sinners see reality. But who is this Jesus Christ and what has he revealed to this self-proclaimed ἀπόστολος of God? One possible way to pursue this conversation is to imagine the Enochic author reading a passage in which Paul considers the content of this divine apocalypse. The remainder of this essay will attempt this interpretive exercise, teasing out the theological tensions between Paul and the epistle by offering a reading of Romans 3:21-24 in dialogue with Enoch

36. Election language is somewhat rare in the Enochic literature. 1 Enoch 51:2 refers to the Son of Man figure choosing the "righteous and holy ones from among (the risen dead)." Similarly, the Apocalypse of Weeks indicates that in the seventh week—the week in which the epistle situates itself—"there will be chosen the chosen righteous ones from the eternal plant of righteous" (93:10). R. Bauckham, "Apocalypses," in *Justification and Variegated Nomism: The Complexities of Second Temple Judaism*, ed. D. A. Carson, P. T. O'Brien, and M. A. Seifrid (Tübingen: Mohr Siebeck, 2001), 1:145.

as an exegete.[37] I will take as an entry point four questions the author of the epistle would likely raise as he read Paul: (1) When did this apocalypse occur? (2) What does "apart from law" mean? (3) How can you say there is no anthropological distinction? (4) How can you coordinate the revelation of divine justice with the obviously unjust justification of sinners?

But When?

The Enochic apocalypse is fundamentally future-oriented. The "now" of the epistle is the location of the crisis. Now is the time of injustice. Now is when the righteous suffer and the wicked experience the covenant blessings. Now is the problem. This "now" is confronted with the eschatological "but then." The coming judgment is the time of hope and the time of justice. Now the righteousness of God is hidden. "But then" the righteousness of God will be revealed.

Paul, by contrast, locates the revelation of the righteousness of God in the now: Νυνὶ δὲ δικαιοσύνη θεοῦ πεφανέρωται (Rom 3:21). One can almost sense the Enochic author rereading the sentence. How can Paul locate the enactment of God's righteousness within temporal history when the manifestation of eschatological justice is supposed to take the form of an end-time judgment that overturns the injustices of the present? The temporal transposition of the Enochic "but then" into the Pauline "but now" appears to endorse the present by declaring it to be the arena of divine righteousness. Such a reading, however, misses the bipartite structure of the divine apocalypse. The gospel that reveals God's righteousness (1:16–17) is a word of judgment (Rom 1:18–3:20) before it is a word of grace (3:21–26). The "but now" of 3:21 is an affirmation of 1:18–3:20 before it is its antithesis. The first word of the present revelation of the divine righteousness is one of diagnosis: πάντες γὰρ ἥμαρτον καὶ ὑστεροῦνται τῆς δόξης τοῦ θεοῦ (Rom 3:23; cf. 3:9). This word is the judgment of the sinner and the justification of God (cf. Rom 3:4). "But now" does not consecrate the present. It confronts it.

Within the movement of this apocalypse, however, the judgment of the sinner contains within it, not as its complement but as its consequence, the justification of the judged (Rom 3:24).[38] The Pauline "but now" is both the logical

37. Limiting our discussion to Romans 3:21–24 leaves the following analysis relatively immune to criticism on tradition-historical grounds. Following E. Lohse, *Der Brief an die Römer*, KEK 4 (Göttingen: Vandenhoeck & Ruprecht, 2003), 131–32, Paul's use of traditional material, if present, does not begin until 3:25.

38. Karl Barth traces this soteriological sequence when, commenting on Romans 3:21, he says that the "but now directs our attention to the . . . impossible possibility . . . to ac-

antithesis to the universal condemnation of Romans 3:9, 19–20 and the temporal antithesis to the epoch of which 1:18 is the thesis and 3:19–20 the conclusion.[39] As the first word of the eschatological present, "but now" acknowledges the correctness of the old era's self-referencing eulogy (3:19–20) even as it proclaims a divine righteousness that judges sin and justifies the sinner.[40]

The Enochic context for this sort of divine action—though the epistle would always distinguish between the judged and the justified—is an end-time judgment. For Paul, the judgment and justification of the sinner, as well as the revelation of divine righteousness that they instantiate, are linked to an event whose content takes the form of a human history (Rom 1:3–4) and especially, at least in this context (3:24–25), a human death. From the Enochic perspective, Paul's claim could not be more bizarre. The past-tense death of the one whom Paul calls Jesus Christ (3:24–25) has taken on the theological function the epistle attributes to the future judgment.[41] The handing over of Jesus to death is, for Paul, the present (ἐν τῷ νῦν καιρῷ) enactment of divine righteousness, an act of divine judgment that justifies God even as God justifies sinners (3:25–26).

This means that Paul locates the revelation of God's righteousness in the temporal and circumstantial contexts which, for the epistle, constitute the theological problem. For the epistle, the present is the scene of the crime, not least because it is characterized by the death of the righteous (e.g., 99:15; 102:4–11; 103:3, 9–10, 15). In striking contrast, Paul links the demonstration of divine righteousness to the death of a righteous person, thereby establishing the now as the eschatological. The Enochic exegete's first impression is no doubt that this is a peculiar righteousness. But peculiarity is likely to become

---

quittal in condemnation." *The Epistle to the Romans*, trans. E. Hoskyns (London: Oxford University Press, 1933), 92.

39. U. Wilckens, *Der Brief an die Römer*, 3 vols, EKKNT (Zurich: Benziger; Neukirchen-Vluyn: Neukirchener, 1978–82), 1:184: "Die Offenbarung der Gerechtigkeit Gottes geschielt als Gegensatz zur Offenbarung seines Zornes." See also, Käsemann, *Commentary on Romans*, trans. G. Bromiley (Grand Rapids: Eerdmans, 1980), 92.

40. F. Watson, *Paul, Judaism and the Gentiles: Beyond the New Perspective* (Grand Rapids: Eerdmans, 2007), 219–31, argues that the conclusion of 3:19–20, following on as it does from the scriptural catena of 3:10–18, is the voice of the law speaking through its canonical interpreters, announcing the failure of its own project and thereby testifying to the righteousness apart from law.

41. M. A. Seifrid, *Christ, Our Righteousness: Paul's Theology of Justification*, NSBT 9 (Leicester: Apollos, 2000), 47: "That which is to take place at the day of judgment . . . is manifest here and now in the crucified and risen Christ." Or again, "The cross is the prolepsis of that day of judgment" (66).

scandalous as Paul makes his second impression by asserting that this divine righteousness is revealed χωρὶς νόμου.

APART FROM LAW?

It is regularly observed that the Enochic literature emphasizes revealed Wisdom where other early Jewish texts are inclined to speak of Torah.[42] This raises the possibility that the Pauline χωρὶς νόμου might catch the attention of the Enochic author, but the way in which the epistle's author would likely hear "apart from law" in the context of Romans 3:19–24 is quite different than the Enochic tradition of locating revelation in Wisdom rather than covenant legislation. The "but then" of the epistle addresses the injustice of the present with the promise of eschatological adjudication. This implies a standard of justice that is able to both diagnose the present as a problem and shape a theological solution. That this required standard of justice is both informed by and conceptually consistent with the structures of the Torah is evident in the epistle's employment of the language of the covenant curses (especially Deut 28) to describe the suffering of the righteous (cf. 1 En. 103:9–15). As argued above, divine justice demands that the present links between sinners and blessing and the righteous and curses (i.e., the inversion of the Deuteronomic formula) be eliminated and replaced by the straight lines of justice that connect, on the one hand, the righteous with blessings and, on the other hand, sinners with the covenant curses (i.e., the eschatological realization of the Deuteronomic formula). For the epistle, the plight is present injustice; the solution is (Deuteronomy-shaped) eschatological justice.

For Paul, the problem is justice and the solution, because it is a justice that is apart from law, looks like injustice. It is easy to miss the contextual absurdity of Paul's claim. Paul is saying that divine righteousness is revealed apart from the very thing that, in his tradition, was the revelation of divine

---

42. G. W. E. Nickelsburg, *1 Enoch 1*, 50: "To judge from what the authors of 1 Enoch have written, the Sinaitic covenant and Torah were not of central importance for them. . . . 1 Enoch employs a different paradigm or set of categories as the primary means of embodying the double notion that God has revealed the divine will to humanity and will reward and punish right and wrong conduct. Law and its interpretation are embodied in the notion of revealed 'wisdom.'" See also the reviews of Nickelsburg's commentary by J. J. Collins and P. Tiller, both in J. Neusner and A. J. Avery-Peck, eds., *George W. E. Nickelsburg in Perspective: An Ongoing Dialogue*, vol. 2 (Leiden: Brill, 2003). The lack of covenantal and nomistic themes makes "covenantal nomism" an odd classification for 1 Enoch (*pace* Sanders, *Paul and Palestinian Judaism*, 422; cf. 361–62).

righteousness. This is, in other words, a manifestation of justice that operates apart from the received canons of justice.[43] The final word of the law,
its illocutionary act of justice, is the announcement that ἐξ ἔργων νόμου οὐ
δικαιωθήσεται πᾶσα σὰρξ ἐνώπιον αὐτοῦ (3:20). The righteousness of the law
is the judgment of the sinner. And yet Paul announces a righteousness that
effects the justification of the sinner. To Enochic ears, this can only be heard
as a confused claim that divine justice has been revealed, not just apart from,
but in opposition to divine justice. This is only half right. As argued above, the
righteousness of the "but now" is an affirmation of the law's justice (3:23) before
it is its antithesis (3:24). The divine grace that Paul cites as the ground of the
justification of the sinner (3:24) does not circumvent the law's verdict. Rather
it takes the shape of an atoning death for those whom the law has rightly condemned (3:24–25).[44] The law's demand for the death of transgressors (cf. Rom
1:32; 6:23) is not set aside. It is carried out in the death of the one whom God
put forward for transgressors.[45] Grace, here, is an event—more specifically
the Christ-event—that reveals God's justice (3:21–22, 26) even as it justifies the
ungodly (3:24, 26).[46] The righteousness apart from the law can therefore be
called the righteousness of grace or, more properly, the divine righteousness

43. It is often supposed that the radicality of this statement is qualified by Paul's "balanc-
ing" clause in 3:21b: μαρτυρουμένη ὑπὸ τοῦ νόμου καὶ τῶν προφητῶν. But it is unlikely that
νόμος has the same reference in 3:21a and 3:21b. The latter refers to the entire Pentateuch,
as is evident from its use within a common taxonomy referring to the Jewish scriptures
as a whole ("the law and the prophets"; cf. Matt 7:12; John 1:15; Acts 13:15). The former, by
contrast, takes its cue from 3:20 in which the νόμος in question is the same as in Romans 2
where it is qualified by verbs such as ποιέω (v. 13), πράσσω (v. 25), and τελέω (v. 27) and
understood as a series of commandments, all taken from the Decalogue in 2:20–23, which
one can transgress (παραβάτης, 2:25, 27). This νόμος is therefore better understood in the
more limited sense of the Sinaitic legislation. Paul is thus saying that the entire sacred corpus, including the Pentateuch (νόμος), witnesses to the revelation of God's righteousness
apart from the law given at Sinai (νόμος).

44. Seifrid, *Christ, Our Righteousness*, 66: "In justifying the sinner God does not set
aside his contention with humanity. He brings it to completion in his own Son." Without
arguing for too specific an interpretation of ἱλαστήριον, this reading assumes that the (pre)-
Pauline usage reflects some conceptual dependence on the atonement traditions associated
with *Yom Kippur*, cf. Lev 16; see K. Haacker, *Der Brief des Paulus an die Römer* (Leipzig:
Evangelische Verlagsanstalt, 1999), 99–100, for a concise review of the interpretative issue.

45. Wilckens, *Römer*, 186: "Die Ausschaltung des Gesetzes bedeutet nicht seine Umge-
hung." This implies that, in this context, law is fulfilled in what has been traditionally called
the "passive obedience" of Christ.

46. Compare R. Bultmann, *Theology of the New Testament*, trans. K. Grobel (Waco, TX:
Baylor University Press, 2007), 1:288–314.

διὰ πίστεως Ἰησοῦ Χριστοῦ (3:22). This is a saving righteousness that moves through—not around—the necessary "no" of judgment to the mysterious and merciful "yes" of justification. The paradox here, as Rudolf Bultmann recognizes, is that the act of justifying grace that reveals God's righteousness apart from law is applied to those whom the justice of the law calls sinners.[47]

No Distinction?

For the epistle, the righteousness of the law (i.e., the Deuteronomic pattern of blessing and curse) means the judgment of sinners and the justification of the righteous. From this perspective, Paul's statement that ἐξ ἔργων νόμου οὐ δικαιωθήσεται πᾶσα σάρξ is an overstatement insofar as the πᾶσα σάρξ ignores the bipartite structure of the law's promise and threat. The epistle is predicated on an anthropological distinction. Justice demands that the righteous are blessed and the wicked are cursed. It is precisely the fact that these two groups exist and yet do not presently correspond to their respective soteriological counterparts that necessitates the writing of the epistle and shapes its announcement of an eschatological reestablishment of the straight lines of Deuteronomic justice.

Not so Paul: οὐ γάρ ἐστιν διαστολή, πάντες γὰρ ἥμαρτον καὶ ὑστεροῦνται τῆς δόξης τοῦ θεοῦ (Rom 3:22b–23). For Paul the problem is not that there is an anthropological distinction which ought to but presently does not correspond to blessings and curses. The problem rather is that there is no distinction: all are, to use the Enochic label, "sinners" (3:9, 23). As such the eschatological reestablishment of the link between sinners and curses for which the epistle longs can only mean universal condemnation (Rom 3:20; cf. Gal 3:10–11).[48] The epistle's solution is Paul's problem. The πᾶσα σάρξ of 3:20 is not an inadvertently one-sided reading of the law's two words. It is the only applicable word of the law to an anthropological situation in which "all sinned" (πάντες ἥμαρτον, 3:23). If, as Paul's apostolic announcement reveals, οὐκ ἔστιν δίκαιος (3:10), then it follows necessarily that ἐξ ἔργων νόμου οὐ δικαιωθήσεται πᾶσα σάρξ (3:20). If there is no anthropological distinction, there can be no soteriological distinction. The justice of the law can only take the form of judgment, never justification.

Such is the Pauline diagnosis: divine justice according to law means universal judgment.[49] Νυνὶ δὲ χωρὶς νόμου δικαιοσύνη θεοῦ πεφανέρωται . . .

---

47. Bultmann, *Theology of the New Testament*, 1:282: "The paradox in 'grace' is that it is precisely *the transgressor, the sinner*, to whom it applies."

48. Haacker, *Der Brief des Paulus an die Römer*, 96: "vor dem Urteil Gottes besteht für Paulus kein Unterschied."

49. See S. Westerholm, *Perspectives Old and New: The "Lutheran" Paul and His Critics* (Grand Rapids: Eerdmans, 2004), 388–90.

δικαιούμενοι δωρεὰν τῇ αὐτοῦ χάριτι. If the gospel reveals the righteousness of God and is "the power of God for salvation (1:16–17), this is its form: it is χωρὶς νόμου and τῇ αὐτοῦ χάριτι. It is a divine justice that justifies those whom, in the first instance, it judges. This triangulation of divine justice, judgment, and justification (cf. 3:26) raises the final and central question.

THE GOD WHO JUSTIFIES WHOM?

The homiletical thrust of the epistle is that the present problem of the apparent justification of the ungodly will give way to the eschatological enactment of divine justice in the form of mercy for the righteous and fitting judgment for the wicked. Put simply (and heuristically): the problem is the present justification of the ungodly; the solution is the eschatological justification of the righteous.

Paul has a different problem. If no one is righteous (3:10) then by works of law no flesh will be justified (3:20). Thus spoke the law. But Paul also has a different gospel: now the righteousness of God apart from law speaks. Its message is one of judgment (3:23) and justification (3:24), of the justification of the judged. The objects of the divine saving action implied in the passive participle δικαιούμενοι (3:24) are the sinners of 3:23.[50] As Dunn remarks, "it is precisely those who have sinned and fallen short of God's glory who are justified."[51] In other words, words that would scandalize the epistle's author, the objects of divine judgment are also the objects of divine justification.[52] The questions the Enochic interlocutor has asked along the way seem to have sensed that the theological momentum initiated by the "but now" was unavoidably moving toward this shocking declaration. "But now" calls the injustices of the present divine justice. "Apart from law" defines divine righteousness independently of its revealed definition. "No distinction" requires divine justice to execute universal judgment. And yet Paul has declared that

50. Following C. E. B. Cranfield, *A Critical and Exegetical Commentary on the Epistle to the Romans*, 2 vols., ICC (Edinburgh: T&T Clark, 1975), 1:205, it is most natural to take as the subject of 3:24 the "all" of 3:23 while recognizing that 3:24 continues the main theme from 3:21–22. D. Campbell, *The Rhetoric of Righteousness in Romans 3.21–26*, JSNTSup (Sheffield: Sheffield Academic Press, 1992), 86–92, is probably correct to see the anthropological statement of 3:23 as an elaboration of the "all the believing ones" of 3:22 such that the subject of the passive form of δικαιόω in 3:24 is doubly qualified by the "all of faith" and the "all who have sinned."

51. J. D. G. Dunn, *Romans 1–8*, WBC 38A (Waco, TX: Word, 1998), 168. So also Wilckens, *Römer*, 1.188: "die Sünde aller also der Ort, an dem die Gottesgerechtigkeit wirksam wird."

52. Bultmann picks up this paradox when he says that "the 'grace of God' is the grace of the judge who rightwises the guilty" (*Theology of the New Testament*, 289).

the gospel which discloses God's righteousness is unto salvation (εἰς σωτηρίαν, 1:16). From an Enochic perspective, the pieces of the Pauline puzzle simply do not fit together. What Paul calls the revelation of divine righteousness, the epistle calls the temporal crisis of empirical injustice. Just as the Enochic promise turned out to be the Pauline problem, so the Pauline gospel takes the shape of the Enochic plight.

It is at this point that our imaginary theological dialogue, however heated along the way, turns into an outright debate. The Enochic apocalypse is fundamentally about the eschatological unveiling of the real. The injustice of the present is less real than the justice of the future precisely because it is injustice rather than justice. In other words, the soteriological judgment implied in the observable flourishing of sinners at the expense of the righteous lacks reality because it is inaccurate. For the epistle, ontology is tied to eschatology because the future judgment promises to be the accurate divine description of reality. Sinners will be called sinners and the righteous will be called righteous and both groups will encounter the appropriate—that is, the just—soteriological consequence. To borrow some terms, the Enochic judgment is analytical and descriptive in that it rightly assesses the objects of its scrutiny and renders a verdict that identifies and recompenses in accordance with the real and the right. The "but then" of the epistle points away from the present to an eschatological future in which divine justice is evident in God's judicial correctness. God, as the judge, gets it right—and that is what's real.

From this perspective, the Pauline announcement of a divine righteousness that justifies the sinner is a theological oxymoron. In a shocking display of forensic schizophrenia, the judge identifies sinners as sinners (3:23) and then immediately overturns this accurate verdict with the seemingly unjust word of justification (3:24). The epistle insists that at the judgment the righteous οὐ μὴ εὑρεθῆτε ὡς οἱ ἁμαρτωλοί (104:5). This, presumably, implies the inverse: sinners will not be found as righteous. But Paul, by linking πάντες ἥμαρτον and δικαιόω, is arguing exactly the opposite: sinners are found as righteous. For Paul, of course, the justice of this apparently unjust justification is tied to a grace that is the atoning death of Jesus that secures the redemption of sinners (3:24–25). From the perspective of the epistle, however, this explanation only takes things from bad to worse. To the Enochic author, Paul's explanation looks like an attempt to justify an act of divine injustice—calling sinners righteous—by grounding it in a prior act of injustice—the death of a righteous person. But two wrongs rarely make a right, and it is wholly unlikely that our Enochic exegete would concede to what would sound like a Pauline claim that two wrongs make God righteous. If Romans 3:23 is correct, then there can be no Romans 3:24. If the divine justice has been revealed, then sinners have been judged. For the epistle, this is the end of the soteriological story.

"But," Paul might appeal to a shared theological conviction, "for the God who resurrects, nothing is the end."[53] As the Enochic author reads Romans 3:21–24, it is the injustice rather than the justice of God that is revealed. The divine judge gets it wrong. Or rather, God gets it wrong (3:24) after getting it right (3:23).[54] This tension is suggestive. What Paul thinks is right, the Enochic author calls wrong. What Paul calls justice, the Enochic author labels injustice. This seems to indicate that we are confronted with two different notions of divine rightness, with two different notions of divine righteousness. The descriptive, accurate justice that defines the epistle's hope is for Paul the righteousness of the law (3:19–20). For the epistle, the enactment of this justice means life for the righteous. For Paul, because no one is righteous (3:10), the enactment of this justice means only death. "But now the righteousness of God has been revealed apart from law." This is a new righteousness, a different righteousness, as peculiar as is it paradoxical. This righteousness is descriptive insofar as it identifies the object of its saving action as a sinner (3:23), but it is declarative and creative in that it renames sinners as the righteous. It is the one diagnosed as a sinner who is declared righteous. The divine righteousness that Paul proclaims locates and labels unrighteousness only in order to create its opposite: πάντες ἥμαρτον . . . δικαιούμενοι.

Slipping in the word "create" here, does, perhaps, move out of Romans 3 into Romans 4. But it does so in order to identity a possible Pauline response to the Enochic charge that Paul's God gets it wrong. If the real is determined by empirical human status, whether ascribed or achieved, then calling sinners righteous is forensically inaccurate and ontologically vapid. But Pauline theology does not anchor reality in the empirical. The God "who justifies the ungodly" (Rom 4:5) is the God "who gives life to the dead and calls nonbeings into being" (4:17). The linking of these liturgical predications of God suggests an analogous form of divine activity in the acts of creation, resurrection, and justification.[55] Justification is an act of the creator. God

53. M. Volf, *Free of Charge: Giving and Forgiving in a Culture Stripped of Grace* (Grand Rapids: Zondervan, 2005), 30.

54. To say that Romans 3:23 is right from the Enochic perspective is not to imply that the epistle would approve of its universalizing diagnosis, but only to note that in identifying sinners as sinners God judges justly.

55. Seifrid, *Christ, Our Righteousness*, 68: "The two characterizations are materially linked: justification is necessarily a *creatio ex nihilo*." See also, Käsemann, *Romans*, 123; Barth, *Romans*, 102.

does not call the sinner righteous even though he or she is not. God calls the sinner righteous and thereby constitutes him or her as such. God's forensic word is right, not because it describes the empirical, but because, as God's word, it establishes reality. Justification, to borrow Simon Gathercole's borrowing of Karl Barth, is *creatio e contrario*—a re-creation of the sinner as the righteous.[56]

In the context of Romans 3:21–26, however, the first movement of this re-creation is an act of de-creation: the judgment of the world in the cross. The justification of the sinner takes place on the far side of judgment. According to the righteous decree of the righteous judge (Rom 2:5; 3:5–6), sinners deserve death (Rom 1:32; cf. 6:23). The cross, at least in the first instance, is the revelation of divine righteousness because it is the enactment of this decree: the death of Christ for sinners is the death of the sinner (cf. Rom 6:3–11; 2 Cor 5:14; Gal 2:20). But the God who judges the ungodly, as the one who raises the dead, also justifies the ungodly. In the eschatological judgment that is the cross, sinners are destroyed. But out of their post-judgment nothingness, the resurrecting God re-creates.

The Pauline apocalypse, like its Enochic counterpart, can be said to reveal the real. But unlike the epistle, this revelation is not located in the accurate eschatological description of reality. It is tied, rather, to a revelation of God's righteous creation of the real. For Paul, reality is a result of divine creativity (Rom 4:17; 11:36). As such, real righteousness is not what people inherit or do but what God, as creator, says. This suggests that the grace of Romans 3:24— the gift that is the ground of the justification of the sinner—is not merely the divine willingness to suffer the injustice of treating sinners "as if" they were righteous. Such a construal would be open to the Enochic critique. But the gift of Christ is an agent of re-creation, God's grace that, in the death of Christ, reveals the rightness of God's presently revealed righteousness as it confronts the sinner and reconstitutes him or her as—not as if, but as—the righteous.

Conclusion

The debate, therefore, is over what we might call diagonal δικαιοσύνη, a divine righteousness that is somehow demonstrated rather than disqualified by the apparent injustice that connects sinners and soteriological blessing.

56. S. J. Gathercole, "The Doctrine of Justification in Paul and Beyond," in *Justification in Perspective: Historical Developments and Contemporary Challenges* (Grand Rapids: Baker Academic, 2006), 219–41.

For the epistle, the observable link between the wicked and the covenantal blessings, implying as it does the inversion of the Deuteronomic formula, raises the fundamental question of divine justice. Responding to this crisis, the author announces a coming judgment in which the diagonal line between sin and blessing will be erased and the straight lines between, on the one hand, righteousness and blessing and, on the other, wickedness and curse will be redrawn (compare 1 En. 103:9–15 with 104:1–6). Put another way, the judgment functions as an act of judicial recalibration which overturns the apparent justification of the ungodly that constitutes the problem of the present. Paul, by contrast, delights in the diagonal. Having eliminated the category of "the righteous" (Rom 1:18–3:20), Paul overcomes the straight line of justice (χωρὶς νόμου, Rom 3:21)—the line that links sinners exclusively with curses and condemnation—with the diagonal tangent of grace (χάρις, Rom 3:24)—the line that links the ungodly with justification (Rom 3:23–24; cf. 4:5). In both cases, the line that connects saving justice with its beneficiaries is conceived of as mercy or grace. But the contrasting recipients of that mercy imply incompatible definitions of the common concept. While the Enochic author locates justice and mercy in the deconstruction of the unjust diagonal that connects sinners and salvation, for Paul the good news of God's righteousness is the revelation that through the gift of Christ God has created out of the opposite: from sin, righteousness and from death, life.

CHAPTER 8

Scandalous and Foolish

DEFINING GRACE WITH PSEUDO-SOLOMON AND ST. PAUL

Without the atonement, the grace of God is a beautiful dream.

—Paul Zahl, *Grace in Practice*

Love in the Ruins. The title of Walker Percy's 1971 novel captures the book's setting and theme—Thomas More's *Utopia* this is not. But the phrase also catches a moment in the marriage of its protagonist, a Dr. Tom More:

"Don't you see" [says his wife] "that people grow away from each other.
. . . We're dead."
"I love you dead. At this moment." . . .
"Dead, dead," she whispered. . . .
"Love," I whispered.[1]

The poignancy of this exchange is the paradox, the surprising where, when, and who of this whispered love: it is *in the Ruins*, "at this moment" of despair, this dead end, and it is "love" for "you"—for the "dead."

The gift that Paul calls "the grace of God" (Rom 5:15; cf. Gal 2:21) is a similar—and no less surprising—embodiment of love. The *Ruins* are "the present evil age" (Gal 1:4), the "moment" is "at the right time, while we were still sinners," and the "you"—the "us"—that God loves there and then are identified, in addition to "sinners," as "weak," "enemies," and "ungodly" (Rom 5:6–10).

If Walker Percy's words give us occasion to pause, Paul's news invited ridicule and incited riots: "scandalous and foolish," taunted his contemporaries (1 Cor 1:23); he has "turned the world upside down," claimed a mob (Acts 17:6).

---

1. W. Percy, *Love in the Ruins* (New York: Picador, 1971), 68.

To feel the surprise of "the word of the cross" (1 Cor 1:18), two aspects of Paul's language of grace need to be brought into focus: grace, as Paul defines and preaches it, is both particular and distinctive. Grace is particular because, for Paul, it is not a given; it is given—it is a specific gift: "the grace of God" is the son "God did not spare, but sent" (Rom 8:32), it is "the son of God who loved me and gave himself for me" (Gal 2:20). And this grace is distinctive because—against the grain of economies of both divine and human giving in Greco-Roman society and early Jewish theology—the gift of Christ is not given to those who are socially, morally, intellectually, or religiously worthy. Rather, strangely and mercifully, Christ is given to the unworthy—to the slave, to the social failure, to the sinner. To speak the Pauline gospel is therefore to announce a gift that is christological and incongruous: God's grace is God's son given at the grave—"I love you dead." But this grace is also an Easter sermon that rolls away the stone: God, says Paul, is the one the who "gives life to the dead" (Rom 4:17).

This chapter is an attempt to hear the scandal and folly of Paul's proclamation of the gift of Christ by listening to Paul in conversation with another emphatic announcement of divine grace: *Wisdom of Solomon*. When Paul insists that "to the one who works, the reward is not reckoned according to grace" (Rom 4:4), it is easy to assume that this is contextual commonsense, a sort of cultural or theological proverb. As this comparison with *Wisdom of Solomon* will suggest, however, Paul's understanding of grace is anomalous rather than obvious. Paul's definition of grace is not taken from the lexicons of his cultural or religious contexts. Rather, Paul's definition of grace is distinctive—it is scandalous and surprising—because it is deduced from and descriptive of God's act of justifying sinners in Jesus Christ.[2]

This chapter is thus an exegetical correlation of two theses about grace: "Grace is one-way love"; and because this grace—so surprising that it comes "unprevented, unimplor'd, unsought" (*Paradise Lost* 3.231)—is grounded in the particular and personal gift of God's son, "Neither can the power of grace be understood except by a description of the gospel."[3]

---

2. For an extended comparison of Romans and *Wisdom of Solomon*, see J. A. Linebaugh *God, Grace, and Righteousness in Wisdom of Solomon and Paul's Letter to the Romans: Texts in Conversation*, NovTSup 152 (Leiden: Brill, 2013). For an understanding of comparison as a relationship that requires engagement and invites response, see chap. 5 of this volume, "Relational Hermeneutics and Comparison as Conversation."

3. Zahl, *Grace*, 36; Philip Melanchthon, *Loci communes theologici* (1521), in *Melanchthon and Bucer*, ed. W. Pauck, trans. L. J. Satre, LCC (Philadelphia: Westminster, 1981), 70. The phrase "one-way love" is borrowed from Zahl's *Grace in Practice: A Theology of Everyday Life* (Grand Rapids: Eerdmans, 2007) and is used in this chapter to define grace as a divine

Congruous and Conditioned Χάρις: *Wisdom* and the Fitting Gift

Wisdom of Solomon is a sermon addressed to sufferers.[4] While it is difficult to reconstruct the socio-historical details alluded to and addressed by *Wisdom*, the tone and content of the pastoral address indicate that whatever the specific *Sitz im Leben*, the occasion was serious enough to generate a series of questions about the stability of the cosmos, the patterns of history, and the past, present, and future justice of God. Into this crisis—a crisis that appears to be characterized by the present flourishing of the ungodly and the suffering of the righteous (Wis 2–5)—the author of *Wisdom* announces a word of hope: the God of illimitable love is immutably just.

For the author of *Wisdom,* sometimes referred to as "Pseudo-Solomon" because the text speaks with the famously wise king's voice (see 9:7–8), the most basic of all realities is that God is just. As 12:15 sings, "You are just and you rule all things justly." Within this song, however, justice (δικαιοσύνη) has a specific definition: God's just rule is evident in the non-condemnation of the righteous (12:15) and the "fitting judgment" of the unrighteous (12:26). Put another way, divine justice is located in the correspondence between the form (wrath or grace) and object (ungodly or righteous) of divine action. For Pseudo-Solomon, the defining event of divine justice is the Red Sea crossing. As the account is retold in *Wisdom* 10:15–21, a humanity divided into "us" and "them" along religious and moral lines (δίκαιοι and ἀσεβεῖς, 10:20) encounters, respectively, deliverance and destruction: "Sophia led the righteous through

---

gift whose giving is neither conditioned by the worth nor disqualified by the absence of the worth of the recipient: grace as one-way love is grace as an incongruous gift. This definition, however, does not entail a denial that God's grace creates a real relationship and so evokes and engenders a response. Much of Zahl's book is an exploration of the thesis that the reality of being loved gives birth to a life of loving (see, e.g., 1 John 4:19; cf. William Cowper's poem, "Love Constraining to Obedience"). For a further consideration of the relationship between God's unconditioned and categorical grace and the "counter-gift of the creature," see O. Bayer, "The Ethics of Gift," *LQ* 24 (2010): 447–68. As Bayer argues, if a "counter-gift" is "understood as a condition" of the gift or as "its *causa finalis,*" then the "gift of response depotentializes the gift." But the "unconditioned and unobligated Giver" is also the creator whose "categorical giving does not exclude the counter-gift of the creature, but rather empowers the creature to [the] counter-gift" of faith and love (458).

4. Hereafter *Wisdom*. The consensus, which is probable though not definitive, places the composition of *Wisdom* in Alexandria between 220 BCE and 50 CE; see C. Larcher, *Le Livre de la Sagesse, ou La Sagesse de Salomon* (Paris: Gabalda, 1983) 1:141–61; D. Winston, *The Wisdom of Solomon*, AB 43 (Garden City, NY: Doubleday, 1979), 20–25; H. Hübner, *Die Weisheit Salomons*, ATD Apokryphen 4 (Göttingen: Vandenhoeck and Ruprecht, 1999), 15–19.

deep waters, but she drowned their enemies" (10:18–19).[5] This paradigmatic event exemplifies the theological confession that God "arranged all things by measure, number, and weight" (11:19) and it anchors the promise that the eschaton will look like the exodus: the injustice of the present will be overturned as the God who acted in the past with grace toward the righteous and wrath toward the unrighteous acts again in accordance with human worth (see Wis 2–5).

The good news according to *Wisdom* is thus an announcement that the end will be like the beginning; or to adapt a prayer: *Wisdom* preaches a sermon to sufferers that says "as it was in the beginning . . . it will be." The good news, in other words, is that God will act with fitting judgment (ἀξίαν θεοῦ κρίσιν, 12:26) and so condemn the ungodly and redeem the righteous. The salvific side of this divide is what *Wisdom* calls "grace" (χάρις).[6] While grace is not synonymous with justice, neither is it antithetical: God's grace operates within the pattern of correspondence that defines God's justice and so exhibits an affinity between God's saving gifts and the worth of their human recipients. For example, in *Wisdom* 4:15, God's χάρις is directed toward "his holy ones" (τοῖς ὁσίοις αὐτοῦ; cf. 3:9), and in 3:14, it is the law-observant and faithful eunuch to whom God gives (δίδωμι) God's χάρις. In both cases the justness of God's beneficence is displayed in the identifiable congruence between benefit and beneficiary.

It is important to observe, however, that within *Wisdom*'s theology—and in keeping with the social and theological patterns of *Wisdom*'s cultural and religious contexts—the justice of grace in no way disqualifies the graciousness of grace. Seneca, in his famous treaties on gift (*De Beneficiis* 1.15.6), and Philo (e.g., *Post.* 142–47) both insist that it is the absence of a careful and discriminate matching between gift and recipient that renders a gift a non-gift. The conceptual context for *Wisdom*'s grace discourse is the social and theological realm of "gift," and as Seneca and Philo indicate, in this frame of reference gifts are properly gifts when they are carefully distributed to the worthy or fitting (*dingus* in Seneca's Latin and ἄξιος in Philo's Greek).[7] Within this pattern of gift exchange, a gift is a gift because it is voluntary rather than contractual and unearned in the sense of not being the payment of wages. As Philo reads

5. For *Wisdom*'s anthropological distinction between Israel and the nations as the difference between non-idolatry and idolatry, see chap. 6, "Announcing the Human."

6. God's love (ἀγαπάω, 11:24) and mercy (ἐλεέω, 11:23) are said to extend to the objects of God's judgment, but this mercy, rather than saving the ungodly, takes the form of decelerated destruction (12:8–11; cf. 12:2).

7. For χάρις in conjunction with the ἄξιο- word group in Philo, see, e.g., *Cher.* 84; *Somn.* 2.177; *Deus* 104–10; *Leg.* 3.14, 27, 164; *Mut.* 52, 58, 268; *Spec.* 1.43; 2.219; *Mos.* 2.242.

the story of the five daughters of Zelophehad (Num 27:1–11), although they are "considered worthy" (ἀξιόω), the χάρις which they receive is emphatically not a payment (οὐδ' ἀποδώσεις) but "a gift" (δόμα).[8] And yet the principle of justice—the bedrock conviction that righteousness operates "according to worth" (κατ' ἀξίαν)—demands that the human beneficiaries of God's grace are in some sense a worthy or fitting recipient, thus ensuring that the gift-loving God (φιλόδωρος, see, e.g., *Conf.* 182; *Leg.* 3.166), rather than being capricious or chaotic, is stable, just, and good.[9]

This theological concern to maintain the fundamental and unalterable justice of God shapes *Wisdom*'s celebration of divine grace. For *Wisdom*, Sophia or Lady Wisdom is God's ultimate gift (ἡ χάρις, 8:21), and precisely as χάρις, Sophia operates within the parameters of the just cosmic and moral order she established and sustains (7:22). This means, in exodus-like fashion, she avoids the ungodly (1:4; cf. 7:25) and associates with the righteous (6:12; 7:27; 10:4, 5, 6, 10, 13). As Sophia's repeated rescue of the righteous characters from Genesis exemplifies in *Wisdom*'s telling (10:1–14), she "delivers from trouble those who serve her" (10:9) and, even more basically, "seeks those who are worthy (ἄξιος) of her" (6:16). This single criterion of "worth" or "fittingness" (ἄξιος) can be met by a variety of human actions directed toward Sophia: for instance, seeking (6:12, 17; 8:2), desiring (6:13, 17, 20; 8:2), requesting (7:7; 8:21; 9:1–18), loving (6:12, 17; 8:2), serving (10:9). But in every instance of divine benefaction there is an identifiable point of correspondence between God's gift and the worth of the human recipient. This does not mean that saving grace is accomplished by human worth. But it does mean that while it is emphatically Sophia who saves (τῇ σοφίᾳ ἐσώθησαν, 9:18), her saving benevolence is for the worthy. In other words, while the moral, social, or intellectual fittingness of the human cannot be properly called the cause of grace, such fittingness is a condition of grace: God's grace, according to *Wisdom*, is conditioned and characterized by correspondence—God's gifts are congruent with the worth of their recipients.

This pattern is evident in the two paradigmatic moments of divine grace. First, in the case of Solomon, his attainment of Sophia came as a genuine gift (χάρις) and required an authentic act of divine giving (δίδωμι, 8:21). This gift, however, was conditioned by correspondence: Solomon was a suitable recipi-

---

8. *De Vita Mosis* 2.242. Philo, like *Wisdom* (see the discussion of Wis 10:17 below) is able to refer to divine χάρις as a reward (γεραίροντος) for the pious (e.g., *Praem.* 126). But, also like *Wisdom*, this does not signal a transition to a pay-economy; it indicates the congruence or fit between gift and recipient.

9. For Philo's insistence that justice, by definition, operates "according to worth" (κατ' ἀξίαν, see, e.g., *Leg.* 1.87; *Mos.* 2.9).

ent of Sophia because he was good (ἀγαθὸς ὤν, 8:20). Similarly, and in terms of the forthcoming comparison with Paul more significantly, *Wisdom*'s narration of the Red Sea crossing depicts the beneficiaries of Sophia's rescue as a "holy people and blameless race" (λαὸν ὅσιον καὶ σπέρμα ἄμεμπτον, 10:21). For *Wisdom* this is the paradigmatic moment of justice, the climatic event of mercy for Israel and judgment upon the Egyptians. And it is this saving act of Sophia— this grace of God—that *Wisdom* 10:17 describes as a "reward" (μισθός, 10:17) for their labors. This succinctly captures *Wisdom*'s understanding of grace: the exodus event is an unearned and divinely given deliverance (it is grace); but because the God of the exodus is "just and rules all things justly," God's rescue is reserved for the righteous—not primarily because they are righteous, but because God is righteous. It is this bedrock conviction about the goodness and ultimate justice of God that determines *Wisdom*'s definition of grace: the God who is good and gracious is not arbitrary or unfair; God is just and so grace is necessarily defined and conditioned by a correspondence between gift and recipient. Grace, according to *Wisdom*, is God giving—abundantly, generously, savingly. And grace, because God is "just and rules all things justly," is God giving fittingly, giving to those whose worth is congruent with God's gifts.

Incongruous and Unconditioned Χάρις: Paul and the Unfitting Gift of Christ

"To the one who works, the reward (μισθός) is not reckoned according to grace" (χάρις, Rom 4:4). Returning to these words from *Wisdom*'s depiction of the saving grace of the exodus as a reward (μισθός) for Israel's labors (Wis 10:17), Paul's claim no longer sounds like contextual commonsense. To put Paul's insistence that a reward for work is not grace next to *Wisdom*'s description of the gracious rescues at the Red Sea as a "reward for labor" (μισθὸν κόπων αὐτῶν, Wis 10:17) is to read Romans 4:4 as a surprise. If, as listening to *Wisdom* indicates, it is not axiomatic or proverbial to say that a reward for work is not grace, why does Paul make this categorical claim? If the definition of grace articulated in Romans 4:4 is not a given, where does Paul's redefinition of grace come from?

One indication of an answer to this question comes in the antithesis between Romans 4:4 and 4:5. Grace is not reward for work; grace is the justification of the ungodly. This is a provocation, not an *a priori*. To identify the God of Abraham as the one who "justifies the ungodly" is not, as James Dunn suggests, to "restate a theologoumenon."[10] Read in dialogue with *Wisdom*'s notion of fitting grace—of grace that is conditioned and characterized by correspon-

---

10. J. D. G. Dunn, *The Theology of Paul the Apostle* (Grand Rapids: Eerdmans, 1998),

dence—Paul's definition of grace as the justification of the ungodly sounds, to let *Wisdom* quote Paul against Paul, "scandalous and foolish" because it cuts the congruence between God's gifts and their human recipients that ensures that in grace God is just. But it is just here, at the point of potential tension between justice and grace, that Paul's dangerous definition of grace shows itself to be deduced from an event that compels him to confess God as the "one who justifies the ungodly" (Rom 4:5). The antithesis between Romans 4:4 and 4:5, together with the new definition of grace that it announces, point back to the specific gift that grounds it, to the grace that Paul calls "the redemption that is in Christ Jesus" (Rom 3:24).

Romans 2:11–3:20, in part, operates within *Wisdom*'s theological cosmos. Romans 2:6–10, 13 describe a judgment according to the criterion of correspondence: "God will repay each person according to (κατά + accusative) their works" (2:6); and again, "it is the doers of the law who will be justified" (2:13). For Paul, however, the revelation of unrighteousness—the reality that "all are under sin" and "not one is righteous" (3:9–10; 1:18)—means that the soteriological conclusion of correspondence can only be condemnation: "by works of law no flesh will be justified" (3:20). It is out of this ineluctable movement from the criterion of correspondence to universal condemnation that Paul announces the impossible: "But now, apart from law, the righteousness of God is revealed. . . . All sinned . . . and are justified freely by his grace through the redemption that is in Christ Jesus" (Rom 3:21, 23–24).

For *Wisdom*, the righteousness or justice of God is evident in the correspondence between the form and object of God's action: God delivers the righteous and judges the ungodly. From this vantage point, Romans 3:21–24, to quote Immanuel Kant, can only sounds like a "moral outage," a proclamation that promises, in Nietzsche's phrase, "a revaluation of all antique values."[11] Rather than locating "the righteousness of God" (δικαιοσύνη θεοῦ) in the congruence between the righteous and God's declaration of righteousness, Paul announces what Alan Badiou calls "an unheard-of possibility," a righteousness that is revealed in the disjunction between sin and salvation (πάντες ἥμαρτον . . . δικαιούμενοι).[12] This is a daring deduction. A received defini-

---

367. For the repeated prohibition against justifying the ungodly, see Exod 23:7; Prov 17:15; 24:24; Isa 5:3; Sir 9:12; CD 1.19.

11. I. Kant, *Religion within the Limits of Reason Alone* (New York: Harper & Row, 1960), 164; F. Nietzsche, *Beyond Good and Evil: Prelude to a Philosophy of the Future*, trans. R. J. Hollingdale (London: Penguin Books, 1973), 75.

12. Following C. E. B. Cranfield, *A Critical and Exegetical Commentary on the Epistle to the Romans*, 2 vols., ICC (Edinburgh: T&T Clark, 1975), 1:205, I take the "all" of 3:23 as the

tion of justice might assume the affinity and order between inheritance and achievement, on the one hand, and status and worth, on the other.[13] But Paul sees the meaning of God's justice revealed (φανερόω, Rom 3:21) in an event that calls sinners righteous—an event that is simultaneously the demonstration (ἔνδειξις, 3:25–26) of God's own righteousness and the defining moment of God's grace (δικαιούμενοι δωρεὰν τῇ αὐτοῦ χάριτι, 3:24). God, incongruously, gives Christ at the site of sin and death; and God, impossibly, creates righteousness and life.

The basic incommensurability between Pseudo-Solomon and St. Paul sits on this christological fault-line. In *Wisdom* the exodus is the paradigmatic exemplification of justice and grace because it instantiates the pattern of correspondence Sophia built into the cosmos. In Romans, by contrast, the justice and grace of God are not ideas or even divine dispositions that can be illustrated. Rather, justice and grace are mutually interpreting ways of describing the death of Jesus and the redemption and righteousness it accomplishes. In Rudolf Bultmann's words, "Righteousness . . . has its origin in God's grace—i.e., in His act of grace accomplished in Christ."[14] It is from this "act of grace"—from the incongruous giving of Jesus for the justification of the ungodly—that Paul's definition of grace in Romans 4:4–5 is derived. As Karl Barth observed, for Paul, "Grace is the gift of Christ," and it is because this gift is characterized by contradiction rather than a correspondence between benefit and recipient that Paul redefines grace in antithesis to reward and as the justification of the ungodly.[15] Paul does not insist that a reward (μισθός) for work is not grace (χάρις) because such claim is true by definition. Rather he cuts the connection between μισθός and χάρις because the "Christ-gift" is an instance of incongruous grace: it is given to sinners.[16] Romans 4:4–5, in other words, does not argue from a definition of grace. It argues for a definition of grace, one that is deduced from the disjunctive declaration that Christ's cross is the enactment of God's judgment

---

subject of 3:24. See A. Badiou, *Saint Paul: The Foundation of Universalism*, trans. R. Brassier (Stanford, CA: Stanford University Press, 2003), 43.

13. For the persistence of this understanding and order, see, e.g., Aristotle (*Eth. Nic.* 2.1.4) and Jean-Paul Sartre, *Existentialism and Humanism*, trans. P. Mairet (London: Methuen, 1949), 28: "man is nothing else but that which he makes of himself."

14. R. Bultmann, *Theology of the New Testament*, trans. K. Grobel (Waco, TX: Baylor University Press, 2007), 284.

15. K. Barth, *The Epistle to the Romans*, trans. E. C. Hoskyns (Oxford: Oxford University Press, 1933), 31.

16. For the phrase "Christ-gift," see J. M. G. Barclay, "Grace within and beyond Reason: Philo and Paul in Dialogue," in *Paul, Grace and Freedom: Essays in Honour of John K. Riches*, ed. P. Middleton, A. Paddison, and K. Wenell (London: T&T Clark, 2009), 17.

upon sin and also—strangely and scandalously—the justification of the sinner (Rom 3:25–26). This is both what Eberhard Jüngel calls "the deepest secret of God's righteousness" and what Bultmann describes as "the paradox of grace" because "it is precisely the transgressor, the sinner, to whom it applies."[17]

It is this paradox that Paul parades in Romans 5:6–10. The gift to which Romans 5:15–17 refers is named in Romans 5:6–10. It is the justifying (5:9) and disjunctive (5:6–8) death of Christ. As in Romans 3:23–24, it is the recipients of grace that signal its surprise. The grammar of 5:6–8 makes this point. The explanatory γάρ that opens Romans 5:7 promises an explication of the claim of Romans 5:6, but the adversative δέ of Romans 5:8 indicates that this explanation is made by way of antithesis: the grace which Paul proclaims is not self-sacrifice for the righteous or the good.[18] As with Romans 4:4, however, this antithesis is not obvious. Rather than being something other than grace, the "gift of death" for noble persons and righteous causes was regularly regarded as the epitome of benefaction.[19] But this is merely to raise again the question about the peculiarly Pauline definition of χάρις: if self-sacrifice for the righteous or good is celebrated as gracious, why does Paul contrast (δέ) divine grace with this hypothetical act of heroism (5:7)? The answer is not that the gift of one's life for a worthy person cannot be a gift. The answer is that *the gift* is not a death for the righteous or the good. *The gift* is Christ crucified for the ungodly (5:6).

In antithesis to the fitting gift of Romans 5:7, Paul announces the utter incongruity of God's grace in Christ. The *kairos* of the cross—the fact that Christ died for the ungodly while they were still (ἔτι) ungodly—excludes the possibility of prior human worth as it announces, in Ernst Käsemann's words, "Christ did his saving work at an unexpected and, morally considered, even inappropriate moment."[20] "Christ died for the ungodly," writes Calvin, "when we were in no way worthy (*dignus*) or fit (*idoneus*)."[21] Entering the "still" (ἔτι) of history east of Eden (5:12–19), the gift of Christ cannot come as a "correspondingly." It comes as a

---

17. E. Jüngel, *Justification: The Heart of Christian Faith*, trans. J. F. Cayzer (London: T&T Clark, 2001), 87; Bultmann, *Theology of the New Testament*, 282.

18. Jewett, *Romans*, 360.

19. Jewett, *Romans*, 360n158, cites Isocrates, *Arch.* 107; Lycurgus, *Leoc.* 86.2; Philo, *Agr.* 3.156; Diodorus Siculus, *Hist.* 9.2.6.3; cf. Plato, *Apology* 32a; Dio Cassius, 80.20; Sir 4:28; 1 Clem. 55:1. The phrase "the gift of death" is taken from the title of Derrida's essay on gift, *The Gift of Death* (Chicago: University of Chicago Press, 1995).

20. E. Käsemann, *Commentary on Romans*, trans. G. W. Bromiley (Grand Rapids: Eerdmans, 1980), 137.

21. Calvin, *Romans*, 195. Benefits given to those who are not *dignus* is exactly the social problem Seneca's *De beneficiis* attempts to redress (cf. 1.1.2).

"nevertheless."²² Rather than locating the worthy (as Sophia does in Wis 6:16), the grace Paul announces encounters the ungodly (ἀσεβής, 5:6), the sinner (ἁμαρτω-λός, 5:8), and the enemy (ἐχθρός, 5:10), and renames its receipts *e contrario*: out of sin, righteousness (5:9); out of enmity, reconciliation (5:10).²³

The tension with *Wisdom* is acute. Paul locates the demonstration of divine love (5:8) and righteousness (3:21) in a gift given to those whom *Wisdom* consistently depicts as the fitting recipients of divine judgment. While the righteous are rescued, their ungodly (ἀσεβής, 10:20) and sinful (ἁμαρτωλός, 19:13) enemies (ἐχθρός, 10:19) are destroyed. Paul can grant the deservedness of this destruction (τὰ ὀψώνια τῆς ἁμαρτίας θάνατος, Rom 6:23a; cf. 1:32), but the gift he announces does not "fit": it is given to those whose proper payment is death, but the incongruous gift (χάρις) is eternal life in Christ Jesus (6:23b). It is thus, in *Wisdom*'s terms, those who are the fitting objects of God's judgment (death) who are identified by Paul as the recipients of God's unfitting grace (life).

Pseudo-Solomon is a theologian of grace. But not this grace. This is something new: a sermon for the sufferers and also for sinners that announces the miracle of God's incongruous and life-giving grace rather than the common-sense of correspondence that leads only to condemnation. For Paul, the death of Jesus for the justification of sinners and the liberation of captives is the gift (Rom 3:24). It is the cross, with the redemption and the righteousness it effects, that grounds Paul's radical redefinition. As Martin Luther might say, "omnia vocabula in Christo novam significationem accipere."²⁴ From the incongruous giving of God's son, Paul derives his surprising definition: grace is not conditioned by any human canons of worth; grace is Jesus Christ given to the unworthy—to those in bondage and under sin. And this grace, the particular and personal gift that is the crucified and risen Christ given into the nothingness of slavery, sin, and death, creates freedom, righteousness, and life.

THE GOSPEL OF GRACE

This chapter opened by saying that it would correlate two theses about grace: "Grace is one-way love" and "Neither can the power of grace be understood ex-

22. K. Barth, *Christ and Adam: Man and Humanity in Romans 5*, trans. T. A. Smail (Edinburgh: Oliver and Boyd, 1956), 2: "In the death of Christ God has intervened on our behalf in the 'nevertheless' of His free grace."

23. As Cranfield suggests, the eschatological salvation of those whom God calls righteous is "very easy" when compared to the "really difficult thing" that is the creative and incongruous gift that grounds this renaming (*Romans*, 1:266).

24. M. Luther, *Disputatio de divinitate et humanitate Christi* (1540; WA 39/2:94).

cept by a description of the gospel."[25] These two theses are forced together by the incompatible understandings of grace articulated by *Wisdom* and Paul: the Pauline definition of grace is strange—its incongruous shape stands out—because the Pauline definition of grace is derived from and is finally "a description of the gospel" that announces and gives God's son despite human unworthiness.

E. P. Sanders's 1977 book, *Paul and Palestinian Judaism*, was a watershed. As Sanders demonstrates, Pauline scholarship had long operated with an antithetical understanding of the relationship between early Judaism and Pauline Christianity: the former, according to this configuration, exhibits a soteriology of Selbsterlösung, whereas the latter preaches a gospel of Gnadenerlösung. Sanders, who set out "to destroy" this "view" and "to establish a different view," offers a fundamentally different portrait: "on the point at which many have found the decisive contrast between Paul and Judaism—grace and works— Paul is in agreement with Judaism."[26] This conclusion created something of a shibboleth: "Christianity and Judaism are both religions of grace." *Wisdom*'s sermon to sufferers is certainly an emphatic announcement of God's grace, and Sanders's corrective was both necessary and constructive: the pages of early Jewish texts are flooded with celebrations and proclamations of the grace of God. The problem, however, as the juxtaposition of *Wisdom* and Paul has uncovered, is that grace is not a univocal concept. It is one thing to note that there is little difference between Paul and other early Jewish texts in terms of the degree of grace, but that leaves unexplored the question of the definition of grace. Sanders, for instance, assume a definition of grace: grace is "groundless," "free," and "unmerited."[27] This same tendency is evident in James Dunn's remark that after Sanders early Judaism "can now be seen to preach good Protestant doctrine: that grace is always prior; that human effort is ever the response to divine initiative; that good works are the fruit and not the root of salvation."[28] A gift that is unconditioned and incongruous—"one-way love," to borrow Zahl's formulation—it seems, has been presupposed to be the one, the only, and the obvious meaning of grace.

25. Zahl, *Grace*, 36; Melanchthon, *Loci communes theologici* (1521), 70.

26. E. P. Sanders, *Paul and Palestinian Judaism: A Comparison of Patterns of Religion* (Minneapolis: Fortress, 1977), xii, 543.

27. Sanders, *Paul and Palestinian Judaism*, 394–96.

28. J. D. G. Dunn, "The Justice of God: A Renewed Perspective on Justification by Faith," in *The New Perspective on Paul*, rev. ed. (Grand Rapids: Eerdmans, 2005), 199. For a further example of an assumed definition of grace, see D. A. Carson, "Divine Sovereignty and Human Responsibility in Philo," *NovT* 23 (1981): 148–64, who "corrects" Philo's phrase "worthy of grace" with an incredulous "*sic*" because the phrase is a "fusion of opposites" (160–62).

But this is what the comparison of *Wisdom* and Romans indicates is categorically not the case. For *Wisdom*, grace is unearned, but never ungrounded; grace is not payment, but it can be called reward; grace is free, but always conditioned; grace is benevolent, but not incongruous with the worth of its recipient. This requires an analysis that is not, in the first instance, focused on the question of degree but on the question of definition: the crucial point of comparison is not the quantity of or even the emphasis on grace; the core question is about the character and content of grace.

This line of comparative questioning opens a new possibility: *Wisdom* and Paul both proclaim God's grace (à la Sanders), but the grace they proclaim is understood differently (*pace* Sanders). To define grace as an incongruous gift is not to speak from an available dictionary or to repeat a proverb. It is to follow Paul as he daringly—and from *Wisdom*'s perspective, dangerously—derives a new definition of grace from the gift of God's Son: the son "God did not spare, but gave" (Rom 8:32), the son who "loved me and gave himself for me" (Gal 2:20). The surprising character of this grace—incongruity—is grounded in the specific content of this grace—Jesus Christ.[29]

Paul Zahl, like Paul the apostle, offers a startlingly definition of grace: "Grace is one-way love. That is the definition of grace."[30] What this means, for Zahl, is that God's gift of Christ bestows rather than responds to or rewards human worth; it is a gift given not according to but in the absence of prior markers of social or moral value. Like St. Paul's christological definition of grace, however, this understanding of grace is not an *a priori*. It is, as this essay's epigram shows, anchored in the atonement: "Without the atonement, the grace of God is a beautiful dream."[31] But this dream has become news: "God's grace exists in relation to the human world" as one-way love "because of . . . Christ's final love on the cross."[32] This is a definition of grace that *Wisdom*, as 1 Corinthians 1:23 suggests, would regard as scandalous and foolish. But it is a definition of grace deduced from that one thing St. Paul determined to know: "Christ and him crucified" (1 Cor 2:2).

---

29. This essay was written before the publication of John Barclay's *Paul and the Gift* (Grand Rapids: Eerdmans, 2015), but Barclay captures this comparative and christological dynamic: "grace is everywhere in the theology of Second Temple Judaism, but not everywhere the same" (565). For Barclay, Paul's distinctive "perfection" of grace—"incongruity," or the mismatch between God's gifts and the unworthiness of their recipients—is derived from the particular grace that is "the Christ-gift, given without regard to worth" (6; cf. 565).
30. Zahl, *Grace*, 36.
31. Zahl, *Grace*, 114.
32. Zahl, *Grace*, 258.

The "word of the cross," it seems, is forever spoken as a surprise. It is something other than what Bob Dylan calls "the song you strum," the "weary tune" that weighs a person's worth according to their pedigree or their past, the record of what the *Book of Common Prayer* calls "things done and left undone." The gospel, rather, invites us to "rest yourself 'neath the strength of strings" that whisper what Thomas Cranmer calls the "comfortable words": the gift of Christ is not indexed to but is given in the absence of any human tokens of worth. God's grace calls the poor, the low, the weak, the foolish (1 Cor 1:26–29); Christ is given to the sinner, the ungodly, the enemy (Rom 5:6–10). To borrow Walker Percy's language, it is "at this moment" of sin and fear and "in the ruins" of bondage and death that God gives the crucified and risen Christ who justifies and gives peace, who sets free and makes alive. Used to describe this pattern of giving, incongruity points in two directions: it identifies the contradiction between the content of God's gift and the condition of its recipients even as it signals the impossible overcoming of that contradiction and that condition: enemies are reconciled, the abandoned and alone are adopted, those in captivity are redeemed, the ungodly are called righteous, and the dead, by grace, are summoned from the grave. In Luther's words, "the love of God does not find but creates that which is pleasing to it."[33] What God finds, according to Paul's diagnosis, is the nothingness of bondage, sin, and death. What God's love creates—incongruously and impossibly—is freedom, righteousness, and life. If Luther had read Walker Percy, he may have put it like this: "'Dead, dead,' whispered the law. 'Love,' whispered the gospel." But this love that is the incongruous grace of God also whispers, "Wake." It says, "I love you dead," and it also shouts, "rise from the dead and Christ will shine on you" (Eph 5:14).

---

33. LW 31:41; WA 1:354–35: "Amor dei non invenit, sed creat suum diligibile."

PART THREE

Reading Paul with Readers of Paul

CHAPTER 9

THE GRAMMAR OF THE GOSPEL

JUSTIFICATION AS A THEOLOGICAL CRITERION IN THE REFORMATION AND IN PAUL'S LETTER TO THE GALATIANS

Theology is a grammar of the language of Holy Scripture.

—Johann Georg Hamann

"The Reformation fought and conquered in the name of Paul."[1] So begins Albert Schweitzer's *Paul and His Interpreters*. As the subtitle to the English translation suggests, however, this is a "critical history," and Schweitzer's opening is both a critique of the Reformers and a diagnosis of Pauline scholarship: "Reformation exegesis reads its own ideas into Paul, in order to receive them back again clothed with Apostolic authority" and "the study [of Paul] continues to be embarrassed by a considerable remnant of the prepossessions with which the interpretation of Paul's doctrine was approached in the days of the Reformation."[2] The only way behind this apostle of Reformation faith and back to the Paul of history, as Schweitzer told the story, was for "the spell which dogma had laid upon exegesis to be broken."[3]

For Schweitzer, dispelling Reformation dogma meant, in part, demoting the doctrine of justification from its reformational rank of *articulus stantis et cadentis ecclesiae* to being "merely a fragment of a doctrine of redemption."[4] William Wrede had already insisted that justification was Paul's *Kampfeslehre*, a polemical teaching that Paul used to argue against the imposition of the

1. A. Schweitzer, *Paul and His Interpreters: A Critical History*, trans. W. Montgomery (New York: Schocken Books, 1964), 2.
2. Schweitzer, *Paul and His Interpreters*, 2, 33.
3. Schweitzer, *Paul and His Interpreters*, 2.
4. A. Schweitzer, *The Mysticism of Paul the Apostle*, trans. W. Montgomery (New York: Seabury, 1931), 220–21.

Jewish law onto the religious lives of his gentile converts.[5] Krister Stendhal later extended Wrede's thesis: "justification by faith was hammered out by Paul for the very specific and limited purpose of defending the rights of Gentile converts."[6] For E. P. Sanders, like Schweitzer before him, the "real bite of Paul's theology"—the originating hub—is not justification but rather "the participatory categories" that express the christological interpretation of the triumph of God.[7]

In each case, this decentering of justification—its movement from *die Mitte* to the margins of Paul's theology—is part of Schweitzer's summons to break the spell of Reformation dogma. Wrede's concern was that too many readings of Paul were filtered through "die Seelenkämpe Luthers."[8] For Stendahl, "we all, in the West, and especially in the tradition of the Reformation cannot help reading Paul through the experience of persons like Luther or Calvin. And this is the chief reason for most of our misunderstanding."[9] In Sanders's words, "Luther's problems were not Paul's, and we misunderstand him if we see him through Luther's eyes."[10] For Wrede, and especially for Schweitzer, Stendahl, and Sanders, exegesis is a way of exorcizing the spirits of the Reformation.

This dethronement of the Reformation's doctrinal *rex* continues to pose a question to readers of Paul: What is the "center" of Paul's theology?[11] Faced with the range of cultural-religious caches from which Paul's language seems to spring, readers of the Pauline letters are forced to ask if and how the different linguistic registers cohere and whether a particular tradition-historical back-

5. W. Wrede, "Paulus," in *Das Bild des Paulus in der neueren deutschen Forschung*, ed. K. H. Rengstorf, WdF 24 (Darmstadt: Wissenschaftliche Buchgesellschaft, 1982), 69, 71. The *Religionsgeschichtliche Schule* tended to marginalize justification because its Jewish origins failed to match their identification of the Hellensitic mystery cults as the religio-historical background to Paul. It is worth noting in this regard that Käsemann's reassertion of the significance of Paul's *Rechtfertigungslehre* included an argument for Jewish apocalyptic, and particularly that tradition's understanding of the "righteousness of God," as the conceptual wellspring for Paul's theology of justification, "'The Righteousness of God' in Paul," in *New Testament Questions Today*, trans. W. J. Montague (London: SCM, 1969), 168–82; cf. E. Käsemann, "Die Anfänge christlicher Theologie," ZTK 57 (1960): 162–85.

6. K. Stendhal, *Paul among Jews and Gentiles* (Philadelphia: Fortress, 1976), 2.

7. E. P. Sanders, *Paul and Palestinian Judaism: A Comparison of Patterns of Religion* (Minneapolis: Fortress, 1977), 5, 502, 549.

8. Wrede, "Paulus," 42.

9. Stendahl, *Paul among Jews and Gentiles*, 12.

10. E. P. Sanders, *Paul: A Very Short Introduction* (Oxford: Oxford University Press, 1991), 53, 57–58.

11. See, e.g., R. P. Martin, "Center of Paul's Theology," in *The Dictionary of Paul and His Letters*, ed. G. Hawthorne, R. P. Martin, and D. Reid (Downers Grove, IL: InterVarsity, 1993), 92–95, and J. Plevnik, "The Center of Paul's Theology," CBQ 51 (1989): 460–78.

ground and/or soteriological metaphor functions as a kind of hermeneutical hub—the center of the Pauline wheel from which the various spokes radiate. Put this way, the elevation of one context or image can appear arbitrary. Why the legal language of righteousness rather than the political and military motif of reconciliation? Why the participatory image of being in Christ rather than the liberative metaphor of redemption? Why the cultic language of temple sacrifice and atonement rather than the legal and familial vocabulary of adoption?[12] Not surprisingly, some have refused to pick one from the list, either denying the coherence of Paul's theology,[13] or locating it in something more general like "the triumph of God"[14] or "the kerygmatic story of God's action through Jesus Christ."[15]

But perhaps there is a way through this post-Schweitzer stalemate. Prompted by a line in Luther, the eighteenth-century provocateur Johann Georg Hamann wrote, "theology is a grammar of the language of Holy Scripture."[16] If we let this sentence reframe our research, the question is not so much which image, linguistic register, lexical set, or religio-historical context is the "center" of Paul's theology. Rather the question is: Does Paul write all his words and metaphors according to a common grammar? Do the sentences that draw on diverse conceptual traditions share a shape? Is there a Pauline pattern of speech, an evangelical grammar, that governs the way the words run when sentences speak the Pauline gospel? The various vocabularies Paul employs throughout his letters are united in the single apostolic task of preaching "the gospel of Christ" (Gal 1:7). Different vocabulary emphatically does not entail a different gospel, for as Paul seems to shout in Galatians, a "different gospel" is in fact "no gospel" (1:6–9). A new question then: what is the grammar of the Pauline gospel? An old answer: justification.

12. Among those who have argued for the centrality of justification in Paul are M. A. Seifrid, *Justification by Faith: The Origin and Development of a Central Pauline Theme* (Leiden: Brill, 1992), and H. Hübner, "Pauli Theologiae Proprium," *NTS* 26 (1980): 445–73.

13. H. Räisänen, "Paul's Theological Difficulties with the Law," in *Studia Biblica 1978* (Sheffield: JSOT Press, 1980), 3:301–20.

14. J. C. Beker, *Paul the Apostle: The Triumph of God in Life and Thought* (Philadelphia: Fortress, 1980).

15. R. B. Hays, "Crucified with Christ: A Synthesis of 1 and 2 Thessalonians, Philemon, Philippians, and Galatians," in *SBL Literature 1988 Seminar Papers*, ed. D. J. Lull (Atlanta: Scholars Press, 1988), 324.

16. J. G. Hamann, *Sämtliche Werke*, 6 vols., ed. J. Nadler (Vienna: Herder, 1949–57), 2:129, 7–9. Hamann passed the "remarkable quote from Luther" onto his brother in a letter from 1760. Luther's words, which Hamann encountered in Bengel's *Gnomon*, were "Theology is nothing but a grammar of the words of the Holy Spirit"; see Johann Georg Hamann, *Briefwechsel*, ed. W. Ziesemer and A. Henkel, 8 vols. (Wiesbaden: Insel Verlag, 1956), 2:10, 2–8.

To make this case in relation to Galatians, I will make recourse to the Reformation dogma that Schweitzer tried to dispel. First, I will revisit the Reformation claim that justification is the "lord, ruler, and judge of every kind of doctrine" and argue, mostly with reference to Luther, that such rhetoric does not deny the polemical function of justification in Paul, nor does it imply that justification is the exclusive or even primary vocabulary of the gospel. Rather this is a grammatical argument from the "not, but" structure of Paul's justification formulae, a claim that justification—specifically justification "not by works of law" but "by faith in Christ"—functions as an evangelical criterion: it says "no" to not-gospels while norming the saying of the gospel.[17] With this understanding of the function of justification in view, I will, second, turn to Galatians in an effort to sketch the grammar of justification in Galatians 2:16 and argue that the "not, but" grammar of justification relates to the rest of the letter as both a critical and hermeneutical criterion: it functions critically to enable Paul to identify other- or not-gospels (Gal 1:6–7), and hermeneutically to give the grammar according to which he proclaims "the gospel of Christ" (Gal 1:7).[18]

RECTOR ET IUDEX: JUSTIFICATION IN REFORMATION RHETORIC

"It is well-known that the . . . reformers proclaimed [justification] as the doctrine by which the church 'stands or falls.' It is, one fears, not so well-known why they would have done so."[19] Robert Jenson wrote these words in 1978, but they still invite an under-asked question: What did the reformers mean when they said

17. In G. A. Lindbeck's terms, justification is criteriological not because the juridical metaphor it evokes should be privileged over other soteriological images, but because of the way its "grammar . . . informs the way the story [of the gospel] is told," *The Nature of Doctrine: Religion and Theology in a Postliberal Age* (Philadelphia: Westminster, 1984), 80. This requires a distinction between identifying justification as criterological because of its grammar and because of its metaphor. See, e.g., E. Jüngel, *Justification: The Heart of the Christian Faith*, trans. J. F. Cayzer (London: T&T Clark, 2001), 48: "the doctrine of justification has this strength of a hermeneutical category because it brings all of theology in the dimension of a legal dispute." This chapter is making only the former (grammatical) claim, which means that other instances of this antithetical and christological grammar in Paul's letters (e.g., the identification as Christ as "our wisdom" in exclusionary contrast to human wisdom in 1 Cor 1:18–30) do not need to be read as derived from justification, but rather as parallel instances of the same grammar.

18. It is worth noting that an appendix to the *Joint Declaration on the Doctrine of Justification* includes the following: "the criteriological significance of the doctrine of justification . . . still deserves to be studied further."

19. E. W. Gritsch and R. W. Jenson, *Lutheranism: The Theological Movement and Its Confessional Writings* (Philadelphia: Fortress, 1978), 36.

things like justification is the "main hinge on which religion turns"[20] or that "when this article stands the church stands; when it falls the church falls"?[21]

Part of the answer to this question is that justification names the site of a sixteenth-century battle and the flag the reformers followed when they "fought and conquered in the name of Paul." For Luther, however, justification was more than just a battle site or standard. It was the "single solid rock."[22] This is, at its core, a pastoral claim, as justification identifies God's unconditioned grace as the only ground of "rest" for "your bones and mine."[23] But it is also a statement about the distinctive theological function of justification:

> The doctrine of justification must be learned diligently. For in it are included all other doctrines of our faith; and if it is sound, all the others are sound as well.[24]

> [Justification is] the lord, ruler, and judge of every kind of doctrine, which preserves and governs Christian teaching.[25]

> Nothing in this article can be given up. . . . On this article rests all that we teach and practice against the pope, the devil, and the world.[26]

It is as an interpretation of these kinds of sentences that the specification of justification as a doctrinal "center" develops. Martin Kähler had already called justification the *evangelische Grundartikel*, but according to Risto Saarinen, it was Hans Iwand's *Glaubensgerechtigkeit nach Luthers Lehre* (1941) that shaped the subsequent language of *Mitte* and *Zentrum*.[27] As Iwand read Luther, justification stands as the "immovable center."[28] This description, however, is

20. J. Calvin, *Institutes of the Christian Religion*, ed. J. T. McNeill, trans. F. L. Battles (Philadelphia: Westminster, 1960), 3.11.1.

21. WA 40.3:352.

22. WA 40.1:33, 16; LW 27:145.

23. LW 26:27.

24. WA 40.1:441.29; LW 26:283.

25. WA 39.1:205.

26. *Smalcald Articles* (1537), BSLK 415–16.

27. R. Saarinen, "Die Rechtfertigungslehre als Kriterium: Zur Begriffsgeschichte einer ökumenischen Redewendung," *Keryma und Dogma* 44 (1998): 98. For Kähler's language, see *Die Wissenschaft der christlichen Lehre von dem evangelischen Grundartikel aus im Abrisse dargestellt* (Neukirchen: Neukirchener Verlag, 1996 [1905]), 67–79.

28. H. J. Iwand, *The Righteousness of Faith according to Luther*, ed. V. F. Thompson, trans. R. H. Lundell (Eugene, OR: Wipf & Stock, 2008), 15.

interpreted by a contrast and a series of supplementary images: justification occupies the "center" rather than the "periphery"; justification is "critical" as opposed to "secondary"; justification is the "core" and functions as the "critical axis from which we can decide whether or not the church preaches the gospel."[29] These images invited a proliferation of centralizing characterizations of justification: it is the theological "discrimen," the "Grund und Grenze," and the "Mitte und Grenze reformatorisher Theologie."[30] But just as Iwand used the language of "center" to indicate the function of justification as a "critical axis from which we can decide whether or not the church preaches the gospel," words like *Mitte* and *Zentrum* are ways of describing "Die Rechtfertigungslehre als Kriterium" or, in the words of Gerhard Gloege, "als hermeneutische Kategorie."[31] Within this language-game, the predicate "center" does "not," as Gerhard Ebeling insists, "give preference to one Christian doctrine amongst many others." Rather it points to "the proper function of the doctrine of justification," identifying it as the "touchstone of theology" or the "standard of theological judgment."[32] Justification is a criterion, an evangelical canon that makes possible the judgment: this is or this is not the gospel.

For Luther, the distinctive significance of justification is tied to its critical and hermeneutical function. Justification "preserves and governs all Christian teaching" and "if it is sound, all the other [doctrines] are sound as well."[33] As a critical criterion, "nothing in this article can be given up" because "on this article rest all that we teach and practice against the pope, the devil, and the world."[34] As a hermeneutical criterion, justification is "the lord, ruler, and judge of every kind of doctrine."[35] In Eberhard Jüngel's phrase, justification is

---

29. Iwand, *The Righteousness of Faith according to Luther*, 15.

30. For "discrimen," see M. C. Mattes, *The Role of Justification in Contemporary Theology* (Grand Rapids: Eerdmans, 2004), 15; for "Grund und Grenze," see O. Bayer, *Leibliches Wort: Reformation und Neuzeit im Konflikt* (Tübingen: Mohr Siebeck, 1992), 19–34; see also E. Wolf, "Die Rechtfertigungslehre als Mitte und Grenze reformatorische Theologie," in *Peregrinatio*, vol. 2, *Studien zur reformatorische Theologie, zum Kirchenrecht und zur Sozialethik* (Munich: Chr. Kaiser Verlag, 1965), 11–21; and E. Jüngel, *Das Evangelium von der Rechtfertigung des Gottlosen als Zentrum des christlichen Glaubens*, 3rd ed. (Tübingen: Mohr Siebeck, 1999).

31. G. Gloege, "Die Rechtfertigungslehre als hermeneutische Kategorie," in *Gnade für die Welt: Kritik und Krise des Luthertums* (Göttingen: Vandenhoeck & Ruprecht, 1964), 34–54.

32. G. Ebeling, *Luther: An Introduction to His Thought*, trans. R. A. Wilson (Minneapolis: Fortress, 2007), 111, 113.

33. WA 39.1:205; WA 40.1:441, 29.

34. *Smalcald Articles* 1537, BSLK 415–16.

35. WA 39.1:205.

"the heart of the heart" because it is hermeneutical: "the best way to express the central function of justification is to highlight its hermeneutical significance for the whole of theological knowledge."[36]

But hermeneutical how? In what sense does all "we teach and practice against the pope, the devil, and the world" rest on justification? How does justification rule, judge, preserve, and govern theology? The answer: as an antithesis. Justification is a critical and hermeneutical criterion because it is "the either/or article."[37] Because justification is both "not by works of law" and "by faith in Jesus Christ"—because it specifies both what the gospel is not as well as what the gospel is—it says a "no" and a "yes." And it is as an antithetical grammar, not as one soteriological image among many, that justification relates to theological discourse as *rector et iudex*. As Robert Jenson puts it, "It is the mission of the church to speak the gospel. . . . Theology is the hermeneutic of this work. Theology must therefore have norms by which to make the judgment, 'this is/is not the gospel.'"[38] The Reformation contention is that justification, with its "not, but" structure, is this norm. Because it is "not by works of law" it enables the identification of not-gospels; because it is "by faith in Jesus Christ" it authenticates and makes audible the preaching of the gospel.

Implicit here is a distinction between first-order and second-order discourse. The first-order language of faith, for the reformers, is preaching, praise, and prayer. In this register, justification takes its place alongside other biblical motifs and metaphors. But as second-order discourse—as the critical and hermeneutical shaping of the sentences of faith—justification relates to preaching, praise, and prayer as a grammatical rule: to speak the gospel, do not condition the grace of God by any human criteria; rather give Jesus Christ in the form of an unconditioned promise.[39] It is as this kind of grammar that Paul Tillich calls justification "the central doctrine of the Reformation," or in his preferred phrase, "the first and basic expression of the Protestant principle": the "not, but" grammar of justification means that "in relation to God, God alone can

36. Jüngel, *Justification*, 47.

37. Iwand, *Righteousness of Faith*, 15.

38. Cf. R. W. Jenson, *Systematic Theology* (Oxford: Oxford University Press, 1997), 1:23; Lindbeck, *The Nature of Doctrine*, 79–84.

39. Cf. Jenson, *Systematic Theology*, 1:13–20. I prefer Oswald Bayer's alternative to first- and second-order discourse, what he calls the distinction and relationship between "monastische und scholastische Theologie," because it focuses theology on "das Klarwerden von Sätze der Verkündigung in ihrem bestimmten Sitz im Leben"; see Bayer, *Handbuch: systematischer Theologie* (Gütersloh: Gütersloh Verlagshaus, 1994), 27–31, 439.

act and that no human claim . . . no intellectual or moral or devotional 'work,' can reunite us with him."[40]

The extent to which these formulations capture what Paul's "not" excludes and what his "but" names will be considered below. For now, the crucial point is that it is as a reading of the grammar of Paul's justification discourse that the reformers identify the unique criteriological function of justification. The Geneva Bible of 1560, for example, can call Galatians 2:16 "the principal scope" of the letter, because Paul's argument against the "other gospel" (Gal 1:6) and for "that which I preached to you" (1:8) has both its "no" and its "yes" in Galatians 2:16: not works of the law, but faith in Jesus Christ.[41] Similarly, Luther can state the *argumentum* of Galatians as "the difference between Christian righteousness and all other kinds of righteousness" because the Pauline "not by works of the law" says an anthropological "no" even as "by faith in Jesus Christ" says a christological "yes": "do we do nothing and work nothing in order to obtain this righteousness? I reply: Nothing at all"—that is the "no." "Christ . . . is my righteousness"—that is the "yes."[42]

It is also the case that the "not, but" grammar of justification often does this theological work without the specific vocabulary of justification. Luther's catechisms and sermons, for instance, often surprise readers with the paucity of references to justification, and yet the shape of both reflect the relationship between and movement from justification's "no" to its "yes": the excluding and including grammar of justification functions as an evangelical gold pan, separating and filtering out all human criteria such that all that remains as gospel is the pure gold that is the grace of God in Jesus Christ.[43] It is, to cite a final example, not in terms of a focusing on a single metaphor but in relation to "the shape of the liturgy" that Thomas Cranmer's 1552 Holy Communion service

40. P. Tillich, *Systematic Theology* (London: SCM, 1978), 3:223–24.

41. *The Geneva Bible: A Facsimile of the 1560 Edition* (Peabody, MA: Hendrickson, 2007), 87 verso.

42. LW 26:4, 8–9.

43. This is evident both in the division of the catechism according the distinction between law and gospel (i.e., between the Decalogue on the one hand and the Creed, Lord's Prayer, and sacraments on the other) and in the way the language of justification is used to interpret other aspects of theology. The explication of the first article of the Creed in the Small Catechism, for example, says, "God has created me together with all creatures . . . purely because of fatherly, divine goodness and mercy without any of my merit and worthiness" (BSLK 510.33–5.11.8). This brings the language of mercy and merit from the disputes about justification to the doctrine of creation and interprets *creatio ex nihilo* as creation by grace and thus creation as gift.

has been described as "the only effective attempt ever made to give liturgical expression to the doctrine of 'justification by faith alone.'"[44]

These examples indicate that the identification of justification as an evangelical criterion is not a claim about justification being the exclusive or even primary vocabulary of the gospel. Rather, it is the "not, but" grammar of justification that enables it to function as a criterion: because it says what the gospel is not and also what the gospel is, justification functions both critically and hermeneutically. This means that justification's criteriological significance is tied to its occasional character as a *Kampfeslehre*. It is as Pauline polemic that justification says "no" to the not-gospel and sets this excluded alterative in antithesis to "the gospel of Christ" (Gal 1:7). An "other-gospel" (Gal 1:6) occasioned Paul's "not, but" grammar in Galatians, and it is this grammar that gives justification its criteriological function: as a critical criterion the "not" of justification identifies "other-gospels" as "not-gospels"; as a hermeneutical criterion the "but" of justification both picks out and guides the proclamation of "the gospel of Christ."

JUSTIFICATION AND THE GRAMMAR OF GALATIANS

The grammar of Galatians is antithetical. Paul is an "apostle, not from human beings or through a human being, but through Jesus Christ and God the Father" (Gal 1:1). The gospel Paul preaches is not κατὰ ἄνθρωπον but "through a revelation of Jesus Christ" (1:12–13). Paul's autobiography is also antithetical, shaped by the christological apocalypse that interrupts his "former life in Judaism" with the call to "preach the faith he once tried to destroy" (1:13, 23) and polarized by a crucified past and a christological present: "I no longer live" but "Christ lives in me" (2:20). The gospel Paul received and is sent to proclaim, moreover, announces the act of God in Christ that delivers sinners and slaves from "the present evil age," crucifying the old cosmos and inaugurating a "new creation" (1:4; 6:14–15). And this contrast between the old cosmos and

44. D. G. Dix, *The Shape of the Liturgy* (Westminster: Dacre, 1945), 672. This grammatical or architectural function is more legible when the distinction between law and gospel is read as a translation of the grammar of justification into a theological hermeneutic. See, e.g., Ebeling, *Luther*, 113: "the proper function of the doctrine of justification . . . can only be understood as Luther saw it if it is identical with what is implied by the distinction between law and gospel." In this respect, the *Heidelberg Catechism* is another exemplar of the grammatical function of justification: "the catechism . . . may be divided as the doctrine of the church, into the law and the gospel"; see Z. Ursinus, *The Commentary on the Heidelberg Catechism*, trans. G. W. Williard (Phillipsburg, NJ: Presbyterian and Reformed, 1852), 13.

the new creation contains still more polarities: the flesh and slavery belong to the old; the Spirit and freedom are part of the new. With these "newly minted distinctions," as John Barclay writes, "Paul's letter to the Galatians . . . remaps reality."[45]

But this raises a question: What criterion shapes Paul's cartography? Is there a source—an event, tradition, idea, or experience—that shapes the antitheses that dot the map of Pauline theology? It would be easy to assume the obvious reformational answer: justification. But to single out justification as the antithesis that sources and shapes all the others is, at least as a reading of Paul, to skip a step. All of the antitheses that Paul articulates in Galatians occur as part of an argument against the "other gospel" (1:6) and for "the gospel of Christ" (1:7). The "other gospel" is in fact no gospel because it cuts off from Christ and so enslaves in the present evil age (5:2–4). "The gospel of Christ" is good news because it gifts the one "who loved me and gave himself for me" and thereby effects life and freedom in the new creation (2:20; 5:1; 6:15). Read within the either/or between the "other gospel" and "the gospel of Christ," Paul's antithetical remapping of reality appears to operate according to an evangelical and christological criterion: "the gospel of Christ," in antithesis to any "other gospel" (cf. 1:8–9), is the "canon" of Paul's cartography of the new creation (6:14–16).

This, however, still leaves one crucial question: according to what evangelical criterion is Paul able to make the judgment "this is the gospel of Christ" or "this is a different gospel"? How does Paul know that the gospel of the agitators is a "different gospel" than "the gospel of Christ"? It is as an attempt to answer these kinds of questions that the antithesis of Galatians 2:16 stands out: justification is not ἐξ ἔργων νόμου but ἐκ πίστεως Χριστοῦ (Gal 2:16). This lexical set (i.e., righteousness, law, faith) is not the only language Paul speaks when speaking the gospel. In Galatians, salvation is figured as deliverance, participation, forgiveness, liberation, and adoption. But what is distinctive about justification is that it is articulated as an antithesis: not ἐξ ἔργων νόμου but ἐκ πίστεως Χριστοῦ. This either/or alternative is introduced as an argument against the "other gospel" and as an argument for "the truth of the gospel" (2:14). And it is in this context—both polemical and proclamatory—that justification functions in Galatians as a critical and hermeneutical criterion: when Paul says justification is "not by works of law" he identifies and says no

---

45. J. M. G. Barclay, *Paul and the Gift* (Grand Rapids: Eerdmans, 2015), 338; cf. J. L. Martyn, "Apocalyptic Antinomies in Paul's Letter to Galatia," *NTS* 31 (1985): 410–24.

to the other gospel; when Paul says justification is "by Christ-faith" he picks out and preaches "the gospel of Christ."[46]

To interpret the antithesis of Galatians 2:16 is therefore to identify, at least in the context of the crisis that occasioned Galatians, both what the gospel is not and what the gospel is. For Paul, as regards justification, ἔργα νόμου and πίστις Χριστοῦ are antithetical: justification is not by ἔργα νόμου "but" (ἐὰν μή) by πίστις Χριστοῦ (16a); Paul and other Jewish Christians (ἡμεῖς) trust in Christ to be justified on the basis of πίστις Χριστοῦ "and not" (καὶ οὐκ) on the basis of ἔργα νόμου (16c).[47] As Martinus de Boer notes, the effect of this antithesis is a kind of grammatical chemistry, "separating justification" from ἔργα νόμου "and binding it instead and exclusively to" πίστις Χριστοῦ.[48] As part of Paul's evangelical *Kampf* this antithesis is an argument (or announcement) about "the truth of the gospel" (2:14). It is not only that justification is not ἐξ ἔργων νόμου but ἐκ πίστεως Χριστοῦ. Paul's contention is also that justification ἐξ ἔργων νόμου is not the gospel whereas justification ἐκ πίστεως Χριστοῦ is. But why?[49]

46. This distinction between "the gospel of Christ" as the canon of Paul's theological cartography and justification as Paul's evangelical criterion suggests that the identification of justification as the "center" of Paul's theology is imprecise: "the gospel of Christ" is the theological *radix*; justification relates to that gospel both critically and hermeneutically, naming not-gospels and norming the articulation of the gospel. It is thus possible to heed Karl Barth's warning not to let justification "be absolutized and given a monopoly" (*CD* IV/1, 528) and at the same time argue that such a concern misfires as a criticism of the criteriological function of justification.

47. Paul's use of ἐὰν μή to articulate this antithesis is a source of much scholarly discussion, as ἐὰν μή is almost always exceptive rather than contrastive; see, e.g., A. A. Das, "Another Look at ἐὰν μή in Galatians 2:16," *JBL* 119 (2000): 529–39; de Boer, *Galatians* (Louisville: Westminster John Knox, 2011), 144–45. The exceptive sense can be read within the overall antithesis, taking ἐὰν μή with the opening clause (i.e., "a person is not justified . . . except through πίστις Χριστοῦ), but de Boer is right to insist that however ἐὰν μή is translated, in Galatians 2:16 the phrase is part of Paul's articulation of an antithesis: πίστις Χριστοῦ is set in explicit contrast (καὶ οὐκ) to ἔργα νόμου at the end of 2:16 (*Galatians*, 144).

48. De Boer, *Galatians*, 155; cf. Martyn, *Galatians*, 251; D. J. Moo, *Galatians* (Grand Rapids: Baker Academic, 2013), 154.

49. This question is, in part, about the interpretation of ἔργα νόμου and πίστις Χριστοῦ, but it is less concerned with what de Boer calls their "referential meanings" and focuses instead on what he terms their "theological ones" (*Galatians*, 144n209). In the case of ἔργα νόμου, the referential meaning takes its bearings from Ἰουδαϊκῶς in 2:14 and the ongoing argument about the time and purpose of the Mosaic law in God's promissory and christological economy. This suggests that νόμος refers to the whole law (cf. 5:3) and ἔργα, as the references to ποιέω from the quotations of Deuteronomy and Leviticus indicate (Gal 3:10, 12), refers to the observance of the law.

As noted above, the "Protestant Principle" answers this question by reading the negation of ἔργα νόμου, in Tillich's words, as a "no" to any "human
claim"—that is, to any "intellectual or moral or devotional 'work.'" This interpretation, which is especially strong in the tradition stemming from Augustine (and including Luther), emphasizes the ἔργα in the phrase ἔργα νόμου:
"works" names the fundamental form of idolatry that is the identification
of the self as the subject of salvation.[50] Paul, however, at least in Galatians,
abbreviates ἔργα νόμου as νόμος, suggesting to some that the accent is on
the law and, given the situation in Galatia, particularly on the way the law
erects boundaries between Jew and non-Jew.[51] But Paul's "no" seems both
more comprehensive and more christological. The occasionally formulated
"no" to "works of law" occurs in an antithesis that rhymes—grammatically—
with other antitheses in Galatians that negate all that is anthropological and
old: the "gospel of Christ" is neither "from a human source" nor "in accord
with human norms" (1:11–12); the cross of Christ crucifies the old cosmos and
renders the religious and cultural criteria of that world irrelevant (6:14–15).
These not-clauses limn the negative grammar of the gospel: "the gospel of
Christ" is *un*conditioned by the criteria of the old age and the predicates of the
old ἄνθρωπος.[52] For Paul, this cosmic and anthropological "no" is spoken in
the cross. Both the cosmos and the human "I" are crucified with Christ (6:14;
2:20). Paul's negations are therefore a christologically grounded reduction to
nothing—the "no" is de-creation and death.[53]

"But": this adversative, which lives in Paul's antitheses at the site of nothingness and death, opens clauses that name Christ as the one who contradicts

50. Cf. Martyn, *Galatians*, 271, who speaks of Paul setting "an act of God" (πίστις Χριστοῦ) "over against . . . an act of the human being" (ἔργα νόμου). This critique of human
agency is distinguishable from, though often linked with, an argument about the impossibility of keeping the law—a point Paul does seem to make in Galatians: see, e.g., the insertion
of σάρξ in the echo of Ps 142:2 LXX in Gal 2:16d, the scriptural logic of Gal 3:10–12, and the
denial that righteousness comes through the law because the law is unable to give life (3:21).

51. See, e.g., J. D. G. Dunn, *The Theology of Paul the Apostle* (Grand Rapids: Eerdmans,
1998), 354–59.

52. Martyn is right to hear the "harmony" between the antitheses of Galatians 1:1, 11–12,
and 2:16, but he unnecessarily limits the anthropological/christological either/or to an an-
tinomy of agency (*Galatians*, 271). Paul's polarity certainly includes a negation of human
action *qua* a condition of the gospel, but it also includes a "no" all other anthropological
predicates, whether inherited or acquired.

53. To distinguish this negative work of God against the old from the gospel that creates
the new, the reformers called it the *opus alienum dei* in distinction from the *opus proprium
dei* and argued that God does these two works through two words: law and gospel.

the conditions of the old cosmos. Where the old age ends: "new creation" (6:14–15). Where the human "I" dies: "Christ lives in me" (2:20). The grammar of the gospel, in its antithetical expression, is a grammar of nothingness and creation—a grammar of death and life. This is evident in Galatians 2:16 in the incongruity between the gift that gives righteousness and its recipients: it is not given to those considered righteous by the law but to those the law diagnoses as "sinners" (Gal 2:15, 17). The divine action communicated by the verb δικαιόω is thus necessarily creative rather than confirmatory: God does not ratify a righteousness regulated by the law; he gives Christ to those whom the law labels sinners and thereby re-creates them as righteous. The antithetical grammar of Galatians 2:16, therefore, expresses a fundamental contrast between the old and the new, between death and life. Within the dispute about the law that occasioned Galatians, "not by works of law" is the contextual way of saying "no" to the old and the anthropological. But if the range of Paul's "no" is as wide as the old world, the rationale for this negation is as specific as a single name: Jesus Christ, the gift who contradicts the old and creates the new.

Galatians 2:21 concludes the paragraph of 2:15–21 with the same contrast that opens it: "I do not reject the grace of God, for if righteousness is through the law, then Christ died in vain" (2:21). The terms νόμος, Χριστός, and δικαιοσύνη pick up the antithesis of Galatians 2:16. But this is more than a restatement. It is a theological interpretation: justification ἐξ ἔργων νόμου invalidates the gift of Christ and voids the cross; justification ἐκ πίστεως Χριστοῦ names Christ crucified as the gift that gives righteousness. This suggests that the rationale for Paul's rejection of ἔργα νόμου as the basis or source of justification is "charismatic" and christological—that is, it is about "the grace (χάρις) of God" and the death of Christ (Χριστός). Galatians 1:6 and 5:4 confirm this: for Paul, the Galatians' attraction to "works of law" (3:3, 5) amounts to an abandoning of "the one who called you in the grace (χάρις) of Christ" (Χριστός, 1:6), and to allow circumcision and so to be "justified by the law" is to be "cut off from Christ" (Χριστός) and to "fall away from grace" (χάρις, 5:3–4). For Paul, "the truth of the gospel" in Galatia, as in Jerusalem and Antioch before (2:5, 14), is either/or: either the law and its works or the divine gift that is the self-giving of Christ (cf. 1:4; 2:20). It is the death of Christ, not the law, that justifies, and it is this christological gift—the cross—that is "the grace of God" (2:21). The antithetical grammar of justification therefore poses a mutually exclusive alternative: either not-Christ or Christ. Justification ἐξ ἔργων νόμου is not the gospel because the gospel is always and only "the gospel of *Christ*."

In saying that justification is not by "works of law," then, Paul is saying what the gospel is not: the gospel is not all that is not-Christ. The other side of the antithesis in Galatians 2:16 says what the gospel is: Christ. In Galatians 2:15–21, Paul uses the language of righteousness and justification to interpret the death of Christ. "If righteousness is through the law," Paul argues, "then Christ died for nothing" (2:21; cf. 2:16–17). It is this "grace of God"—the death of Christ—that Paul does not "reject" (2:21), because whereas justification by "works of law" voids the cross, justification ἐκ πίστεως Χριστοῦ confesses "the one who loved me and gave himself for me" as the justifying gift. It is in this sense that the phrase "but by Christ-faith" says the gospel. Justification ἐκ πίστεως Χριστοῦ means "to be justified in Christ" (2:17), it means that the gift that justifies is Christ crucified (2:21; cf. 1:4; 2:20). This suggests that πίστις Χριστοῦ is a way of naming Jesus Christ as the gift that gives righteousness—or better: as the gift who is "our righteousness" (cf. 1 Cor 1:30). In the theology and exegesis of the Reformation, the translation "faith in Christ" means exactly this: it identifies Jesus Christ as the *one* by, in, and on the basis of whom God justifies the ungodly.[54] But however πίστις Χριστοῦ is translated, it articulates "the gospel of Christ" in antithesis to a "different gospel" because it proclaims rather than rejects "the grace of God" that is the cross of Christ. It is as an antithesis—as the mutually exclusive alternative of either not-Christ or only Christ—that justification gives the grammar of the gospel. As the reformers might put it, πίστις Χριστοῦ, in antithesis to ἔργα νόμου, is a Pauline way of saying *solus Christus*.[55]

The grammar of the gospel, then, as it comes to expression in the antithesis of Galatians 2:16, is christological and just so charismatic, incongruous, and creative. It is Christ crucified: an unconditioned gift, given to sinners, which re-creates them as righteous. This grammar says "no" to any "other gospel": anything that is not Christ is not the gospel. But this grammar also says "the gospel of Christ": at the site of sin, slavery, nothingness, and death, God gives Christ as the gift that creates *e contrario*: righteousness, freedom, new creation, and life.

A CRITICAL CRITERION

Galatians repeatedly says "no" to not-gospels; to the agitators, the ψευδάδελφοι; and to Peter. But how does Paul distinguish "the truth of the gospel" from a

---

54. See chap. 11, "The Christocentrism of Faith in Christ."

55. The reformers used a term from Latin grammar, *particulae exclusivae*, to express the excluding function of Paul's antithesis. Martin Chemnitz put it this way in the Solid Declaration of the Formula of Concord (1576): "This is the apostle Paul's position when he so diligently and urgently insists on *particulae exclusivae*, that is, on terms through which human works are excluded . . . that is, by grace, without merit, apart from works, not by works, etc. These exclusive terms are all summarized when one says, 'by faith alone.'"

"different gospel"? What criterion enables the critical judgment that something is not the gospel?

The occasion of Galatians can only be tentatively reconstructed, but Paul says enough to indicate the correspondence between the prior events in Jerusalem and Antioch and the current crisis in Galatia (2:1–10, 11–14). While the majority of the believers in Galatia are of non-Jewish origin (4:8), there is a compulsion to join their commitment to Christ with the observance of the Torah. Paul's use of the phrase "another gospel" (1:6), his appeal to analogous disputes in Jerusalem and Antioch with Jewish believers in Christ (2:1–14), the language of "starting" and "finishing" (3:1–5), and his extended engagement with Israel's scriptures in Galatians 3–4 all suggest that those Paul perceived as opponents were Jewish Christ followers.[56] This means that their message was likely one of complementation rather than competition: Paul's opponents likely argued that it is not Christ or Torah; it is Christ and Torah. It is here, where a Pauline "or" confronts an unevangelical "and," that the grammar of justification functions as a critical criterion.[57]

Paul's "no" to the "different gospel" takes the form of saying "no" to justification by works of the law.[58] The occasion helps to account for the specific language Paul employs: the terms "righteousness," "law," and "faith" have Israel's scripture as their source (Gal 3:6, 10–12) and the gentile mission as their *Sitz im Leben*. The vocabulary of Galatians 2:16, in other words, is occasional and traditional. The grammar, however, is uniquely Pauline: justification is *not* by works of law, *but* by Christ in faith.[59] This "not, but" grammar, as argued above, poses an evangelical either/or: either not-Christ or only Christ. It is as this mutually exclusive alternative that justification functions in Galatians as a critical criterion. Where the agitators put an "and," Paul puts an antithesis: not Christ and the law, but Christ. Righteousness comes either through the law or the death of Christ (2:21). "To be justified by the law"—in this case,

---

56. For a different view, that "the influencers" were non-believing Jews local to Galatia, see M. D. Nanos, *The Irony of Galatians: Paul's Letter in First-Century Context* (Minneapolis: Fortress, 2002), 62–72.

57. For the theology of Paul's opponents, see J. M. G. Barclay, *Obeying the Truth: A Study of Paul's Ethics* (Edinburgh: T&T Clark, 1988), 45–60.

58. Galatians 2:15–21 is lexically and thematically connected to both 2:11–14 and 3:1–25. For the former, see Barclay, *Paul and the Gift*, 370. For the latter, see H.-J. Eckstein, *Verheissung und Gesetz: Eine exegetische Untersuchung zu Galater 2,15–4,7* (Tübingen: Mohr Siebeck, 1996), 79. Galatians 2:15–21 should therefore be read both within the context of the incident in Antioch and as part of Paul's argument against the "different gospel" that has come to Galatia.

59. Cf. Martyn, *Galatians*, 264n158; Campbell, *The Deliverance of God*, 842–47.

to undergo circumcision—does not complement or complete "the gospel of
Christ;" it "cut[s] off from Christ" (5:4). "In place of the agitators' synthesis of
faith in Christ and the law," writes Douglas Moo, "Paul insists on an antithesis:
it is Christ and therefore not the law."[60]

There is little indication, however, that Paul's antithesis between Christ
and the law is grounded in an opposition to the law *per se*: uncircumcision,
just as much as circumcision, is "not worth anything" (οὔτε . . . τι ἰσχύει, 5:6;
cf. 1 Cor 7:17–19). As Luther might put it, the question is not whether the law
is good; the question is whether the law is the gospel. In Barclay's words, "to
require circumcision . . . is to place the Christ-event within the parameters of
worth defined by the Jewish tradition, and that would make the Christ-gift
conditioned by something outside and before itself."[61] The problem, in other
words, is that the agitators' "and" erases the gospel's "alone"—*solus Christus*.
Paul's critique is an application of this grammatical rule in the opposite direction. "Christ alone" erases any "and" that is a nonchristological condition of
the gospel: neither uncircumcision nor circumcision, neither Jew nor Greek,
neither slave nor free, neither male nor female (5:6; 3:28). To condition the gift
of Christ by any religious, cultural, moral, or social criteria is to disqualify its
essential character an unconditioned gift. "The gospel of Christ," Paul insists,
is only and exclusively Christ.

It is as an expression of this exclusivity—that is, as a grammar that excludes—that the antithesis of Galatians 2:16 functions as a critical criterion.
The terms of Paul's argument target the situation in Galatia (and recall the
disputes in Jerusalem and Antioch). The not-clause of the antithesis identifies and critiques the "other gospel": justification is not by works of the law.
This "not," however, is not grounded in a "no" to the law. "Not by works of
law," rather, is the contextual spelling of the "un-" that defines Christ as an
unconditioned gift. It is as an expression of this either/or that the "not, but"
grammar of justification is a critical criterion. The grammar of Galatians 2:16,
as an antithesis, says Christ alone.

A HERMENEUTICAL CRITERION

Justification functions as a critical and hermeneutical criterion in Galatians
because it says "no" to the "other gospel" even as it says "the gospel of Christ."
As an argument against the "other gospel" and for "the gospel of Christ," Ga-

---

60. Moo, *Galatians*, 154.
61. Barclay, *Paul and the Gift*, 392.

latians 2:16 says what the gospel is not and what the gospel is: the gospel is not conditioned by any of the non-christological criteria of the old cosmos; the gospel is Jesus Christ, the gift who contradicts the old and creates the new. The previous section considered the critical side of this criteriological function. This section will demonstrate that justification also functions as a hermeneutical criterion.

"Hermeneutics," as Jenson puts it, concerns the fusion of two horizons that occurs "where past hearing turns to new speaking."[62] Paul's letter to the churches of Galatia is "new speaking," but it includes the interpretation of "past hearing." Israel's scripture is listened to and reread, the gospel the Galatians once heard is recalled and re-preached, and Paul's "former life" is remembered and retold. The hermeneutical function of justification is traceable, in a limited way, as Paul uses terms from the "semantic domain" of justification to interpret these texts and histories: the language of law, righteousness, and faith permeate Paul's engagement with Israel's scripture, his account of the Galatians' reception of the Spirit is cast in terms of the contrast between faith and "works of law" (3:1–5), and the paradigmatic "I" of Galatians 2:19–20 dies "to the law" and lives "in faith."[63] For Paul, however, these are not just discrete histories; they fuse at the horizon he calls "the gospel of Christ": Israel's canonical texts "pre-preach the gospel" (3:8), the Galatian believers are being drawn toward a "different gospel" and away from "the gospel of Christ" (1:6–10), and Paul's "calling through grace" (1:15) culminates in Paul "preaching the gospel" (1:23). Justification is therefore a hermeneutical criterion in Galatians not only as it

---

62. Jenson, *Systematic Theology*, 1:14.

63. This language is native to Israel's scripture, as Paul's quotations from Genesis, Leviticus, Deuteronomy, and Habakkuk indicate (Gal 3:6, 10–13). But Paul's selection of these texts—and not others—and his distinctive reading of them (i.e., distinguishing law from promise and faith) suggest that his personal and missionary experience and his antithetical theology of justification inform his scriptural interpretation. The source of Paul's justification-vocabulary is Israel's scripture. The origin of Paul's justification-grammar, however, is theological and experiential—that is, the antithesis of justification and the specific experience of the self-giving of Christ to sinners *qua* sinners (both Paul and the gentiles, 1:13–15; 2:16–17, 19–20; 3:1–5; 4:8–9). This theology and experience, however, establish a hermeneutical frame within which Paul does not so much create as discover the antithetical grammar of the gospel within his canonical tradition, a discovery that in turn informs the shape of his theology and the interpretation of his experiences. In this sense, justification functions as a hermeneutical criterion in a mutually interpretative relationship with Paul's calling in grace, the gentile mission, and Israel's scripture, all of which source and shape his justification formulae even as his theology and grammar of justification inform his re-narrations and re-readings of those events and texts.

informs Paul's interpretations, but also (and especially) as his interpretations identify these pasts as promises and paradigms of the gospel.

Justification functions in just this way as a grammar. It is as an antithesis that Galatians 2:16 gives the grammar of the gospel: not not-Christ but only Christ. This is not an isolated antithesis, however. It is a Pauline pattern of speech—it is the grammar of the gospel according to which Paul writes Galatians. Even in those places where the vocabulary of justification is (largely) absent, the christological and antithetical grammar of Galatians 2:16 molds Paul's stories and readings of scripture into the shape of the gospel: not the old cosmos, but the unconditioned and creative gift of Christ.

Graham Stanton has noticed this hermeneutical function of Galatians 2:16: the "antithesis between those who are ἐξ ἔργων νόμου and those who are ἐκ πίστεως" introduces "key musical notes in contrasting thematic phrases." For Stanton, the "sound map" of Galatians is divided by this antithesis, with some "satellite words and phrases" going with πίστις (e.g., ἡ ἐπαγγελία, ἡ κληρνομία, υἱοί and τέκνα of Abraham or of God, and the δικ- word group) and others going with νόμος (e.g., ἡ κατάρα and δοῦλος).[64] This list of "satellites" could be expanded, with terms such as "grace," "Christ," "Spirit," and "calling" dotting one side of the Pauline map, while "curse," "flesh," "cosmos," στοχεῖα, and ἄνθρωπος dot the other. This is what Stanton means when he suggests, quoting the words of G. S. Duncan, that Galatians 2:16 "is the text on which all that follows in the Epistle is commentary."[65] The antithesis of Galatians 2:16 plays the "key notes" that shapes the "sound map" of the letter—that is, the antithesis between "works of law" and "faith in Christ" functions as a hermeneutic as it provides the headings under which other parts of the letter can be grouped.

Applied to the stories Paul recounts and the scriptures he interprets, the antithetical grammar of Galatians 2:16 shapes Paul's speech as it splits each story he tells into two. There is, in Galatians, no unbroken story of the self or of salvation history. There is an old story and a new story, an old self and a new, an old cosmos and a new creation, a time "before" and "the fullness of time" (4:4). Paul can narrate history κατὰ ἄνθρωπον, but that means talking about his "former" (ποτέ, 1:13) life, remembering the condition of the Galatians "then" (τότε, 4:8), and tracing the history of Israel "before" (πρό, 3:23). This side of the stories consists of what Stanton calls the "satellites" that correspond to Paul's negation of νόμος in Galatians 2:16. Paul's "former life" is situated

---

64. G. Stanton, "The Law of Moses and the Law of Christ: Galatians 3:1–6:2," in *Paul and the Mosaic Law*, ed. J. D. G. Dunn (Tübingen: Mohr Siebeck, 1996), 101.

65. Stanton, "Law of Moses and the Law of Christ," 103n11.

within a cultural, ethnic, familial, and religious context identifiable as "Judaism" (1:13). Within this sphere he is the subject of his own existence and his progress and zeal are measurable both according to a standard ("the traditions of my ancestors") and relative to his peers ("I advanced beyond many of my people of the same age," 1:14). For the Galatian believers, their "then" was a time of theological ignorance and enslavement: they were slaves both to "beings that by nature are not gods" and to "the elements of the cosmos" (4:3, 8). Similarly, if more surprisingly, Israel's time "before"—their time "under the law"—is interpreted as an era of "captivity," a time of being "imprisoned until . . ." (3:21–25; cf. 4:21–31).

In Paul's telling each of these old stories ends. Paul's autobiography is interrupted: "but when God" (1:15). The Galatians' time of "not knowing God" is contradicted and overcome: "But now you have come to know God, or rather to be known by God" (4:9). Israel's imprisonment under the law ends: "But now that faith has come" (3:25). On the far side of these adversatives, Paul's new stories consist of the "satellites" that correspond to the but-clause of Galatians 2:16. Paul is "called through grace" (1:15), just as the Galatians are "called by grace."[66] The Galatian believers, like those formerly under the Jewish law, are "set free" or "redeemed" (4:5; 5:1), they are made children of Abraham or the promise and so of God—they are no longer slaves but adopted children who have received the Spirit and so say "Abba" (3:26–4:7; cf. 4:8–9).

The grammar of Galatians 2:16, however, does more than play two contrasting notes. As an antithesis, the "not, but" grammar of justification names and negates the old as it identifies and announces the new. Paul's theology, in other words, is not about balance, an equilibrium indicated by the word "and": old and new, death and life, sin and righteousness. As an antithesis, Galatians 2:16 does not say "and"; it says "not, but." This is a grammar that both names a battle and proclaims the victor: the end of the old cosmos and from that nothingness, new creation (6:14–15); the old I "no longer lives," but from that death, resurrection—"Christ lives in me" (2:20). This unconditioned and creative grace patterns Paul's stories and reading of scripture. Paul's "calling through grace" occurs without regard to his "former life in Judaism," because God's act of setting Paul apart took place before there was a Paul (1:15).[67] The

66. On the connection between 1:6 and 1:15, see O. McFarland, "The One Who Calls in Grace: Paul's Rhetorical and Theological Identification with the Galatians," *HBT* 35 (2013): 151–65.

67. In 1 Corinthians 15:8–10, Paul's former life is interpreted as a condition of unworthiness that is met with an incongruous and vocation-creating grace: "I am unworthy to be called an apostle, because I persecuted the church, but by the grace of God, I am what

Galatians were "called by grace" (1:6) while they were still enslaved and theologically ignorant (4:3, 8–9), just as Israel was still imprisoned under the law when they were redeemed from the curse of the law (3:21–4:7; cf. 3:13).[68] In Paul's stories the old self, sin, and slavery are terms that name the nothingness from which God's grace creates out of the opposite: a new "I" (1:13–16; 2:19–20), righteousness (2:16; 3:8; 5:5), and freedom (4:5; 5:1).

The grammar of Paul's stories and scriptural interpretation is, like the grammar of Galatians 2:16, antithetical. There is a rupture between the old and the new, there is a death and a resurrection. The grammar of Galatians 2:16—that is, the grammar of the incongruous and creative gift—is the grammar according to which Paul reads scripture and writes stories. The language of death and resurrection, however, is not just a metaphor of reversal. It identifies an event: the crucifixion and resurrection of Christ. For Paul, it is through the cross of Jesus Christ that the old cosmos is crucified (Gal 6:14) and the new creation that exists out of this nothingness (6:15) only is "in Christ" (3:28; 5:6; cf. 2:20; 4:16). As argued above, while Paul's language of justification is scripturally sourced and occasionally situated, the origin of his antithetical grammar is christological. Similarly, as he retells the histories of Israel, the Galatians, and himself, the caesura is always christological. Paul's apostleship is "through Jesus Christ" (1:1), and he received the gospel "through a revelation of Jesus Christ" (1:12). It is this event that interrupts his past and re-creates him as a preacher of the gospel: "But when God . . . was pleased to reveal his son to me" (1:13–24). The Galatians' time of ignorance and enslavement ends with Paul's proclamation, an instance of "hearing" that makes present the crucified Christ (3:1–5; 4:13–14).[69] Israel's captivity under the law was an imprisonment "until faith came"—that is, "until Christ" (3:23–25).

For Paul, however, Christ does not just contradict and crucify the old. He is the gift that creates the new. The deep grammar of the gospel, the incongruity

I am." For the theological shape and function of Paul's autobiographical remarks, see J. H. Schütz, *Paul and the Anatomy of Apostolic Authority* (Cambridge: Cambridge University Press, 1975), 114–58; B. R. Gaventa, "Galatians 1 and 2: Autobiography as Paradigm," *NTS* 28 (1986): 309–26.

68. This unconditioned grammar is echoed in the antithetically structured depiction of the calling of the Corinthians in 1 Corinthians 1:26–31: "Consider your calling. . . . Not many were wise . . . not many were powerful . . . not many were of noble birth. . . . But God chose." A similarly antithetical dynamic shapes Paul's interpretation of the genesis of Israel: Isaac is not a child of the flesh but of the promise, Jacob is chosen not on the basis of works but by the one who calls (Rom 9:7–13).

69. See E. Güttgemanns, *Der leidende Apostel und sein Herr: Studien zur paulinischen Christologie* (Göttingen: Vandenhoeck & Ruprecht, 1966), 185.

and creativity of grace, is seen most sharply at the point of radical cosmological and anthropological discontinuity. The old cosmos ends; the old ἄνθρωπος dies. But there is, to borrow from the Song of Songs, a "love as strong as death" (Song 8:6). As Barclay writes, "at the human level, the Christ-event is a matter of discontinuity," it is "God's counter-statement to the previous conditions of the possible" and "narrates disjunction, not progress."[70] The discontinuity, to use Pauline language, is as deep as death. But as Paul's antithetical grammar signals, there is also a reversal as radical as resurrection: from immaturity and captivity to adoption (3:19; 4:1–7), from ignorance to being known (4:8–9), from sin to righteousness (2:16–21), from slavery to freedom (4:21–5:1), from the crucifixion of the old cosmos to new creation (6:14–15), from death to life (2:19–20). For the old ἄνθρωπος, in J. Louis Martyn's metaphor, there are "no through trains from" the old cosmos "to the gospel of God's son."[71] The old ἄνθρωπος does not survive her or his own salvation. The old ἄνθρωπος dies (2:20). But the gospel gives a gift to the dead—this is its full incongruity. The gospel also gives a gift that makes alive—this is its full creativity. The old ἄνθρωπος dies, but the gospel of Christ says, in the words of the novelist Walker Percy, "I love you dead."[72]

This love has a surprising way of holding together the histories it also fractures. For Paul, this love is enacted in the self-giving of Christ, the "one who loved me and gave himself for me" (2:20). It is this christological gift that Paul calls "the grace of God" (2:21). This "grace of God," however, also fulfills the promise of God (3:8, 14, 16) and accomplishes the purpose of God (note the ἵνα-clauses in 3:22, 24; 4:5). "The Christ-gift," as Barclay puts it, "is both entirely congruous with the promise of God and wholly incongruous with the prior conditions of human . . . history."[73] But, as love and gift, it is not wholly incongruous with the human. That Christ "loved *me* and gave himself for *me*" gestures toward a continuity of the self: not in the sense that the "I" lives, but in that the "I" is loved—"strong as death." There is, for Paul, an "I" that is killed, but this is also a "me" for whom Christ loved and gave himself (2:20). There is an "us" whose deliverance from "the present evil age" goes through death, and yet this "us," again, names those for whom "Christ gave himself" (1:4).[74] The grace of God is there before Paul's former life, just as the promise to Abraham

---

70. Barclay, *Paul and the Gift*, 412–13.

71. J. L. Martyn, "Paul and His Jewish-Christian Interpreters," *USQR* 42 (1987–88): 6.

72. W. Percy, *Love in the Ruins* (New York: Picador, 1971), 68.

73. Barclay, *Paul and the Gift*, 413.

74. This begins to address Daphne Hampson's concern that a soteriology of death and resurrection is inherently misanthropic, *Christian Contradictions: The Structures of Lutheran*

that includes Israel and the gentiles (3:8, 14) "pre-preaches the gospel" (3:8). These histories, broken into before and after by the advent of Christ, also have Christ as their beginning and end.

This grammar patterns the paradigmatic account of the "I" in Galatians 2:20. The biography of the "I" is both broken into two and connected through the incongruous and creative gift of Christ. The "I" dies ("I no longer live"), yet there is life out of this death: "the life I live in the flesh I live by faith." What fractures this story of the self is the cross of Christ: "I have been crucified with Christ." And yet the life out of death is also christological: "Christ lives in me." For Paul, this evokes a dialectical confession: I no longer live, but I am loved. The hermeneutical function of the "not, but" grammar of Galatians 2:16 is traceable here as this christological death and life is articulated as an antithesis: "I no longer live, but Christ lives in me." Death and life with and in Christ is "not, but": it is not I, but Christ. And this, in Galatians, is the grammar of the gospel: a "no" to all that is not Christ, and a "yes" to only Christ. This antithetical grammar, as the reformers insisted, functions as both a critical and hermeneutical criterion: it identifies and negates any "other gospel" even as it picks out and proclaims "the gospel of Christ." The "no" here is death—"I no longer live." But: there is a "love as strong as death," a love for "me," a love that says, incongruously, "I love you dead," and a love that says, creatively, "Wake up, sleeper, rise from the dead."

---

and Catholic Thought (Cambridge: Cambridge University Press, 2001), 239–40. For a consideration of this theme, see chap. 4, "'The Speech of the Dead.'"

CHAPTER 10

THE TEXTS OF PAUL AND
THE THEOLOGY OF THOMAS CRANMER

> *[A] notable qualitie or virtue he hadd: to be benficiall unto his*
> *enemyes. . . . For whosoever he hadd byn that hadd reportid evil of*
> *hym, or otherwaies wrought or done to hym displeasure, were the*
> *reconciliation never so meane or simple on the behalf of his adver-*
> *sarye . . . the matter was both pardoned and clerelie forgotten, and*
> *so voluntarily caste into the sachell of oblivioin behind the backe*
> *parte, that it was more clere nowe out of memorie, than it was in*
> *mynde before it was either commensid or committed.*

> —J. G. Nicholas, *Narratives of the Days of the Reformation*

This reminiscence from Ralph Morice, Thomas Cranmer's secretary, offers more than a description of Cranmer's character. It captures the core of his evangelical theology.[1] In his 1538 annotations to King Henry VIII's corrections to the Bishop's Book, Cranmer asks, "What were we, when [Jesus] gave his most precious life and blood for us?" And he answers: "horrible sinners and his enemies."[2] Like the apostle Paul in Romans 5:6–10, Cranmer emphasizes the simultaneity of human unworthiness and the definitive embodiment of divine love. "God demonstrates his love for us in this way," writes Paul, "that while we were still sinners Christ died for us"—"while we were enemies we were reconciled to God by the death of his son" (Rom 5:8, 10a). "Sinners" and

---

1. For "evangelical" and the related label "gospellers" as the original designation for reformers like Cranmer in England, see A. Null, "Thomas Cranmer and Tudor Evangelicalism," in *The Advent of Evangelicalism: Exploring Historical Continuities*, ed. M. A. G. Haykin and K. J. Stewart (Nashville: B&H Academic, 2008), 226–30.

2. J. E. Cox, *Miscellaneous Writings and Letters of Thomas Cranmer* (Cambridge: Parker Society, 1846; repr., Vancouver: Regent College Publishing), 110. Hereafter page references to this work are given in parentheses in the text.

"enemies": Paul's words flow from Cranmer's pen as he characterizes the recipients of the love and grace that is the cross of Christ. God, as Cranmer sees in the act of the one "who did not spare his own son but gave him up for us all" (Rom 8:32a), is "always ready to forgive us" (110). Humans may be haunted by the memory of sin and shame, but Cranmer's habit of forgiving and forgetting offense—of casting it "into the sachell of oblivion"—is anchored in what he takes to be a Pauline announcement: the sin we cannot forget, the forgiving God cannot remember.[3]

God, in Christ, forgives his enemies. This is both a summary of Cranmer's reformational theology and the main motif in his reading of Paul. But it is also what might be called the heart of his "theology of the heart."[4] In Cranmer's words, "if the profession of our faith of the remission of our own sins enters within us into the deepness of our hearts, then it must needs kindle a warm fire of love in our hearts towards God, and towards all other[s]" (86). Here, then, is the ground and catalyst for Cranmer's "notable qualitie." Forgiving his enemies was not a personality quirk of Cranmer's, nor was it, to his mind, a simple matter of obedience to Christ's command. To be sure, Cranmer considered it "a true rule of our Saviour Christe to do good for evill," but he was likewise convinced that "it is above our frail and corrupt nature to love our enemies."[5] What "kindled a warm fire of love" in his heart for his enemies was that his own belovedness as an enemy "entered within [him] into the deepness of [his] heart." Pointing to this pattern of God's merciful love producing a mimetic love, Cranmer advised, "if any peradventure will think it to be a hard thing to suffer and forgive his enemy . . . let him consider again, how many hard storms our Saviour Christ suffered and abode for us" (110). For Cranmer, the divine "I love you" spoken in the "I forgive you" of the cross creates its own echo: faith in God and forgiveness for others. Cranmer's habit of forgiveness, therefore, at least as he would tell his own story, was the fruit of having been forgiven.

Understood this way, Cranmer's "notable qualitie," so memorably portrayed in a line from Shakespeare's *Henry VIII*—"Do my Lord of Canterbury / a shrewd turn, and he is your friend forever"—is an X-ray revealing the heart of Cranmer's theology: "God's gracious love," as Ashely Null puts it, "inspires a grateful love in his children."[6]

3. This is, for Cranmer, a distinctively but not exclusively Pauline theme. It is also rooted in texts such as Psalm 103:8–12, Isaiah 43:23, and Hebrews 8:12.
4. For this theme, see A. Null, "Thomas Cranmer's Theology of the Heart," *TJTM* 1 (2007): 18–34.
5. Nicholas, *Narratives*, 247.
6. A. Null, "Conversion to Communion: Thomas Cranmer on a Favourite Puritan Theme,"

This chapter will interact with this core of Cranmer's theology as it is articulated as a reading of Paul. For Cranmer, the identification of God as the one who forgives his enemies is, at least in part, an interpretation of Paul's language of justification. Similarly, the insistence that the experience of being forgiven engenders a willingness to forgive is worked out, again in part, as exegesis of the Pauline expression "faith active in love" (Gal 5:6). These shared Cranmerian and Pauline *loci*—that is, the nature and basis of justification and the meaning, source, and liveliness of faith—will function as icebreakers of sorts, conversation starters that will enable us to eavesdrop on a dialogue between the texts of Paul and the theology that Cranmer confessed as a reading of them.

THE QUEST FOR THE EXEGETICAL CRANMER

Cranmer did not write a commentary. He wrote prayer books and sermons, kept extensive notebooks organizing the discoveries unearthed in the books in his famously vast library, offered marginal comments during the formative stages of what would become public documents, penned a preface to the Bible (1540), maintained prolific correspondences with political players at court and religious reformers on the continent, participated in the crafting of a theological confession, and engaged in (transcribed) debates related to the Lord's Supper and other topics *du jour*. This means that locating texts or passages that can be called readings of Paul is not as easy as pulling a commentary on Galatians or Romans off the shelf.

Further complicating this quest for the exegetical Cranmer is the reality of political constraints on his publications during the Henrician period. It was not until the death of Henry VIII and the subsequent accession of the nine-year-old Edward VI on January 28, 1547, that Cranmer's theological publications could match his theological positions. Edward VI reigned for just over six years, but his short rule witnessed a proliferation of public Protestant formularies. In addition to the *Book of Common Prayer* (1549 and 1552), the *Articles of Religion* appeared in 1553. Cranmer's first publication project, however, was the *Book of Homilies* (1547), which as Null says, "was designed to be both a manifesto of the Edwardian regime's theological agenda and the means of implementation."[7] It is here in the homilies, especially the third, fourth, and

---

Churchman 116 (2002): 250. For an extended discussion of this theme, see A. Null, *Thomas Cranmer's Doctrine of Repentance: Renewing the Power to Love* (Oxford: Oxford University Press, 2000). The Shakespeare quotation is from *Henry VIII*, act 5, scene 3, lines 176–77.

7. See A. Null, "Thomas Cranmer's Reading of Paul's Letters," in *Reformation Readings of Paul*, ed. M. Allen and J. A. Linebaugh (Downers Grove, IL: IVP Academic, 2015).

fifth, which address "Salvation," "Faith," and "Good Works," respectively, that we come closest to a sustained interpretation of Paul. That Cranmer is the author of these three public, serial sermons is evident from their derivation from his research notebooks, known as the "Notes on Justification"[8] and "Cranmer's Great Commonplaces."[9] These three homilies, together with the research notes upon which they are dependent and Cranmer's aforementioned annotations to Henry VIII's corrections to the Bishop's Book, will serve as the main textual sources for this consideration of Cranmer's reading of Paul.

The Justice of God the Father and the Justification of God's Ungodly Children

Having just cited Romans 3:20, 22, 23–24; 8:3–4; 10:4; and Galatians 2:16, Cranmer writes, "In these foresaid places the apostle toucheth specially three things, which must concur and go together in our justification" (128–29). His enumeration is a summary of his exegesis: (1) "upon God's part, his great mercy and grace"; (2) "upon Christ's part, justice, that is, the satisfaction of God's justice" by the "shedding of his blood"; (3) "upon our part, true and lively faith in the merits of Jesus Christ" (129). What Cranmer calls "our part" will be considered below as Cranmer's notion of a "true and lively faith" converses with Paul's phrase πίστις χριστοῦ ("faith in Christ") and the antithesis that helps to define it ("not by works of the law"). This section, however, will let Cranmer's claims about "God's part" and "Christ's part"—that is, the coming together of divine justice and grace in the sending and self-giving of the Son—talk to the texts of which they purport to be an interpretation. Put heuristically: If the Cranmerian references to the justice and grace of God in Christ are readings of the Pauline announcement of "the righteousness of God" and the justification it effects, what might the Pauline texts that make this announcement say to the theology derived from them?

That Cranmer understands himself to be interpreting Paul's phrase "the righteousness of God" (δικαιοσύνη θεοῦ) when he says that "in our justification"

8. The "Notes on Justification" are included in Cox, *Miscellaneous Writings and Letters of Thomas Cranmer.*

9. My access to "Cranmer's Great Commonplaces" (hereafter CGC) is facilitated by Ashley Null, who has either translated or transcribed extensive portions in his various publications on Cranmer. Null is currently engaged in a project to produce a critical edition of "Cranmer's Great Commonplaces." As Cox notes, there is also strong and "nearly contemporary" external evidence attributing these homilies to Cranmer (*Miscellaneous Writings*, 128n1).

there is a convergence of "God's mercy and grace, but also his justice" is evident in the way he ends the sentence: "which the apostle calleth the justice of God." For Cranmer, what Paul calls "the righteousness of God" is revealed in "the mystery of our redemption" (cf. Rom 3:24)—that is, the cross of Christ upon which God "tempered his justice and mercy together," leaving sinners neither in the "prison of hell, remediless for ever," nor "delivered . . . without justice" (129).

It is worth recalling that in Cranmer's carefully ordered collection of homilies, the "Homily of Salvation" followed the homily on the "Misery of Mankind." This reflects Cranmer's reformational understanding of the order and function of the law and the gospel:

> The commandments of God lay our faults before our eyes, putteth us in fear and dread, and maketh us see the wrath of God against our sins, as St Paul saith [referring to Rom 3:20b]. . . . The gracious and benign promises of God by the mediation of Christ sheweth us, (and that to our great relief and comfort,) . . . that we have the forgiveness of our sins, be reconciled to God, and accepted, and reputed just and righteous in his sight. (113)

This sequencing of the homilies also allows Cranmer to open the "Homily of Salvation" with an assumption: "Because all men be sinners and offenders against God . . ." (128). The result of this hamartiological starting point is that "no man can be justified by his own good works because that no man fulfilleth the law" (130), a conclusion Cranmer offers as a reading of Galatians 2:21b and 3:21b. This "excludeth the justice of man" (129) and means that the only hope for justification—that is, the pronouncement that one is judged righteous by God—is the miracle of "another righteousness," a *iustitia aliena* "received from God's own hands" in the form of the "forgiveness of sins" (128).[10]

It is this miracle, this promise of the "impossible," that Cranmer hears in Paul's proclamation that "the righteousness of God has been revealed" (Rom 3:21a). With Paul's Abraham, he is "hoping against hope" (Rom 4:18), crying out from the conclusion that "all, both Jews and Greeks, are under sin" (Rom 3:9), that "no one is righteous" (Rom 3:10), that "all sinned" (Rom 3:23a), and that therefore "by works of the law no human being will be justified" (Rom 3:20a). To Cranmer's exegetical ears, Paul's "word of the cross" (1 Cor 1:18) is at once a confirmation and a contradiction of this conclusion,

---

10. For Cranmer's understanding justification in terms of the pronouncement of righteousness, see CGC 2, 84r: "*Iustificare subinde significat, iustum pronuntiarie, declarare, aut ostendere.*"

the announcement of an event that goes through "the wrath of God revealed from heaven against all ungodliness" and to a new and antithetical conclusion: "there is now no condemnation" (Rom 8:1). For Cranmer, the name of this new conclusion effected by the cross is justification. The death of Jesus weaves a heretofore unimagined tapestry as the "justice and mercy of God [are] knit together": the curse of the law is carried out (Gal 3:13), and yet those who "have offended, and have need of the glory of God" are "justified freely by his grace" (129). Cranmer's quotation of Romans 3:23–24 indicates that this underlining of the disjunction between the divine verdict—"righteous"—and the inherent status of the justified—"unrighteous"—is offered as an interpretation of Paul.

In emphasizing this contradiction, Cranmer captures the core of Paul's announcement in Romans 3:21–24. As Paul pivots from the impossibility of justification (Rom 3:20) to the promise of justification (Rom 3:21–26), he dramatizes the disjunction between the universality of human sin and the somehow stronger word of justification: "All sinned . . . and are justified" (πάντες ἥμαρτον . . . δικαιούμενοι; Rom 3:23–24). Grammatically, the objects of the divine saving action implied in the passive participle δικαιούμενοι (3:24) are the sinners of 3:23.[11] And thus, as James Dunn construes this Pauline paradox, "it is precisely those who have sinned and fallen short of God's glory who are justified."[12] In Cranmer's words, "God justified us when we were sinners."[13]

The "scandal and folly" (1 Cor 1:23) is not lost on Cranmer. "Here," he says, "may man's reason be astonished" (129) because what Paul calls "the justice of God" appears to be an instance of injustice in which, with apparent forensic schizophrenia, God locates and labels unrighteousness (Rom 3:23) only to create its opposite with the word of justification (Rom 3:24). For Cranmer, then, justification, as a forensic word, is a creative word—a *verbum efficax*, to use Luther's phrase.[14] Searching for an analogous action to the "infinite benefits of God, shewed and exhibited unto us mercifully and without deserts," Cranmer sees a consistent pattern of grace in the economy of the one "who not only created us from nothing . . . but also, whereas we were condemned to hell and death eternal, hath given his eternal Son . . . to the intent to justify us and

---

11. Following C. E. B. Cranfield, *A Critical and Exegetical Commentary on the Epistle to the Romans*, 2 vols., ICC (Edinburgh: T&T Clark, 1975), 1:205, I take as the subject of 3:24 the "all" of 3:23 while recognizing that 3:24 continues the main theme from 3:21–22.

12. J. D. G. Dunn, *Romans 1–8*, WBC 38A (Waco, TX: Word, 1988), 1:168.

13. "*Iustificavit nos deus cum peccatores essemus*," CGC 2, 104v. Cf. Romans 5:6–10.

14. Cf. LW 5:140.

restore us to life everlasting" (134).[15] This echoes Paul's language in Romans 4: God is "the one who justifies the ungodly" (4:5), "gives life to the dead," and "calls non-being into being" (4:17). The linking of liturgical predications suggests an analogous form of divine activity in the acts of creation, resurrection, and justification.[16] Nothingness, death, and sin are the site at which God utters a creative counterstatement: creation, life, salvation. Following this Pauline pattern, Cranmer hears God's justifying verdict as a reality-determining declaration: justification is a word spoken to us "while we were [God's] enemies" (Rom 5:10) that "mak[es] us [God's] dear beloved children" (134).[17]

For both Paul and Cranmer, however, justification is not a groundless divine fiat. Rather, justification, understood as God's creative counterstatement to sin, is a word of new creation anchored in the cross. "All the world being wrapped in sin," writes Cranmer, "God sent his only Son our Saviour Christ into this world . . . and by the shedding of his most precious blood, to make a sacrifice and satisfaction . . . to his Father for our sins." Jesus's "'for us' fulfilling [of] the law perfectly and thoroughly" to which Cranmer refers climaxes as the curse of the law is carried out in the "condemning of sin in the flesh of [God's] son" (128). This reading runs with the grain of a passage like Galatians 3:10–13 in which the law's conditional promise of life (Gal 3:12, quoting Lev 18:5b) is contravened by the universality of the deuteronomic curse: "Cursed be everyone who does not abide by all things written in the Book of the Law" (Gal 3:10, quoting Deut 27:26).[18] In this context, redemption from the curse is a consequence of Christ "becoming a curse for us" (Gal 3:13a). On the cross, the deuteronomic curse is not cast aside. It is carried out: "cursed is everyone who is hanged on a tree" (Gal 3:13b, quoting Deut 21:23). When addressing the *locus* of atonement, however, the Pauline texts Cranmer gathers are predominately from Romans, especially Romans 3 (though references to

---

15. Cf. the quotation from Augustine in CGC 2, 255r: "*Gratis creati, gratis et iustificati sumus.*" For the relationship between creation *ex nihilo* and justification *sola gratia*, see chap. 4, "'The Speech of the Dead.'"

16. J. A. Linebaugh, *God, Grace, and Righteousness in Wisdom of Solomon and Paul's Letter to the Romans: Texts in Conversation*, NovTSup 152 (Leiden: Brill, 2013), 152–54; cf. E. Käsemann, *Commentary on Romans*, trans. G. W. Bromiley (Grand Rapids: Eerdmans, 1980), 123.

17. For Cranmer's filial understanding of justification, especially in his reading of Romans 8 in the annotations, see the section entitled "Paul for Cranmer the Solafidian" in Null, "Thomas Cranmer as a Reader of Paul," in *Reformation Readings of Paul*.

18. For this reading of Leviticus 18:5b in early Judaism and Paul, see P. M. Sprinkle, *Law and Life: The Interpretation of Leviticus 18.5 in Early Judaism and in Paul*, WUNT 2.241 (Tübingen: Mohr Siebeck, 2008).

Romans 8 and 10 appear as well).[19] This suggests that his description of the movement from condemnation to no condemnation via Jesus's substitutionary suffering of the law's curse upon the cross is offered, in part, as a reading of Romans 3:21–26. And this Pauline passage, I think, has something to say to Cranmer's reading of it.

As noted above, Cranmer is singing in a Pauline key when he characterizes justification as a creative contradiction effected by the cross: the unrighteous are called righteous through the redemption that is in Christ Jesus (3:23–24). There is, however, what might be called a Pauline harmony that Cranmer does not seem to hear: the disjunctive and reality-determining word of justification is, for Paul, a forensic word from the future. Reading Romans 3:25–26 in conversation with Romans 2:4–5 will explain what I mean.

The oft-noted lexical link between Romans 2:4 and 3:26a (ἀνοχή) occurs within parallel plotlines. In both Romans 2:4–10 and 3:24–26, ἀνοχή is used to characterize an era in contrast to a time defined by the disclosure of divine righteousness (δικαιοκρισία τοῦ θεοῦ, 2:5; δικαιοσύνη αὐτοῦ, 3:26). As Günther Bornkamm observes, in Romans "the periods of salvation history" are "placed in contrast to each other as the time of patience and the time of the showing of righteousness."[20] This observation is offered by Bornkamm as an exegesis of Romans 3:25–26, but, as it stands, it functions as an equally apt description of the implicit plotline of Romans 2:4–5. The present is the time of God's kindness and patience and concludes with the coming apocalypse of God's righteous judgment (2:5). Within this narrative sequence, the end of the era of divine patience is the arrival of the eschaton in the form of a future judgment (2:5–10).

Romans 3:24–26 tells a sequentially similar yet surprising story. Romans 2:4–6 contrasts the present era of patience with the future enactment of justice in the form of a judgment "according to works." Romans 3:25–26,

19. Cranmer organized his research notes and homilies by *loci communes* ("commonplaces" or recurring and significant topics), thus participating in the humanist practice of Erasmus and Melanchthon. In Cranmer, this means that a discussion of a particular *locus* is often followed by quotations from or references to numerous texts that address the given topic. The preceding explanation, therefore, functions as a synthetic reading of multiple texts rather than a detailed exegesis of a particular passage. For Cranmer's use of the *loci* method, see A. Null, "Official Tudor Homilies," in *Oxford Handbook of the Early Modern Sermon*, ed. P. McCullough, H. Adlington, and E. Rhatigan (Oxford: Oxford University Press, 2011), 353–54.

20. G. Bornkamm, "The Revelation of God's Wrath," in *Early Christian Experience* (New York: Harper and Row, 1966), 49.

on the other hand, presents the past as the time of the ἀνοχή τοῦ θεοῦ ("the patience of God"), the time in which God delayed the revelation of his righteous judgment "by passing over former sins," and juxtaposes this era, not with the future "day of wrath" but with the present demonstration of divine righteousness that is the cross. Thus, in narrative terms, God's act of putting Jesus forward as a ἱλαστήριον is functionally parallel to "the revelation of God's righteous judgment." In other words—and here we arrive at the Pauline harmony Cranmer seems not to have heard—the "now-time" (νῦν καιρῷ) of Jesus's death is the eschatological enactment of the future judgment. The cross, to borrow from Hans Urs von Balthasar, is "the full achievement of the divine judgment."[21] Expressed in terms of the parallel between Romans 2:5 and 3:25–26a, the present "demonstration of divine righteousness" (ἔνδειξιν τῆς δικαιοσύνης αὐτοῦ, 3:25, 26a) is the occurrence of the promised "revelation of God's righteous judgment" (ἀποκαλύψεως δικαιοκρισίας τοῦ θεοῦ, 2:5). The "now" of the cross is the "day of wrath" (2:5), the day God shows himself "to be just" (εἰς τὸ εἶναι αὐτὸν δίκαιον, 3:26; cf. 3:5).

The cross, however, is not the justification of God alone. As the καί that links the predicates "just" and "justifier" (Rom 3:26b) indicates, the death of Jesus is simultaneously the event of divine judgment *and* human justification; it is, to borrow Justyn Terry's phrase, "the justifying judgment of God."[22] According to the righteous decree of the righteous God (Rom 2:5; 3:5–6), sinners "are worthy of death" (Rom 1:32; cf. 6:23a). The death of Jesus, in the first instance, is the demonstration of divine righteousness because it is the enactment of this decree: the cross is the condemnation of sin and as such the fulfillment of "the righteous decree of the law" (Rom 8:3–4; cf. Gal 3:10–13). In other words, the gracious sending and self-giving of Jesus (Rom 3:24–25; 8:32; Gal 2:20), is not the circumvention of God's contention with sinful humanity (Rom 1:18; 3:9–20). It is, rather, the completion of that contention in the eschatological judgment that is God's condemnation of sin in the flesh of his son. But—and here we return to the linking of "just" and "justifier"—the condemnation of sin (Rom 8:3) grounds the non-condemnation of the sinner (Rom 8:1). The cross, then, is the "correspondingly" that connects human unrighteousness and God's wrath (Rom 1:18; 3:5), but the "correspondingly" of divine judg-

21. H. U. von Balthasar, *Mysterium Paschale*, trans. A. Nichols (Edinburgh: T&T Clark, 1990), 119.

22. J. Terry, *The Justifying Judgement of God: A Reassessment of the Place of Judgement in the Saving Work of Christ*, Paternoster Theological Monographs (Milton Keynes: Paternoster, 2007).

ment—mysteriously and mercifully—contains and effects the "nevertheless" of justification (Rom 3:24, 26). The arrival of God's eschatological judgment in the "now" of Jesus's death rewrites God's future word of justification (Rom 2:13; 3:20) in the present tense (Rom 3:24, 28; cf. the aorist in 5:1). Justification is not a separate verdict from the one God will speak at final judgment, nor is it only "an anticipation of the future verdict."[23] Justification is the final verdict: a forensic word from the future spoken in the arrival of God's eschatological judgment that is the "now" of Jesus's death (and resurrection; cf. Rom 4:25).

A forensic word from the future: Cranmer does not indicate that he hears this harmony. But he never tires of singing the melody: the God who judges ungodliness on the cross is, in that way, the God "who justifies the ungodly" (Rom 4:5).

FAITH AS THE FINGER OF JOHN THE BAPTIST

Translations of the Pauline phrase πίστις Χριστοῦ have become a litmus test. This exegetical debate, as some construe it, marks a fundamental divide. The interpretive alternatives—"faith in Christ" or "the faith(fulness) of Christ"— entail a more basic set of contrasts: fictional and forensic as opposed to real and participatory, anthropological rather christological (and so, by implication, Pelagian rather than Augustinian).[24] As Richard Hays diagnoses the problem of translating Paul's genitive phrase "faith in Christ," this "understanding of 'faith' and 'justification' in Paul . . . offers no coherent account of the relation between the doctrine of justification and Christology."[25] But Cranmer is likely to ask Karl Barth's question: "What is the *sola fide* other than a faint echo of the

23. N. T. Wright, "New Perspectives on Paul," in *Justification in Perspective: Historical Developments and Contemporary Challenges*, ed. B. L. McCormack (Grand Rapids: Baker Academic, 2006), 260.

24. Richard Hays introduced the "anthropological-Christological" contrast; see *The Faith of Jesus Christ: The Narrative Substructure of Galatians 3:1–4:11*, 2nd ed. (Grand Rapids: Eerdmans, 2002), xxv–xxvi. The expansion of the contrast to include "anthrocentric-theocentric" is most notable in the work of Douglas Campbell, who also employs the distinction between "contractual and covenantal" as well as "Arian-Athanasian," which he borrows from James Torrance's critique of Federal Theology. For Campbell, see especially *The Deliverance of God: An Apocalyptic Rereading of Justification in Paul* (Grand Rapids: Eerdmans, 2009). For Torrance, see "Covenant and Contract: A Study of the Theological Background of Worship in Seventeenth-Century Scotland," *SJT* 23 (1970): 51–76; "The Covenant Concept in Scottish Theology and Politics and Its Legacy," *SJT* 34 (1981): 225–43.

25. Hays, *Faith of Jesus Christ*, xxix. Hays refers in this context to Gerhard Ebeling, "Jesus and Faith," in *Word and Faith* (London: SCM, 1963), 203. Suggestively, in this essay Ebeling

solus Christus?"[26] For Cranmer, the final and comforting answer—nothing—points to a christological understanding of "faith in Christ" that unsettles the theological alternatives some claim the different translations represent.

The question is whether this contrast resonates with Cranmer's reading of Paul. Does Cranmer's rendering of πίστις Χριστοῦ as "faith in Christ" untie the Pauline knot that links justification and Jesus? Is the notion of "righteousness by faith" that Cranmer articulates as a reading of Paul anthropocentric? Cranmer does say that "faith," the third of the "three things" the "apostle toucheth ... which must concur and go together in our justification," is "our part" (129). To place these words within an anthropocentric context, however, would be to commandeer a Cranmerian phrase against Cranmer, for whom "justification is not the office of man, but of God" (131).[27] To the point: for Cranmer, "faith in Christ" is Christocentric.[28] The *sola fide*, which for Cranmer is an interpretation of a Pauline antithesis—"not by works of the law, but through faith in Jesus Christ"—is an anthropological negation and a christological confession: "Faith alone" excludes the human as the subject of salvation and confesses Christ, "who is now the righteousness of all them that truly do believe," as the one by, in, and on the basis of whom God justifies the ungodly (130).

Paul does not consider faith in the abstract; he presents it in an antithesis: "a person is not (οὐκ) justified by works of law (ἐξ ἔργων νόμου) but through faith in Jesus Christ" (διὰ πίστεως Ἰησοῦ Χριστοῦ, Gal 2:16; cf. Rom 3:28). For Cranmer, this formulation indicates what faith is not: "faith in Jesus Christ" is not a "work of the law." According to his "Notes on Justification," Cranmer concludes that "when St Paul said, 'We be justified freely by faith without works,' he meant of all manner of works of the law, as well of the Ten Commandments, as of ceremonials and judicials" (207–8).[29] For Cranmer, then, whatever faith is (see below), it is emphatically not a work—not even, to quote Hays, a "bizarre sort of work in which Christians jump through the entranceway of salvation."[30]

anticipates this rhetorical situation and warns that we must "not let ourselves be impressed by the labels . . . like 'anthropological approach'" ("Jesus and Faith," 202n1).

26. K. Barth, *Church Dogmatics*, IV/1: *The Doctrine of Reconciliation*, ed. G. W. Bromiley and T. F. Torrance, trans. G. W. Bromiley (Edinburgh: T&T Clark, 1956), 632.

27. Cf. CGC 2, 226v.

28. For a parallel argument in relation to Luther's understanding of "faith in Christ," see chap. 11, "The Christocentrism of Faith in Christ."

29. Cranmer cites passages from Romans 2, 3, 4, 5, 7, 8, 9; 2 Corinthians 3; Galatians 2, 3; Ephesians 2; Philippians 3; and Titus 3.

30. R. B. Hays, "ΠΙΣΤΙΣ and Pauline Christology: What Is at Stake?," in *Pauline Theology*, vol. 4: *Looking Back, Pressing On*, ed. D. M. Hay and E. E. Johnson (Atlanta: Scholars, 1997),

Romans 4:3–5 can clarify Cranmer's point. As Paul's citations of Genesis 15:6 indicates, Abraham is the unambiguous subject of the verb πιστεύω (4:3), and yet the antithesis of Romans 4:4–5 makes it impossible to interpret this human act as a "work." Precisely as the subject of πιστεύω, Abraham is ὁ μὴ ἐργαζόμενος ("the one who does not work"; 4:5)—he is χωρὶς ἔργων ("without works"; 4:6)—and his justification is therefore the act of "the one who justifies the ungodly" (4:5). Faith, it seems, as an anthropological action, is an anthropological negation. It is the act of the ungodly in the absence of "works" (4:5, 6). It is what is present as impossibly possible when and where works are not. In this sense, and to borrow from Barth again, faith is "the great negation," the site of nothingness, death, and sin at which God operates out of the opposite, speaking creation (Rom 4:17b), life (4:17b), and salvation (4:5).[31] Faith, in other words, is a "yes" to the divine "no" that is God's judgment against sin in the death of Jesus. Cranmer joins voices with Paul to say that "boasting is excluded" (see Rom 3:27) because the one who has faith "doth not boast himself . . . but knowth himself certainly to be unworthy" and therefore "advanceth not himself for his own righteousness, but knowledgeth himself to lack true justice and righteousness" (130, citing Phil 3). Faith says "no" to the human. That is what the excluded option ("not by works of law") in the Pauline antithesis teaches Cranmer.

But, to return to the argument above, the one whom faith trusts is the God who acts in Jesus to judge and justify the ungodly. Faith lives in this contradiction: it is an anthropological "no" because it says "yes" to the eschatological judgment of the cross. But, to anticipate Cranmer's positive definition of faith, it is also a theological "yes" because it hears in God's "no" of judgment the merciful surprise that is the "yes" of justification. This "no" and "yes" that Cranmer hears in the Pauline formula "justified by faith without works of the law" (Rom 3:28; Gal 2:16) is expressed in the "Homily of Salvation" as exegesis of Paul's words:

> This proposition, that we be justified by faith only, freely, and without works, is spoken for to take away clearly all merit of our works, as being insufficient to deserve our justification at God's hands, and thereby most plainly to express the weakness of man, and the goodness of God; the great infirmity of ourselves, and the might and power of God; the imperfectness of our own works, and the most abundant grace of our Saviour Christ; and

---

56. For further engagement with Hays and contemporary Pauline research on this point, see Linebaugh, *God, Grace, and Righteousness*, 155–60.

31. Barth, *CD* IV/1, 621.

thereby to ascribe the merit and deserving of our justification unto Christ only . . . this doctrine advanceth and setteth forth the true glory of Christ, and suppresseth the vain-glory of man. (131)

Faith acknowledges one's "weakness," "infirmity," and "imperfectness"— that's the anthropological "no." But this same faith confesses God's "goodness," "might and power," and the "grace our Saviour Christ"—that's the christological "yes." And this, for Cranmer, is "the very true sense of [Paul's] proposition." It "excludeth the justice of man" as it sings the sings *solus Christus*: "We put our faith in Christ, that we be justified by him only" (129, 132). Justification by faith, for Cranmer, is a way of saying and safeguarding the soteriological cornerstone: justification by Jesus.

The only alternative Cranmer can see to this exclusively christological confession is a soteriology that is in fact an expression of original sin. To make "justification . . . the office of man," either "in part, or in the whole," is the "greatest arrogancy and presumption of man," and makes the sons of Adam and daughters of Eve who have been seduced by the serpent's whisper, "you will be like God" (Gen 3:5), "adversar[ies] of Christ and his gospel" (131). Faith, however, is the opposite of idolatry. It affirms the dependence of the creature in both creation and redemption and therefore says, "justification is the office of God only, and it is not a thing which we render unto him but which we receive of him; not which we give to him, but which we take of him" (131). Faith, then, is not what justifies. Rather, faith is the confession that nothing and no one but Christ justifies. In Cranmer's words:

> The true understanding of this doctrine, that we be justified freely by faith . . . is not, that this our own act to believe in Christ, or this our faith in Christ, which is within us, doth justify us, and merit our justification unto us (for that were to count ourselves to be justified by some act or virtue that is within ourselves): but the true understanding and meaning thereof is, that although we hear God's word, and believe it; although we have faith . . . we must renounce the merit of all our said virtues, of faith, hope, charity, and all our other virtues and good deeds . . . as things far too weak and insufficient and unperfect to deserve remission of our sins, and our justification. (131)

Faith, in other words, does not trust in faith; it "trust only in God's mercy." As Cranmer records in his the "Notes on Justification," "neither faith nor charity be the worthiness and merits of our justification, but that is to be ascribed only to our Saviour Christ, which," and here Cranmer quotes Romans 4:25, "was offered upon the cross for our sins, and rose again for our justification" (209).[32]

This reading of the Pauline antitheses catches their christological confession. In Romans 4:4–5, for example, as Halvor Moxnes observes, the antithesis between "works" and "faith" is unbalanced by the addition of the predication "the one who justifies the ungodly," which directs the reader "not to faith *per se*, but to God, in whom one believes."[33] The salvific subject here is not believing Abraham—he is "the one who does not work"—but the justifying God. This pattern reverberates throughout the chapter. Abraham's faith lives at the disjunction between the content of God's promise ("so shall your offspring be," Rom 4:18) and empirical reality ("his body was as good as dead" and "Sarah's womb was dead," 4:19). The grounds for this "hope against hope" (4:18), however, is not Abraham's faith but the one in whom Abraham believes: "the God who makes alive the dead and calls non-being into being" (Rom 4:17), the God who "raised from the dead Jesus our Lord (4:25).[34] Similarly, the contrast between "law" and "faith" in Romans 3:21–22 is made asymmetrical by the identification of faith's object: Jesus Christ. Faith, because it is "apart from law," is a pointing away from self and, because it is "faith in Jesus Christ," is a pointing to the singular saving subject that Cranmer calls God's "most dearly-beloved Son" (131). In Cranmer's most precise (and deeply Pauline) formulation, it is not that faith justifies but that "Christ is now the righteousness of all them that truly do believe in him" (130).[35]

For Paul, to say that "the righteousness of God" is "the righteousness of God through faith in Jesus Christ" is to say that God's eschatological act of judgment and justification is irreducibly and exclusively singular: it is Jesus Christ. Cranmer, as a reader of Paul, put it this way: "We put our faith in Christ, that we be justified by him only" (132). Rather than qualifying Paul's christological singularity (*solus Christus*) and his announcement of God's unconditioned grace (*sola gratia*), Cranmer said *sola fide* as their echo and affirmation (cf. Rom 4:16; 11:6).[36] Expressed with Paul's pen, faith's motto is "not I, but Christ"

32. Cranmer also cites Titus 3:5 at this point in the "Notes."

33. H. Moxnes, *Theology in Conflict: Studies in Paul's Understanding of God in Romans*, NovTSup 53 (Leiden: Brill, 1980), 42.

34. The passive forms of ἐνδυναμόω and πληροφορέω in 4:20 and 4:21 suggest that even Abraham's believing is generated by God through the promise (cf. Rom 10:17). Cranmer can make a parallel point, saying "a true and lively faith . . . is the gift of God" and is therefore "not ours, but God's working in us." Cf. CGC 2, fols. 251v, 252r.

35. Cf. 1 Corinthians 1:30: "Christ is our righteousness."

36. In the "Homily of Salvation," Cranmer cites Romans 11:6 as "the sum of all Paul's disputation in this" (130).

(Gal 2:20). Cranmer's image is of faith as the finger of "St John Baptist," which "put the people from him, and appointed them," not merely with assent but with "sure trust and confidence," "unto Christ" (132–33).

It's Alive: Faith Active in Love

The homilies on faith and good works are officially entitled "A Short Declaration of the True, Lively, and Christian Faith" and "An Homily or Sermon of Good Works Annexed unto Faith." Together they center on two characteristics of faith: "First, that this faith doth not lie dead in the heart, but is lively and fruitful in bringing forth good works. Second, that without it no good works be done, that shall be acceptable and pleasant to God" (136). For Cranmer, this is a mutual necessity: good works inevitably flow from faith; in the absence of faith there is an absence of good works. In this sense, Cranmer's phrase "lively faith" is a double entendre: faith is both alive and life-giving—it "worketh by charity" and it "doth give life to works" (135).

Galatians 5:6 provides Cranmer with an antithesis to the "idle, unfruitful, and dead" "persuasion . . . whereby [a person merely] knoweth that there is a God, and assenteth unto all truth of God's most holy word." Whereas this *fides historica* (i.e., faith in the facts of history) is a "dead faith," "a sure trust and confidence of the mercy of God through our Lord Jesus Christ, and a steadfast hope of all good things to be received at God's hand" is a "lively faith" (135).[37] Cranmer can therefore identify the "faith which is wholesome and clearly evangelical" by quoting Paul: it is "the faith which he says works by love" (Gal 5:6).[38] In its Pauline context, faith is both freedom from the curse of the law (Gal 3:13, 22–26) and freedom for the love of others (Gal 5:13). The law "locked up everything under sin" (3:22), but the coming of faith (3:23, 25), which is the coming of Christ (3:24), establishes a filial freedom ("you are children of God," 3:26) and unlocks love for others (5:6, 13).

In his "Great Commonplaces," Cranmer, with help from Augustine, traces this Pauline transition from slavery to sonship, insisting that while fear is a sign of slavery, faith lives in the space of filial freedom.[39] Cranmer can both join Paul is saying, "Whatsover work is done without faith, it is sin" (Rom 14:23) and follow the Pauline move from faith to love: faith is "the ground of all good works" (141–42). Reading Romans 14:23 and Galatians 5:6, it seems, compels a

37. For Cranmer's understanding of faith as *fiducia* (sure, personal trust), see Null, *Thomas Cranmer's Doctrine of Repentance*, 165–66.

38. CGC 2, 261v.

39. CGC 247r; cf. Null, *Thomas Cranmer's Doctrine of Repentance*, 167.

double confession (143): "nothing is good without faith" (an interpretation of Rom 14:23); "faith of itself is full of good works" (an interpretation of Gal 5:6). Following Augustine, Cranmer understands "good deeds to be measured . . . by the ends and intents for which they be done." Because faith is the antithesis of the "antichrist" ambition to justify oneself, "faith it is that doth commend work to God" (131).[40] Faith, in other words, extracts works from the satanic scheme of self-salvation and locates them within the responsive gratitude that is the echo created by God's prior and unconditioned grace.

The logic here is related to what might be called Cranmer's affective anthropology. Echoing Philipp Melanchthon's first edition of the *Loci communes* (1521), Cranmer understands the decisions of the will to be determined by the desires of the affections: we choose what we love. This means that any reorienting of the human will results from a replacing of the human heart. No wonder Cranmer confesses, "we have no power of ourselves to help ourselves" (collect for the second Sunday in Lent). If death and resurrection are required for the will's redirection, then as Cranmer's collect for the fourth Sunday after Easter prays, it is "Almighty God who alone canst order the unruly wills and affections of sinful men." For Paul, as the parallel between Galatians 5:6 and Galatians 6:14–15 suggests, the reality of a faith that is active in love results from the cosmos-crucifying-and-re-creating event that is the cross of Christ (5:14–15). "Lively faith," to combine Cranmerian and Pauline language, is a "new creation" (Gal 6:15) In Cranmer's words, "a loving heart" is what "doth follow" from "true Christian faith" (133). It is the "great and merciful benefits of God" that "move us to render ourselves to God" and "for his sake also to be ever ready to give ourselves to our neighbours" (134). As Null summarizes: "When the good news of justification by faith was proclaimed, the Spirit, working through God's Word, assured believers of their salvation. This new confidence in God's gracious goodwill towards them reoriented their affections, calming their turbulent hearts and inflaming in them a grateful love in return."[41]

Faith, for Cramner, is the opposite of fear. It is "sure trust and confidence in God's merciful promises."[42] It is, in other words, the presence of "the profession of our faith of the remission of our own sins" in "the deepness of our hearts." Faith is being loved. And such belovedness, for Cranmer, "must kindle a warm

---

40. "For man cannot justify himself by his own works . . . that were the greatest arrogancy and presumption of man that the antichrist could erect against God, to affirm that a man might by his own works take away and purge his own sins, and so justify himself" (131).

41. Null, *Thomas Cranmer and Tudor Evangelicalism*, 241.

42. CGC 2, fol 247; Cox, *Miscellaneous Writings*, 133.

fire of love in our hearts towards God, and towards all other[s]" (86). Cranmer's "notable qualitie" is a parable of this, a biographic reading of Romans 5:10 and Galatians 5:6 you might say. His "sure trust" in God's reconciliation of him "while [he] was an enemy" (Rom 5:10) was active in love (Gal 5:6)—or, in this case, leniency. The fruit of having been forgiven as an enemy was a habit of being "benficiall unto his enemyes." This, as Cranmer understands himself within the Pauline grammar of "faith," is "freedom." And "freedom" is faith active in love: it is the march of love cascading from the divine "I love you" (gospel) to the affective certainty of being love by God (faith), which in turn "must kindle a warm fire of love" for others.

LET US PRAY

Thomas Cranmer's 1552 *Book of Common Prayer* is "the only effective attempt ever made to give liturgical expression to the doctrine of 'justification by faith alone.'"[43] This is the opinion of Gregory Dix, and to the extent it is correct it can also be said that Cranmer's second prayer book is, in part, a liturgical expression of his reading of Paul, the apostle of justification by faith. Paul, in other words, is among those who taught Cranmer to pray. The words of absolution, for example, are littered with Pauline language; the inclusion of the reading of the Decalogue with the refrain "Lord, have mercy on us" reflects Romans 3:20 ("through the law comes the knowledge of sin"); the Pauline pattern of the word creating the faith that communes with it (see Rom 10:17; 1 Cor 10:16) is followed in the elimination of the epiclesis, a change that makes the reception of the bread and wine—the "feeding on him in your hearts by faith"—the immediate response to the words of institution; one of the four "comfortable words" comes from the Pauline corpus (1 Tim 1:15); all self-offering is reserved for the post-Communion prayer, making the presentation of one's self as a "living sacrifice" a response to having received "God's mercies" in the "full, perfect and sufficient sacrifice, oblation, and satisfaction" of Christ "once offered." (cf. Rom 12:1).[44]

The thesis is confirmed: Cranmer, in part, learned to pray from Paul. It seems fitting, therefore, to conclude this conversation by inviting Paul to join Cranmer in a prayer that employs his theological grammar. Pauline texts regu-

43. G. Dix, *The Shape of the Liturgy* (Westminster: Dacre, 1945), 672.

44. For a full consideration of these changes to the liturgy, see Null, *Thomas Cranmer's Doctrine of Repentance*, 236–47, who concludes by describing "the solafidian shape of the liturgy as a whole" (244).

larly turn on an adversative: "I am unworthy . . . but (δέ) by the grace of God I am what I am" (1 Cor 15:9–10); "by works of the law no human being will be justified . . . but (δέ) now the righteousness of God has been disclosed" (Rom 3:20–21; cf. Gal 1:13–16; 2:16; Eph 2:1–6). This Pauline pattern shapes the "Prayer of Humble Access." I can hear Cranmer saying, "Let us pray." And (I think) I can hear Paul joining him:

> We doe not presume to come to this thy table (O mercyfull Lorde) trusting in our owne righteousnesse, *but* in thy manifolde and great mercies: we bee not worthye, so much as to gather up the crommes under thy table: *but* thou are the same Lorde whose propertie is always to haue mercye.

CHAPTER 11

THE CHRISTOCENTRISM OF FAITH IN CHRIST

MARTIN LUTHER'S READING OF GALATIANS 2:16, 19–20

> *This [is] the reason our theology is sure: it snatches us away from*
> *ourselves and places us outside ourselves, so that we do not depend*
> *on our own strength, conscience, experience, person, or works but*
> *depend on that which is outside ourselves, that is, on the promise*
> *and truth of God.*

—Martin Luther

"What," asked Karl Barth, "is the *sola fide* other than a faint echo of the *solus Christus?*"[1] In implicit answer to this question, an increasing number of Pauline scholars have failed to see what, for Barth, was the obvious and inextricable connection between faith in Christ and the person and work of Christ. Referring to an essay by Gerhard Ebeling, Richard Hays has suggested that the great weakness of the reformational "understanding of 'faith' and 'justification' in Paul is that it offers no coherent account of the relation between the doctrine of justification and Christology."[2] Within this rhetorical context, the πίστις Χριστοῦ debate is a line in the sand. Translate the genitive phrase as "faith in Christ" and your reading of Paul is anthropological, anthropocentric, contractual, and now even Arian. But interpret πίστις Χριστοῦ as "the faith/faithfulness of Christ," and thus as a compressed reference to the narrative of Jesus's life and death, and your exegesis is christological, theocentric, covenantal, and Athanasian.[3]

1. K. Barth, *Church Dogmatics*, IV/1: *The Doctrine of Reconciliation*, ed. G. W. Bromiley and T. F. Torrance, trans. G. W. Bromiley (Edinburgh: T&T Clark, 1956), 632.
2. R. Hays, *The Faith of Jesus Christ: The Narrative Substructure of Galatians 3:1–4:11*, 2nd ed. (Grand Rapids: Eerdmans, 2002), xxix; quoting G. Ebeling, "Jesus and Faith," in *Word and Faith* (London: SCM, 1963), 203.
3. Hays introduced the "anthropological-Christological" contrast with Bultmann as the

This chapter is not a defiant attempt to plant my flag in an unpopular camp, taking a stand with those influenced by Heidegger or even Arius in defense of a *sola fide* that somehow drives a wedge between justification and Jesus. Rather, I will argue that this semantic debate, as it is currently construed, poses false theological alternatives. Contrary to the criticism of some opponents of the subjective genitive interpretation, the notion of Christ exercising faith is not theologically dubious.[4] Borrowing a formulation from Michael Allen, I regard "the faith of Christ" as both christologically coherent and soteriologically necessary.[5] That said, I also regard "the faith of Christ" to be a mistranslation of Paul's πίστις Χριστοῦ phrases and the theological correction it claims to offer to betray a fundamental misunderstanding of reformational readings of Paul. The stress of this chapter falls on the latter contention, and it will therefore argue historically about Reformation reception of Paul rather than grammatically about the translation of πίστις Χριστοῦ. The specific focus is Martin Luther's reading of Galatians 2:16, 19–20. My thesis can be stated simply: For Luther, "faith in Christ" is Christocentric.[6] More fully expressed, the *sola fide*, as an interpretation of a Pauline antithesis—"not by works of the law, but through faith in Jesus Christ"—is an anthropological negation and a christological

named polemical target (*Faith of Jesus Christ*, xxv–xxvi). The expansion of the contrast to included "anthrocentric-theocentric" is most notable in the work of Douglas Campbell, as are the "contractual-covenantal" and "Arian-Athanasian" distinctions that he borrows from James Torrance's critique of Federal Theology. For Campbell, see especially *The Deliverance of God: An Apocalyptic Rereading of Justification in Paul* (Grand Rapids: Eerdmans, 2009). For Torrance, see "Covenant and Contract: A Study of the Theological Background of Worship in Seventeenth-Century Scotland," *SJT* 23 (1970): 51–76, and "The Covenant Concept in Scottish Theology and Politics and Its Legacy," *SJT* 34 (1981): 225–43. Interestingly, in the essay Hays quotes, Ebeling anticipated this rhetorical situation and warned that we must "not let ourselves be impressed by the labels . . . like 'anthropological approach'" ("Jesus and Faith," 202n1).

4. See, e.g., D. J. Moo, *The Epistle to the Romans*, NICNT (Grand Rapids: Eerdmans, 1996), 225. Moo's opinion reflects Aquinas's insistence that the infused knowledge of the incarnate Son negates Jesus's need for faith, see Thomas Aquinas, *Summa theologiae*, III a. 7, 3. References to the *Summa theologiae* are to the Blackfriars edition, 60 vols. (New York: McGraw-Hill, 1963–76).

5. R. M. Allen, *The Christ's Faith: A Dogmatic Account*, T&T Clark Studies in Systematic Theology (London: T&T Clark, 2009).

6. S. Chester, "It is No Longer I Who Live: Justification by Faith and Participation in Christ in Martin Luther's Exegesis of Galatians," *NTS* 55 (2009): 315–37, reaches a similar conclusion by considering the relationship between justification and participation in Luther's reading of Galatians.

confession: it excludes the human as the subject of salvation and confesses Christ, who is present in faith, as the *one* by, in, and on the basis of whom God justifies the ungodly.[7]

NOT BY WORKS OF THE LAW

As Luther reads Galatians 2:16, he notes that Paul does not consider faith in the abstract. Rather, Paul presents faith in an antithesis: "a person is not justified by works of law but through faith in Jesus Christ" (οὐ δικαιοῦται ἄνθρωπος ἐξ ἔργων νόμου ἐὰν μὴ διὰ πίστεως Ἰησοῦ Χριστοῦ). This antithesis, as Barry Matlock observes, reflects a Pauline pattern: a form of *pistis* is set in contrast to law and/or works with δικαιόω or δικαιοσύνη as the middle term.[8] For Luther, this syntactical structure becomes theologically significant at Galatians 2:16: justification is both "not by works of law" and "through faith in Jesus Christ," and therefore, as Luther interprets Galatians, Paul "is contrasting the righteousness of faith with the righteousness of the law."[9] According to the summative *argumentum* to the 1531/5 lectures on Galatians, Luther regards this distinction between "two kinds of righteousness" as "the argument of the

7. Once the theological objections are addressed, the strong semantic case for something like the objective genitive can be heard: (1) Paul's instrumental faith clauses are derived from the ἐκ πίστεως of Habakkuk 2:4, which does not (*pace* R. B. Hays, *The Conversion of the Imagination: Paul as Interpreter of Israel's Scripture* [Grand Rapids: Eerdmans, 2005], 119–42) employ ὁ δίκαιος as a christological title but as a reference to the generic, believing human, a point confirmed by the appeal to Abraham in Romans 4 and Galatians 3; so F. Watson, *Paul, Judaism and the Gentiles: Beyond the New Perspective* (Grand Rapids: Eerdmans, 2007), 240. (2) In Paul, Jesus is never the subject of the verb πιστεύω and Paul's habit of interpreting an instance of the verb in a citation with reference to the noun (e.g., Rom 4:3, 5; 9:32–33 10:5–11, 16–17) indicates that the meaning of the noun and verb have not drifted apart; so R. B. Matlock, "Detheologizing the ΠΙΣΤΙΣ ΧΡΙΣΤΟΥ Debate: Cautionary Remarks from a Lexical Semantic Perspective," *NovT* 42 (2000): 13–14; cf. Watson, *Paul, Judaism and the Gentiles*, 243. (3) The question of redundancy in Romans 3:22; Galatians 2:16; 3:22; and Philippians 3:9 points to "a much wider pattern of repetition of πίστις/πιστεύω in Galatians and Romans, rooted in Genesis 15:6 and Habakkuk 2:4" that functions to disambiguate the genitive phrase; so R. B. Matlock, "Saving Faith: The Rhetoric and Semantics of πίστις in Paul," in *The Faith of Jesus Christ: Exegetical, Biblical and Theological Studies*, ed. M. F. Bird and P. M. Sprinkle (Peabody, MA: Hendrickson, 2009), 89.

8. Matlock, "Saving Faith," 77, notes Galatians 2:16, 19, 20, 21; 3:2, 5, 7, 8, 9, 10, 11, 12, 14, 18, 21, 22, 24, 26; 5:4, 5; Romans 3:20, 22, 25, 26, 27, 28, 30, 31; 4:3, 6, 11, 13, 14, 16; 5:1; 9:30, 32; 10:5, 6; Philippians 3:9; cf. Romans 4:4–5; 9:32 (Eph 2:8–9).

9. Martin Luther, *Lectures on Galatians* (1531/5) (LW 26:122; WA 40.1:218, 15–18).

epistle."[10] The antithesis between "works of the law" and "faith in Jesus Christ" is read as expressing an essential contrast between active and passive righteousness. In explicit disagreement with Jerome and Erasmus who interpret the phrase "works of the law" as a restricted reference to the ceremonial law, Luther, based on the subsequent argument of Galatians which he understands to concern the whole law (see, e.g., Gal 3:10–26; 5:3), insists that "works of the law be taken in the broadest possible sense."[11] Law names the divine demand and therefore the entire Mosaic legislation. Thus, in his reading, the excluded option in Galatians 2:16—justification by works of the law—is a reference to the establishment of righteousness before God on the basis of works performed in accordance with the law: it specifies a justification that is grounded in human action rather than divine giving.

While this "active righteousness" has its proper place—after justification and before the world in service to one's neighbor—it oversteps its limits if and when the topic is the righteousness that avails before God. To paraphrase Luther, justification is outside the law's jurisdiction. Nevertheless, in what he refers to as an "unhappy habit," "reason cannot refrain from looking at active righteousness."[12] Human history is haunted by the serpent's words: "Did God really say? You will be as God." For Luther, the unbelief evoked by the serpent's question has as its inevitable consequence the self-righteous idolatry suggested by the serpent's promise: failing to live from the word of the creator and thus outside oneself in faith toward God and love for others, human existence is characterized by the incurvation associated with attempting to live from and for the self—what Luther called the *ambitio divinitatis*.

Within this theological frame, "justification by works of the law" specifies the fundamental form of human bondage: disbelief in the giftedness of creation and salvation and a corresponding (and idolatrous) attempt to establish and save oneself. While this may be a theological expansion rather than a focused exegesis of Galatians 2:16, Luther indicates his awareness of the particularity of Paul's polemical target and thus the distance between the first and sixteenth centuries. In his words, "For if according to the testimony of

10. LW 26:4; WA 40.1:40, 25–26. While this chapter will focus on the 1531 lectures, it is worth noting that this basic contrast is present in the 1519 revision of his 1516–17 *Lectures on Galatians* as well: "There are two ways in which a man is justified. . . . In the first place, there is the external way, by works. . . . This is the kind of righteousness the Law of Moses, even the Decalogue itself, brings about. . . . In the second place, there is the inward way, on the basis of faith and of grace" (LW 27:219–20).

11. LW 26:122; WA 40.1:217, 27–28.

12. LW 26:5; WA 40.1:42, 18–19.

the apostle, no one is justified by the works of the divine law, much less will anyone be justified by the rule of Benedict or Francis?"[13] Put another way, if the Mosaic Law, which Luther can refer to as the "best of all things in the world"[14] and the "most salutary doctrine of life," "cannot," as he says in the Heidelberg Disputation, "advance humans on their way to righteousness,"[15] then, *mutatis mutandis*, merits and masses certainly do not justify. The issue, for Luther, is not primarily "what" people do (that is, which laws) or even "who" performs the works (the human or the Holy Spirit). For Luther, Paul's critique centers on "why" works of the law are performed. As he puts it, "good works and love must also be taught; but this must be in its proper time and place. . . . But when we are involved in a discussion of justification, there is no room for speaking about the law."[16]

The reason for this totalizing claim, as noted above, is that Luther regards the righteousness of the law, and thus justification by works of the law, as fundamentally "active": human beings, bound to exist as "unhappy and proud gods," are tethered to their "own righteousness" (which, as Luther notes, appears as a synonym to "the righteousness of the law" in Romans 10 and Philippians 3).[17] The negation of justification by works of the law in Galatians 2:16 is therefore, according to Luther's reading, the exclusion of the human as the subject of salvation.[18] This excluded soteriological option is essential to understanding the corresponding Pauline phrase: διὰ πίστεως Ἰησοῦ Χριστοῦ. The coordination of these mutually interpreting assertions suggests that the negation of justification by works of the law provides a negative definition of the phrase "faith in Jesus Christ." In other words, for Luther, "by works of the law" is a soteriological antonym to "faith in Christ" and thus, as its excluded opposite, entails and partially defines the debated phrase: not by works of the law indicates that the human is not the subject of salvation; faith in Christ identifies Jesus as the savior.

It is precisely this observation—that it is Jesus rather than the believer who justifies—that motivates the translation of the genitive phrase as the faith or faithfulness of Jesus Christ. As Richard Hays remarks, "the Christological

13. LW 26:140; WA 40.1:245.
14. LW 26:5; WA 40.1:42, 22.
15. M. Luther, *Heidelberg Disputation* (1518), LW 31:39, 42.
16. LW 26:137; WA 40.1:240, 17–19.
17. M. Luther, *Work on the Psalms*, WA 5:128, 36.
18. For my understanding of what Paul's "not by works of law" clause excludes in Galatians and the extent to which this does and does not correspond to Luther's interpretation of the phrase, see chap. 9, "The Grammar of the Gospel."

[that is, subjective] reading highlights the salvific efficacy of Jesus Christ's faithfulness . . . the anthropological [that is, objective] reading stresses the salvific efficacy of the human act of faith."[19] If Paul's antithesis excludes the human as a co-operative saving agent—as Luther reads the negated reference to justification by works of the law—and if the translation of διὰ πίστεως Ἰησοῦ Χριστοῦ as "faith in Jesus Christ" stresses the efficacy of a human act, turning faith, as Hays says, into a "bizarre sort of work," then the subjective reading would appear to provide a necessary soteriological solution.[20] But here's the surprise: the current concern to ensure the singularity of the salvific subject (*solus Christus*) is exactly what Luther and his Protestant heirs thought they were purifying and proclaiming with their insistence that justification is by grace alone, through faith alone, on account of Christ alone. In other words, for the reformers, the *sola fide* was consistent with, and as we will see necessary to, the *solus Christus*. This invites a fresh consideration of Luther's Christocentric understanding of faith in Christ.

THROUGH FAITH IN JESUS CHRIST

Whatever Luther thought faith in Jesus Christ was, he certainly did not regard it as the human contribution to salvation—as "a bizarre sort of work in which Christians jump through the entranceway of salvation," to quote Hays again.[21] In a series of Disputations on Romans 3:28, a parallel to Galatians 2:16, Luther repeatedly critiques the thesis that faith is a work and therefore works justify. First, just as law and promise are distinct, so works and faith are distinct. Works relate to law; faith relates to promise. It is therefore a category mistake to label faith a work. Second, faith is more properly called a divine work than a human work because it is given by the Holy Spirit in the speaking of the promise. As the 1519 *Lectures on Galatians* puts it, "Faith comes through the Word of Christ."[22] For Luther, faith is not a work because it is oriented to God's promise and because God creates faith by the promise.[23] As Oswald Bayer summarizes, "turning toward salvation, which is what faith is, is in no way the work of the human being; it is the work of God—just as the divine

19. R. B. Hays, "ΠΙΣΤΙΣ and Pauline Christology: What Is at Stake?," in *Pauline Theology*, vol. 4: *Looking Back, Pressing On*, ed. D. M. Hay, and E. E. Johnson (Atlanta: Scholars, 1997), 35–60.

20. Hays, "ΠΙΣΤΙΣ and Pauline Christology," 293.

21. Hays, "ΠΙΣΤΙΣ and Pauline Christology," 293.

22. LW 27:220.

23. *The Disputation Concerning Justification* (1536), LW 34:189; WA 39.1:120.

promise that creates faith is solely the work of God."[24] Thus, in distinction
to the active righteousness of the law, Luther calls the righteousness of faith
passive or receptive and insists that "here we work nothing, render nothing to
God; we only receive and permit someone else to work in us."[25] This language
is reminiscent of Luther's earlier definition of faith in his 1522 preface to his
published lectures on Romans: "Faith is a divine work in us. It changes us and
makes us to be born anew of God. It kills the old Adam and makes altogether
different people."[26] For Luther, then, the first thing to say about the righteousness of faith is that "we do not perform but receive."[27] He can therefore answer
his own question, "do we do nothing and work nothing in order to obtain this
righteousness?" with an emphatic, "I reply: nothing at all."[28]

This interpretation of "through faith" in Galatians 2:16 is informed by a
reading of Romans 4. As Paul's citation of Genesis 15:6 in Romans 4:3 indicates, Abraham is the unambiguous subject of the verb πιστεύω, and yet the
antithesis of Romans 4:4–5 makes it impossible to interpret this human act as
a "work." Precisely as the subject of πιστεύω, Abraham is "the one who does
not work" (ὁ μὴ ἐργαζόμενος)—he is, as verse 4 says, "without works" (χωρὶς
ἔργων)—and his justification is therefore the act of the one who justifies the
ungodly.[29] Here, as in Luther's reading of Galatians 2:16, πίστις, as an anthropological action, is an anthropological negation: faith is the act of the ungodly
in the absence of works and what is present as the impossibly possible when
works are excluded.[30] According to this interpretation, faith is not a human
contribution or a new point of correspondence between divine saving action
and the believing human subject. It is an affirmation of the contradiction between the form and recipient of God's activity: God justifies the ungodly, gives
life to the dead, and calls non-being into being (Rom 4:5, 17). In Barth's words,
the *"sola fide* is the great negation,*"* it is the site of ungodliness, deadness, and
nothingness at which the creative and gracious God operates out of the op-

---

24. O. Bayer, *Martin Luther's Theology: A Contemporary Interpretation*, trans. T. H. Trapp
(Grand Rapids: Eerdmans, 2008), 188.

25. LW 26:5; WA 40.1:41, 1–2.

26. M. Luther, *Preface to the Epistle of St. Paul to the Romans* (1522), LW 35:370; WA
DB, 7:11.

27. LW 26:6; WA 40.1:43, 15–16.

28. LW 26:8; WA 40.1:47, 15–16.

29. For a reading of Romans 4, see chap. 2, "Promises beyond the Possible."

30. This theme is already present in the 1519 lectures, where Luther insists that righteousness "on the basis of faith and of grace" occurs "when a man utterly despairs of his former
righteousness" (LW 27:220).

posite.[31] In this sense, as Bayer puts it, "the human being who believes thus speaks in *via negationis*—not about God but about himself."[32] For Luther, the exclusion of justification by works of the law and the announcement of justification by faith in Jesus Christ means that "faith" is an anthropological "no": it takes God's side in the divine judgment against the sinner. But, to anticipate the argument, it is also a theological "yes" because it is directed to the God who speaks and, as Luther would insist, thereby effects (*verbum efficax*), the merciful "yes" of justification.[33]

Luther, as was his rhetorical and pastoral habit, celebrates the power of faith with great diversity. Faith is the fulfillment of the first commandment; faith is the receptive posture of the creature in distinction from and dependence on the creator; faith clings to and is created by the promise; faith is a living, daring confidence in God's grace; faith lets God be God. Despite this variety, however, when answering the specific question why the righteousness of faith avails before God, Luther's answer is consistently christological. Commenting on Galatians 2:16 Luther says, "faith justifies because it takes hold of and possesses this treasure, the present Christ," and therefore "the true Christian righteousness" is not the human act of believing; it is "the Christ who is grasped by faith . . . and on account of whom God counts us righteous."[34] This recalls the marriage imagery from *The Freedom of the Christian*, where Luther relates faith to a wedding ring and grounds justification in the marriage union between Christ and the sinner such that the Christian can say with the Song of Solomon, "My beloved is mine and I am his."[35] The intimacy of this account is anchored in the "joyous exchange," a communion of persons (not just properties) in which Christ takes the believer's sin and gives his righteousness such that justification is

---

31. Barth, *CD* IV/1, 621.

32. Bayer, *Martin Luther's Theology*, 172; cf. 191: "faith, for Luther, is in forgetting the self completely."

33. Cf. H. J. Iwand, *The Righteousness of Faith according to Luther*, trans. R. H. Lundell (Eugene, OR: Wipf & Stock, 2008): "in faith a person takes a decisively judging position *for* God and *against* himself."

34. LW 26:130; WA 40.1:229, 22–30. This theme is repeated again and again in Reformation and post-Reformation texts. See, e.g., the Heidelberg Catechism (61): "Question. Why do you say that you are righteous by faith alone? Answer. Not because I please God by virtue of the worthiness of my faith, but because the satisfaction, righteousness, and holiness of Christ alone are my righteousness before God." Cf. the Westminster Larger Catechism 73. For Thomas Cranmer's understanding of Paul's language of faith in Christ, see chap. 10, "The Texts of Paul and the Theology of Thomas Cranmer."

35. M. Luther, "Freedom of a Christian," in *Three Treatises*, trans. W. A. Lambert, revised by H. Grimm (Philadelphia: Fortress, 1970), 286–87.

participation in the present Christ. Because Christ "took upon himself our sinful person and granted us his innocent and victorious person," because he became "Peter the denier, Paul the persecutor . . . David the adulterer" and "the person of all people," Luther invites us to sing, "mine are Christ's living and dying."[36] As Luther comments on Galatians, "faith takes hold of Christ in such a way that Christ is the object of faith, or rather not the object but, so to speak, the One who is present in faith itself."[37] It is therefore Christ, who is present in faith, that is "our righteousness" (a point Luther repeats throughout the Galatians lectures). This means that justification is, as the reformers consistently affirmed, *propter Christum*: it is by, in, and on the basis of Christ alone. And therefore, as Luther remarks, the expression "faith alone" is a shorthand for a three-part affirmation: "These three things are joined together: faith, Christ, and imputation. Faith takes hold of Christ and God accounts you righteous on account of Christ."[38]

This christological focus continues in Luther's comments on Galatians 2:19–21. As Luther notes, the terms "law," "faith," and "righteousness" in these verses indicate that the subject matter has not shifted, but the imagery, as Gerhard Forde captures it, has moved from the courtroom to the cemetery.[39] Justification, as Luther reads Galatians 2:19–20, is a matter of life and death—or perhaps more accurately, of death and life.[40] Through the law one dies to the law so that one might live to God. Luther reads these references to death and life realistically, and the result is what we might call a relational re-creation of the self. The demand of the law condemns and kills the sinner, first in the event of the cross in which Christ is crucified under the curse (cf. Gal 3:13) and also in the hearing of "the word of the cross" which makes present the crucified Christ to faith. In other words, it is the event and proclamation of Christ crucified, a moment and message that is both judgment and justification, that kills the sinner in their soteriological relationship to the law and resurrects the Christian in righteous (that is, Christ-defined) relationship to God. In this sense, the life of the Christian, as Luther expresses Paul's confession "not I, but Christ," is an "alien life" and Christian righteousness is therefore an alien righteousness (*iustitia aliena*).[41] Because the believer is crucified with Christ

36. LW 26:280–84; *Freedom of the Christian*, 287.

37. LW 26:129; WA 40.1:228, 31–229, 15. For the "joyous exchange" in the Galatians lectures, see LW 26:284; WA 40:443, 23–4.

38. LW 26:132; WA 40.1:233, 16–19.

39. G. Forde, *Justification by Faith: A Matter of Death and Life* (Philadelphia: Fortress, 1982).

40. For a reading of the themes of death and life in Galatians 2:19–20, see chap. 4, "'The Speech of the Dead.'"

41. LW 26:170; WA 40.1:287, 30–288, 2.

and alive only in Christ and through faith in Christ, the Christian possesses, though does not own, the righteousness that remains *extra nos*.[42] Righteousness before God is ever extrinsic and always christological.[43]

This interpretation of justification in terms of death and life reinforces the anthropological negation and christological confession indicated by Luther's reading of the antithesis between works of the law and faith in Christ. As in Romans 4, where the justification of the ungodly is related to God's acts of raising the dead and creating out of nothing (see Rom 4:5, 17), Luther reads the recurrence of righteousness language in Galatians 2:21 as indicating that the references to death and life denote and describe God's act of judging and justifying the sinner. What Luther is tuned into is the way the disjunction in Paul between what God says and those to whom he speaks suggests that words like καλέω and δικαιόω function as verbal verbs—works of God enacted as words of God.[44] God's calling, for instance, calls into being: where there was a "not my people" God calls and thereby creates "my people"; to those who were "not loved" God calls and so creates the "loved" (Rom 9:24). Or again, to those who are sinners and unrighteous, God does the verbal verb δικαιόω and thereby creates the opposite: "all sinned . . . and are justified" (Rom 3:23–24; cf. 4:5; 5:6–10; Gal 2:15–21).[45]

In a series of disputations on Romans 3:28, Luther interprets justification as life from death and creation from nothing: in the "divine work of justification" the negation of works and the incongruity between human unrighteousness

---

42. H. Oberman, *The Dawn of the Reformation: Essays in Late Medieval and Early Reformation Thought* (Edinburgh: T&T Clark, 1986), 120–25, indicates Luther's awareness of the distinction in Roman law between the right to use (*possessio*) and ownership (*proprietas*).

43. Cf. Chester, "It Is No Longer I Who Live," 317: "In his exegesis of Paul, Luther displays a profoundly participatory understanding of justification in which human faith is of salvific significance solely because it is itself christocentric." Imputation is therefore never something from or on account of Christ that is somehow given apart from Christ. Imputation, rather, is anchored to Christ, who is given in the gospel and present in faith.

44. According to Bayer's reconstruction, Luther's reformation breakthrough is tied up with a development in his understanding of language: rather than a word functioning only as a sign (*signum*) that refers to a reality (*res*), Luther came to see that God's words (*verba Dei*) are God's work (*opera Dei*), that divine speech establishes rather than merely refers to reality; see O. Bayer, *Promissio: Geschichte der reformatischen Wende in Luthers Theologie*, 2nd ed. (Darmstadt: Wissenschaftliche Buchgesellschaft, 1989).

45. Consider this line from a Lutheran hymn: "Thy strong word bespeaks us righteous." Cf. U. Wilckens, *Der Brief an die Römer*, 3 vols., EKKNT (Zurich: Benziger; Neukirchen-Vluyn: Neukirchener, 1978–82), 1:188n39: "die Sünde aller [ist] also der Ort, an dem die Gottesgerechtigkeit wirksam wird."

and God's pronouncement of righteousness forces us to "say with Paul that we are nothing at all, just as we have been created out of nothing." In being justified, the *homo peccator* is, from this "nothing," "called righteous" and so, *ex nihilo* and from the grave, constituted as "a new creature."[46] As Luther argues in *The Babylonian Captivity*, it is nothing less than "death and resurrection that is full and complete justification."[47] The consequence of this diagnosis of the human "under sin" and "in Adam" is that the *homo peccator* is not alive as an agent who could have faith but is depotentiated as deeply as death.

The self that remains alive to the law, the old Adam, is, as Luther put it in his 1526 interpretation of Jonah 1:5, able to know that there is a God, but to know who God is and that God is "for me" belongs only to faith.[48] Thus, for Luther, the "for me" of Galatians 2:20 cannot be confessed by the old Adam. It is a confession of the one who has been crucified with Christ and who lives as Christ and in Christ. Faith as an affirmation that Christ gave himself for me is an impossible possibility: it is a reality only on the other side of resurrection.[49]

For Luther, the divine act of self-giving that is the death of Jesus is the gift that grounds justification. In other words, it is the story of Jesus, of the one who loved me and gave himself for me, that is the gift of righteousness. As Luther put it, "It was 'the Son of God who loved me and gave Himself for me.' It was not I who loved the Son of God and gave myself for Him."[50] In this sense, the *solus Christus* is the content of the *sola gratia*: grace is the self-giving of Christ for me (Gal 2:20; or "for our sins," 1:4).[51] The faith that, in one of Luther's favorite pastoral phrases, properly applies the pronoun—the faith that believes that God in Christ is *pro me*—in no way qualifies the singularity or unconditionality of this christological gift.[52] Rather, the *sola fide* points to the presence of the self-giving Christ in the promise that creates and is clung to by faith.[53] According to "Luther's Paul, " justification through faith

46. LW 34:113, 156. For more on this theme in Paul and in Luther, see chap. 4, "'The Speech of the Dead.'"

47. LW 36:67; cf. LW 34:113: "Justification is in reality a kind of rebirth in newness."

48. *Lectures on Jonah* (1525/6), LW 19:11; WA 13:246. For a penetrating reading of this text, see Bayer, *Martin Luther's Theology*, 133.

49. For Luther on the *pro me*, see LW 26:176–79; WA 40.1:295–300.

50. LW 26:172; WA 40.1:291, 3–4.

51. Cf. Chester, "It Is No Longer I Who Live," 321: "Christ himself is the gift received by the believer."

52. On this theme, see S. D. Paulson, *Lutheran Theology*, Doing Theology (London: T&T Clark, 2011), 136–37.

53. E. Käsemann, *Commentary on Romans*, trans. G. W. Bromiley (Grand Rapids: Eerdmans, 1980), 101: "Precision is given to *sola gratia* by *sola fide*."

in Jesus Christ is therefore not, as Richard Hays and others fear, a stressing of the salvific efficacy of the human act of faith. Justification through faith in Christ is a confession of the soteriological singularity of Jesus: the *sola fide* is the confession of the *solus Christus*. And this, for Luther, is why what he calls "our theology" is good news: rather than focusing on faith, justification through faith in Jesus Christ "snatches us away from ourselves and places us outside ourselves, so that we do not depend on our own strength, conscience, experience, person, or works but depend on that which is outside ourselves, that is, on the promise and truth of God."[54]

54. LW 26:387; WA 7:69, 12–13.

CHAPTER 12

Until Christ

ADVENT AGAIN AND AGAIN IN MARTIN LUTHER'S INTERPRETATION
OF GALATIANS

> *It is surely a terrible charge to bring against a religious system,*
> *that in the conflict which has to be waged by every son of Adam*
> *with disease, misfortune, death, the believers in it are provided*
> *with neither armour nor weapons. Surely a real religion, handed*
> *down from century to century, ought to have accumulated a store of*
> *consolatory truths which will be of some help to us in time of need.*
> *If it can tell us nothing, if we cannot face a single disaster any the*
> *better for it, and if we never dream of turning to it when we are in*
> *distress, of what value is it?*

—Mark Rutherford, *The Revolution in Tanner's Lane*

In the summer of 1518, Martin Luther wrote a set of theses. As an academic disputation, the first half of the title is standard: *Pro veritate inquirenda* (*For the Inquiry into Truth*). The second half, however, is more of a surprise: *et timoratis conscientiis consolandis* (*For the Comfort of Troubled Consciences*).[1] Luther had been asking after the truth for more than a decade, first as a theology student in Erfurt (from 1507) and then, from 1512, as a *doctor in biblia* at the still young university in Wittenberg. During these years of study, however, Luther was, to borrow some of his later words, "plagued" by the "two monsters" of "the power of the law and the sting of sin." Rather than consolation for his "troubled conscience," Luther speaks of "despair" and "deep anxiety," of "weary bones" and an experience of exhaustion and fear that caused him, like the heroine of George Eliot's novel *Janet's Repentance*, to cry out, "Is there any comfort—any hope?"[2]

---

1. WA 1:629–33.
2. LW 26:5, 26–27, 445; G. Eliot, *Janet's Repentance* (London: Hesperus, 2007 [1858]), 138.

Some years later, commenting on Galatians, Luther offers an unqualified "yes" to this question. "The distinction between the law and the gospel," he says, is a "sure comfort": it knows the limits of the law and so "sets before" the despairing—before the dead—only "the promise of Christ, who came for the afflicted and for sinners."[3] These two words, the law and the gospel, are, according to Luther, "the sermon which we should daily study," the "sermon" that speaks of, and as God's word accomplishes, "both imprisonment and redemption, sin and forgiveness, wrath and grace, death and life."[4] But this distinction, this daily sermon that is a "sure comfort," is the one thing the early Luther "lacked." In words from the *Tischreden*, Luther recalls:

> I lacked nothing before this except that I made no distinction between the law and the gospel. I regarded both as one thing and said that there was no difference between Christ and Moses except time and perfection. But when I discovered the proper distinction, that the law is one thing and the gospel is another, I broke through.[5]

This reminiscence tells the story of this chapter. Luther began his study and teaching of scripture as an heir of a long interpretative tradition. Included in this inheritance is an understanding of the relationship between the Old and New Testaments that might be summarized by the phrase *concordia legis et evangelii*—the "concord of law and gospel."[6] But the problem for Luther, as he read and lived with this hermeneutical inheritance, was both exegetical and experiential. The harder he "pounded upon" the pages of scriptures, the more the texts turned on the tradition. And the longer he heard the gospel preached in harmony with the law, the more "desperate and disturbed" he became. The *concordia*, in other words, offered no comfort.[7] What finally "broke through"— what gives "rest" to "your bones and mine," says Luther—was the "discovery" of a distinction: "the law is one thing and the gospel is another."

This discovery happens as Luther turns to lecture on Paul's letters, first Romans and then Galatians. This chapter will trace this exegetical and pastoral ref-

3. LW 26:7, 445.

4. WA 45:3.19.

5. LW 54:442; WATr 5:210.6, no. 5518: "Zuuor mangelt mir nichts, denn das ich kein discrimen inter legem et euangelium machet, hielt es alles vor eines et dicebam Christum a Mose non differre nisi tempore et perfection. Aber do ich das discrimen fande, quod aliud esset lex, aliud euangelium, da riß ich her durch."

6. See E. Herrmann's chapter in J. A. Linebaugh, *God's Two Words: Law and Gospel in the Lutheran and Reformed Traditions* (Grand Rapids: Eerdmans 2018).

7. LW 34:337; WA 54:186.3–16.

ormation, considering first the tradition that Luther was schooled in and finally came to criticize before sketching Luther's new reading of Paul. Galatians 3–4 is a touchstone for this change: law and gospel are no longer related only as the before and after of two historical epochs but as the recurrent movement from "the time of the law" to "the time of the gospel" that occurs as the Christ who came once comes again and again through the word that creates faith. The final question, however—a question Luther would insist we ask as we follow the "brook" of his exegesis back to "the spring" of scripture—is not what Luther wrote about Galatians, but rather: do Luther's words about Galatians help us hear the word of God that is Galatians?[8] That, for Luther, is the definitive question of reception history, and it will be the final question of this chapter.

No Difference between Christ and Moses

When Luther began his first lectures on the Psalms in 1513, he "regarded" the "law and the gospel" as "one thing and said," in his words, "that there was no difference between Christ and Moses except time and perfection." "The law," he told his students, "was the beginning of the gospel," and the gospel "perfects the law."[9] The language here—law and gospel as one yet differentiated by history and degree— situates Luther within and also epitomizes an interpretive tradition.

To make a long and rich story too short and too simple, the basic framework for relating the Old and New Testaments that Luther inherited was, at once, the temporal movement of *Heilsgeschichte* and the hermeneutical distinction between letter and spirit.[10] If, in Tertullian's phrase, the *seperatio legis et evangelii* was the "proper and principal work of Marcion" (*proprium et principale opus est Marcionis*), the dominant patristic and medieval tendency was to counter this *seperatio* with the *concordia*: law and gospel are, to quote Luther again, "one thing."[11] One terminological indication of this continuity is

8. WA 50:519, 33–520.

9. WA 3:605, 21.

10. This tradition is analyzed in detail by E. Herrmann, "'Why Then the Law?' Salvation History and the Law in Martin Luther's Interpretation of Galatians 1513–1522" (PhD diss., Concordia Seminary, 2005); cf. Hermann's essays in Linebaugh, *God's Two Words* and in *The Oxford Handbook of Martin Luther's Theology*. This section and the next are informed by and indebted to Herrmann's research. This tradition and Luther's relationship to it in his first Psalms lectures is also considered by J. Preus, *From Shadow to Promise: Old Testament Interpretation from Augustine to the Young Luther* (Cambridge, MA: Harvard University Press, 1969), and G. Ebeling, "Die Anfänge von Luthers Hermeneutik," *ZTK* 48.2 (1951): 172–230.

11. Tertullian, *Adversus Marcionem.*

the word νόμος or *lex*. Adjectives change, but the noun is constant: the old law (παλαίος νόμος, *vetus lex*) gives way to the new law (καινὸς νόμος, *nova lex*), and Moses ends where the ministry of Christ, the new lawgiver (νομοθέτης), begins. Law, in this sense, is a thread that ties the two testaments together.

What accounts for the different adjectives, however, is advent: "the law," writes Paul in Galatians, "was until Christ" (Gal 3:24). Within the movement of history, law and gospel are understood as old and new, as the before and after of two successive times. The "difference," to return to Luther, is a matter of "time"—it is an historical divide that can be dated: BC names the years of the old; *anno Domini* announces the arrival of the new. According to Luther, however, the difference is also one of degree, of "perfection." As Erik Herrmann puts it, the distinction between law and gospel—as the distinction between old and new—is "quantitative and chronological": from "temporal and carnal" to "eternal and spiritual," from an externality that commands the hand to an interiority that commands the heart, from a slave-like obedience motivated by fear to the obedience of children prompted by love.[12] There is, in Herrmann's phrase, a "graduated continuity" between the testaments, between the time of the law and the time of grace: *lex* remains even as it shifts temporally from old to new and by degree from preparation to perfection.[13]

Paul's letters relate to this hermeneutical tradition as something of a riddle. According to the apostle, law ends when Christ comes. Encouraged by Paul's references to the "law of faith" and "the law of Christ," however, exegetes have often found it possible to distinguish between the law *per se* and the law in particular. "Christ is the end of the law," writes Paul (Rom 10:4), and therefore this law is only "until Christ" (Gal 3:23–24). But this law, the *vetus lex*, is interpreted (by the majority tradition) as the Mosaic legislation specific to the people of Israel for the time between exodus and advent. In Jerome's words, Paul preaches "the cessation of the old law and the introduction of the new law," though as he is quick to qualify: the old law that ends consists of ceremonies such as "Sabbath" and "circumcision."[14] A passage like Galatians 3–4, then, with its language of "before" and "until" and its suggestion that the

12. Herrmann, "'Why Then the Law?,'" 6, 8.

13. E. Herrmann, "Luther's Absorption of Medieval Biblical Interpretation and His Use of the Church Fathers," in *The Oxford Handbook of Martin Luther's Theology* (Oxford: Oxford University Press, 2014), 83.

14. Jerome, *Commentarius in Epistolam S. Pauli ad Galatas*, PL 26, 333, C–334, A. As Herrmann observes, this ceremonial law was often linked with the New Testament references to law as a "yoke" (e.g., Matt 11:29–30; Acts 15:10; Gal 5:1) and the mention of ordinances that are "not good" in Ezekiel 20:25; see Herrmann, "'Why Then the Law?,'" 15–16.

law has both a beginning and a temporal limit, is taken to indicate that the harmony of law and gospel is that of *Heilsgeschichte*: the law of Moses is until and the law of Christ.

This historical distinction, however, raises a hermeneutical question: How does the *vetus lex*, which is past, speak as scripture in the present? If the difference between old and new is, as Luther notes, one of "time," then the historical distance between then and now is also, to borrow from Lessing, an ugly hermeneutical ditch between text and reader. Paul's temporal language raises this question; his distinction between the letter and the spirit is read as answering it (2 Cor 3:6).

Following Origen, Paul is interpreted as moving not just along the timeline of sacred history but from that history to that which is timeless—from the earthly to the eternal, from an occasional text to its perennial truth, from, that is, the letter to the spirit. Within this pattern of reading, the letter of the law—the rites and ceremonies specific to Israel—are past. But as spirit these rituals and words still speak, they are figures and types that promise and prepare for Christ. As one popular medieval saying delineates, "the law was given as a *signum*" (a sign pointing to a deeper reality or *res*), "a *flagellum*" (a scourge that, as Paul says, "was added because of transgressions"), and, again in Paul's language, "a *paedagogum*" (a pedagogue that uses the ceremonial law as lessons that finally lead to Christ).[15] Expanding this binary difference between letter and spirit, readers of Paul placed his references to the law's temporal limit and pedagogical office within a fourfold distinction between the one literal and the three spiritual senses of scripture. The *vetus lex*, read as letter, is a set of ceremonies that cease. But interpreted spiritually, these old rites and words are always young: allegorically, they prefigure Christ and inform faith; tropologically, they pattern moral judgment and shape love; anagogically, they indicate the glories of heaven and engender hope.

As a student of scripture, Luther was, in his own words, after "the flesh of the nut," and, as Gerhard Ebeling puts it, the interpretative "nutcracker" that Luther uses "to pry open the hard shell of scripture" in the *Dictata super Psalterium* of 1513–1515 is the historical distinction between old and new and the hermeneutical distinction between letter and spirit.[16] In accordance with his

15. For a discussion of the use and provenance of this dictum, see Herrmann, "A Lutheran Response," 162nn18, 19.

16. WABr 1:17, 39–44 §5; Ebeling, "The Beginning of Luther's Hermeneutic," *LQ* 7 (1993): 452. There are some exegetical moments in the *Dictata* that are, with retrospect, sometimes read as seeds of reformation: Luther's christological focus often elides the distinction between the literal and allegorical senses and an eschatological and effective concept of God's

later recollection, the early Luther still regarded law and gospel as "one thing," differentiating them only by date and by degree. The *vetus lex* relates to the new as past to future; it is only, he writes, "until another age comes" (*usque ad alterum saeculum futurum in Christo*). And, as Luther comments on Psalm 35, this movement from old to new—from before to after—is at the same time the movement from imperfect to perfect: *Nam imperfectio ad perfectionem est sicut lex vetus ad novam.*[17]

In the course of these comments on the Psalms, Luther references Galatians 3 to indicate both the historical boundary of the law and its pedagogical function: the *vetus lex* is, at once, temporary and, in Luther's term, concerned with *temporalia*.[18] Just so, however, it relates to the timeless and the true not only as old to new, but also as *figura* to *impleta*, as *umbra* to *vera*, and, most fundamentally, as *littera* to *spiritus*. As Herrmann summarizes the interpretation of Galatians in the *Dictata*, "Luther consistently" reads law as referring to "the *vetus lex* and its function in the Old Testament," a function that is indicated by a preparatory and prefigurative interpretation of the Pauline image of the παιδαγωγός.[19] Law, in the historical movement from old to new, functioned "until Christ." And law, in the hermeneutical movement from letter to spirit, points "to Christ."[20]

Old and new, spirit and letter: for the early Luther and the interpretive tradition he inherited, these Pauline distinctions signal the history and hermeneutic according to which the apostle—the one who would later teach Luther to distinguish law and gospel—establishes the *concordia legis et evangelii.*[21]

The Law Is One Thing and the Gospel Is Another

Near the origin of the scholarly investigation of Luther's "Auslegungskunst," Karl Holl observed a relationship between Luther's exegesis and his experience.[22] The *doctor* at the lectern was also the preacher in the pulpit, and these

---

promissio develops as a dominate theme. See, respectively, Ebeling, "Die Anfänge von Luthers Hermeneutik" and Preus, *From Shadow to Promise.*

17. WA 55.1:316.

18. WA 55.2:536, 46–51.

19. Herrmann, "'Why Then the Law?,'" 110.

20. Both phrases translate Paul's statement, ὁ νόμος . . . εἰς Χριστόν, but their different emphases exploit the semantic potential of Paul's preposition.

21. For the medieval tradition that celebrates Paul as the theologian that models scriptural interpretation and harmonizes law and gospel, see H. de Lubac, *Medieval Exegesis: The Four Senses of Scripture*, trans. E. M. Macierowski (Grand Rapids: Eerdmans, 2000), 2:223.

22. K. Holl, "Luthers Bedeutung fur den Fortschritt der Auslegungskunst," in *Gesammelte Aufsätze zur Kirchengeschichte*, vol. 1: *Luther* (Tübingen: Mohr Siebeck), 547–49.

roles were inseparable both from each other and from Luther himself—professor and pastor, and also and always a person before God. Within this tightly woven life, to "lack nothing except" the distinction between "the law and the gospel" is, to borrow a phrase, to lack the "one thing needful." Luther read, taught, and preached the Old and New Testaments as the before and after of *Heilsgeschichte* and so understood the gospel as the new and perfect law, the *lex evangelii*. In this new time—the *tempus gratiae*—the gospel, as Paul announced, reveals God's righteousness, but this, to quote Heiko Oberman, is both gift and demand: it is the gift of the "*iustitia Christi*" that moves "*the viator*" toward the goal of the "*iustitia Dei*," the "*Gegenüber*" or "standard according to which" life "will be measured in the Last Judgment." The result is that what the gospel proclaims—the possibility but also the requirement of righteousness—is not "the stable basis" but "the uncertain goal of life."[23] In the encounter between this theology and Luther's life, the one word that promised peace and consolation—the good news that is the gospel—only deepened Luther's confusion and amplified his question: "Is there any comfort—any hope?"

Luther launched a new course of lectures on Romans in 1515, the same year he seems to have begun reading Augustine's anti-Pelagian writings. "This shift in exegetical sources," Herrmann suggests, is among the "most significant moments in Luther's theological development."[24] The impact, however, was not immediate. Luther knew the Pauline phrase νυνὶ δέ named the time when the old became the new, but, as he later confessed, this movement of history seemed only to say that "God adds sorrow to sorrow through the gospel." Living and reading in the "time of grace," Luther found himself, as he put it, "with a desperate and disturbed conscience."

23. H. Oberman, "*Iustia Christi* and *Iustia Dei*: Luther and Scholastic Doctrines of Justification," *HTR* 59.1 (1966): 19, 20, 25. Cf. E. Herrmann, "Luther's Divine Aeneid: Continuity and Creativity in Reforming the Use of the Bible," *Lutherjahrbuch* 85 (2018): 85–109: Because the Old Testament law belongs to the past, "the Christian has only the gospel which must perform the conflicting offices of judgment and consolation . . . it is the gospel that brings . . . both the revelation of sin and absolution. . . . Because the gospel is the only 'law' in the New Testament, it is simultaneously a demand" (*iudicium*) as well as "that which fulfills the demand" (*iustitia*)—"both the source of angst and the only bearer of comfort" (103).

24. Complete additions of patristic authors were newly available, including an edition of Augustine's *Opera* from 1506. For the significance of having complete works rather than the collections of quotations found in the *florilegia* and the *Glossa ordinaria*, as well as the importance of Luther's turn to Paul and Augustine, see Herrmann, "Luther's Absorption of Medieval Biblical Interpretation and His Use of the Church Fathers," 77–79.

As he continued to study Paul alongside Augustine, however, the letters that first intensified Luther's *Anfechtung* finally offered "an open gate into paradise." Augustine was, according to Luther, Paul's "*interpres fidelissimus*": he understood that the justice of God justifies, that law is not limited to ceremonies, and that the letter is the law that demands righteousness and exposes its absence whereas the spirit identifies the gifts that make the law's imperatives newly possible. In Augustine's own words, "the law was given that we might seek grace, and grace was given that we might fulfill the law."[25] These new yet ancient interpretations emerged for Luther as he "persistently pounded on Paul." "At last," Luther remembers, "God being merciful," he "began to understand" both that God's righteousness is the grace that gives righteousness and, to return to the *Tischreden*, that "the law is one thing and the gospel is another."[26]

Luther continued to lecture on Paul's letters from 1515 to 1517. As he did so, Paul's texts seemed to question the tradition that claimed him as the champion of the *concordia legis et evangelii*. According to Paul, the law is not only before the gospel; the law is not the gospel. To quote Romans and Galatians, if the promise is "through law," then it is "not according to grace" (Rom 4:14), and "no one is justified by the law" because "the law is not of faith" (Gal 3:11–12). The distinction is not only chronological, it is categorical: "the law is one thing and the gospel is another."

For Luther, this realization that the law is not the gospel meant that the law could be what it actually is: the law. This entails both a broadening of its scope and a specifying of its function. The law, for Luther, is the *totus lex Mosi* and its office is "until Christ," not so much as a *figura* but because it performs a theological function: the law discovers and diagnoses sin.[27] Paul's answer to his own question—"why then the law?"—is not, "as typology," but rather "because of transgressions" (Gal 3:19). For Paul, the law operates εἰς Χριστόν not mainly by prefigurement but by imprisonment: it "reveals sin" (Rom 3:19–20), "works wrath" (Rom 4:15), and "imprisoned everyone" (Gal 3:22). As Luther wrote to Emser—the "Leipzig Goat"—the distinction between letter and spirit in 2 Corinthians is "not" about "two meanings," but "two kinds of preaching": the "ministry of the letter" which diagnoses sin and is therefore not dead but deadly, and the

---

25. Augustine, *De spiritu et littera* 19.34.

26. WA 54:186.3–16; LW 34:337; LW 54:442; WATr 5:210.6 no. 5518. For a full and informative examination of the significance of the turn from the Psalms to Paul's letter in Luther's hermeneutical development from 1513 to 1522, see Herrmann, "'Why Then the Law?'"

27. WA 56:197, 7–8; WA 57.2: 59, 18–20.

"ministry of the Spirit" that, by giving "Christ" and "grace" to "those who are burdened" and "killed" by "the law," "forgives sin" and "gives life."[28]

During these years, Luther was, in his phrase, learning Paul's language: the *modus loquendi Apostoli*. As he did so, however, he read the apostle with but also beyond Augustine. For Augustine, the hermeneutical distinction between letter and spirit occurs within the historical movement from old to new. For Luther, however, law and gospel no longer name only two times; they are two words of God that are and enact the works of God. The *verba Dei*, according to Luther, are not reducible to a system of signs that refer to some nonlinguistic *res*. "God spoke and it was done," says Psalm 33:9. For Luther, this means that God's word, as Hebrews puts it, is "living and active" (Heb 4:12), that divine speech does not merely correspond to but actually creates reality.[29] As two *verba Dei* that are and accomplish the *opera Dei*, law and gospel cannot be distinguished only by date. They are, Luther says, the "sermon we should study daily"—they are, that is, the definitive but also the day-by-day words that do the divine work. God's word of law condemns and seals the tomb of the old; God's word of gospel redeems and rolls away the stone.

The echo of Easter is not incidental. For Luther, the resurrection of the crucified remains the hinge of history. The law, Paul says, is until Christ. But now, Luther adds, that advent is not only once for all; it is again and again: the law was, but also and always is, until Christ. As Luther writes in the 1535 Galatians commentary, Paul's language of "before," "until," and "no longer" indicates "how long the law should last." This "duration of time," however, is interpreted by Luther "both in a literal and in a spiritual sense": "until Christ" announces "what happened historically and temporally when Christ came" and also what "happens personally and spiritually every day" as God's words

---

28. LW 39:182–83; cf. G. Forde, "Law and Gospel in Luther's Hermeneutic," *Int* 37 (1983): 240–52: 2 Corinthians 3:6 "is not about an attribute of the text but an activity"; "Luther saw . . . what the tradition had overlooked: 2 Corinthians 3:6 is about ministry and preaching, not about interpretation" (246–48).

29. According to Oswald Bayer's reconstruction, Luther's reformation breakthrough is tied up with a development in his understanding of language. Rather than a word functioning only as a *signum* that refers to a *res* (as per Augustine's semiotics), Luther came to see that the *verba Dei* are and perform the *opera Dei*; see O. Bayer, *Promissio: Geschichte der reformatischen Wende in Luthers Theologie*, 2nd ed. (Darmstadt: Wissenschaftliche Buchgesellschaft, 1989). As Robert Kolb notes, it was sometime "in the late 1510s" that "Luther's understanding of God as a God who creates reality through his Word slowly fused with his view of that Word as" law "which condemns sin and" gospel that "promises and creates life"; R. Kolb, *Martin Luther: Confessor of the Faith* (Oxford: Oxford University Press, 2009), 48.

of law and gospel do God's work of death and life.[30] In Luther's words, "the Christian is divided . . . into two times": the "time of law" in which sin is still confronted and condemned, and the "time of grace" in which Christ ends the hour of "sadness" and "death" with the word of mercy and life.[31]

This dialectic is, in part, a symptom of the simultaneity of Christian existence. Living both "by faith" and "in the flesh," the Christian is, in Luther's phrase, *simul iustus et peccator*. The time of the law is thus always translated from the past to the present tense: the old law speaks a new word any time it encounters sin.[32] The effect is that—"in experience" and "in our feelings," as Luther puts it—these two times are "in constant alternation." Yet even this simultaneity is finally asymmetrical: "the time of the law," Luther rejoices, "is not forever, but the time of grace is forever."[33]

This definitiveness, however, does not eliminate the necessity of the daily. Luther recognizes that with the phrase "until Christ" "Paul is speaking" about the one who "came once for all." But the Christ who came definitively at "a specific time" needs to be given "continually" to those who live between the times. Commenting on Galatians 4:4 in the *Weihnachtspostille* of 1522, Luther refers the Pauline words τὸ πλήρωμα τοῦ χρόνου to "the bodily advent of Christ," but insists that this first "advent would have been of no use (*were kein nutz*) if it had not effected" another "advent."[34]

There is a subtle yet significant shift in the basic hermeneutical question here. Luther never stops reading scripture christologically. In his image, "If I find a nut with a shell too hard to crack, I fling it in on the rock [of Christ]."[35] But it is one thing to find Christ; the crucial matter is to "define Christ." In Luther's words, "the highest art . . . is to be able to define Christ" not as "a new lawgiver who, after abrogating the old law, established a new law," but "as the son of God, who . . . because of his sheer mercy and love, gave and offered himself . . . for us." This Christ, according to Luther, "is not Moses . . . or a lawgiver;

---

30. LW 26:317, 340.

31. LW 26:341–42; WA 40.1:526, 2–3.

32. WA 40.1:526, 2–3. Luther distinguishes between the Christian *quatenus caro* and *quatenus spiritus* and correlates these with being at once *sub lege* and *sub Euangelio* (WA 40.1:526, 2–3). Cf. LW 26:350: "as long as we live in a flesh that is not free of sin, so long the law keeping coming back and performing its function."

33. LW 26:340–42, 349–50; WA 40.1:526, 2–3.

34. WA 10.1/1:1, 353, 6–354. Cf. J. Calvin, *Institutes* 3.1.1: "as long as Christ remains outside of us, and we are separated from him, all that he has suffered and done for the salvation of the human race remains useless and of no value for us."

35. WA 3:12.

he is the dispenser of grace, the savior," the "joy and sweetness of a trembling and troubled heart." Defined by way of the distinction between law and gospel, Christ "is nothing but sheer, infinite mercy, which gives and is given."[36]

If Christ "gives and is given," however, the hermeneutical question is "how?" For Luther, it is no longer enough to say that the distance between text and reader is traversed by uncovering the timeless doctrines, demands, and destiny that shape the virtues of faith, love, and hope. Christ, Paul confesses, is "the one who loved me and gave himself for me" (Gal 2:20). But how does that past become present? That, for Luther, is the real "ugly ditch": How, today and tomorrow, is "the one who loved me and gave himself for me" the one who loves me and gives himself to me?

This question is underneath Luther's assertion that "Christ's bodily advent" must "establish . . . a spiritual advent."[37] For Luther, a "spiritual advent," is not a second saving event, another moment in history that surpasses what occurred *sub Pontio Pilato*. "Christ came once for all time," he writes, and in this advent he "abrogated the . . . law, abolished sin, and destroyed death."[38] This is the decisive day, the *kairos* that Johann Georg Hamann calls the "historical truth, not only of . . . past times but also of times to come."[39] In Luther's words, "Everything, from the beginning of the world to the end, must cling to this bodily advent."[40]

But that only rephrases the question: how does the Christ who came once— there and then—come again—here and now? For Luther, to speak of a "spiritual advent" is not to suggest that someone else arrives or that something else is accomplished. The question is both more basic and more profound: how does the one Christ who once gave himself for us, now give himself to us? In the *Weihnachtpostille*, Luther's answer is "spiritual advent": Christ came in flesh; Christ comes in the power of the Holy Spirit. For Luther, Paul's words—"the law, until Christ"—proclaim the day that divides history. But what happened definitively at one time and in one place, occurs "whenever and wherever" (*wenn und wo . . . wilchem*) the Spirit speaks the words that do at all times

36. LW 26:177–78.

37. Luther's terminology draws on the tradition of the *triplex adventus*, but his use of this theme in the 1522 *Weihnachtspostille*, when compared to its appearance in the *Dictata*, reflects similar changes to his broader hermeneutical developments concerning old and new, letter and spirit, and law and gospel. For an analysis of this theme in Luther and in the tradition, see Herrmann, "'Why Then the Law?,'" 111–30, 217–25.

38. LW 26:350.

39. J. G. Hamann, "Golgotha and Sheblimini," 182.

40. WA 10.1/1:1, 353, 6–354.

what Paul says the law and Christ did in "the fullness of time": the law did and always does imprison under sin; the gospel that gives Christ did and always does set the captives free. To use a distinction that recurs throughout Luther's writings, Christ "won" salvation once for all time; the gospel "gives" the savior again and again in all times. In Oswald Bayer's words, for Luther, there is no disjunction between "the facticity of . . . the event *sub Pontio Pilato* and" the Holy Spirit's "imparting of that occurrence" in the gospel. Christ's "presence in the Spirit does not surpass what happened under Pontius Pilate, but reminds us of it . . . recalls it, brings into the present, distributes it, and promises it."[41] The Christ who comes as the Spirit speaks—in sacrament, scripture, and sermon—is the Christ who came once for all. "Christ is not divided," says Paul (1 Cor 1:13). He is, as Luther quotes while commenting on Galatians, "the same yesterday, today, and forever" (Heb 13:8).[42] It is this Christ, the one who gave himself on Golgotha, who now gives himself in the gospel.

When Luther returns to these Pauline texts in the 1530s, he finds himself returning to this theme as well. "Until Christ" announces advent, the event in history that divides history: old and new, before and after—there is a distinction between these times, Luther writes, only because "Christ came . . . at a set time." But again, the advent that is "once for all" is also an advent that is again and again. As Luther comments on Galatians 3:26, "Christ came" definitively; "through the word of the gospel," he adds, "Christ comes . . . daily."[43]

This answer to the hermeneutical dilemma also addresses Luther's more fundamental question: "Is there any comfort—any hope?" The gospel, *qua narratio*, tells the story of the Christ who gave himself for me. The gospel, *qua promissio*, is Christ giving himself to me. But this Christ, as Paul says, is both the one who gave himself for me and the one who loved me (Gal 2:20). According to Luther, these words both distinguish law from gospel and define Christ: "Christ is not Moses;" he is, at once, the one who "gives and is given" and also the one who "loves those who are in anguish, sin and death."[44] This is the truth Luther was asking after, but it is also the consolation for troubled consciences he longed to experience and to share. The time of the law is, in Luther's words, an era of "despair" and "death," a time in which the hours are

41. The Bayer quotes are from "The Word of the Cross," 190, and "Preaching the Word," 205, both of which appear in *Justification Is for Preaching*, ed. V. Thompson (Eugene, OR: Pickwick, 2012). For Luther's distinction between salvation "won" and "bestowed," see LW 40:213–14; LW 37:193; cf. the "Large Catechism," BC 469.31.

42. LW 26:351.

43. LW 26:351.

44. LW 26:178.

marked not by the clock but by the creature's *cri de cœur*. But this time "is not forever." It is only "until": the one who, "at a specific time," loved me and gave himself for me is also and always the one who, through the gospel, loves me and gives himself to me. "When he comes," says Luther, whether once for all or again and again, the law's condemnation stops and its shadows of "fear and sadness" are scattered. The time of the law may be the time of the question: Is there any comfort? But the time of the gospel is the time of grace: Christ, the one who gives and is given, is, in Luther's phrase, the "Comforter."[45]

THE TRUTH OF THE GOSPEL

Luther poses one more question. In lecturing and writing on Paul's letters, he says, "I have had one thing in view . . . that, through my work, those who have heard me explaining the epistles of the apostle might find Paul clearer."[46] For Luther, the final reception historical criterion is, in his metaphor, whether drinking from an exegetical "brook" leads the reader deeper into the "spring" of scripture.[47] According to this image, the text is the touchstone: theological commentary, to borrow a line from Zacharias Ursinus, is to be "taken out of the scriptures" so it can, in his words, "lead us" back "to the scriptures."[48] Asked in these terms: Is Luther's interpretation of Galatians superimposed on or generated by the text; is it a detour around or a possible entrée back into Paul's letter? At root, this question concerns a relationship: Do Luther's comments about Galatians, as was once said of Barth's *Römerbrief*, relate to the text only as a "ruminative overlay," or is the interaction between Paul's letter and Luther's interpretation an instance of the relationship that is reading?[49]

A number of Luther's exegetical developments, though still contested, enjoy significant scholarly support. Many interpreters, for instance, read νόμος

45. LW 26:348.
46. WA 2:449, 27–31.
47. WA 50:519, 33–520.
48. Z. Ursinus, *The Commentary on the Heidelberg Catechism*, trans. G. W. Williard (Phillipsburg, NJ: Presbyterian and Reformed, 1852), 10.
49. For a relational understanding of reading, see J. G. Hamann who refers to the "intimate relation" of "author, book, and reader" and locates "the riddle of a book" not so much in one of these three relative members as in the relationship between them; J. G. Hamann, *Briefwechsel*, ed. W. Ziesemer and A. Henkel, 8 vols. (Wiesbaden: Insel Verlag, 1955–75), 5, Nr. 784, 272:14–18. These questions contain a host of others: Is interpretation only *Nachsprechen* or also *Nachdenken*? Are the effects of a text and the horizon of its readers constitutive aspects of its meaning? Is *Sachkritik* in the service of translating the theology of a text from one time to another a form of exegesis or something other than exegesis?

in Paul as referring to the entire law of Moses and understand its preparatory function not so much in terms of prefiguring salvation as imprison-
ing under sin. But what of Luther's reading of the Pauline prepositions πρό
and εἰς? Is Paul's argument in Galatians 3–4 only about *Heilsgeschichte*, and
if so, does Luther's translation of the epochal into the ever-present have an
exegetical basis?[50]

For Luther, Paul's temporal language registers in at least three tenses. The
movement from the time of the law to the time of grace happened, definitively, as Christ gave himself once for all; decisively, as Christ gave himself *pro
me* in the word that creates faith; and still occurs daily, when and wherever
Christ gives himself as the Spirit speaks the words—and so does the work—of
law and gospel. But is this, as Ebeling suggests, "an unchronological both/
and," a transposition "of the text" that effectively replaces Paul's sequential
account of history with the simultaneity that characterizes human life?[51] Paul's
terms—"until," "before," "no longer"—together with the temporal analogies of
inheritance and maturation, confirm Ebeling's basic claim: for Paul, the coming of Christ is "the turning point," the "unique, epochal event" that "divides
history into two times." Old and new, under law and under grace: these are, in
one fundamental sense, the before and after of a chronological either/or.[52] As
John Barclay writes, "in Galatians 3–4," Paul "decenters the Torah" by limiting
"its role in history to an interlude."[53] The law is distinguished from, and temporally bound on both ends by, the promise: it came "after" the promise and it is
only "until" that promise is fulfilled—that is, "until Christ" (Gal 3:15–17, 24).

If, as John Riches indicates, Luther modulates this historical argument
"into . . . an existential dialectic," then his interpretation risks blunting Paul's
sharp temporal divide.[54] For Luther, however, Paul's "distinction" is not so
much "dislodged from . . . its salvation historical moorings" as it is extended
into multiple tenses.[55] Christ's continuing advents are not cut off from but

50. It is interesting to ask if and to what extent this question is echoed in later debates
within Pauline studies between, for example, dialectical and salvation historical readings of
Paul (e.g., Rudolf Bultmann and Oscar Cullmann) or, in a more recent iteration, apocalyptic
and covenantal interpretations (e.g., J. Louis Martyn and N. T. Wright).

51. G. Ebeling, *The Truth of the Gospel: An Exposition of Galatians*, trans. D. Green
(Minneapolis: Fortress, 1985), 204.

52. Ebeling, *Truth of the Gospel*, 195.

53. J. M. G. Barclay, *Paul and the Gift* (Grand Rapids: Eerdmans, 2015), 401–2.

54. J. Riches, *Galatians through the Centuries* (Oxford: Blackwell, 2013), 194: "The language of the history of salvation is transposed into that of an existential dialectic."

55. Herrmann, "Luther's Absorption of Medieval Biblical Interpretation and His Use of
the Church Fathers," 84.

anchored to "Christ's bodily advent." It is the one who came once for all that comes again and again; and it is what Christ did at a specific time—ending the era of the law and inaugurating the hour of grace—that Christ delivers in every time. This may be more than the historical movement and moment Paul announces with the words, "until Christ." But perhaps this more is still exegetical, a movement beyond the text that stems from living before and beneath the text—from attending, that is, to the details and complex dynamics of Paul's letter and asking after the deep theological springs that flow under and onto Paul's pages. To state this thesis as a question: are there aspects of Paul's letter that suggest that even as Luther moves beyond and says more than Galatians he is still responding to and offering a reading of Galatians?[56]

In Galatians 3–4, Paul writes with what Riches calls "the language of history." Even within these chapters, however, there are features of the text that complicate notions of chronology and temporal linearity. Sometime in the canonical past, "Abraham believed" (Gal 3:6), but this was "before faith came" (3:23). The antitheses between flesh and spirit, slavery and freedom, and law and promise correspond to the before and after of Torah and Christ, and yet these paired contrasts are present in the birth of Abraham's sons: Ishmael is born κατὰ σάρκα and enslaved under the law of Sinai (itself a chronological surprise); Isaac is the child of the "free woman" and his birth is both δι' ἐπαγγελίας and κατὰ πνεῦμα (Gal 4:21–31). For Paul, Christ comes in "the fullness of time." But this advent does not realize the law's latent potential; it is "God's counter-statement to the previous conditions of the possible": curse is overcome by blessing, ignorance gives way to knowledge, slaves are adopted as sons, and at the site of sin and death God gives righteousness and life.[57] The time of the Torah, according to Paul, is an interval of anticipation: a time of waiting until. Strangely, however, the end of this historical vigil is both an arrival and a return. It is "until Christ" and also a hearing again of the gospel

---

56. This question could be asked in terms borrowed from Oliver O'Donovan, *Finding and Seeking: Ethics as Theology* (Grand Rapids: Eerdmans, 2014): Does Luther's interpretation "struggle against the text" and "supplement the text, overlaying it with independent reflections"? Or, as my thesis asks, is Luther's reading of Galatians "the cheerful acceptance of the text's offer of more than lies on its surface, its invitation to come inside, to attune [himself] to its resonances and dynamics, its suggestions and its logic"? The interrogative form of this thesis may indicate that the final section of this essay, to quote Anton Chekhov, resembles more the role of the artist than the task of the philosopher: "It is not the business of the writer to answer the questions—let the philosophers do that if they must—but to state the questions precisely."

57. Barclay, *Paul and the Gift*, 412.

that was announced to Abraham ahead of time (προευαγγελίζομαι, 3:8). Christ may be the "end of the law," as Paul says in Romans, but as the fulfillment of the promise he also marks the boundary of its temporal beginning, the "before" as well as the "until" of the time of Torah. In Galatians, Christ does not only divide chronological time in two. For Paul, it seems, however surprisingly and however strangely, the one who comes in and at time's fullness is both the after and the before—he is, to invert a phrase, the end and the beginning, the last and also the first.[58]

There are also indications in Galatians that the eras of law and grace continue to echo after "the time appointed by the father" (4:2). The coming of Christ is, in one sense, singular, and yet this epochal event occurs again and again as Christ comes to Paul "through the revelation of Jesus Christ" (1:12) and as he later comes to the Galatians as "the one who called you in grace" (1:6). Similarly, the giving of the Spirit is figured as the fulfillment of the promise to Abraham and tied to what occurred "in Christ Jesus" (3:14). That giving, however, happens not only as Christ came in history but also and again as Christ is given in the "word of faith" that Paul preached in Galatia (3:1–5). The gospel, in other words, is both what took place in the fullness of time and also the (pre- and) post-proclamation of that news that now gives the Christ who once gave himself. As Orrey McFarland writes, for Paul, "apostolic proclamation makes the past present" as a "mode by which" the "enacted-in-the-past Christ-gift is" again given and "received."[59]

Those who hear this gospel, moreover, who live "by faith," continue to live "in the flesh" (2:20). The slavery and sin that characterize human captivity during the time of the law still threaten. Paul warns the Galatians not to "gratify" or "sow to" the flesh, a power that is yet present and at war with the Spirit (5:16–21; 6:7–9). There may be "no law" against the fruits of the Spirit, but a law added because of transgressions continues to curse the "works of the flesh" (5:19–23): "You who would be under the law, do you not listen to the law?" (4:21). Indeed, Paul's double-depiction of life in Galatians 2:20 suggests that even as the christological events of the past reach into and determine the present, life is still marked by a *simul*: "I live," says Paul, "in the flesh," and at the same time, "by faith" (2:20).

58. Cf. R. B. Hays, *Echoes of Scripture in the Letters of Paul* (New Haven: Yale University Press, 1993), 109: "The fulfillment precedes the promise."

59. O. McFarland, *God and Grace in Philo and Paul* (Leiden: Brill, 2015), 156–57, 160. Cf. 1 Corinthians 1: the "word of the cross" is the "preaching of Christ crucified," and it is this proclamation of what occurred "under Pontius Pilate" that is identified as "the power of God" (1 Cor 1:18, 23–24; cf. Rom 16–17).

This simultaneity, however, only deepens the strangeness of Paul's confession. Galatians 2:19–20 personalizes the movement from the time of law to the time of grace.[60] "In the fullness of time, God sent forth his son, born of a woman, born under the law, to redeem those who were under the law" (4:4–5). The redemption that is the deep reason for this birth occurs on the cross: "Christ redeemed us from the curse of the law by becoming a curse for us: as it is written, 'Cursed is everyone who is hanged on a tree'" (3:13). What occurred once as Christ came and was crucified, however, happens both for and also to the human person: "I have been crucified with Christ" and "Christ lives in me" (2:20). In Barclay's words, "although the crucifixion of Christ was . . . an event in history, it punctures other times and other stories not just as a past event recalled but as a present event that . . . happens anew for its hearers . . . in 'the revelation of Jesus Christ.'"[61] Christmas and Good Friday, you might say, date the end of the law and the dawn of life. But these holy days are also my history: "I died to the law"; I "live to God"—and all this, Paul confesses, because Christ was and forever is "the one who loved me and gave himself for me."

These features of Galatians open up the possibility that the Pauline sequence—"the law, until Christ"—is, if unambiguously chronological, then also: what's the word. . . . Recurring? Dialectical? The gospel announces the Christ who came "in the fullness of time"; the gospel also gives that same Christ to those who live between the times. This suggestion comes into even sharper focus under a wider lens: not only this or that detail of the text, but especially the occasion and nature of Galatians indicate that the times of law and grace resonate in more than one temporal register.

When Paul writes Galatians, it is, in one fundamental sense, after the day that divides the ages. The law was only "as long as" the interval of imprisonment and immaturity (3:22–24; 4:1–3), and its time was only after, before, and until: it was after the promise, "before faith came" and "until Christ" (3:17, 23–24). "But now," Paul declares, "faith has come" (3:25) and "God has sent forth his son" (4:4). The result is a reversal. The relative adjective ὅσος gives way to the adverb οὐκέτι: "you are no longer a slave, but a son" (4:1, 7; cf. 3:25).[62] Speaking in the present, Paul refers to the time "before faith came"

60. I suspect that "personalize" is not only a useful description of what Paul does in Galatians 2 but also a suggestive way to indicate what Luther does as he translates Paul's declaration about a definitive change in history into the language of recurring human experience.

61. J. M. G. Barclay, "Paul's Story: Theology as Testimony," in *Narrative Dynamics in Paul: A Critical Assessment*, ed. B. W. Longenecker (Louisville: Westminster John Knox, 2002), 146.

62. For Paul's use of language from the sphere of legal adoption and inheritance, and

READING PAUL WITH READERS OF PAUL

as the past: it was the time of the Galatians "then" (τότε) rather than "now" (νῦν, 4:8–9), the period of Paul's "former" (ποτέ) life (1:13), and an epoch of imprisonment that is "now" in the past (3:23–25).

There is, however, another sense in which Galatians, though written in a year marked *anno Domini*, is addressed to a critical hour that seems to back date reality to a time *ante Christum natum*. The law was only until Christ and the era of enslavement is over (3:24–25; 4:8–9). And yet, in Galatia, there is a risk of return. The present may be the age of "freedom," but "another gospel" that imposes the law threatens to relock the prison doors of the past: "do not submit again to a yoke of slavery," Paul urges (5:1). Under the influence of those Paul calls "the ones who trouble you" (5:12), there is a danger that some are now, as was once true of a time before, "obligated to keep the whole law" (5:3; cf. 3:10). For Paul, to "accept circumcision" is both to revert to "righteousness by the law" and to be "cut off from Christ" (5:3–4). As the letter opening laments, to turn to the law is to "turn away from the one who called you in grace" (1:6). And this turning, as Paul interprets the times, is both a turning from "the gospel of Christ" and, precisely as such, a turning back of the hands of time (1:7). "In the past," Paul reminds the Galatians, "you were enslaved," and yet now, in the present, he asks, "how can you return again to captivity" (4:8–9). According to Paul's diagnosis, the Galatians are back in the condition of humanity and history before, that time of waiting "until Christ." The Galatians "long to be under the law" (ὑπὸ νόμον), but if they would only "listen to the law" (4:21), Paul suggests, it would do to its hearers what it did in history: imprison under sin. As before, however, so also now: the law, until Christ. That was Paul's argument about the past. It is also his hope in the present. The Galatians are, again (πάλιν), in that time dated ὑπὸ νόμον; and so Paul is, again (πάλιν), preaching and praying in the age of "until": "I am again in the pains of childbirth," he writes, "until Christ is formed in you" (4:19).[63]

In Galatians, the movement from the era of captivity under the law to the time of freedom in Christ is both, as Luther appears to have noticed, an argument from history (3:15–4:5) and also an announcement of what once happened (3:1–5; 4:8–9) and now needs to happen again in Galatia (4:9–11, 19). "Christ came once for all at a set time," Luther writes, adding, "he also comes"

---

thus the metaphoric appropriateness and inclusiveness of the term "son" in this context, see E. Heim, *Adoption in Galatians and Romans* (Leiden: Brill, 2017).

63. The obvious image: the crisis in Galatia amounts to a type of time travel and Paul's present-tense proclamation of the gospel is a journey "back to the future." (One can only resist the analogy between Paul preaching the gospel in Galatians and a ride in a DeLorean so many times before relegating the entire metaphor to a footnote.)

again and again in every time. In Paul's words, both the time of the law and the time of the Galatian crisis are "until Christ"—until he came in history (3:24) and until he comes again through the word that once gave and, Paul hopes, will again give Christ (3:1–5; 4:19). The rehearsal of history in Galatians 3–4 is aimed at this kerygmatic horizon. "After the promise," "until Christ," "before faith": these are dates from the canonical and christological past, but they are addressed to "the churches of Galatia" in the present. "Another gospel" has arrived and it appears, as Paul represents it, to synthesize Christ and law by adding the word "and": the "other gospel" is Christ and law observance (1:6; 5:1–4).[64] Where the "other gospel" places an "and," however, Paul puts an antithesis: not Christ and the law, but Christ. "The truth of the gospel," as Paul insisted earlier in Jerusalem and Antioch and now argues again in Galatians (2:5, 14), is that it does not say, "Christ and"; it says, "Christ alone": the gospel is, and only is, in Paul's words, "the gospel of Christ" (1:7).[65]

According to Luther's recollection, he was only able to hear the gospel as good news when he realized that "the law is one thing, the gospel is another." Paul's consideration of the relationship between law and promise moves in a similar direction. The law came after and is only until the fulfillment of the promise. For Paul, however, this chronological sequence implies a categorical distinction: "if inheritance is based on the law, it is no longer based on the promise" (3:17–18).[66] In Galatians, this absolute antithesis is part of Paul's argument against the "other gospel," and it joins a refrain by which he clarifies and proclaims again "the gospel of Christ." As Paul says and then says again, "a person is not justified by works of the law, but through faith in Jesus Christ" (2:16; cf. 3:11–12, 21). "If righteousness were through the law," Paul insists, "then Christ died for nothing" (2:21).

---

64. For the theology of Paul's opponents, see J. M. G. Barclay, *Obeying the Truth: A Study of Paul's Ethics* (Edinburgh: T&T Clark, 1988), 45–60.

65. Moo, *Galatians* (Grand Rapids: Baker Academic, 2013), 154: "In place of the agitators' synthesis of faith in Christ and the law, Paul insists on an antithesis: it is Christ and therefore not the law." For an interpretation of Paul's antitheses in relation to the occasion of Galatians and its fundamental argument against the "other gospel" and for "the gospel of Christ," see chap. 9, "The Grammar of the Gospel."

66. There is, in Galatians 3–4, an unmistakable sense in which law and Christ indicate successive historical epochs. But even here, the promise that was before the law (3:17) announced the gospel ahead of time (3:8) and the law that was only "until Christ" still speaks to those who—in the flesh—live east of Eden even as they—in Christ, by grace, and through faith—live east of Easter. This simultaneity seems to be what Luther is responding to when he suggests that the "Christian is divided . . . into two times": living both "by faith" and "in the flesh" entails the "alternation" of the "time of law and the time of grace" (LW 26:340, 342).

But Christ did not die for nothing. The "truth of the gospel" is that he "gave himself for our sins to deliver us from the present evil age" (1:4). This giving happened, in Luther's phrase, "once for all at a set time." As Paul confesses, Christ "loved me and gave himself for me" (2:20). In writing Galatians, however, Paul does more than remember this past gift; he proclaims it and so gives it: "until Christ is formed in you." Here, perhaps, is the deepest resonance between Paul's letter and Luther's interpretation. As Amos Wilder once said, "All about us—yesterday, today, tomorrow—there is an unrecognized court in the hearts of men and women which sifts the arts of an age and gives suffrage to whatever provides us with incentives to go on living."[67] As Luther turned to Paul's letters in 1515, he was sifting texts and traditions, looking and longing for something to which could he give suffrage, something that was—yesterday, today, tomorrow—both "The Truth and For the Consolation of Troubled Consciences." Until this time, Luther recalls, "I lacked nothing except I made no distinction between law and gospel." As he would later comment on Galatians 2:20, however, Paul's words, *pro me*, "define Christ properly": "Christ is not Moses," he is "mercy"; "Christ is not . . . a lawgiver," he was and always is "the one who loved me and gave himself for me."[68] What Luther noticed is that in Galatians the gospel is not only an historical memory about Christ; the gospel is the promise in which this christological past meets a personal pronoun: "Christ give himself for our (ἡμῶν) sins, in order to deliver us (ἡμᾶς) from the present evil age" (1:4); Christ "loved me (με) and he gave himself for me" (με, 2:20). This, for Luther, is the truth that comforts, that gives "rest to your weary bones and mine." And this, for Paul, is "the truth of the gospel": the good news that not only remembers but also gives, in every time, the "grace and peace" (1:3) that come from the one who loved me and gave himself for me "in the fullness of time."

---

67. A. Wilder, *Thornton Wilder and His Public* (Eugene, OR: Wipf & Stock, 2013), 89.
68. LW 26:177–78.

ACKNOWLEDGMENTS

"Righteousness Revealed: The Death of Christ as the Definition of the Righteousness of God." In *Paul and the Apocalyptic Imagination*. Edited by Ben Blackwell, John Goodrich, and Jason Maston. Minneapolis: Fortress, 2016. Used by permission of Fortress Press.

"Not the End: The History and Hope of the Unfailing Word in Romans 9–11." In *God and Israel: Providence and Purpose in Romans 9–11*. Edited by Todd D. Still. Waco, TX: Baylor University Press, 2017. Reprinted by arrangement with Baylor University Press. All rights reserved.

"The Speech of the Dead: Identifying the No Longer yet Now Living I of Galatians 2:20." *NTS* 66.1 (2020): 87–105.

"Relational Hermeneutics and Comparison as Conversation." In *Comparing Traditions*. Edited by John M. G. Barclay. Library for the Study of the New Testament Series. London: T&T Clark, an imprint of Bloomsbury Publishing Plc, 2020.

"Announcing the Human: Rethinking the Relationship between *Wisdom of Solomon* 13–14 and Romans 1.18–32." *NTS* 57.2 (2011): 214–37.

"Debating Diagonal Δικαιοσύνη: The *Epistle of Enoch* and Paul in Theological Conversation." *Early Christianity* 1 (2010): 107–28.

"Scandalous and Foolish: Defining Grace with Pseudo-Solomon and Saint Paul." In *Comfortable Words: Essays in Honor of Paul F. M. Zahl*. Edited by John D. Koch and Todd Brewer. Eugene, OR: Pickwick, 2013. Used by permission of Wipf and Stock Publishers, www.wipfandstock.com.

"The Grammar of the Gospel: Justification as a Theological Criterion in the Reformation and Galatians." *SJT* 71.3 (2018): 287–307.

"The Texts of Paul and the Theology of Cranmer." In *Reformation Readings of Paul*. Edited by R. Michael Allen and Jonathan A. Linebaugh. Downers Grove, IL:

IVP Academic, 2015. Used by permission of InterVarsity Press, P. O. Box 1400, Downers Grove, IL 60515. http://www.ivpress.com.

"The Christo-Centrism of Faith in Christ: Martin Luther's Reading of Galatians 2:16, 19–20." *NTS* 59.4 (2013): 535–44.

Bibliography

Adam, E. "Abraham's Faith and Gentile Disobedience: Textual Links Between Romans 1 and Romans 4." *JSNT* 65 (1997): 47–66.

Agamben, G. *The Time That Remains: A Commentary on the Letter to the Romans.* Translated by P. Dailey. Stanford, CA: Stanford University Press, 2005.

Allen, R. M. *The Christ's Faith: A Dogmatic Account.* T&T Clark Studies in Systematic Theology. London: T&T Clark, 2009.

———. "'It Is No Longer I Who Live': Christ's Faith and Christian Faith." *JRT* (2013): 3–26.

———. *Justification and the Gospel: Understanding the Contexts and Controversies.* Grand Rapids: Baker Academic, 2013.

Aquinas, Thomas. *Commentary on Saint Paul's Epistle to the Galatians by St. Thomas Aquinas.* Translated by F. R. Larcher. Albany: Magi, 1966.

———. *Summa Theologiae.* Blackfriars edition. 60 vols. New York: McGraw-Hill, 1963–76.

Arendt, H. *Eichmann in Jerusalem: A Report on the Banality of Evil.* London: Penguin Books, 2006 [1963].

Auerbach, E. "Figura." Pages 11–71 in *Istanbuler Schriften*, vol. 5, *Neue Dantestudien*. Istanbul, 1944.

Augustine. *On Continence.* Translated by C. L. Cornish. In *Nicene and Post-Nicene Fathers*, series 1, edited by P. Schaff, vol. 3. Christian Literature Publishing Company, 1887.

Avemarie, F. "Israels rätselhafter Ungehorsam. Römer 10 als Anatomie eines von Gott provozierten Unglaubens." Pages 299–320 in *Between Gospel and Election*. Edited by F. Wilk and J. R. Wagner. WUNT 257. Tübingen: Mohr Siebeck, 2010.

Badiou, A. *Saint Paul: The Foundation of Universalism.* Translated by R. Brassier. Stanford, CA: Stanford University Press, 2003.

Bakhtin, M. "Toward a Methodology for the Human Sciences." Pages 159–72 in *Speech Genres and Other Late Essays.* Edited by C. Emerson and M. Holquist. Translated by V. W. McGee. Austin: University of Texas Press, 1986.

Balthasar, H. U. von. *Mysterium Paschale.* Translated by A. Nichols. Edinburgh: T&T Clark, 1990.

Barclay, J. M. G. "Grace within and beyond Reason: Philo and Paul in Dialogue." In *Paul, Grace and Freedom: Essays in Honour of John K. Riches.* Edited by P. Middleton, A. Paddison, and K. Wenell. London: T&T Clark, 2009.

———. "'I Will Have Mercy on Whom I Have Mercy': The Golden Calf and Divine Mercy in Romans 9–11 and Second Temple Judaism." *EC* 1 (2010): 82–106.

———. *Jews in the Mediterranean Disapora: From Alexander to Trajan 323 BCE–117 CE.* Berkeley: University of California Press, 1996.

———. *Obeying the Truth: A Study of Paul's Ethics.* Edinburgh: T&T Clark, 1988.

———. *Paul and the Gift.* Grand Rapids: Eerdmans, 2015.

———. *Paul and the Power of Grace.* Grand Rapids: Eerdmans, 2020.

———. "Paul's Story: Theology as Testimony." In *Narrative Dynamics in Paul: A Critical Assessment.* Edited by B. W. Longenecker. Louisville: Westminster John Knox, 2002.

Barth, K. *Christ and Adam: Man and Humanity in Romans 5.* Translated by T. A. Smail. Edinburgh: Oliver and Boyd, 1956.

———. *Church Dogmatics.* Edited by G. W. Bromiley and T. F. Torrance. Translated by G. W. Bromiley. 14 vols. Edinburgh: T&T Clark, 1936–1977.

———. *Der Römerbrief* (Erste Fassung, 1919). Gesamtausgabe 2: Akademische Werke. Edited by Hermann Schmidt. Zürich: Theologischer Verlag, 1985.

———. *The Epistle to the Romans.* Translated by E. C. Hoskyns. Oxford: Oxford University Press, 1933.

———. *A Shorter Commentary on Romans.* Translated by D. H. van Daalen. London: SCM, 1959.

Barth, M. "Speaking of Sin." *SJT* 8 (1955): 288–96.

Bauckham, R. "Apocalypses." In *Justification and Variegated Nomism: The Complexities of Second Temple Judaism.* Edited by D. A. Carson, P. T. O'Brien, and M. A. Seifrid. Tübingen: Mohr Siebeck, 2001.

Bayer, O. "The Being of Christ in Faith." *LQ* 10 (1996): 135–50.

———. *A Contemporary in Dissent: Johann Georg Hamann as a Radical Enlightener.* Translated by R. A. Harrisville and M. C. Mattes. Grand Rapids: Eerdmans, 2012.

———. "The Ethics of Gift." *LQ* 24 (2010): 447–68.

———. *Freedom in Response.* Oxford: Oxford University Press, 2007.

———. "God as Author: On the Theological Foundations of Hamann's Authorial

Poetics." In *Hamann and the Tradition*. Edited by L. M. Anderson. Evanston, IL: Northwestern University Press, 2012.

―――. *Handbuch: Systematischer Theologie*. Gütersloh: Gütersloh Verlagshaus, 1994.

―――. "Hermeneutical Theology." *SJT* 56.2 (2003): 131–47.

―――. *Leibliches Wort: Reformation und Neuzeit im Konflikt*. Tübingen: Mohr Siebeck, 1992.

―――. *Martin Luther's Theology: A Contemporary Interpretation*. Translated by Thomas H. Trapp. Grand Rapids: Eerdmans, 2008.

―――. "Preaching the Word." In *Justification Is for Preaching: Essays by Oswald Bayer, Gerhard O. Forde, and Others*. Edited by V. Thompson. Eugene, OR: Pickwick, 2012.

―――. *Promissio: Geschichte der reformatischen Wende in Luthers Theologie*. 2nd ed. Darmstadt: Wissenschaftliche Buchgesellschaft, 1989.

―――. *Theology the Lutheran Way*. Edited and translated by Jeffrey G. Silcock and Mark C. Mattes. LQB. Grand Rapids: Eerdmans, 2007.

Beker, J. C. *Paul the Apostle: The Triumph of God in Life and Thought*. Philadelphia: Fortress, 1980.

Bell, R. H. *No One Seeks for God: An Exegetical and Theological Study of Romans 1.18–3.20*. WUNT 106. Tübingen: Mohr Siebeck, 1998.

―――. *Provoked to Jealousy: The Origin and Purpose of the Jealousy Motif in Romans 9–11*. WUNT 2.63. Tübingen: Mohr Siebeck, 1994.

Benjamin, W. "Theses on the Philosophy of History." Pages 253–64 in *Illuminations: Essays and Reflections*. Edited by H. Arendt. Translated by H. Eiland and K. McLaughlin. Cambridge, MA: Harvard University Press, 1999.

Betz, J. R. *After Enlightenment: The Post-Secular Vision of J. G. Hamann*. Oxford: Wiley-Blackwell, 2012.

―――. "Hamann before Kierkegaard: A Systematic Theological Oversight." *Pro Ecclesia* 16.3 (2007): 299–333.

Bietenhard, H. "Natürliche Gotteserkenntnis der Heiden? Eine Erwägung zu Röm 1." *ThZ* 12 (1956): 275–88.

Bird, M. F. *The Saving Righteousness of God: Studies on Paul, Justification and the New Perspective*. Milton Keynes: Paternoster, 2006.

Black, M. *Apocalypsis Henochi Graece*. PVTG 4. Leiden: Brill, 1970.

Bockmuehl, M. *Revelation and Mystery in Ancient Judaism and Pauline Christianity*. WUNT 2.36. Tübingen: Mohr Siebeck, 1990.

Boer, M. de. *Galatians*. Louisville: Westminster John Knox, 2011.

Bonhoeffer, D. *Creation and Fall* (1937). Minneapolis: Fortress, 2004.

Bornkamm, G. "The Revelation of God's Wrath." In *Early Christian Experience*. New York: Harper & Row, 1966.

———. "Sin, Law and Death: An Exegetical Study of Romans 7." In *Early Christian Experience*. New York: Harper & Row, 1969.

Bultmann, R. "αἰσχύνω κτλ." In *TDNT* 1. Edited by G. Kittel. Translated by G. W. Bromiley. Grand Rapids: Eerdmans, 1964.

———. *Theology of the New Testament*. Translated by K. Grobel. Waco, TX: Baylor University Press, 2007.

Calvin, J. "Acts 14–28 and Romans 1–6." In vol. 19 of *Calvin's Commentaries*. Translated by J. Owen. Grand Rapids: Baker, 2003.

———. *Institutes of the Christian Religion*. Edited by J. T. McNeill. Translated by F. L. Battles. Philadelphia: Westminster, 1960.

Campbell, D. *The Deliverance of God: An Apocalyptic Rereading of Justification in Paul*. Grand Rapids: Eerdmans, 2009.

———. *The Rhetoric of Righteousness in Romans 3.21–26*. JSNTSup. Sheffield: Sheffield Academic Press, 1992.

Carson, D. A. "Divine Sovereignty and Human Responsibility in Philo." *NovT* 23 (1981): 148–64.

Cervantes, M. de. *Don Quixote*. Translated by E. Grossman. London: Vintage Books, 2003.

Chester, S. "Apocalyptic Union: Martin Luther's Account of Faith in Christ." In *In Christ in Paul: Explorations in Paul's Theology of Union and Participation*. Edited by M. J. Thate, K. J. Vanhoozer, and C. R. Campbell. Grand Rapids: Eerdmans, 2018.

———. *Conversion at Corinth: Perspectives on Conversion in Paul's Theology and the Corinthian Church*. SNTW. London: T&T Clark, 2003.

———. "It is No Longer I Who Live: Justification by Faith and Participation in Christ in Martin Luther's Exegesis of Galatians." *NTS* 55 (2009): 315–37.

Congdon, D. "Eschatologizing Apocalyptic: An Assessment of the Present Conversation on Pauline Apocalyptic." In *Apocalyptic and the Future of Theology: With and beyond J. Louis Martyn*. Edited by J. B. Davis and D. Harink. Eugene, OR: Cascade, 2012.

Conzelmann, H. "Current Problems in Pauline Research." *Int* 22 (1968): 170–86.

Cosgrove, C. *Elusive Israel: The Puzzle of Election in Romans*. Louisville: Westminster John Knox, 1997.

Cox, J. E. *Miscellaneous Writings and Letters of Thomas Cranmer*. Cambridge: Parker Society, 1846; repr., Vancouver: Regent College Publishing.

Cranfield, C. E. B. *A Critical and Exegetical Commentary on the Epistle to the Romans*. 2 vols. ICC. Edinburgh: T&T Clark, 1975.

Cremer, H. *Die paulinische Rechtfertigungslehre im Zusammenhange ihrer geschichtlichen Voraussetzungen.* Gütersloh: Bertelsmann, 1899.

Dabelstein, R. *Die Beurteilung der "Heiden" bei Paulus.* BBET 14. Bern: Lang, 1981.

Das, A. A. "Another Look at ἐὰν μή in Galatians 2:16." *JBL* 119 (2000): 529–39.

Dawson, J. D. *Christian Figural Reading and the Fashioning of Identity.* Berkeley: University of California Press, 2002.

Derrida, J. *The Gift of Death.* Chicago: University of Chicago Press, 1995.

Dillmann, A. *Das Buch Henoch.* Leipzig: Fr. Chr. Wilh. Vogel, 1853.

Dix, D. G. *The Shape of the Liturgy.* Westminster: Dacre, 1945.

Dodd, C. H. *The Epistle to the Romans.* MNTC. London: Hodder and Stoughton, 1932.

Dodson, J. R. *The "Powers" of Personificaiton: Rhetorical Purpose in the* Book of Wisdom *and the Letter to the Romans.* BZNW 161. Berlin: de Gruyter, 2008.

Donaldson, T. "'Riches for the Gentiles' (Rom 11:12): Israel's Rejection and Paul's Gentile Mission." *JBL* 12 (1993): 81–98.

Dunn, J. D. G. "The Justice of God: A Renewed Perspective on Justification by Faith." Pages 193–211 in *The New Perspective on Paul.* Revised ed. Grand Rapids: Eerdmans, 2005.

———. *Romans 1–8.* WBC 38A. Waco, TX: Word, 1988.

———. *Romans 9–16.* WBC 38B. Waco, TX: Word, 1988.

———. *The Theology of Paul the Apostle.* Grand Rapids: Eerdmans, 1998.

Eastman, S. *Paul and the Person: Reframing Paul's Anthropology.* Grand Rapids: Eerdmans, 2017.

Ebeling, G. "The Beginning of Luther's Hermeneutic." *LQ* 7 (1993): 129–59.

———. "Der Grund christlicher Theologie." *ZTK* 58 (1961): 227–44.

———. "Die Anfänge von Luthers Hermeneutik." *ZTK* 48.2 1951: 172–230.

———. *Dogmatik des christlichen Glaubens.* Tübingen: Mohr Siebeck, 1979.

———. "Jesus and Faith." In *Word and Faith.* London: SCM, 1963.

———. *Luther: An Introduction to His Thought.* Translated by R. A. Wilson. Minneapolis: Fortress, 2007.

———. *The Truth of the Gospel: An Exposition of Galatians.* Translated by D. Green. Minneapolis: Fortress, 1985.

Eckstein, H.-J. "'Denn Gottes Zorn wird vom Himmel her offenbar warden.' Exegetische Erwägungen zu Röm 1,18." *ZNW* 78 (1987): 74–89.

———. *Verheissung und Gesetz: Eine exegetische Untersuchung zu Galater 2,15–4,7.* Tübingen: Mohr Siebeck, 1996.

Elert, W. *The Structure of Lutheranism.* Translated by W. A. Hansen. St. Louis: Concordia, 1962.

Eliot, G. *Essays of George Eliot*. Edited by T. Pinney. Milton Park: Routledge & Kegan Paul, 1968.

———. *Janet's Repentance*. London: Hesperus, 2007 (1858).

Engberg-Pedersen, T. "Self-Sufficiency and Power: Divine and Human Agency in Epictetus and Paul." In *Divine and Human Agency in Paul and His Cultural Environment*. Edited by J. M. G. Barclay and S. J. Gathercole. London: T&T Clark, 2008.

Feldmeier, R. "Vater und Töpfer? Zur Identität Gottes im Römerbrief." Pages 377–90 in *Between Gospel and Election*. Edited by F. Wilk and J. R. Wagner. WUNT 257. Tübingen: Mohr Siebeck, 2010.

Flebbe, J. *Solus Deus: Untersuchungen zur Rede von Gott im Brief des Paulus an die Römer*. BZNW 158. Berlin: de Gruyter, 2008.

Forde, G. *Justification by Faith: A Matter of Death and Life*. Philadelphia: Fortress, 1982.

———. "Law and Gospel in Luther's Hermeneutic." *Int* 37 (1983): 240–52.

Gaca, K. L. "Paul's Uncommon Declaration in Romans 1.18–32 and Its Problematic Legacy for Pagan and Christian Relations." *HTR* 92.2 (1999): 165–98.

Gadamer, H.-G. *Truth and Method*. New York: Continuum, 1997.

———. *Wahrheit und Methode: Grundüzge einer philosophischen Hermeneutik*. Gesammelte Werke 1. Tübingen: Mohr Siebeck, 1990.

Gathercole, S. "The Doctrine of Justification in Paul and Beyond." In *Justification in Perspective: Historical Developments and Contemporary Challenges*. Grand Rapids: Baker Academic, 2006.

———. "Sin in God's Economy: Agencies in Romans 1 and 7." In *Divine and Human Agency in Paul and His Cultural Environment*. Edited by J. M. G. Barclay and S. J. Gathercole. London: T&T Clark, 2006.

———. *Where Is Boasting? Early Jewish Soteriology and Paul's Response in Romans 1–5*. Grand Rapids: Eerdmans, 2002.

Gaventa, B. R. "Galatians 1 and 2: Autobiography as Paradigm." *NTS* 28 (1986): 309–26.

———. "On the Calling-into-Being of Israel: Romans 9.6–29." In *Between Gospel and Election*. Edited by F. Wilk and J. R. Wagner. WUNT 257. Tübingen: Mohr Siebeck, 2010.

———. *Our Mother Saint Paul*. Louisville: Westminster John Knox, 2007.

———. "The Singularity of the Gospel Revisited." In *Galatians and Christian Theology: Justification, the Gospel, and Ethics in Paul's Letter*. Edited by M. W. Elliott et al. Grand Rapids: Baker Academic, 2014.

Gilbert, M. *La critique des dieux dans le Livre del la Sagesse Sg 13–15*. Rome: Biblical Institute Press, 1973.

Gleoge, G. "Die Rechtfertigungslehre als hermeneutische Kategorie." In *Gnade für die Welt: Kritik und Krise des Luthertums.* Göttingen: Vandenhoeck & Ruprecht, 1964.

Gorman, M. *Inhabiting the Cruciform God: Kenosis, Justification, and Theosis in Paul's Narrative Soteriology.* Grand Rapids: Eerdmans, 2009.

Grafe, E. "Das Verhältniss der paulinischen Schriften zur Sapientia Salmonis." Pages 251–86 in *Theologische Abhandlungen: Carl von Weizsäcker zu seinem siebzigsten Geburtstage 11. December 1892 gewidmet.* Freiburg: Mohr Siebeck, 1892.

Griffith-Dickson, G. "God, I, and Thou: Hamann and the Personalist Tradition." In *Hamann and the Tradition.* Edited by L. M. Anderson. Evanston, IL: Northwestern University Press, 2012.

———. *Johann Georg Hamann's Relational Metacriticism.* Berlin: de Gruyter, 1995.

Gritsch, E. W., and R. W. Jenson. *Lutheranism: The Theological Movement and Its Confessional Writings.* Philadelphia: Fortress, 1978.

Güttgemanns, E. *Der leidende Apostel und sein Herr: Studien zur paulinischen Christologie.* Göttingen: Vandenhoeck & Ruprecht, 1966.

———. "'Gottesgerechtigkeit' und strukturale Semantik: Linguistische Analyse zu δικαιοσύνη θεοῦ." Pages 5–98 in *Studia linguistica Neotestamentica.* BEvT 60. Munich, 1971.

Haacker, K. *Der Brief des Paulus an die Römer.* Leipzig: Evangelische Verlagsanstalt, 1999.

Habermas, J. *Knowledge and Human Interests.* Cambridge: Polity, 1987.

———. *Theory and Practice.* London: Heinemann, 1974.

Hahn, F. *Theologie des Neuen Testament.* 2 vols. Tübingen: Mohr Siebeck, 2005.

Hamann, J. G. *Briefwechsel.* Edited by W. Ziesemer and A. Henkel. 8 vols. Wiesbaden: Insel Verlag, 1955–75.

———. "Cloverleaf of Hellenistic Letters, First Letter." In *Hamann: Writings on Philosophy and Language.* Edited by K. Haynes. Cambridge: Cambridge University Press, 2007.

———. "Golgotha and Scheblimini." Pages 164–204 in *Hamann: Writings on Philosophy and Language.* Edited by K. Haynes. Cambridge: Cambridge University Press, 2007.

———. *Sämtliche Werken.* Edited by J. Nadler. 6 vols. Vienna: Verlag Herder, 1949–57.

———. *Writings on Philosophy and Language.* Edited by K. Haynes. Cambridge: Cambridge University Press, 2007.

———. "Zweifel und Einfälle" (1776). In *J. G. Hamann 1730–1788: A Study in Chris-*

tian Existence. Edited and translated by R. G. Smith. New York: Harper & Brothers, 1960.

Hampson, D. *Christian Contradictions: The Structures of Lutheran and Catholic Thought*. Cambridge: Cambridge University Press, 2001.

———. "Luther on the Self: A Feminist Critique." *WW* 8.4 (1988): 334–42.

Hays, R. B. *The Conversion of the Imagination: Paul as Interpreter of Israel's Scripture*. Grand Rapids: Eerdmans, 2005.

———. "Crucified with Christ: A Synthesis of 1 and 2 Thessalonians, Philemon, Philippians, and Galatians." Pages 318–35 in *SBL Literature 1988 Seminar Papers*. Edited by D. J. Lull. Atlanta: Scholars Press, 1988.

———. *Echoes of Scripture in the Letters of Paul*. New Haven: Yale University Press, 1989.

———. *The Faith of Jesus Christ: The Narrative Substructure of Galatians 3.1–4.11*. 2nd ed. Grand Rapids: Eerdmans, 2002.

———. "Have We Found Abraham to Be Our Forefather According to the Flesh? A Reconsideration of Rom 4:1." *NovT* 27.1 (1985): 76–98.

———. *The Moral Vision of the New Testament*. San Francisco: Harper Collins, 1996.

———. "ΠΙΣΤΙΣ and Pauline Christology: What Is at Stake?" In *Pauline Theology*, vol. 4: *Looking Back, Pressing On*. Edited by D. M. Hay and E. E. Johnson. Atlanta: Scholars, 1997.

———. "What Is 'Real Participation in Christ'? A Dialogue with E. P. Sanders on Pauline Soteriology." Pages 336–51 in *Redefining First Century Jewish and Christian Identities: Essays in Honor of Ed Parish Sanders*. Edited by Fabian E. Udoh. Notre Dame, IN: University of Notre Dame Press, 2008.

Heim, E. *Adoption in Galatians and Romans*. Leiden: Brill, 2017.

Hengel, M. *Crucifixion*. London: SCM, 1977.

Herrmann, E. "Luther's Absorption of Medieval Biblical Interpretation and His Use of the Church Fathers." In *The Oxford Handbook of Martin Luther's Theology*. Oxford: Oxford University Press, 2014.

———. "Luther's Divine Aeneid: Continuity and Creativity in Reforming the Use of the Bible." *Lutherjahrbuch* 85 (2018): 85–109.

———. "'Why Then the Law?' Salvation History and the Law in Martin Luther's Interpretation of Galatians 1513–1522." PhD dissertation. Concordia Seminary, 2005.

Hill, W. *Paul and the Trinity: Persons, Relations, and the Pauline Letters*. Grand Rapids: Eerdmans, 2015.

Hoffman, V. *Johann Georg Hamanns Philologie: Hamanns Philologie zwischen enzyklopädischer Mikrologie und Hermeneutik*. Stuttgart: Verlag W. Kohlkammer, 1972.

Holl, K. "Luthers Bedeutung für den Fortschritt der Auslegungskunst." In *Gesam-*

melte Aufsätze zur Kirchengeschichte, vol. 1: *Luther*. Tübingen: Mohr Siebeck, 1932.

Hooker, M. D. "Adam in Romans I." *NTS* 6 (1959–60): 297–306.

Hübner, H. *Das Gesetz bei Paulus. Ein Beitrag zum Werden der paulischen Theologie*. FRLANT 119. Göttingen: Vandenhoeck & Ruprecht, 1978.

———. *Die Weisheit Salomons*. ATD Apokryphen 4. Göttingen: Vandenhoeck & Ruprecht, 1999.

———. *Gottes Ich und Israel*. FRLANT 126. Göttingen: Vandenhoeck & Ruprecht, 1984.

———. "Pauli Theologiae Proprium." *NTS* 26 (1980): 445–73.

Irons, C. L. *The Righteousness of God: A Lexical Examination of the Covenant-Faithfulness Interpretation*. WUNT 2.386. Tübingen: Mohr Siebeck, 2015.

Iwand, H. J. *The Righteousness of Faith according to Luther*. Edited by V. F. Thompson. Translated by R. H. Lundell. Eugene, OR: Wipf & Stock, 2008.

Jenson, R. W. *Systematic Theology*. Oxford: Oxford University Press, 1997.

Jervell, J. *Imago Dei: Gen 1,26f. im Spätjudentum, in der Gnosis und in den paulischen Briefen*. Göttingen: Vandenhoeck & Ruprecht, 1960.

Jewett, R. *Romans*. Hermeneia. Minneapolis: Fortress, 2007.

Joest, W. *Ontologie der Person bei Luther*. Göttingen: Vandenhoeck & Ruprecht, 1967.

Jüngel, E. *Das Evangelium von der Rechtfertigung des Gottlosen als Zentrum des christlichen Glaubens*. 3rd ed. Tübingen: Mohr Siebeck, 1999.

———. *Justification: The Heart of Christian Faith*. Translated by J. F. Cayzer. London: T&T Clark, 2001.

Kähler, M. *Die Wissenschaft der christlichen Lehre von dem evangelischen Grundartikel aus im Abrisse dargestellt*. Neukirchen: Neukirchener Verlag, 1996 [1905].

Kant, I. *Religion within the Limits of Reason Alone*. New York: Harper & Row, 1960.

Käsemann, E. *An die Römer*. HNT 8a. Tübingen: Mohr Siebeck, 1973.

———. *Commentary on Romans*. Translated by G. W. Bromiley. Grand Rapids: Eerdmans, 1980.

———. "Die Anfänge christlicher Theologie." *ZTK* 57 (1960): 162–85; ET, "The Beginnings of Christian Theology." Pages 82–107 in *New Testament Question of Today*. Translated by W. J. Montague. London: SCM, 1969.

———. "The Faith of Abraham in Romans 4." In *Perspectives on Paul*. Translated by M. Kohl. Philadelphia: Fortress, 1971.

———. "Gottesgerechtigkeit bei Paulus." *ZTK* 58 (1961): 367–78.

———. "Justification and Salvation History in the Epistle to the Romans." In *Perspectives on Paul*. Translated by M. Kohl. Philadelphia: Fortress, 1971.

———. "Paul and Israel." In *New Testament Questions of Today*. London: SCM, 1969.

———. "'The Righteousness of God' in Paul." Pages 168–82 in *New Testament Questions Today*. Translated by W. J. Montague. London: SCM, 1969.

Kelsey, D. *Eccentric Existence: A Theological Anthropology*. Louisville: Westminster John Knox, 2009.

Kertelge, K. *"Rechtfertigung" bei Paulus*. Münster: Aschendorff, 1967.

Kierkegaard, S. *Sickness unto Death*. New York: Doubleday, 1954.

Klein, G. "Römer 4 und die Idee der Heilsgeschichte." *EvT* 23 (1963): 424–47.

Klostermann, E. "Die adäquate Vergeltung in Röm 1,22–31." *ZNW* 32 (1993): 1–6.

Kolb, R. *Martin Luther: Confessor of the Faith*. Oxford: Oxford University Press, 2009.

Kuck, D. W. *Judgment and Community Conflict: Paul's Use of Apocalyptic Judgment Language in 1 Corinthians 3.5–4.5*. SNT 66. Leiden: Brill, 1992.

Kummel, W. G. "Πάρεσις und ἔνδειξις. Ein Beitrag zum Verständis der paulinschen Rechtfertigungslehre." Pages 260–70 in *Heilsgeschehen und Geschichte: Gesammelte Aufsätze: 1933–1964*. Marburg: Elwert Verlag, 1965.

Laato, T. *Paul and Judaism: An Anthropological Approach*. Translated by T. McElwain. Atlanta: University of South Florida, 1995.

Lagrange, M.-J. *Saint Paul: Épitre aux Romains*. Ebib 13. Paris: Gabalda, 1922.

Lambrecht, J. "Israel's Future according to Romans 9–11: An Exegetical and Hermeneutical Approach." Pages 34–54 in *Pauline Studies*. Leuven: Peeters, 1994.

———. "Romans 4: A Critique of N. T. Wright." *JSNT* 36.2 (2013): 189–94.

Larcher, C. *Le Livre de la Sagesse, ou La Sagesse de Salomon*. Paris: Gabalda, 1983.

Lessing, G. *Lessing's Theological Writings*. Translated by H. Chadwick. Stanford, CA: Stanford University Press, 1957.

Levison, J. R. "Adam and Eve in Romans 1.18–25 and the Greek *Life of Adam and Eve*." *NTS* 50 (2004): 519–34.

Lietzmann, H. *An die Römer*. 3rd ed. HNT 8. Tübingen: Mohr Siebeck, 1928.

Lindbeck, G. A. *The Nature of Doctrine: Religion and Theology in a Postliberal Age*. Philadelphia: Westminster, 1984.

Linebaugh, J. A. *God, Grace, and Righteousness in Wisdom of Solomon and Paul's Letter to the Romans: Texts in Conversation*. NovTSup 152. Leiden: Brill, 2013.

———. "Participation and the Person in Pauline Theology." *JSNT* 40.4 (2018): 516–23.

———. "Rational or Radical: Origen on Romans 9.10–14." *StPatr* 52 (2011): 63–69.

Linebaugh, J. A., ed. *God's Two Words: Law and Gospel in the Lutheran and Reformed Traditions*. Grand Rapids: Eerdmans, 2018.

Lohse, E. *Der Brief an die Römer*. KEK 4. Göttingen: Vandenhoeck & Ruprecht, 2003.

Longenecker, B. W. "Different Answers to Different Issues: Israel, the Gentiles and Salvation History in Romans 9–11." *JSNT* 36 (1989): 95–123.

———. *Eschatology and the Covenant: A Comparison of 4 Ezra and Romans 1–11.* JSNTSup 57, Sheffield: JSOT Press, 1999.

Lubac, H. de. *Medieval Exegesis: The Four Senses of Scripture.* Translated by E. M. Macierowski. Grand Rapids: Eerdmans, 2000.

Luther, M. *D. Martin Luthers Werke.* Kritische Gesamtausgabe. Edited by J. F. K. Knaake et al. 57 volumes. Weimar: Böhlau, 1883–.

———. "Freedom of a Christian." In *Three Treatises.* Translated by W. A. Lambert. Revised by H. Grimm. Philadelphia: Fortress, 1970.

———. *Luther's Works.* American Edition. 82 vols. Philadelphia: Fortress; St. Louis: Concordia, 1955–.

———. *Preface to the Complete Edition of Luther's Latin Writings.* In LW 34. Edited by L. W. Spitz. Philadelphia: Muhlenberg, 1960.

Luz, U. *Das Geschichtsverständnis des Paulus.* Neukirchen: Neukirchener Verlag, 1968.

Macaskill, G. *Union with Christ in the New Testament.* Oxford: Oxford University Press, 2013.

Martin, F. *Le Livre d'Hénoch: Documents pour l'étude de la Bible, traduit sur le texte Éthiopien.* Paris: Letouzey et Ané, 1906.

Martin, R. P. "Center of Paul's Theology." Pages 92–95 in *The Dictionary of Paul and His Letters.* Edited by G. Hawthorne, R. P. Martin, and D. Reid. Downers Grove, IL: InterVarsity, 1993.

Martyn, J. L. "Apocalyptic Antinomies in Paul's Letter to Galatia." *NTS* 31 (1985): 410–24.

———. *Galatians: A New Translation with Introduction and Commentary.* New York: Doubleday, 1997.

———. "John and Paul on the Subject of Gospel and Scripture." In *Theological Issues in the Letters of Paul.* Edinburgh: T&T Clark, 1997.

———. "Paul and His Jewish-Christian Interpreters." *USQR* 42 (1987–88): 1–15.

———. *Theological Issues in the Letters of Paul.* Nashville: Abingdon, 1997.

Matlock, R. B. "Detheologizing the ΠΙΣΤΙΣ ΧΡΙΣΤΟΥ Debate: Cautionary Remarks from a Lexical Semantic Perspective." *NovT* 42 (2000): 1–23.

———. "Saving Faith: The Rhetoric and Semantics of πίστις in Paul." Pages 73–89 in *The Faith of Jesus Christ: Exegetical, Biblical and Theological Studies.* Edited by M. F. Bird and P. M. Sprinkle. Peabody, MA: Hendrickson, 2009.

———. *Unveiling the Apocalyptic Paul: Paul's Interpreters and the Rhetoric of Criticism.* JSNTSup 126. Sheffield: Sheffield Academic, 1996.

Mattes, M. C. *The Role of Justification in Contemporary Theology*. Grand Rapids: Eerdmans, 2004.

McFarland, A. "The Upward Call: The Category of Vocation and the Oddness of Human Nature." Pages 217–36 in *The Christian Doctrine of Humanity: Explorations in Constructive Dogmatics*. Edited by O. D. Crisp and F. Sanders. Grand Rapids: Zondervan, 2018.

McFarland, O. "The One Who Calls in Grace: Paul's Rhetorical and Theological Identification with the Galatians." *HBT* 35 (2013): 151–65.

———. "Whose Abraham, Which Promise? Genesis 15:6 in Philo's *De Virtutibus* and Romans 4." *JSNT* 35.2 (2012): 107–29.

McGlynn, M. *Divine Judgement and Divine Benevolence in the Book of Wisdom*. WUNT 2.139. Tübingen: Mohr Siebeck, 2001.

Melanchthon, Philip. *Loci communes theologici* (1521). In *Melanchthon and Bucer*. Edited by W. Pauck. Translated by L. J. Satre. LCC. Philadelphia: Westminster, 1981.

Moberly, W. *At the Mountain of God: Story and Theology in Exodus 32–34*. JSOTSup 22. Sheffield: JSOT Press, 1983.

Moo, D. J. *The Epistle to the Romans*. NICNT. Grand Rapids: Eerdmans, 1996.

———. *Galatians*. Grand Rapids: Baker Academic, 2013.

———. "Israel and Paul in Romans 7.7–12." *NTS* 32 (1986): 122–35.

Moxnes, H. *Theology in Conflict: Studies in Paul's Understanding of God in Romans*. NovTSup 53. Leiden: Brill, 1980.

Müller, C. *Gottes Gerichtigkeit und Gottes Volk*. FRLANT 86. Göttingen: Vandenhoeck & Ruprecht, 1964.

Nanos, M. D. *The Irony of Galatians: Paul's Letter in First-Century Context*. Minneapolis: Fortress, 2002.

Neusner, J., and A. J. Avery-Peck, eds., *George W. E. Nickelsburg in Perspective: An Ongoing Dialogue*. Leiden: Brill, 2003.

Nicholas, J. G., ed., *Narratives of the Days of the Reformation*. London: Camden Society, 1859.

Nickelsburg, G. W. E. "The Apocalyptic Message of *1 Enoch* 92–105." *CBQ* 39 (1977): 322–33.

———. *1 Enoch 1: A Commentary on the Book of 1 Enoch, Chapters 1–36; 81–108*. Heremeneia. Minneapolis: Fortress, 2001.

———. "Riches, the Rich, and God's Judgment in 1 Enoch 92–105 and the Gospel According to Luke." *NTS* 25 (1978–79): 324–44.

Nickelsburg, G. W. E., and J. C. VanderKam. *1 Enoch: A New Translation*. Minneapolis: Augsburg Fortress, 2004.

Nietzsche, F. *Beyond Good and Evil: Prelude to a Philosophy of the Future*. Translated by R. J. Hollingdale. London: Penguin Books, 1973.

Null, A. "Conversion to Communion: Thomas Cranmer on a Favourite Puritan Theme." *Churchman* 116: 239–57.

———. "Official Tudor Homilies." Pages 348–65 in *Oxford Handbook of the Early Modern Sermon*. Edited by P. McCullough, H. Adlington, and E. Rhatigan. Oxford: Oxford University Press, 2011.

———. "Thomas Cranmer and Tudor Evangelicalism." Pages 221–51 in *The Advent of Evangelicalism: Exploring Historical Continuities*. Edited by M. A. G. Haykin and K. J. Stewart. Nashville: B&H Academic, 2008.

———. *Thomas Cranmer's Doctrine of Repentance: Renewing the Power to Love*. Oxford: Oxford University Press, 2000.

———. "Thomas Cranmer's Reading of Paul's Letters." In *Reformation Readings of Paul*. Edited by M. Allen and J. A. Linebaugh. Downers Grove, IL: IVP Academic, 2015.

Nygren, A. *Commentary on Romans*. Translated by C. C. Rasmussen. London: SCM, 1952.

Oberman, H. *The Dawn of the Reformation: Essays in Late Medieval and Early Reformation Thought*. Edinburgh: T&T Clark, 1986.

———. "*Iustia Christi* and *Iustia Dei*: Luther and Scholastic Doctrines of Justification." Pages 104–25 in *The Dawn of the Reformation: Essays in Late Medieval and Early Reformation Thought*. Edinburgh: T&T Clark, 1986.

Oepke, A. "Δικαιοσύνη Θεοῦ bei Paulus." *TLZ* 78 (1953): cols. 257–63.

Olson, D. *Enoch: A New Translation*. Richland Hills, TX: BIBAL Press, 2004.

Paulson, S. D. *Lutheran Theology*. Doing Theology. London: T&T Clark, 2011.

Percy, W. *Love in the Ruins*. New York: Picador, 1971.

Plevnik, J. "The Center of Paul's Theology." *CBQ* 51 (1989): 460–78.

Poole, F. J. P. "Metaphor and Maps: Towards Comparison in the Anthropology of Religion." *JAAR* 54 (1986): 411–57.

Porter, C. L. "Romans 1.18–32: Its Role in the Developing Argument." *NTS* 40 (1994): 210–28.

Preus, J. *From Shadow to Promise: Old Testament Interpretation from Augustine to the Young Luther*. Cambridge: Harvard University Press, 1969.

Räisänen, H. "Paul, God, and Israel: Romans 9–11 in Recent Research." Pages 178–208 in *The Social World of Formative Christianity and Judaism*. Edited by J. Neusner et al. Philadelphia: Fortress, 1998.

———. "Paul's Theological Difficulties with the Law." Pages 301–20 in *Studia Biblica 1978 III*. Sheffield: JSOT Press, 1980.

Rehfeld, E. *Relationale Ontologie bei Paulus: Die ontische Wirksamkeit der Christus-*

bezogenheit im Denken des Heidenapostels. WUNT 2.326. Tübingen: Mohr Siebeck, 2012.

Riches, J. *Galatians through the Centuries.* Oxford: Blackwell, 2013.

Ricouer, P. "Erzählung, Metapher und Interpretationstheorie." *ZTK* 84 (1987): 232–53.

Rowe, C. K. "Romans 10:13: What Is the Name of the Lord?" *HBT* 22 (2000): 135–73.

Saarinen, R. "Die Rechtfertigungslehre als Kriterium: Zur Begriffsgeschichte einer ökumenischen Redewendung." *Keryma und Dogma* 44 (1998): 98.

———. "Martin Luther and Relational Thinking." In *Oxford Research Encyclopedia of Religion.* Oxford: Oxford University Press, 2017.

Sanday, W., and A. C. Headlam. *The Epistle to the Romans.* ICC. New York: Scribner's, 1896.

Sanders, E. P. *Paul: A Very Short Introduction.* Oxford: Oxford University Press, 1991.

———. *Paul and Palestinian Judaism: A Comparison of Patterns of Religion.* Minneapolis: Fortress, 1977.

Sartre, Jean-Paul. *Existentialism and Humanism.* Translated by P. Mairet. London: Methuen, 1949.

Schmeller, T. *Paulus und die "Diatribe": Eine vergleichende Stilinterpretation.* Münster: Aschendorf, 1987.

Schumacher, W. W. *Who Do I Say That You Are? Anthropology and the Theology of Theosis in the Finnish School of Tuomo Mannermaa.* Eugene, OR: Wipf & Stock, 2010.

Schütz, J. H. *Paul and the Anatomy of Apostolic Authority.* Cambridge: Cambridge University Press, 1975.

Schweitzer, A. *The Mysticism of Paul the Apostle.* Translated by W. Montgomery. New York: Seabury, 1931.

———. *Paul and His Interpreters: A Critical History.* Translated by W. Montgomery. New York: Schocken Books, 1964.

Seifrid, M. A. *Christ, Our Righteousness: Paul's Theology of Justification.* NSBT 9. Leicester: Apollos, 2000.

———. *Justification by Faith: The Origin and Development of a Central Pauline Theme.* Leiden: Brill, 1992.

———. "Paul's Use of Righteousness Language Against Its Hellenistic Background." In *Justification and Variegated Nomism,* vol. 2: *The Paradoxes of Paul.* Edited by D. A. Carson et al. Tübingen: Mohr Siebeck, 2004.

———. "Unrighteous by Faith: Apostolic Proclamation in Romans 1.18–3.20." In

Justification and Variegated Nomism, vol. 1: *The Paradoxes of Paul*. Edited by D. A. Carson et al. Grand Rapids: Baker Academic, 2004.

Shaw, D. "Romans 4 and the Justification of Abraham in Light of Perspectives New and Newer." *Them* 40.1 (2015): 50–62.

Slenckza, N. "Luther's Anthropology." In *Oxford Handbook of Martin Luther's Theology*. Edited by R. Kolb, I. Dingel, and L. Batka. Oxford: Oxford University Press, 2015.

Smith, J. Z. *Drudgery Divine: On Comparison of Early Christianities and the Religions of Late Antiquity*. Chicago: University of Chicago Press, 1990.

Stanton, G. "The Law of Moses and the Law of Christ: Galatians 3:1–6:2." In *Paul and the Mosaic Law*. Edited by J. D. G. Dunn. Tübingen: Mohr Siebeck, 1996.

Stendhal, K. *Paul Among Jews and Gentiles*. Philadelphia: Fortress, 1976.

Stowers, S. K. *A Rereading of Romans: Justice, Jews, and Gentiles*. New Haven: Yale University Press, 1994.

Stuckenbruck, L. T. *1 Enoch 91–108*. CEJL. Berlin: Walter de Gruyter, 2007.

Stuhlmacher, P. *Gerechtigkeit Gottes bei Paulus*. FRLANT 87. Göttingen: Vandenhoeck & Ruprecht, 1965.

———. *Revisiting Paul's Doctrine of Justification: A Challenge to the New Perspective*. Translated by D. P. Bailey. Downers Grove, IL: IVP Academic, 2001.

Tanner, K. *Christ the Key*. Cambridge: Cambridge University Press, 2010.

Terry, J. *The Justifying Judgement of God: A Reassessment of the Place of Judgement in the Saving Work of Christ*. Paternoster Theological Monographs. Milton Keynes: Paternoster, 2007.

Theissen, G. *Erleben und Verhalten der ersten Christen: Eine Psychologie des Urchristentums*. Munich: Gütersloher, 2007.

———. *Psychological Aspects of Pauline Theology*. Translated by J. Galvin. Edinburgh: T&T Clark, 1987.

Theobald, M. *Studien zum Römerbrief*. WUNT 136. Tübingen: Mohr Siebeck, 2001.

Thompson, V., ed. *Justification Is for Preaching*. Eugene, OR: Pickwick, 2012.

Tillich, P. *Systematic Theology*. London: SCM, 1978.

Torrance, T. F. "Covenant and Contract: A Study of the Theological Background of Worship in Seventeenth-Century Scotland." *SJT* 23 (1970): 51–76.

———. "The Covenant Concept in Scottish Theology and Politics and Its Legacy." *SJT* 34 (1981): 225–43.

Turner, G. "The Righteousness of God in Psalms and Romans." *SJT* 63.3 (2010): 285–301.

Ursinus, Z. *The Commentary on the Heidelberg Catechism*. Translated by G. W. Williard. Phillipsburg, NJ: Presbyterian and Reformed, 1852.

VanderKam, J. C. *Enoch: A Man for All Generations*. Columbia: University of South Carolina Press, 1995.

Vanhoozer, K. J. "From 'Blessed in Christ' to 'Being in Christ': The State of the Union and the Place of Participation in New Testament Exegesis and Systematic Theology Today." In *In Christ in Paul: Explorations in Paul's Theology of Union and Participation*. Edited by M. J. Thate, K. J. Vanhoozer, and C. R. Campbell. Grand Rapids: Eerdmans, 2018.

VanLandingham, C. *Judgment and Justification in Early Judaism and the Apostle Paul*. Peabody, MA: Hendrickson, 2006.

Volf, M. *Free of Charge: Giving and Forgiving in a Culture Stripped of Grace*. Grand Rapids: Zondervan, 2005.

Wagner, J. R. *Heralds of the Good News: Isaiah and Paul "In Concert" in the Letter to the Romans*. NovTSup 101. Leiden: Brill, 2002.

———. "'Not from the Jews Only, but Also from the Gentiles': Mercy to the Nations in Romans 9–11." Pages 417–31 in *Between Gospel and Election*. Edited by F. Wilk and J. R. Wagner. WUNT 257. Tübingen: Mohr Siebeck, 2010.

Watson, F. *Paul and the Hermeneutics of Faith*. London: T&T Clark, 2004.

———. *Paul, Judaism and the Gentiles: Beyond the New Perspective*. Grand Rapids: Eerdmans, 2007.

———. *Text and Truth: Redefining Biblical Theology*. Edinburgh: T&T Clark, 1997.

Way, D. V. *The Lordship of Christ: Ernst Käsemann's Interpretation of Paul's Theology*. Oxford: Oxford University Press, 1991.

Webster, J. "Eschatology, Ontology, and Human Action." *TJT* 7.1 (1991): 4–18.

Wedderburn, A. J. M. "Adam in Paul's Letter to the Romans." In *Studia Biblica 1978*. Vol. 3. JSNTSup 3. Edited by E. A. Livingstone. Sheffield: JSOT Press, 1980.

Westerholm, S. "Paul and the Law in Romans 9–11." Pages 215–37 in *Paul and the Mosaic Law*. Edited by J. D. G. Dunn. Tübingen: Mohr Siebeck, 1996.

———. *Perspectives Old and New: The "Lutheran" Paul and His Critics*. Grand Rapids: Eerdmans, 2004.

Wilckens, U. *Der Brief an die Römer*. 3 vols. EKKNT. Zurich: Benziger; Neukirchen-Vluyn: Neukirchener, 1978–82.

Wilder, A. *Thornton Wilder and His Public*. Eugene, OR: Wipf and Stock, 2013.

Wilder, T. *The Collected Short Plays of Thornton Wilder*. Edited by A. T. Wilder. New York: Theatre Communications Group, 1998.

Wilk, F. *Die Bedeutung des Jesajabuches für Paulus*. FRLANT 179. Göttingen: Vandenhoeck & Ruprecht, 1998.

Williams, S. K. "The 'Righteousness of God' in Romans." *JBL* 99 (1980): 241–90.

Winston, D. *The Wisdom of Solomon*. AB 43. Garden City, NY: Doubleday, 1979.

Wischmeyer, O. "Römer 2.1–24 als Teil der Gerichtsrede des Paulus gegen die Menschheit." *NTS* 52 (2006): 356–76.

Wolf, E. "Die Rechtfertigungslehre als Mitte und Grenze reformatorische Theologie." Pages 11–21 in *Peregrinatio*, vol. 2: *Studien zur reformatorische Theologie, zum Kirchenrecht und zur Sozialethik*. Munich: Chr. Kaiser Verlag, 1965.

Wolter, M. "Das Israelproblem nach Gal 4, 21–31 und Röm 9–11." *ZTK* 107 (2010): 1–30.

Wrede, W. "Paulus." In *Das Bild des Paulus in der neueren deutschen Forschung*. Edited by K. H. Rengstorf. WdF 24. Darmstadt: Wissenschaftliche Buchgesellschaft, 1982.

Wright, N. T. *The Climax of the Covenant: Paul and the Law in Pauline Theology*. London: T&T Clark, 1991.

———. "The Letter to the Romans." Pages 393–770 in *NIB* 10. Edited by Leander E. Keck. Nashville: Abingdon, 2002.

———. "New Perspectives on Paul." Pages 243–64 in *Justification in Perspective: Historical Developments and Contemporary Challenges*. Edited by B. L. McCormack. Grand Rapids: Baker Academic, 2006.

———. *Paul and the Faithfulness of God*. Minneapolis: Fortress, 2013.

———. "Paul and the Patriarch: The Role of Abraham in Romans 4." *JSNT* 35.3 (2013): 207–41.

Yinger, K. *Paul, Judaism and Judgement According to Deeds*. SNTSMS 105. Cambridge: Cambridge University Press, 1999.

Zahl, P. F. M. *Die Rechtfertigungslehre Ernst Käsemann*. Stuttgart: Calwer, 1996.

———. *Grace in Practice: A Theology of Everyday Life*. Grand Rapids: Eerdmans, 2007.

Zahn, T. *Der Brief des Paulus an die Römer*. KNT 6. Leipzig: Deitchert, 1910.

Index of Authors

Index of Subjects

Abraham: faith of, 29–31, 192, 194, 205; family of, 25–27; righteousness of, 23–25, 50, 51

Adam, sin of, 114–16, 120

apocalypse: distinction and judgment of the righteous and sinners in Enoch, 124–33, 138–40; distinction and judgment of the righteous and sinners in *Wisdom*, 91–92, 105–6, 146–47; double-apocalypse of divine righteousness and wrath, 108–11; gift of Christ as the apocalypse, 12–16, 19–20, 135, 189; history-of-religions approach, 5–8

applied Christology, 19

Aquinas, Thomas, 60–61, 70, 200n4

Articles of Religion (1553), 183

Augustine, 31, 43n32, 53, 56, 59, 195, 217–18, 219

Austen, Jane, *Pride and Prejudice*, 89n57

Bacon, Francis, 81

Baumgarten, Siegmund Jakob, 78n2

Berens, Christoph, 79, 80

Biel, Gabriel, 61

body, the, 67n66

Book of Common Prayer, 156, 183, 197

calling. *See* election and calling

Calvin, John, 36, 67, 220n34

catechisms, Reformation, 64, 166, 167n44, 206n34

Cervantes, Miguel de, *Don Quixote*, xvii, xix, 97

Chekhov, Anton, 225n56

Chemnitz, Martin, 172n55

Christ: advent of, 219–23, 224–30; body of, 67n66; death with, 57–58, 60, 61–63, 65–66, 179–80, 207–9; faith in, 16–19, 61, 63, 68–69, 168–69, 172, 190–95, 201–2, 204–7, 209–10; faith of, 190, 199–200, 203–4; life in, 60–63, 65–66, 67–69, 171, 179–80, 208–9; righteousness of God in death of, 10–13, 15–16, 19–20, 142, 189–90, 207–9; righteousness of God revealed in, 4, 8–10, 37, 41, 109–10; union with, 70n82. *See also* crucifixion and death of Christ; grace

Chrysostom, John, 43n32

Coleridge, Samuel Taylor, 24

comparative research: as conversation, 86–90; Hamann's relational hermeneutic, 79–86; Michaelis's approach, 78. *See also* Epistle of Enoch; *Wisdom of Solomon*

Cranmer, Thomas: *Book of Common Prayer*, 156, 183, 197; *Book of Homilies*, 183–84; exegetical texts, 183–84; on faith, 18–19, 190–97; on God's love and forgiveness, 181–82, 197; Holy Communion service, 166–67; on justification, 184–88; on the word, xvi, xviii, 156

creation: and knowledge of God, 101, 111–13; out of nothing, 16–17, 26, 28–29, 39, 64–65, 141–42, 170–71, 187, 205, 208–9

crucifixion and death of Christ: death defined in relation to, 57–58, 60, 61–63,

255

Index of Scripture and Other Ancient Sources